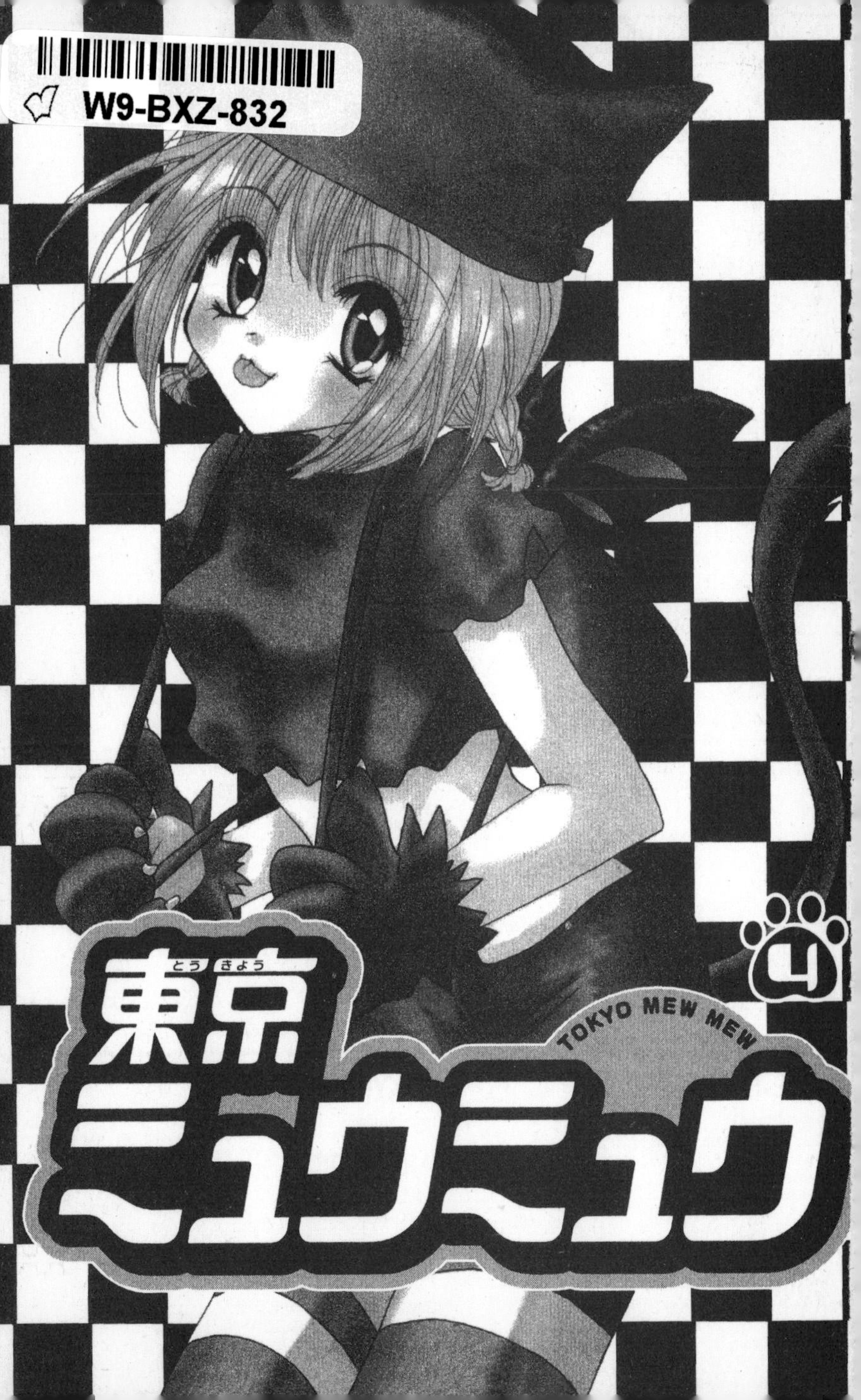
東京ミュウミュウ
とうきょう
TOKYO MEW MEW
4

ALSO AVAILABLE FROM

TOKYO MEW MEW

MIA IKUMI & REIKO YOSHIDA

VOLUME FOUR

TOKYOPOP®

LOS ANGELES • TOKYO • LONDON

Translator - Ikoi Hiroe
English Adaptation - Stuart Hazelton
Contributing Editors - Jodi Bryson and Amy Court Kaemon
Retouch and Lettering - Norine Lukaczyk
Cover Layout - Patrick Hook

Senior Editor -Julie Taylor
Managing Editor - Jill Freshney
Production Coordinator - Antonio DePietro
Production Manager - Jennifer Miller
Art Director - Matt Alford
Editorial Director - Jeremy Ross
VP of Production - Ron Klamert
President & C.O.O. - John Parker
Publisher & C.E.O. - Stuart Levy

Email: editor@TOKYOPOP.com
Come visit us online at www.TOKYOPOP.com

A **TOKYOPOP**® Manga

TOKYOPOP Inc.
5900 Wilshire Blvd. Suite 2000
Los Angeles, CA 90036

ISBN: 1-59182-239-4

First TOKYOPOP® printing: October 2003

10 9 8 7 6 5 4 3 2 1

Printed in the USA

TOKYO MEW MEW

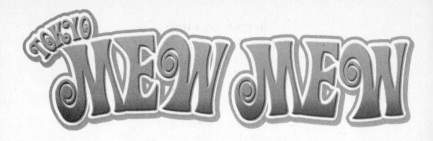

TABLE OF CONTENTS

About this story

Ichigo Momomiya was a normal junior high school student, until a freak accident turned her into superhero Mew Mew! Ichigo and her partners are working hard to save the world!

東京ミュウミュウ

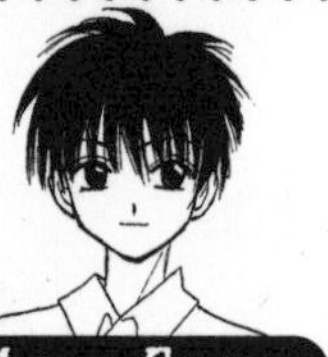

Masaya Aoyama

He's cute, smart and popular! Even better, he's on the kendo team!

CAFE MEW MEW

A mysterious, wealthy high school student.

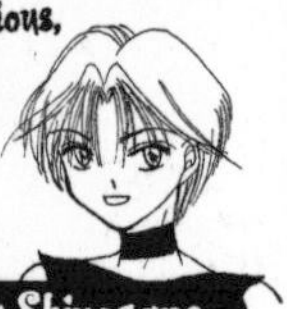

Ryou Shirogane

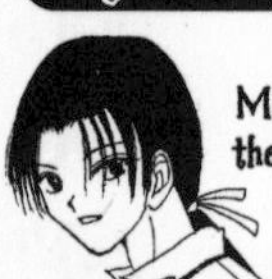

Manager of the café and Ryou's partner.

Keiichiro Akasaka

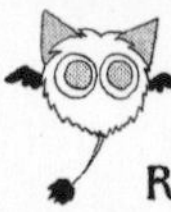

Masha

Ryou's pet robot.

Kish

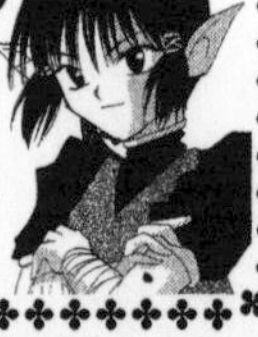

One of the aliens attacking Earth.

TOKYO MEW MEW

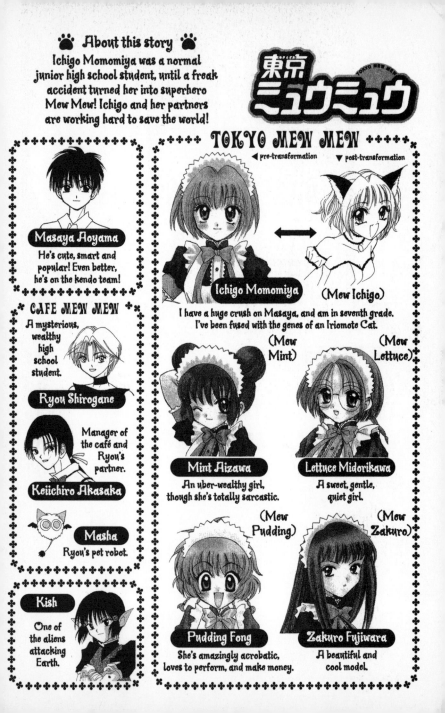

◀ pre-transformation ▼ post-transformation

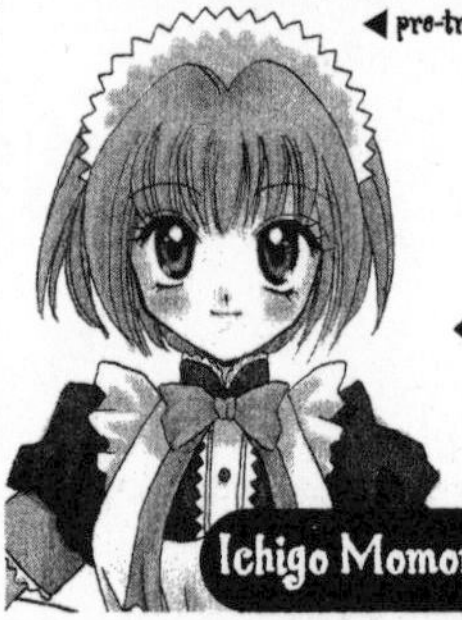

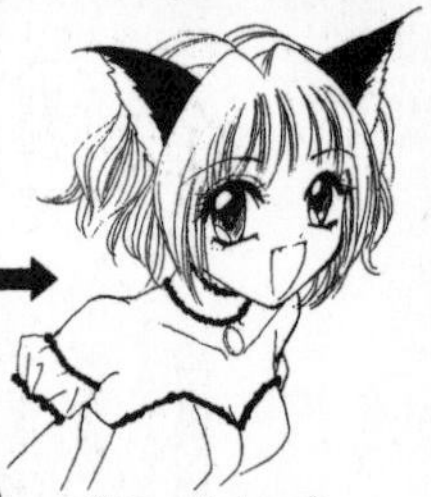

Ichigo Momomiya (Mew Ichigo)

I have a huge crush on Masaya, and am in seventh grade. I've been fused with the genes of an Iriomote Cat.

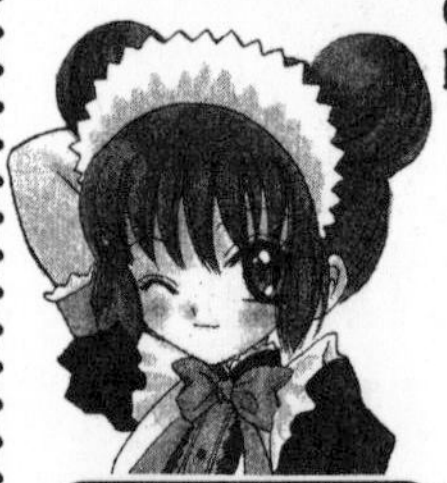

Mint Aizawa (Mew Mint)

An uber-wealthy girl, though she's totally sarcastic.

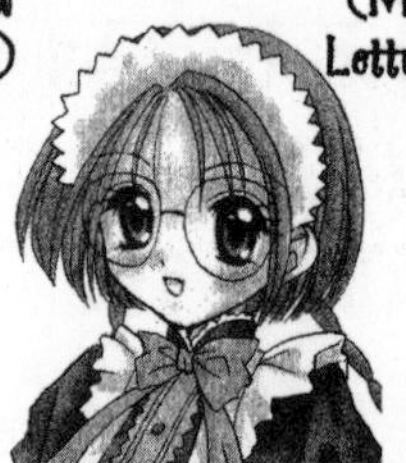

Lettuce Midorikawa (Mew Lettuce)

A sweet, gentle, quiet girl.

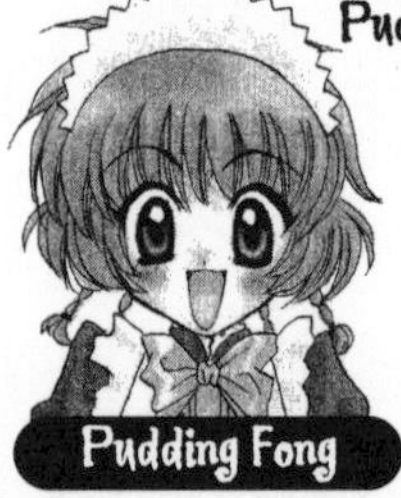

Pudding Fong (Mew Pudding)

She's amazingly acrobatic, loves to perform, and make money.

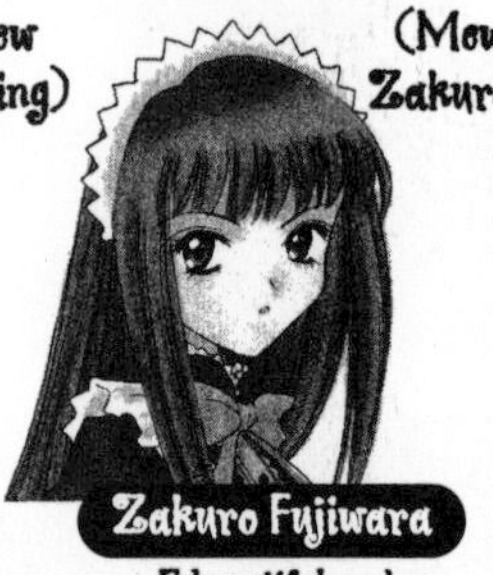

Zakuro Fujiwara (Mew Zakuro)

A beautiful and cool model.

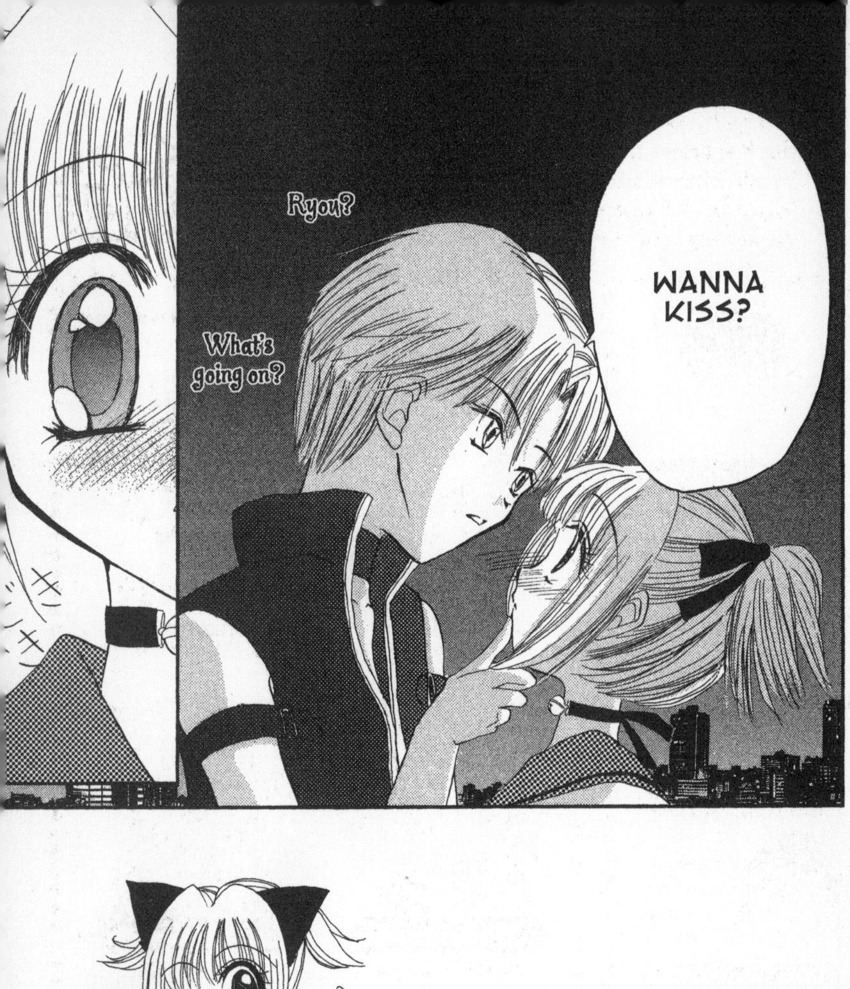
WANNA KISS?
Ryou?
What's going on?

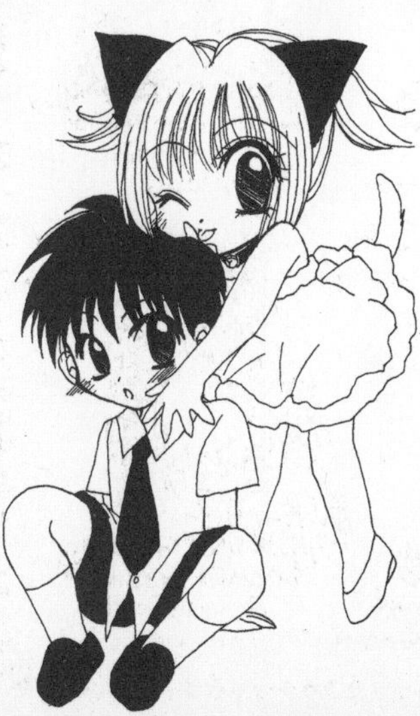

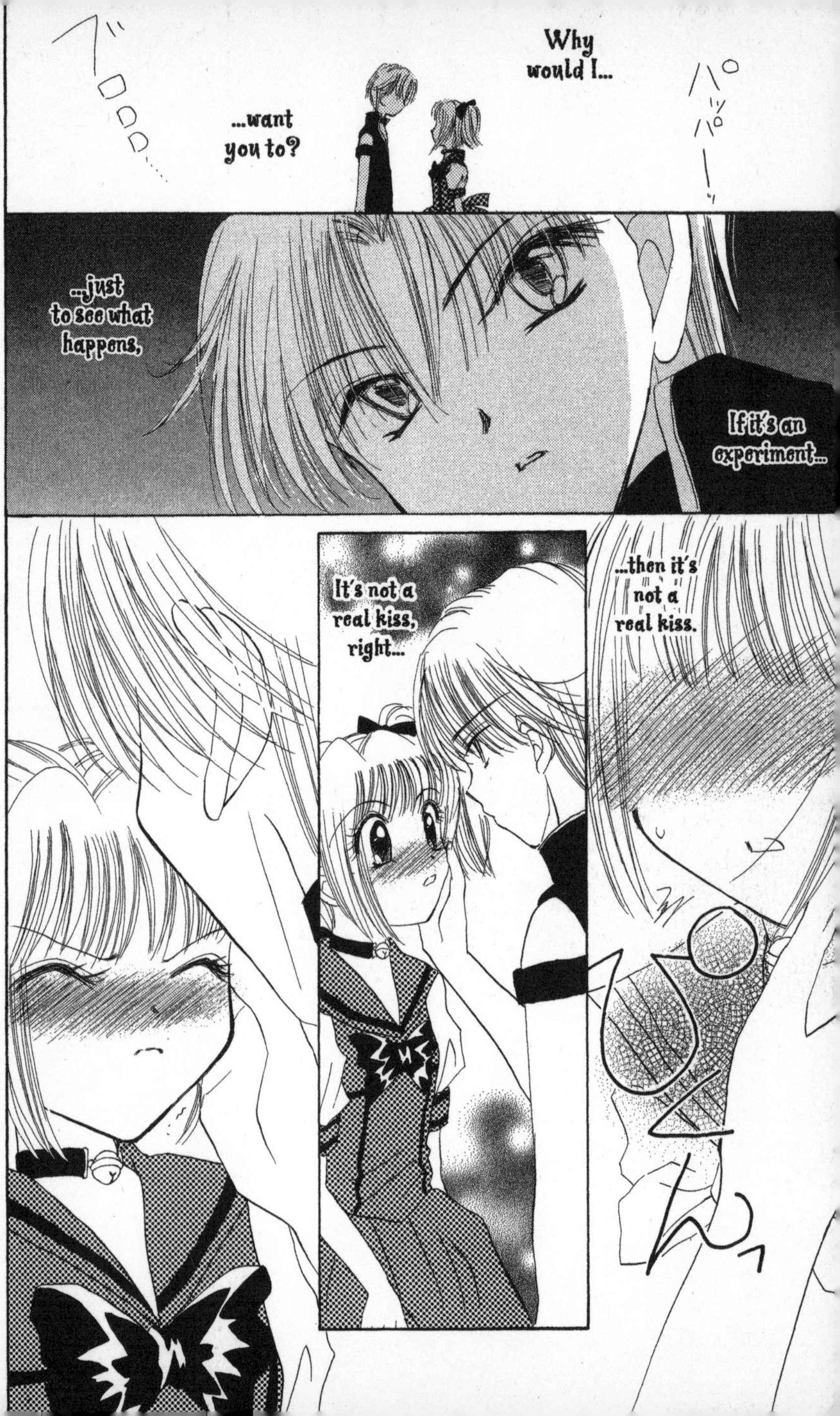
パッパー!!
Why would I...
...want you to?
ブロロロ……
If it's an experiment...
...just to see what happens,
...then it's not a real kiss.
It's not a real kiss, right...

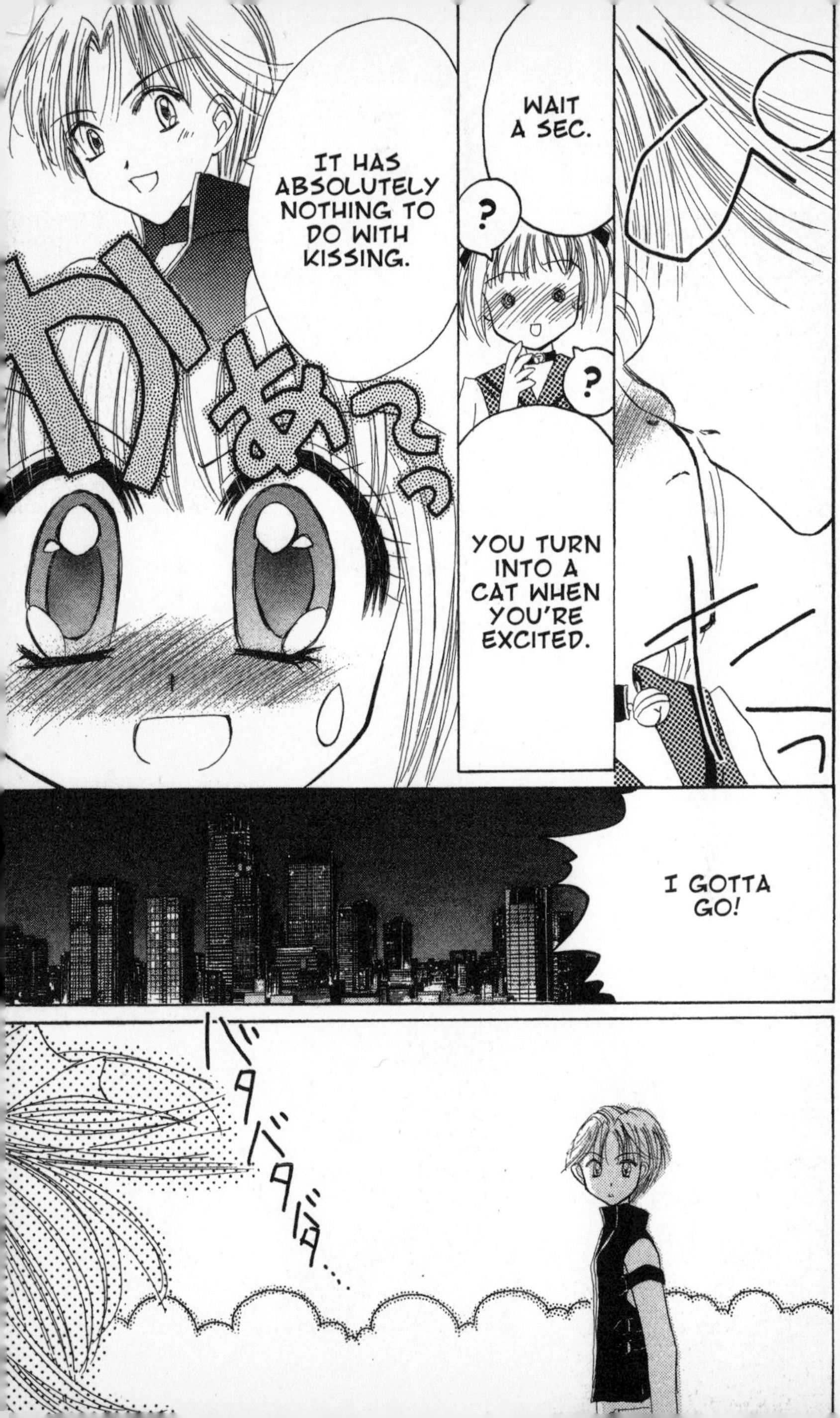
WAIT A SEC.
?
?
YOU TURN INTO A CAT WHEN YOU'RE EXCITED.
IT HAS ABSOLUTELY NOTHING TO DO WITH KISSING.
I GOTTA GO!
バタバタバタ…

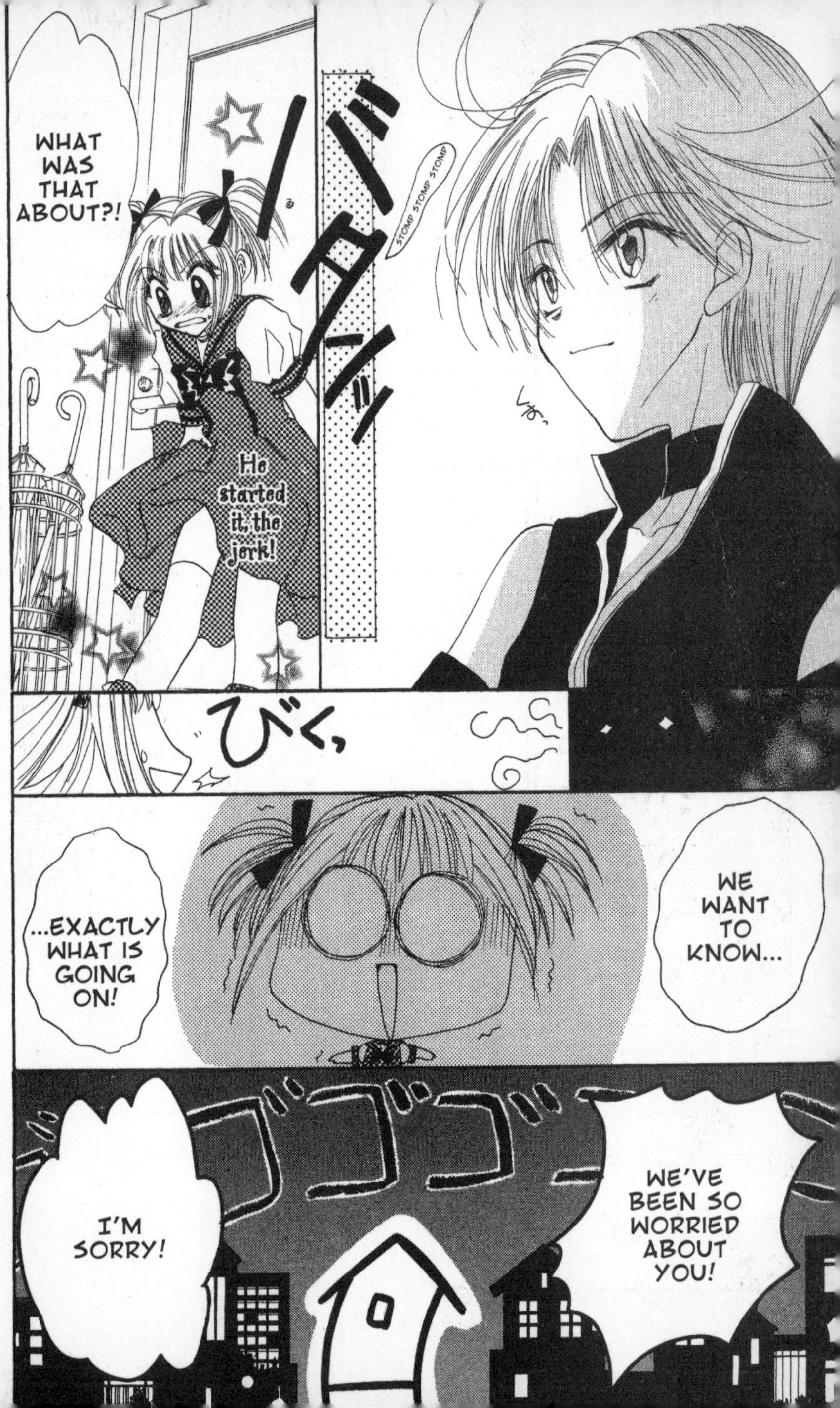
STOMP STOMP STOMP
WHAT WAS THAT ABOUT?!
He started it, the jerk!
WE WANT TO KNOW...
...EXACTLY WHAT IS GOING ON!
WE'VE BEEN SO WORRIED ABOUT YOU!
I'M SORRY!

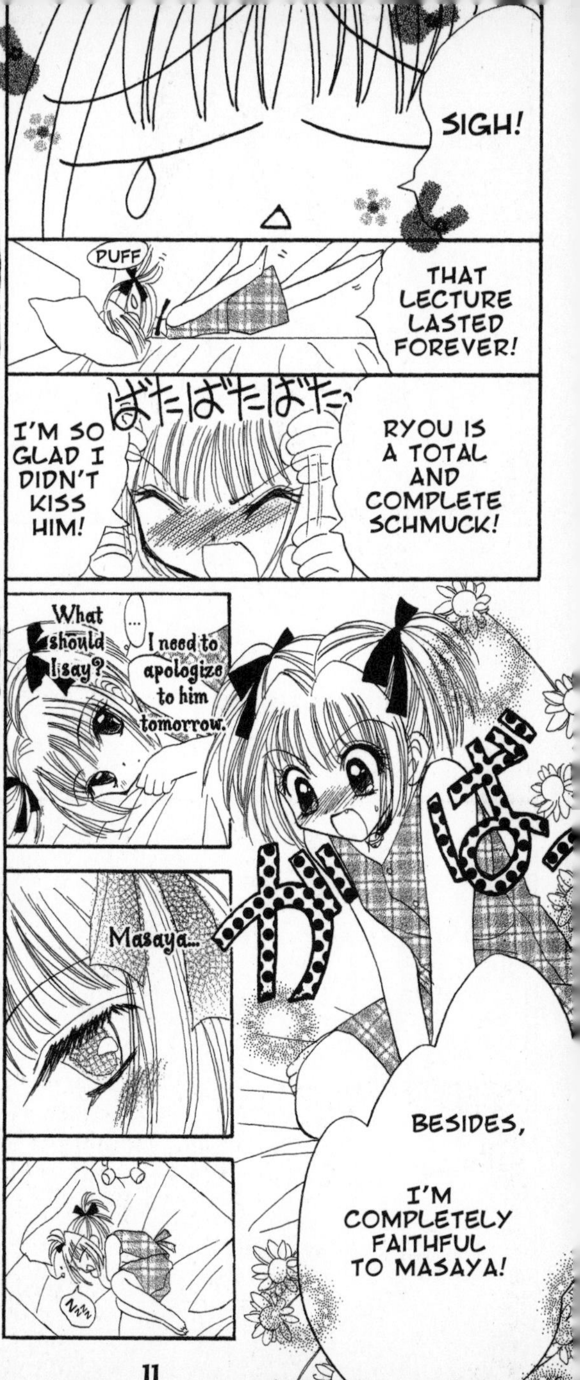
SIGH!
THAT LECTURE LASTED FOREVER!
PUFF
ばたばたばた
RYOU IS A TOTAL AND COMPLETE SCHMUCK!
I'M SO GLAD I DIDN'T KISS HIM!
BESIDES,
I'M COMPLETELY FAITHFUL TO MASAYA!
I need to apologize to him tomorrow.
...
What should I say?
Masaya...

Business Meeting

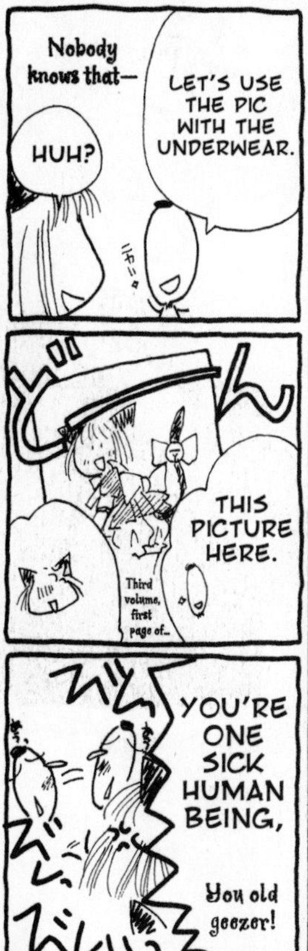
LET'S USE THE PIC WITH THE UNDERWEAR.
Nobody knows that—
HUH?
どーん
THIS PICTURE HERE.
Third volume, first page of...
YOU'RE ONE SICK HUMAN BEING,
You old geezer!
I'VE BEEN HAVING THESE WEIRD DAYDREAMS LATELY.... (LAUGH)
THAT WOULD BE HILARIOUS!
?

★ those are bloomers, not underwear!

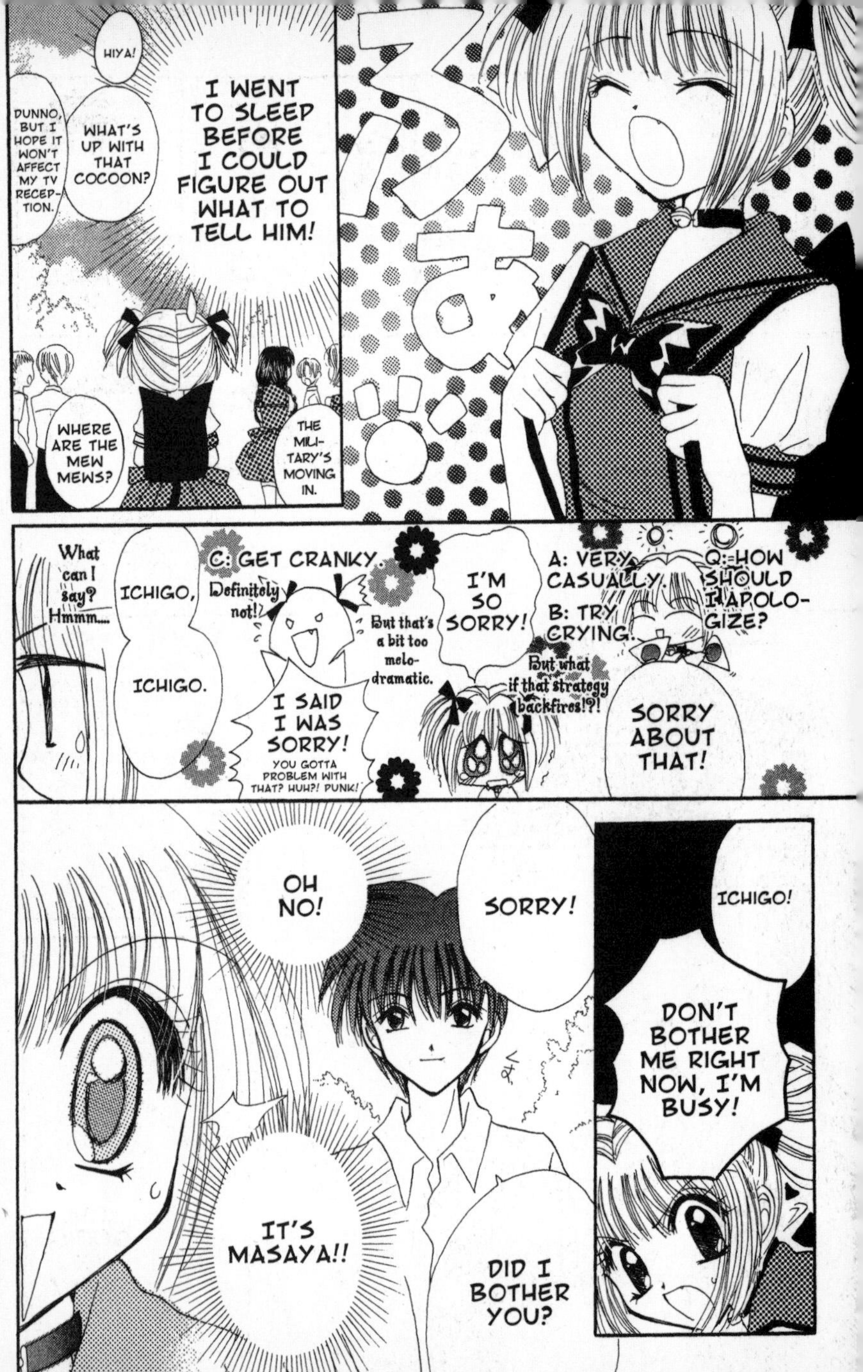
I WENT TO SLEEP BEFORE I COULD FIGURE OUT WHAT TO TELL HIM!
HIYA!
WHAT'S UP WITH THAT COCOON?
DUNNO, BUT I HOPE IT WON'T AFFECT MY TV RECEPTION.
THE MILITARY'S MOVING IN.
WHERE ARE THE MEW MEWS?
Q: HOW SHOULD I APOLOGIZE?
A: VERY CASUALLY.
SORRY ABOUT THAT!
B: TRY CRYING.
I'M SO SORRY!
But what if that strategy backfires!?!
But that's a bit too melodramatic.
C: GET CRANKY.
I SAID I WAS SORRY! YOU GOTTA PROBLEM WITH THAT? HUH?! PUNK!
Definitely not!?
ICHIGO,
ICHIGO.
What can I say? Hmmm....
ICHIGO!
DON'T BOTHER ME RIGHT NOW, I'M BUSY!
SORRY!
DID I BOTHER YOU?
OH NO!
IT'S MASAYA!!

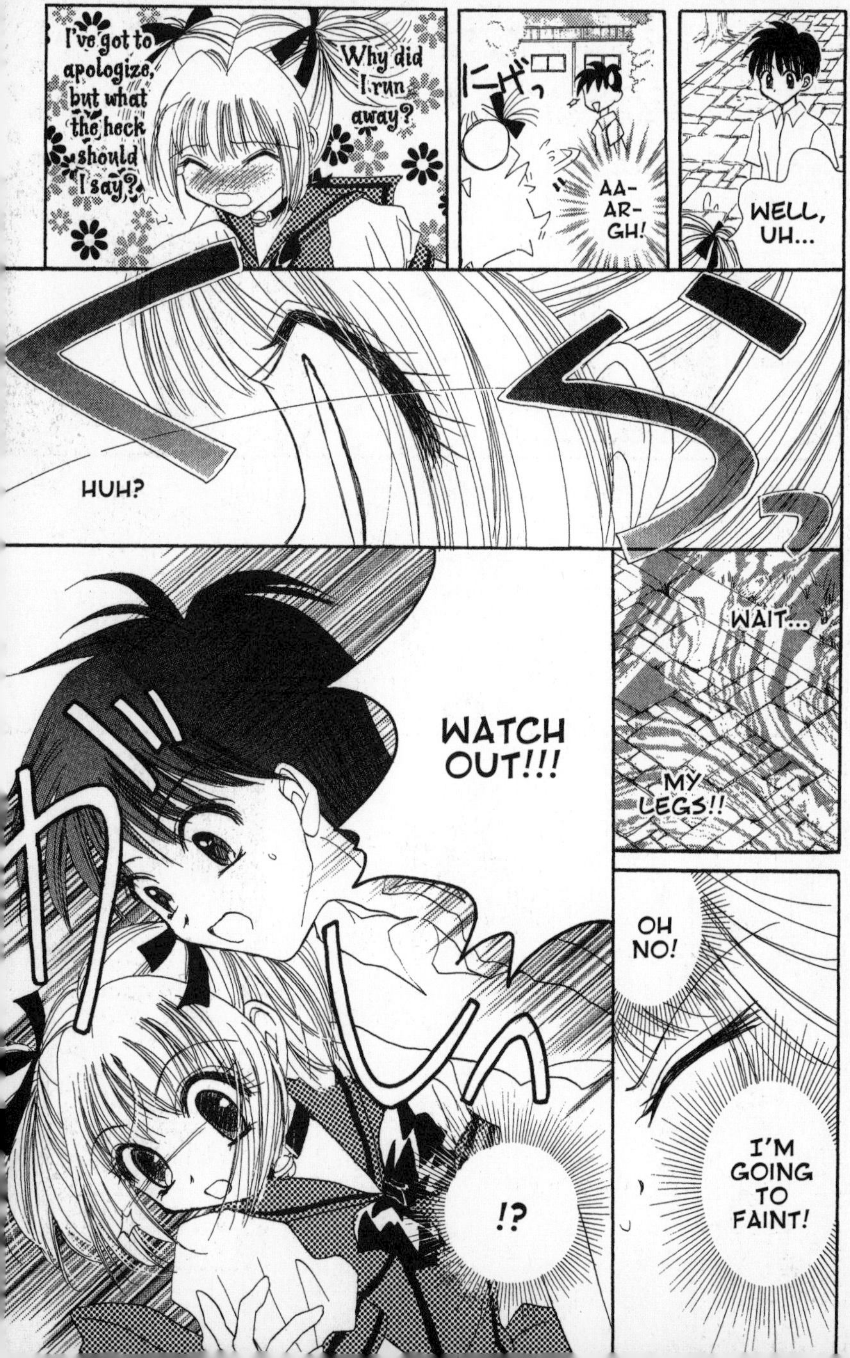
WELL, UH...
AA-AR-GH!
Why did I run away?
I've got to apologize, but what the heck should I say?
くらっ
HUH?
WAIT...
MY LEGS!!
OH NO!
I'M GOING TO FAINT!
WATCH OUT!!!
!?

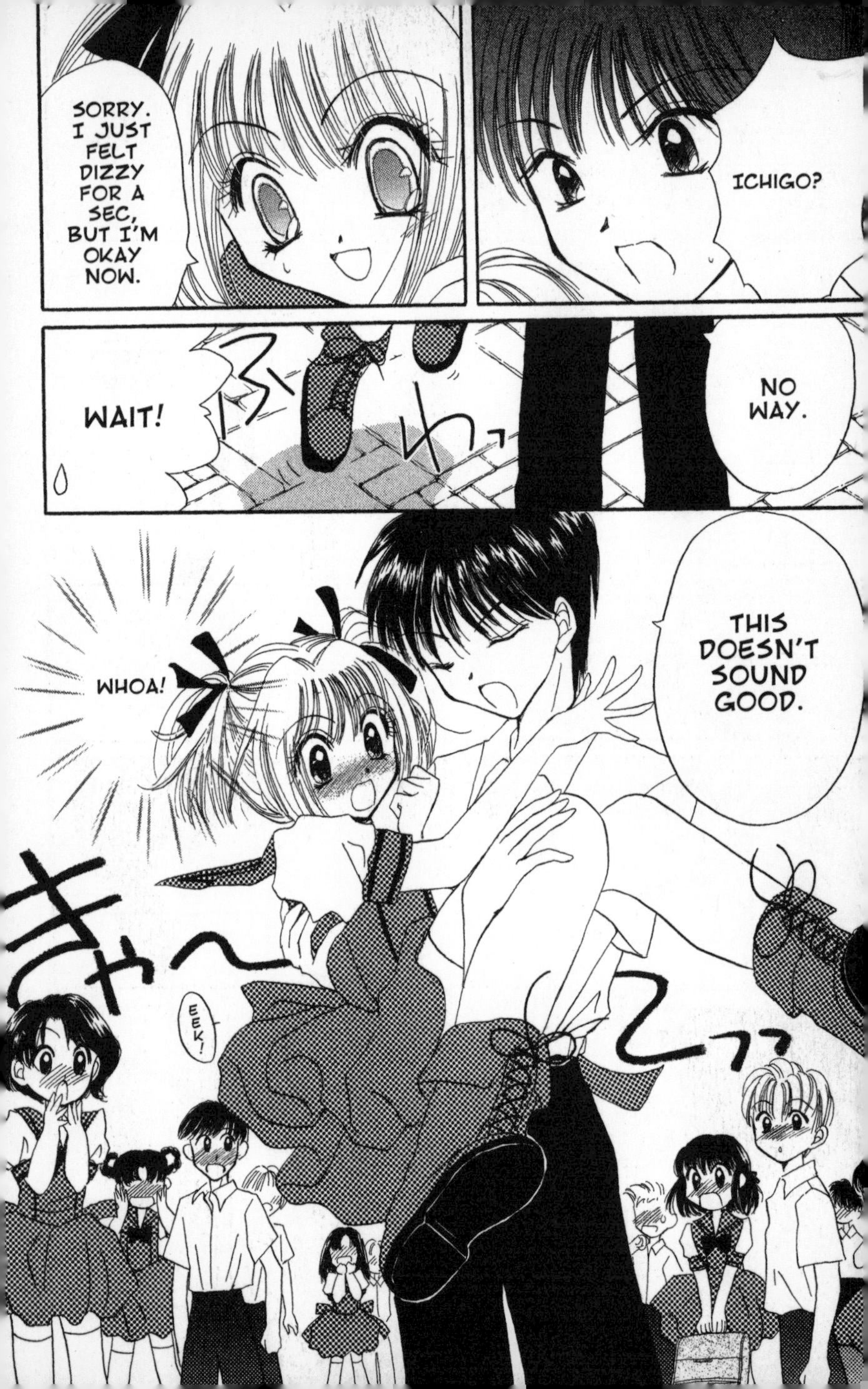
ICHIGO?
SORRY. I JUST FELT DIZZY FOR A SEC, BUT I'M OKAY NOW.
NO WAY.
ふわっ
WAIT!
THIS DOESN'T SOUND GOOD.
WHOA!
きゃ〜
EEK!

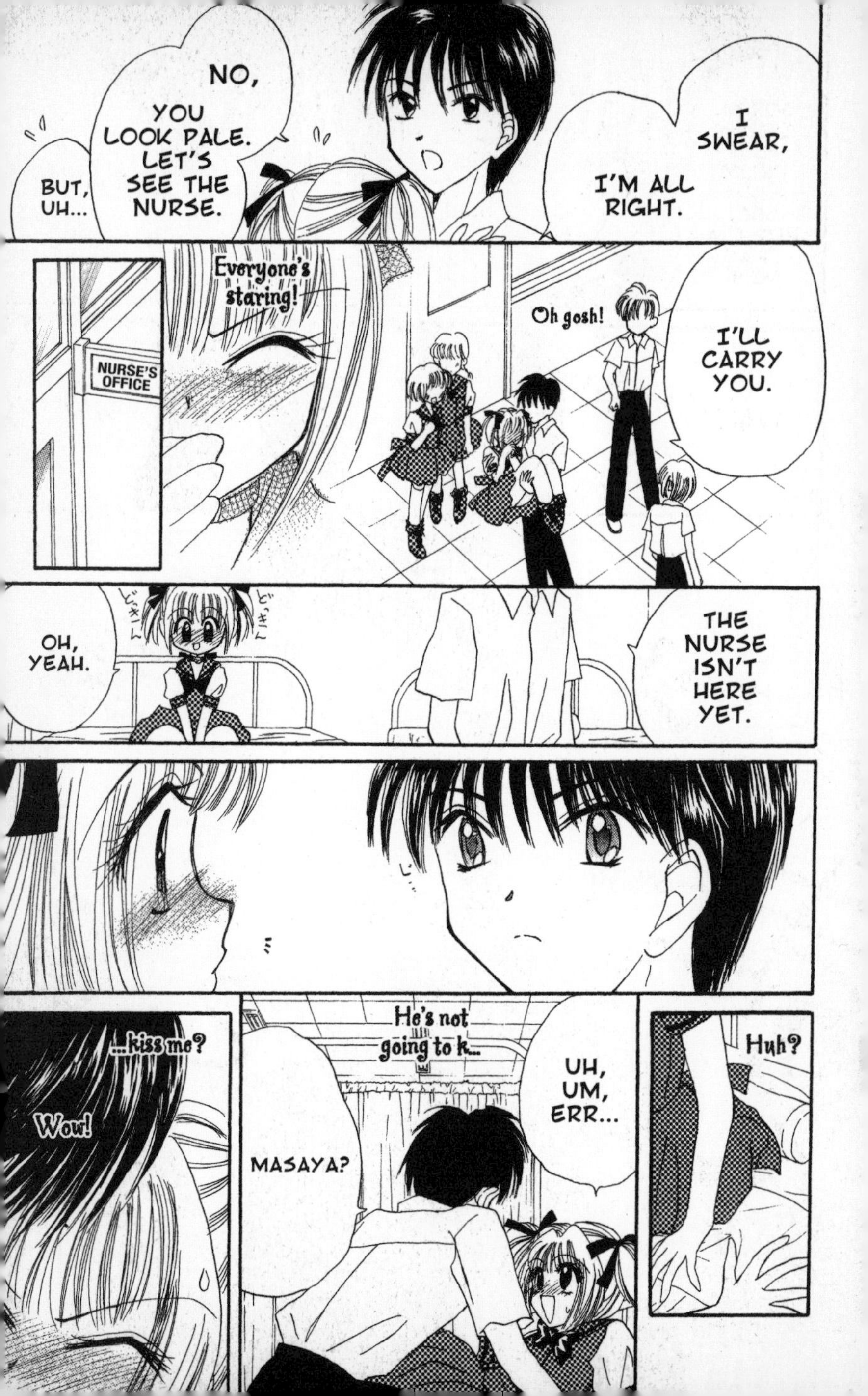
I SWEAR, I'M ALL RIGHT.
NO, YOU LOOK PALE. LET'S SEE THE NURSE.
BUT, UH...
I'LL CARRY YOU.
Oh gosh!
Everyone's staring!
NURSE'S OFFICE
THE NURSE ISN'T HERE YET.
OH, YEAH.
Huh?
UH, UM, ERR...
He's not going to k...
MASAYA?
...kiss me?
Wow!

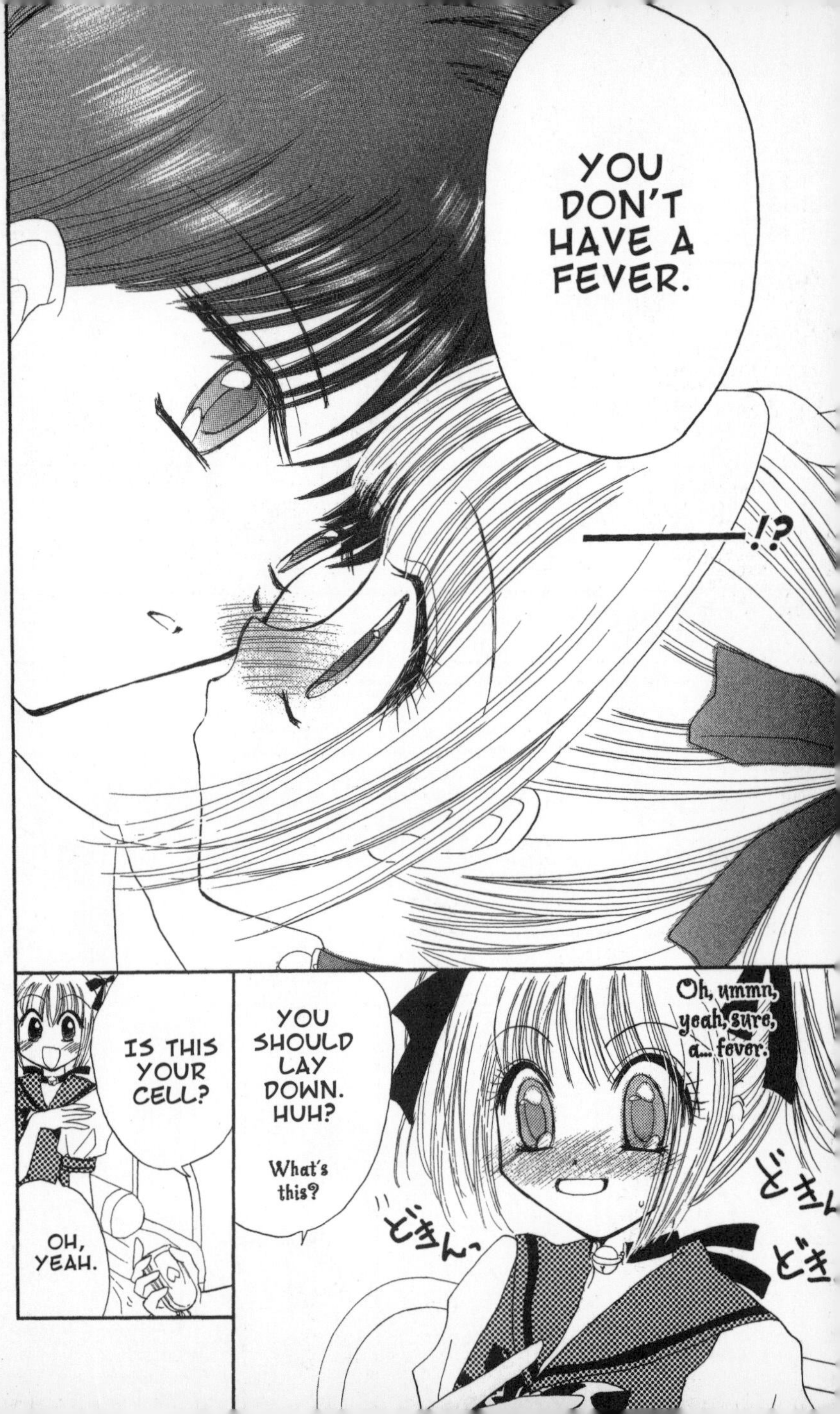
YOU DON'T HAVE A FEVER.
———!?
Oh, ummn, yeah, sure, a... fever.
どきん
どき
どきん
YOU SHOULD LAY DOWN. HUH?
What's this?
IS THIS YOUR CELL?
OH, YEAH.

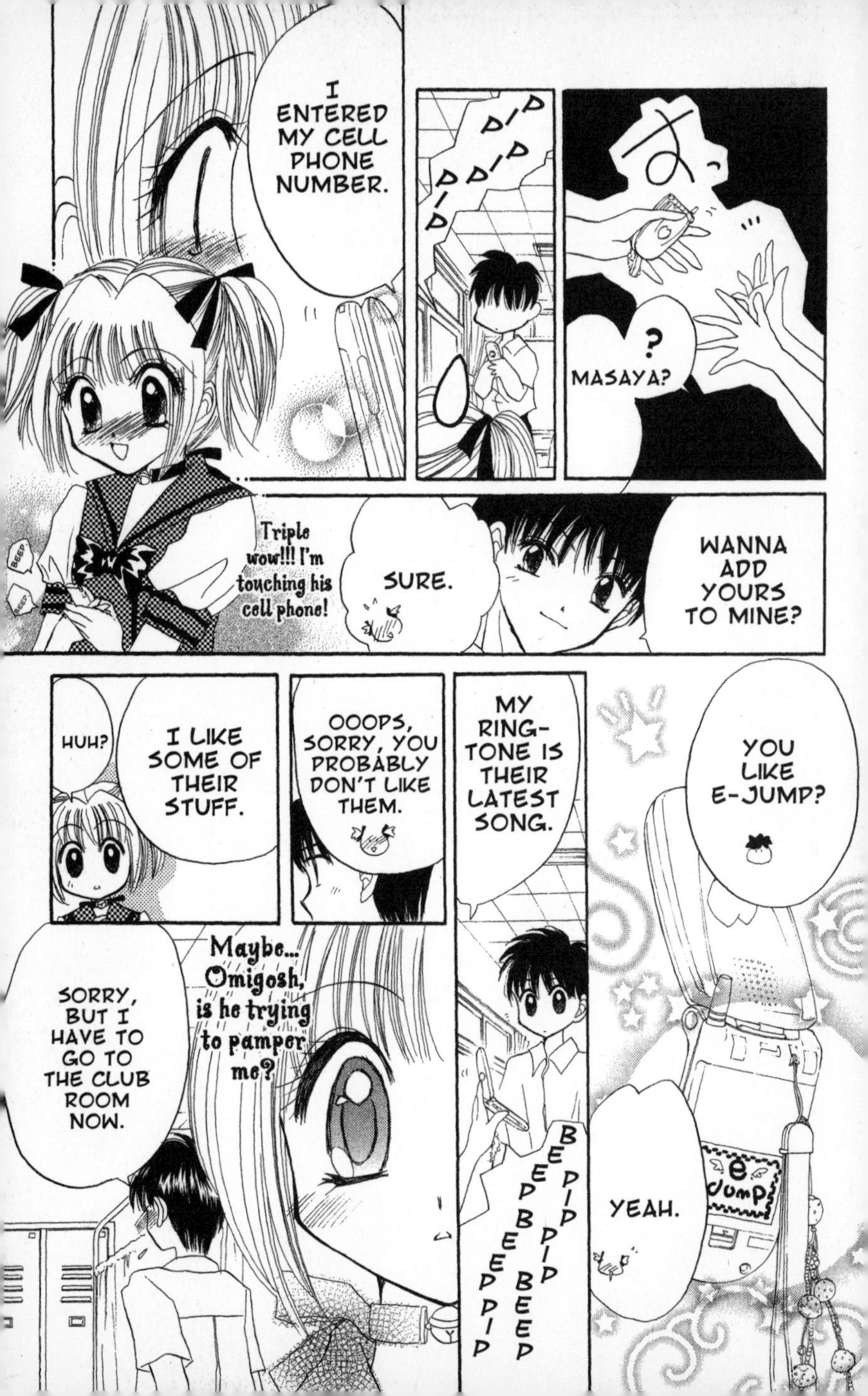
?
MASAYA?
DIDIDIDIDI
I ENTERED MY CELL PHONE NUMBER.
WANNA ADD YOURS TO MINE?
SURE.
Triple wow!!! I'm touching his cell phone!
BEEP
BEEP
YOU LIKE E-JUMP?
YEAH.
e jump
MY RINGTONE IS THEIR LATEST SONG.
OOOPS, SORRY, YOU PROBABLY DON'T LIKE THEM.
I LIKE SOME OF THEIR STUFF.
HUH?
DIP DIP BEEP
BEEP BEEP DIP
Maybe... Omigosh, is he trying to pamper me?
SORRY, BUT I HAVE TO GO TO THE CLUB ROOM NOW.

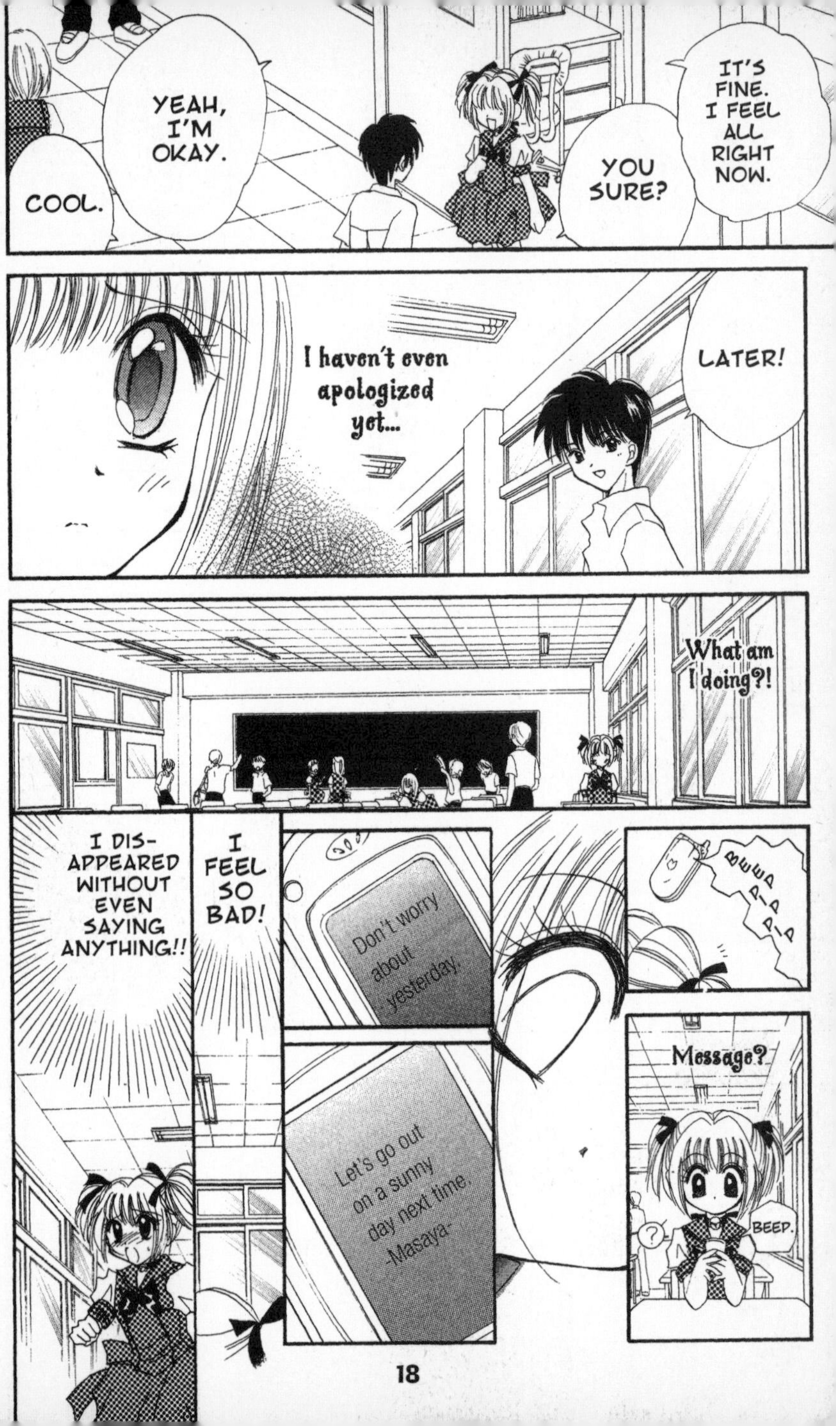
IT'S FINE. I FEEL ALL RIGHT NOW.
YOU SURE?
YEAH, I'M OKAY.
COOL.
LATER!
I haven't even apologized yet...
What am I doing?!
BWWA P-P-P-P
Message?
BEEP.
Don't worry about yesterday,
Let's go out on a sunny day next time. -Masaya-
I FEEL SO BAD!
I DIS-APPEARED WITHOUT EVEN SAYING ANYTHING!!

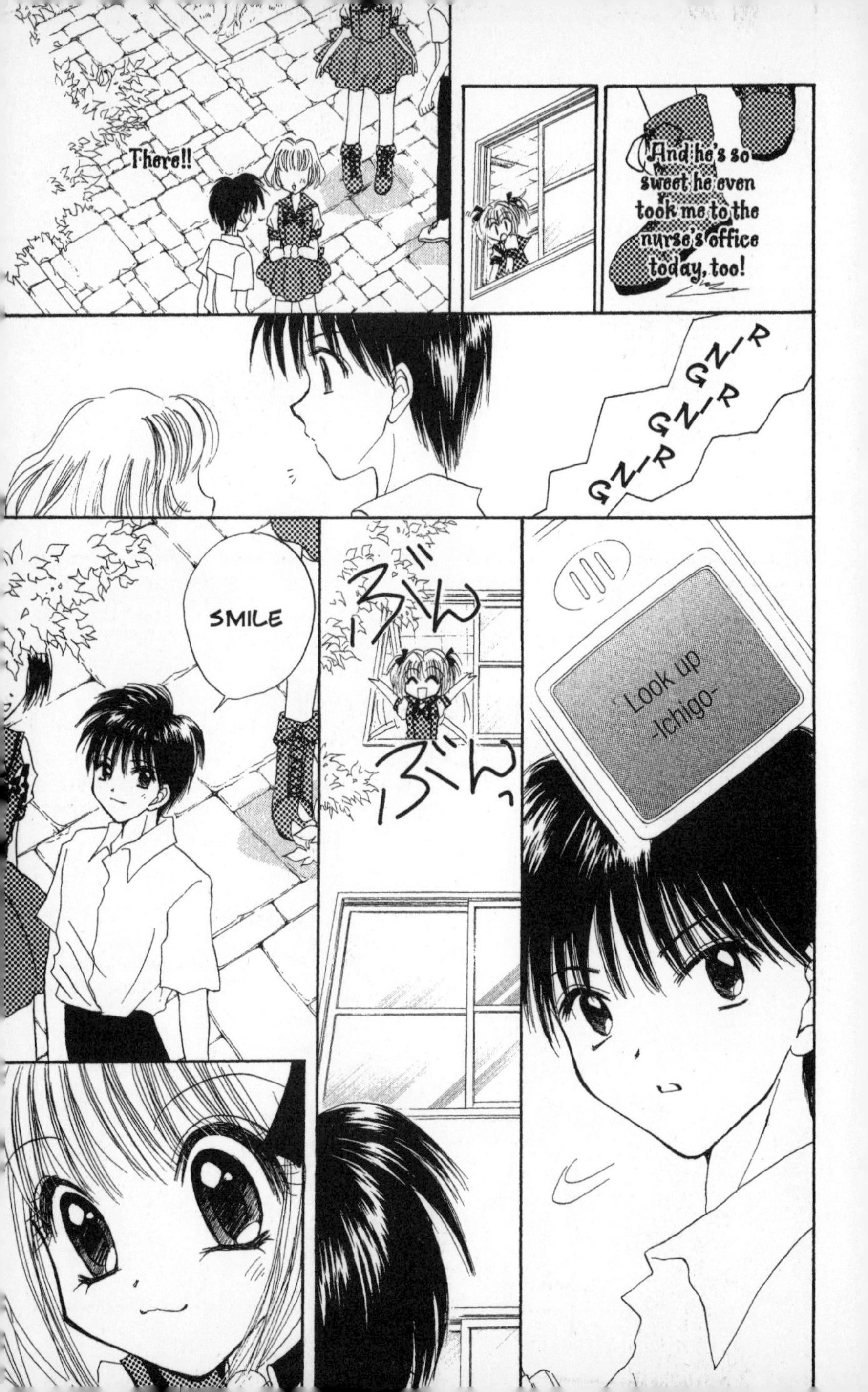
And he's so sweet he even took me to the nurse's office today, too!
There!!
GNIR GNIR GNIR
Look up -Ichigo-
ぶん ぶん
SMILE

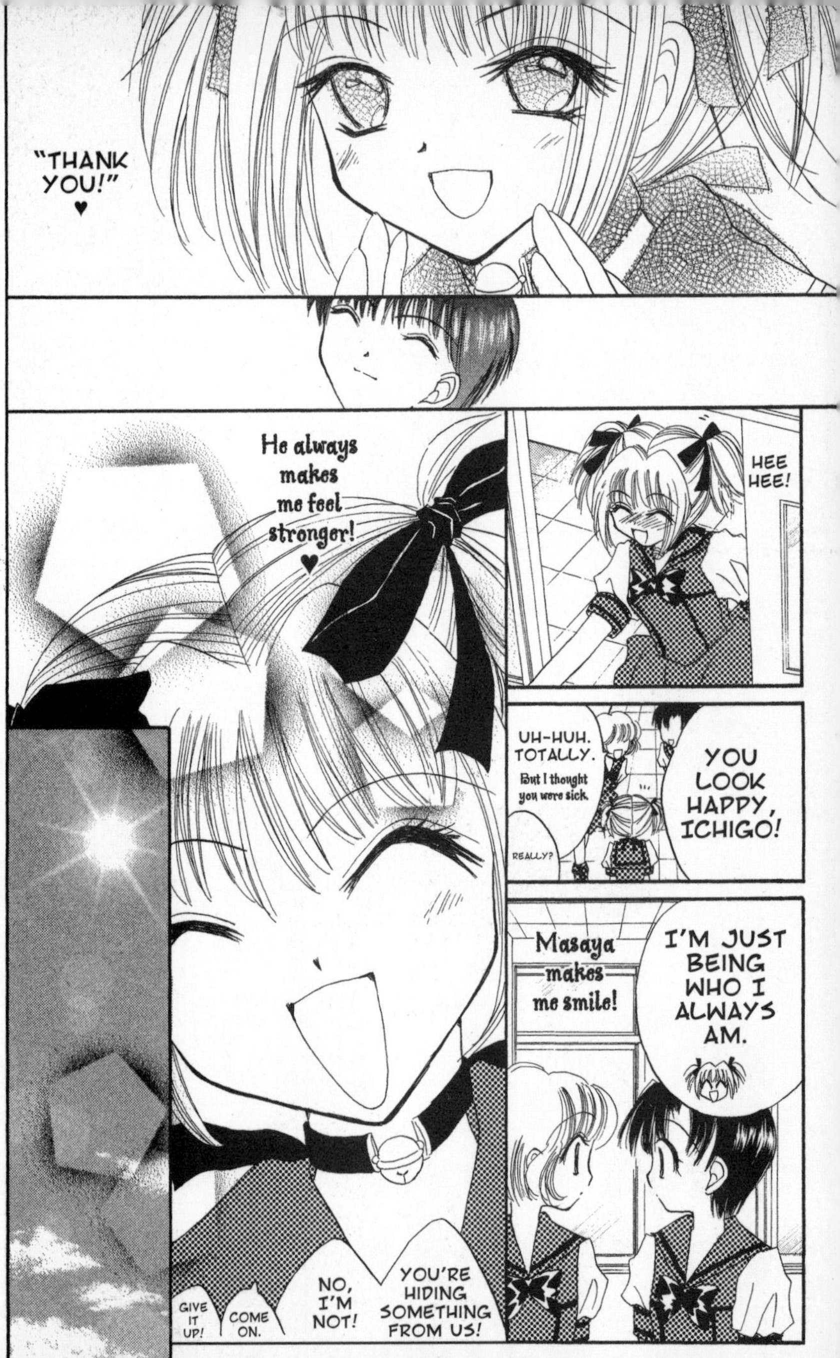
"THANK YOU!" ♥
HEE HEE!
YOU LOOK HAPPY, ICHIGO!
UH-HUH. TOTALLY.
But I thought you were sick.
REALLY?
I'M JUST BEING WHO I ALWAYS AM.
Masaya makes me smile!
He always makes me feel stronger! ♥
YOU'RE HIDING SOMETHING FROM US!
NO, I'M NOT!
COME ON.
GIVE IT UP!

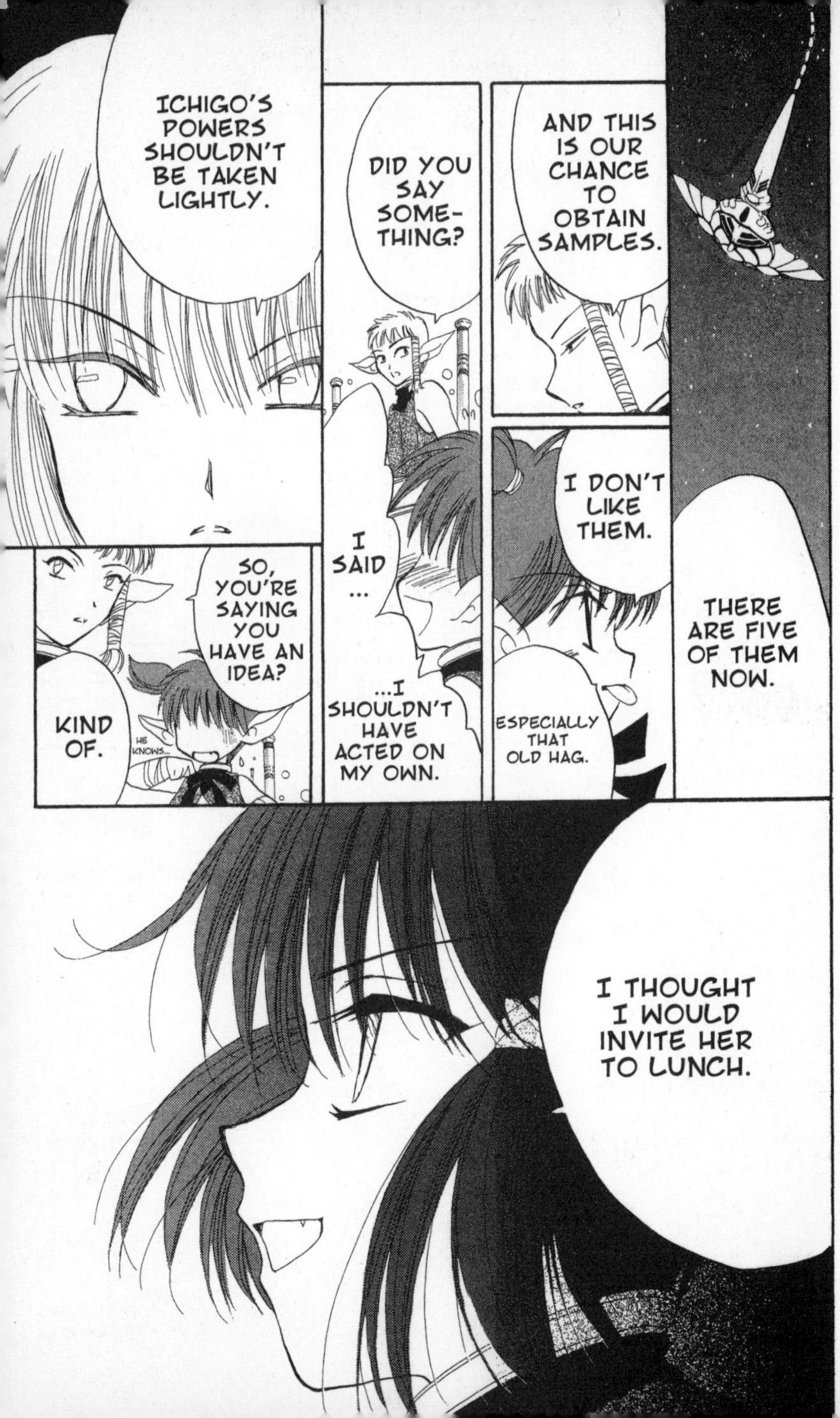
THERE ARE FIVE OF THEM NOW.
AND THIS IS OUR CHANCE TO OBTAIN SAMPLES.
I DON'T LIKE THEM.
ESPECIALLY THAT OLD HAG.
DID YOU SAY SOME-THING?
I SAID ...
...I SHOULDN'T HAVE ACTED ON MY OWN.
ICHIGO'S POWERS SHOULDN'T BE TAKEN LIGHTLY.
SO, YOU'RE SAYING YOU HAVE AN IDEA?
KIND OF.
HE KNOWS...
I THOUGHT I WOULD INVITE HER TO LUNCH.

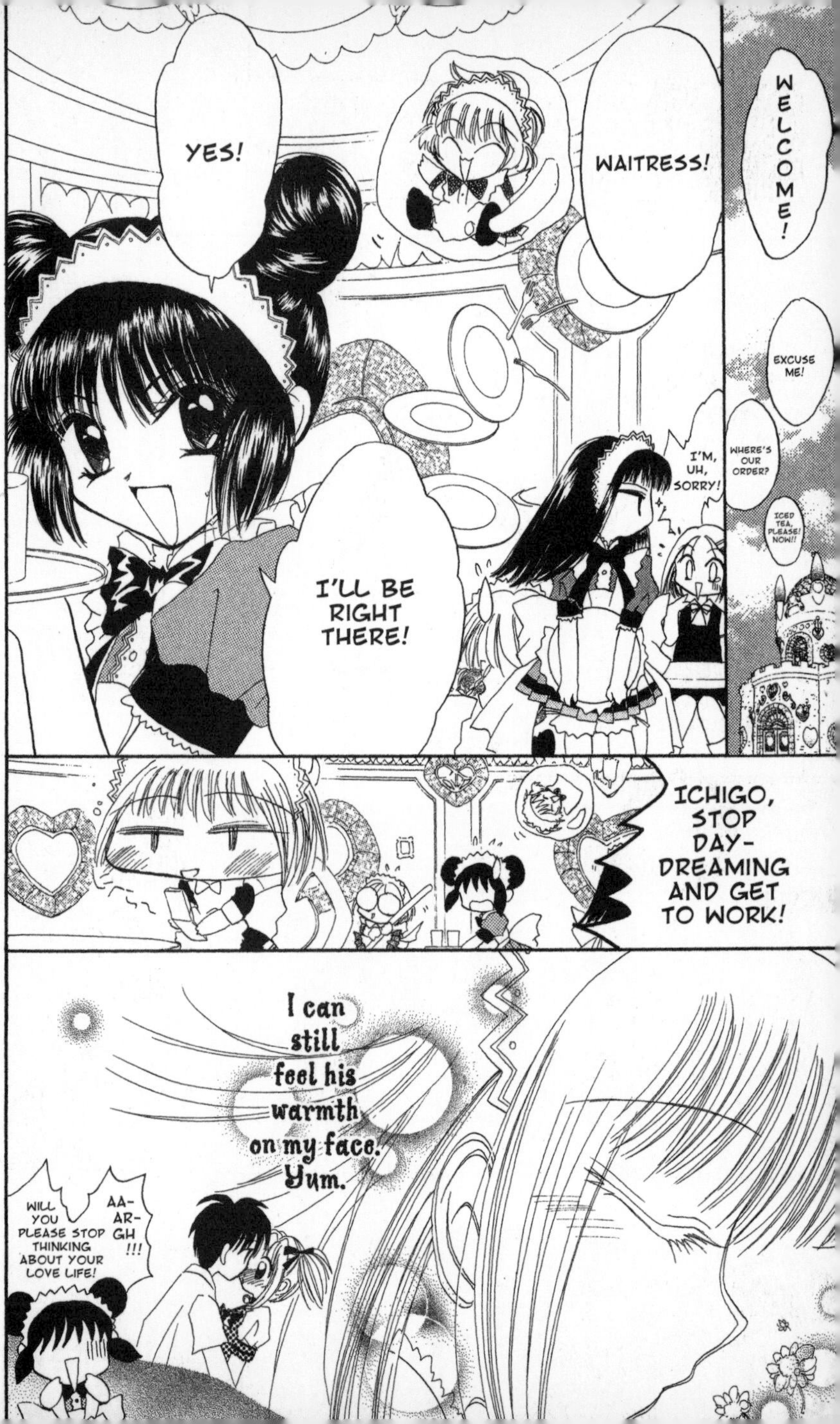
WELCOME!
EXCUSE ME!
WHERE'S OUR ORDER?
ICED TEA, PLEASE! NOW!!
WAITRESS!
YES!
I'M, UH, SORRY!
I'LL BE RIGHT THERE!
ICHIGO, STOP DAY-DREAMING AND GET TO WORK!
I can still feel his warmth on my face. Yum.
AA-AR-GH!!!
WILL YOU PLEASE STOP THINKING ABOUT YOUR LOVE LIFE!

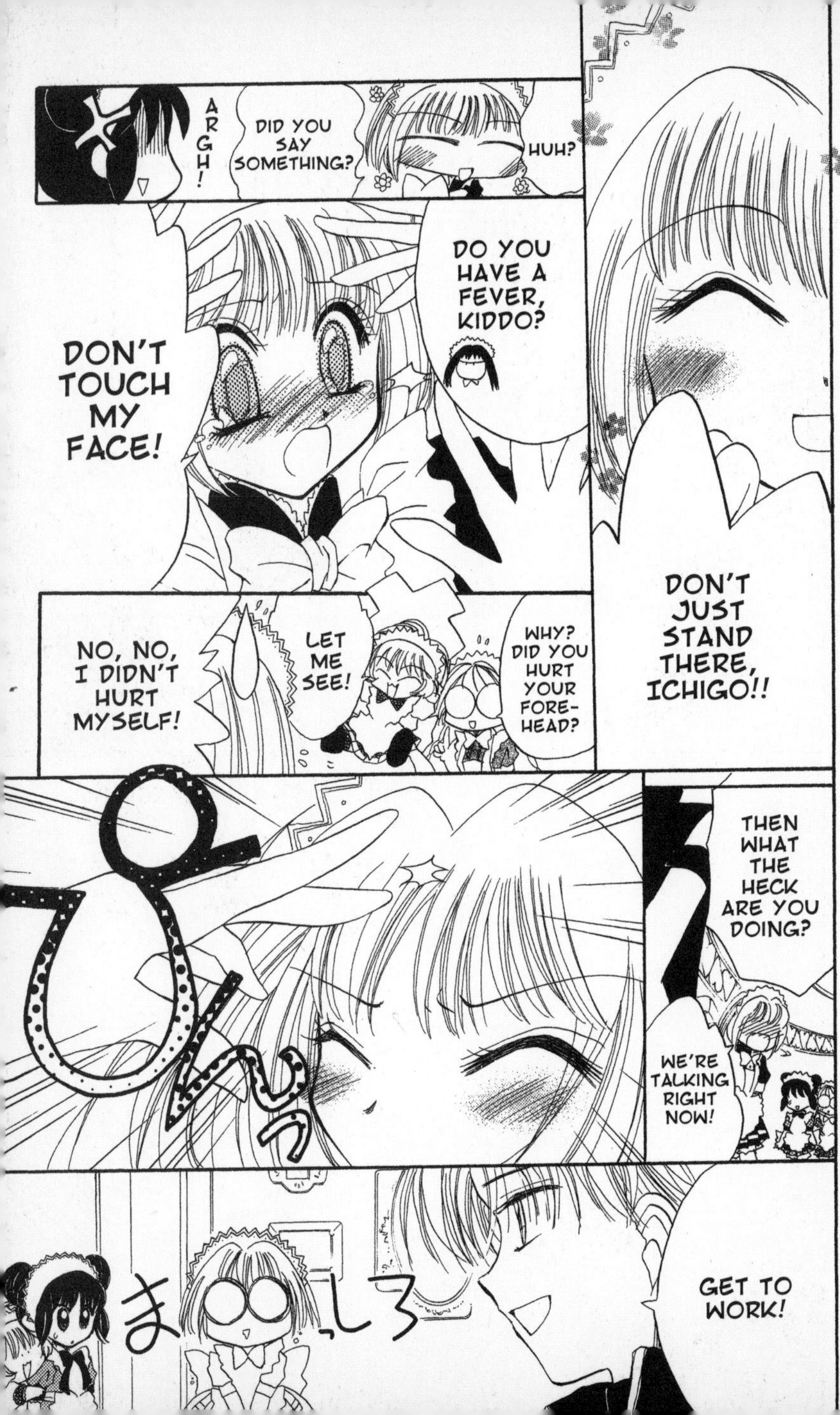
DON'T JUST STAND THERE, ICHIGO!!
HUH?
DID YOU SAY SOMETHING?
ARGH!
DO YOU HAVE A FEVER, KIDDO?
DON'T TOUCH MY FACE!
WHY? DID YOU HURT YOUR FORE-HEAD?
LET ME SEE!
NO, NO, I DIDN'T HURT MYSELF!
THEN WHAT THE HECK ARE YOU DOING?
WE'RE TALKING RIGHT NOW!
GET TO WORK!

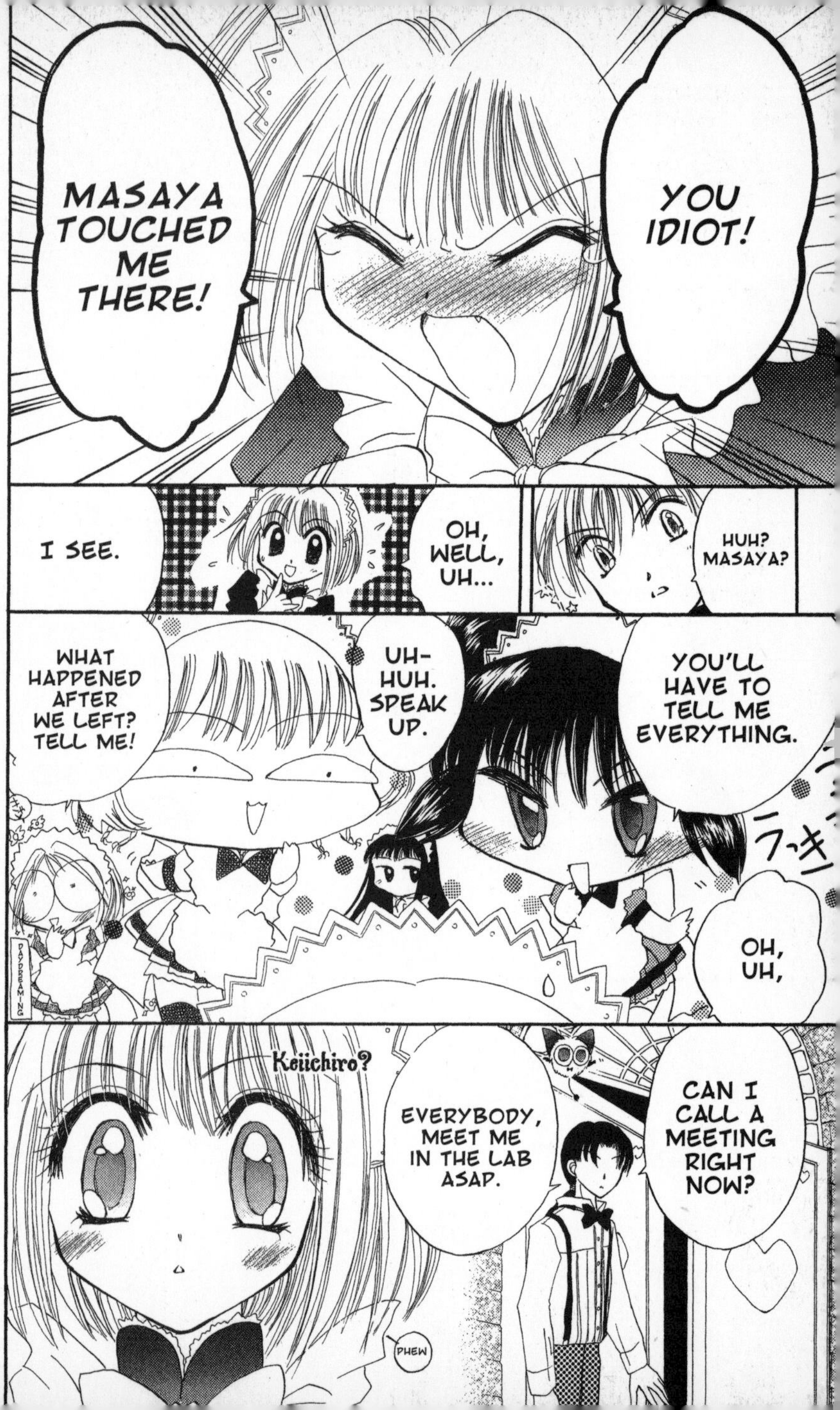
YOU IDIOT!
MASAYA TOUCHED ME THERE!
HUH? MASAYA?
OH, WELL, UH...
I SEE.
YOU'LL HAVE TO TELL ME EVERYTHING.
ラッキ
UH-HUH. SPEAK UP.
WHAT HAPPENED AFTER WE LEFT? TELL ME!
OH, UH,
DAYDREAMING
CAN I CALL A MEETING RIGHT NOW?
EVERYBODY, MEET ME IN THE LAB ASAP.
Keiichiro?
PHEW

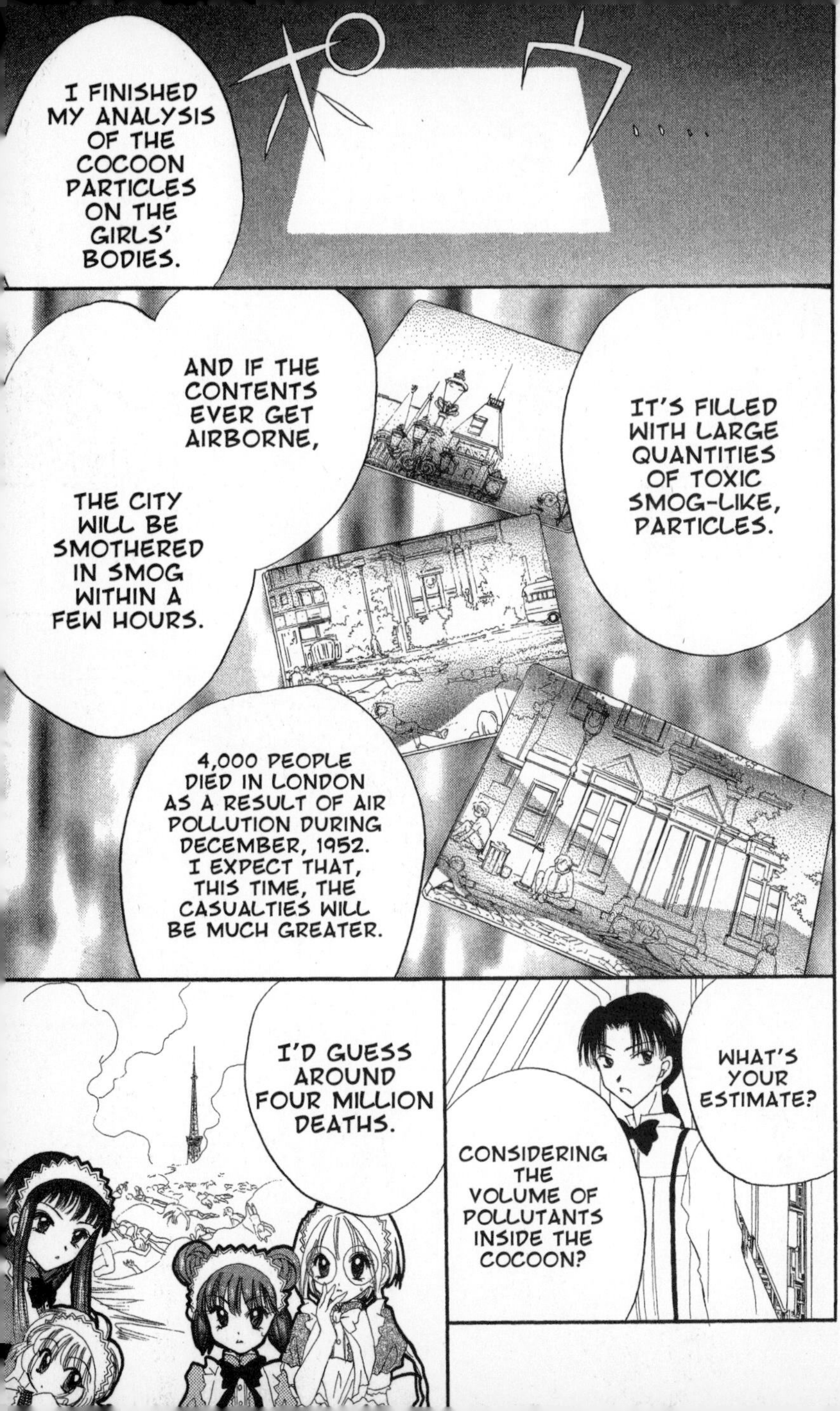
I FINISHED MY ANALYSIS OF THE COCOON PARTICLES ON THE GIRLS' BODIES.
IT'S FILLED WITH LARGE QUANTITIES OF TOXIC SMOG-LIKE, PARTICLES.
AND IF THE CONTENTS EVER GET AIRBORNE,
THE CITY WILL BE SMOTHERED IN SMOG WITHIN A FEW HOURS.
4,000 PEOPLE DIED IN LONDON AS A RESULT OF AIR POLLUTION DURING DECEMBER, 1952. I EXPECT THAT, THIS TIME, THE CASUALTIES WILL BE MUCH GREATER.
WHAT'S YOUR ESTIMATE?
CONSIDERING THE VOLUME OF POLLUTANTS INSIDE THE COCOON?
I'D GUESS AROUND FOUR MILLION DEATHS.

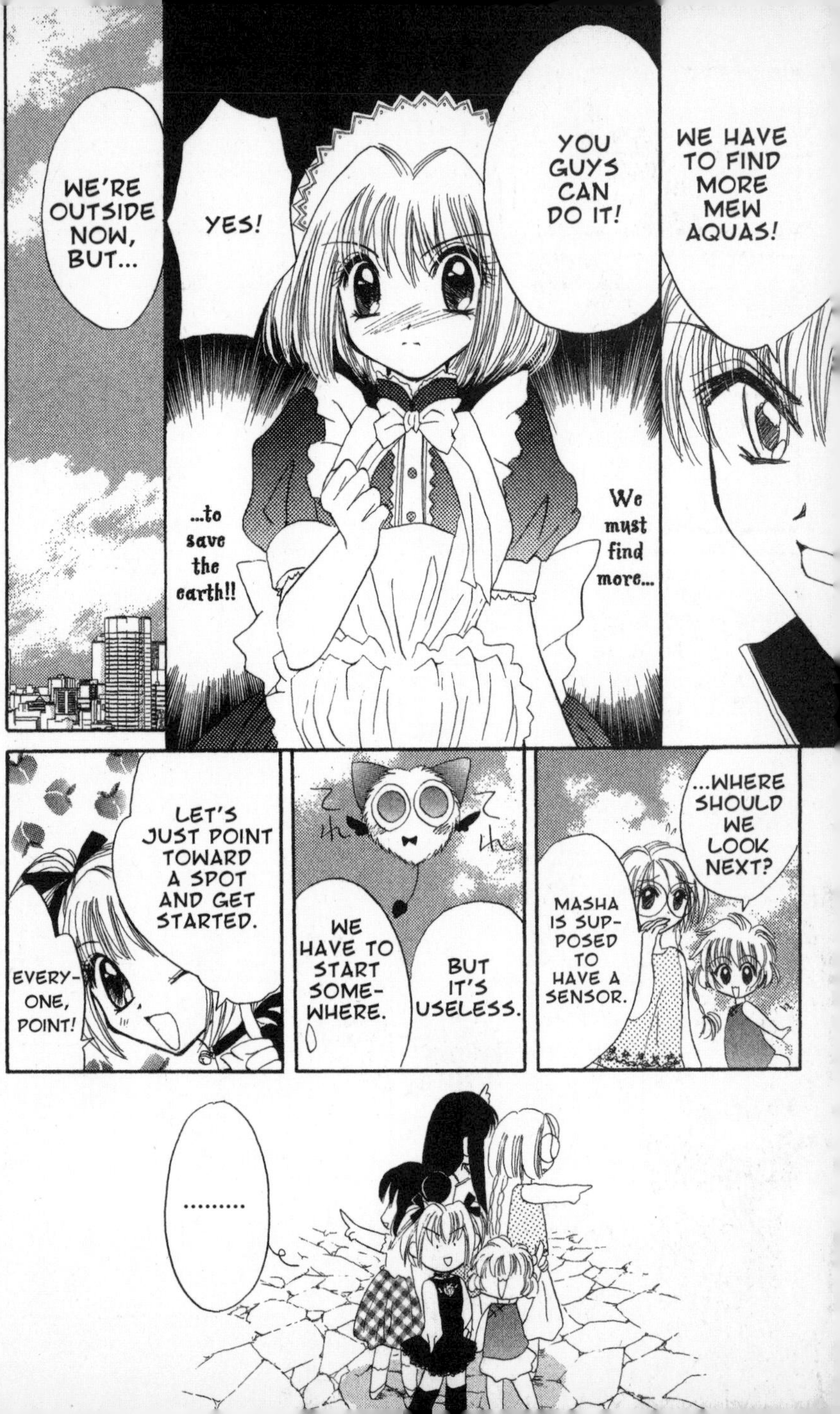
WE HAVE TO FIND MORE MEW AQUAS!
YOU GUYS CAN DO IT!
YES!
We must find more...
...to save the earth!!
WE'RE OUTSIDE NOW, BUT...
...WHERE SHOULD WE LOOK NEXT?
MASHA IS SUP-POSED TO HAVE A SENSOR.
BUT IT'S USELESS.
WE HAVE TO START SOME-WHERE.
LET'S JUST POINT TOWARD A SPOT AND GET STARTED.
EVERY-ONE, POINT!
....

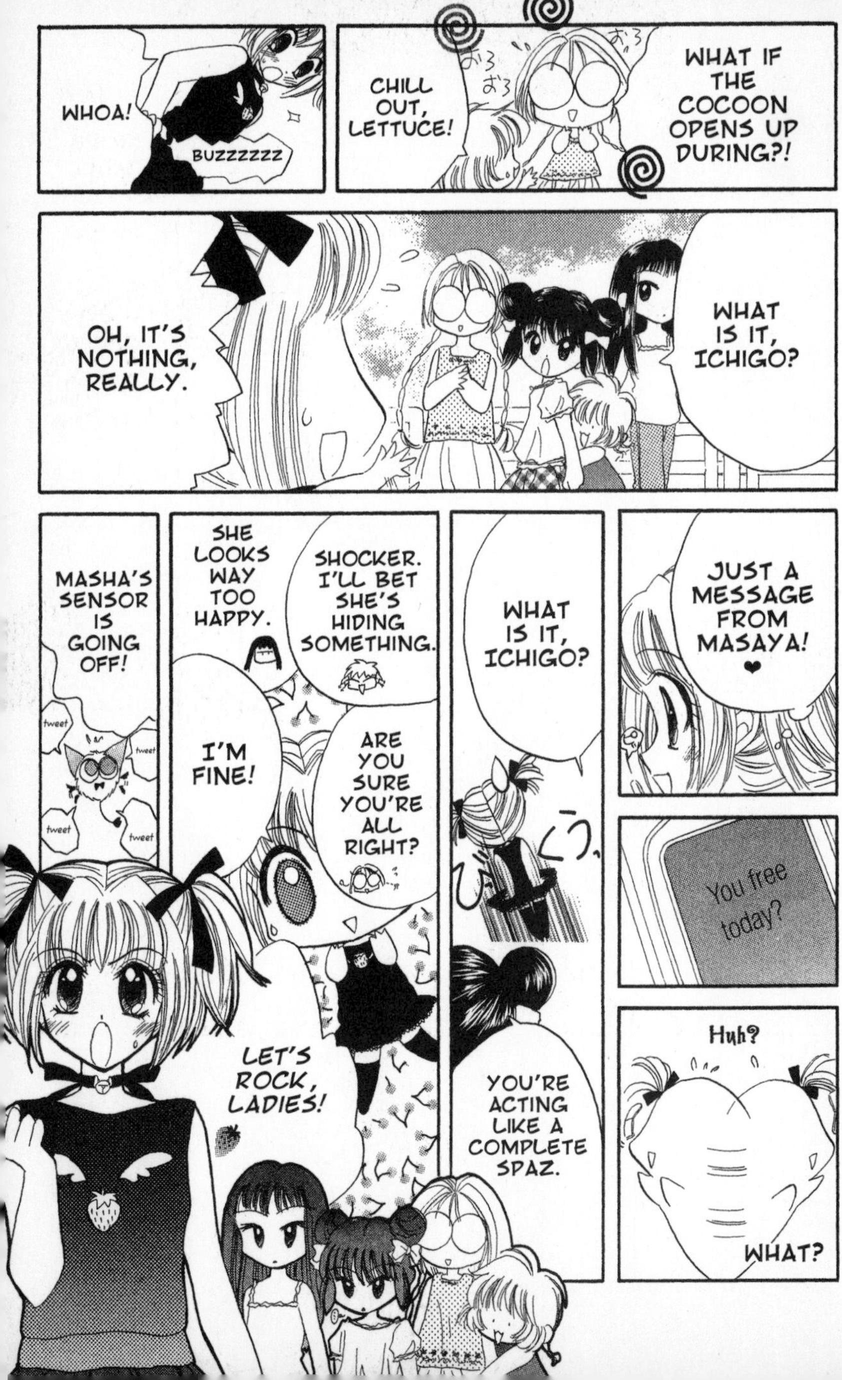
WHAT IF THE COCOON OPENS UP DURING?!
おろ おろ
おろ
CHILL OUT, LETTUCE!
WHOA!
BUZZZZZZ
WHAT IS IT, ICHIGO?
OH, IT'S NOTHING, REALLY.
JUST A MESSAGE FROM MASAYA! ❤
You free today?
Huh?
WHAT?
WHAT IS IT, ICHIGO?
YOU'RE ACTING LIKE A COMPLETE SPAZ.
SHOCKER. I'LL BET SHE'S HIDING SOMETHING.
SHE LOOKS WAY TOO HAPPY.
ARE YOU SURE YOU'RE ALL RIGHT?
I'M FINE!
MASHA'S SENSOR IS GOING OFF!
tweet
tweet
tweet
tweet
LET'S ROCK, LADIES!

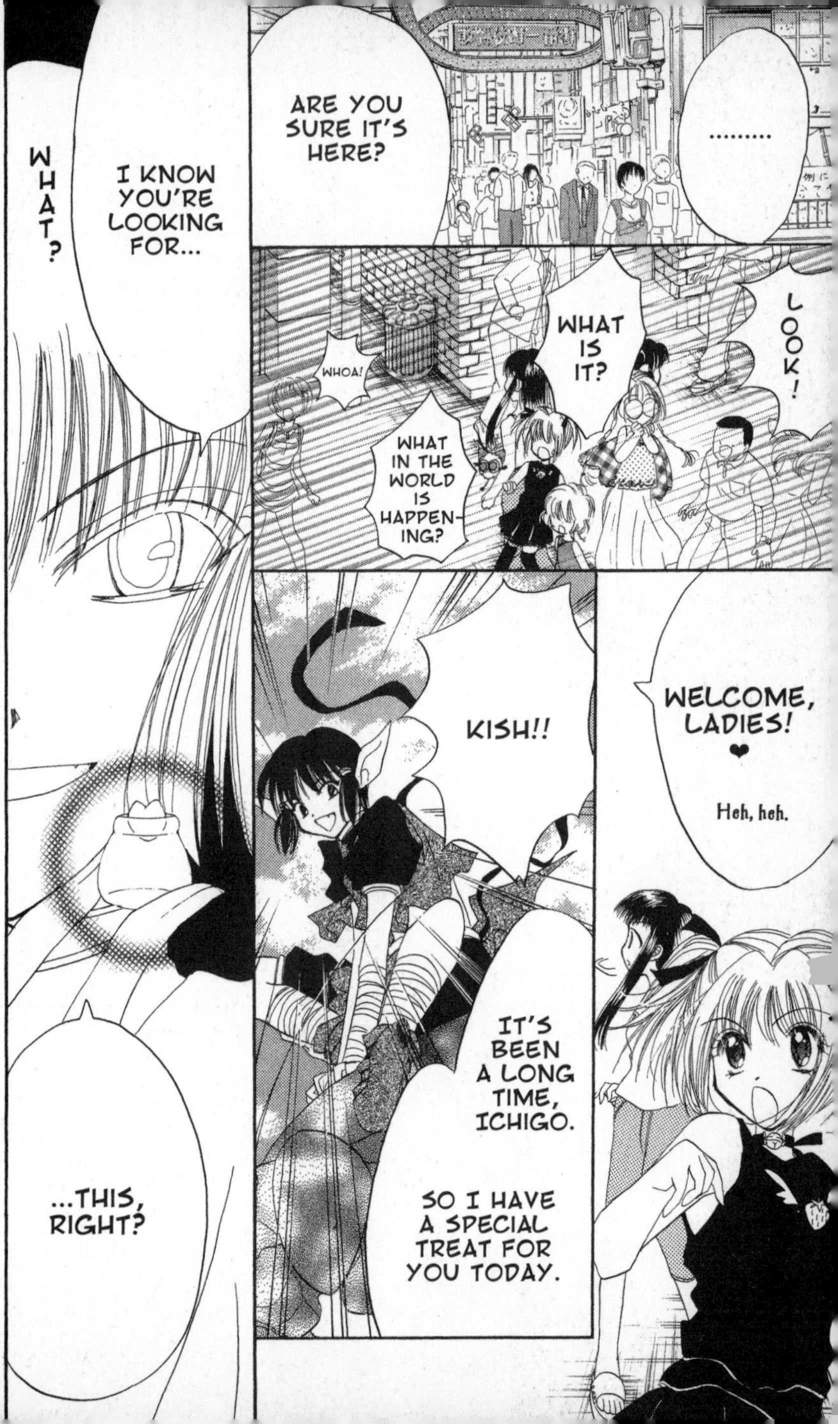
....
ARE YOU SURE IT'S HERE?
LOOK!
WHAT IS IT?
WHAT IN THE WORLD IS HAPPENING?
WHOA!
WELCOME, LADIES! ❤
Heh, heh.
KISH!!
IT'S BEEN A LONG TIME, ICHIGO.
SO I HAVE A SPECIAL TREAT FOR YOU TODAY.
I KNOW YOU'RE LOOKING FOR...
WHAT?
...THIS, RIGHT?

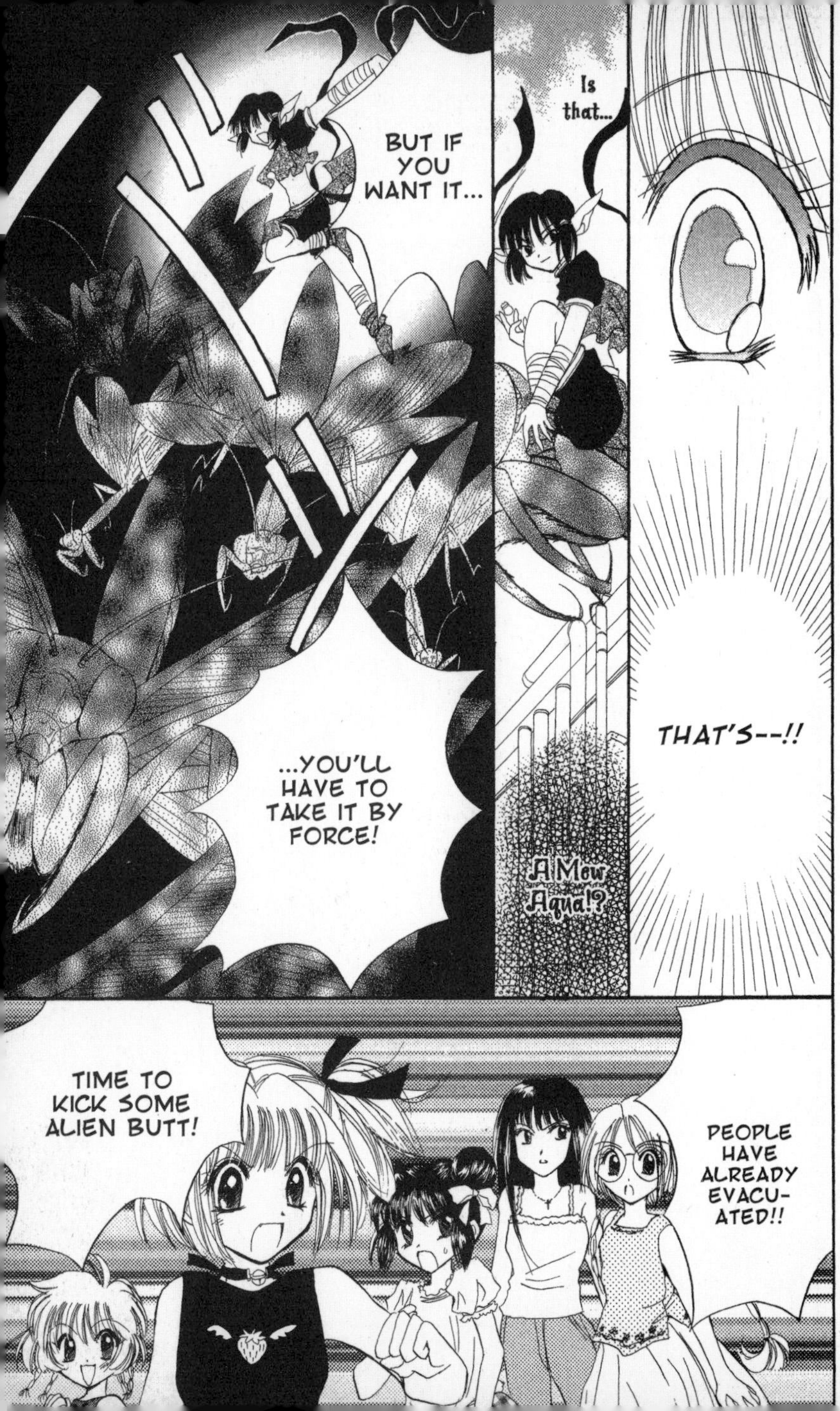
THAT'S--!!
Is that...
A Mew Aqua!?
BUT IF YOU WANT IT...
...YOU'LL HAVE TO TAKE IT BY FORCE!
PEOPLE HAVE ALREADY EVACU-ATED!!
TIME TO KICK SOME ALIEN BUTT!

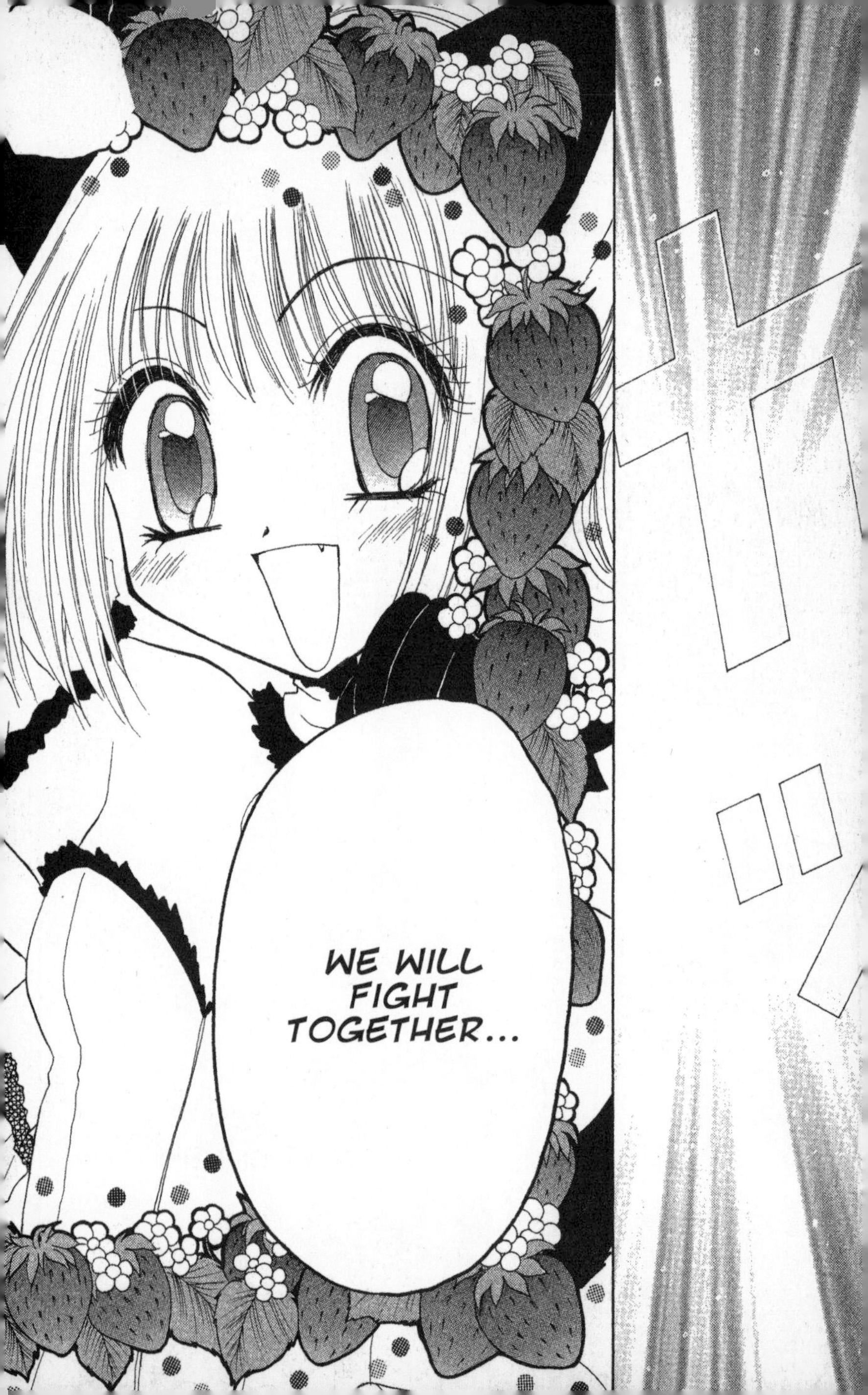
WE WILL FIGHT TOGETHER...

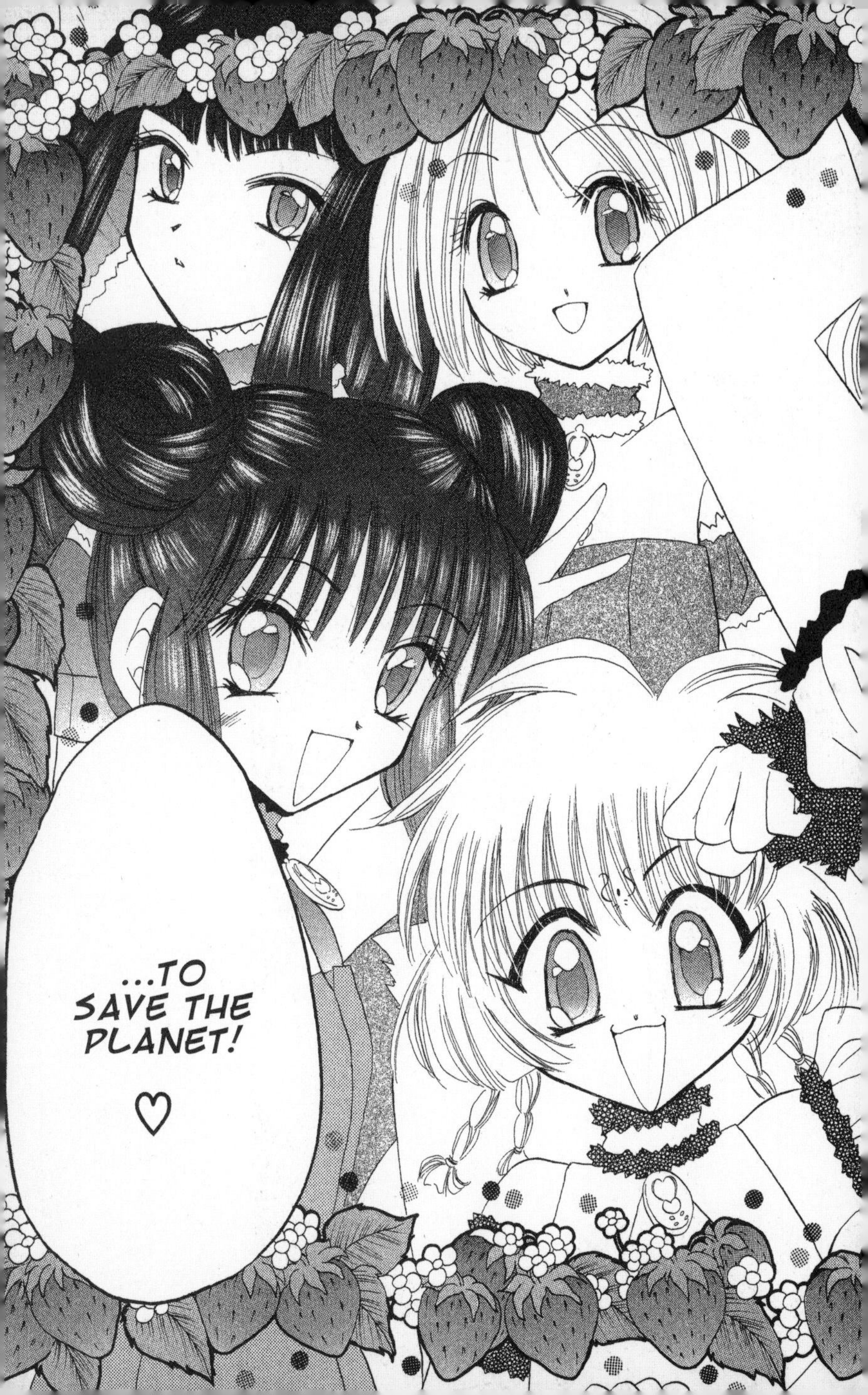
...TO SAVE THE PLANET! ♡

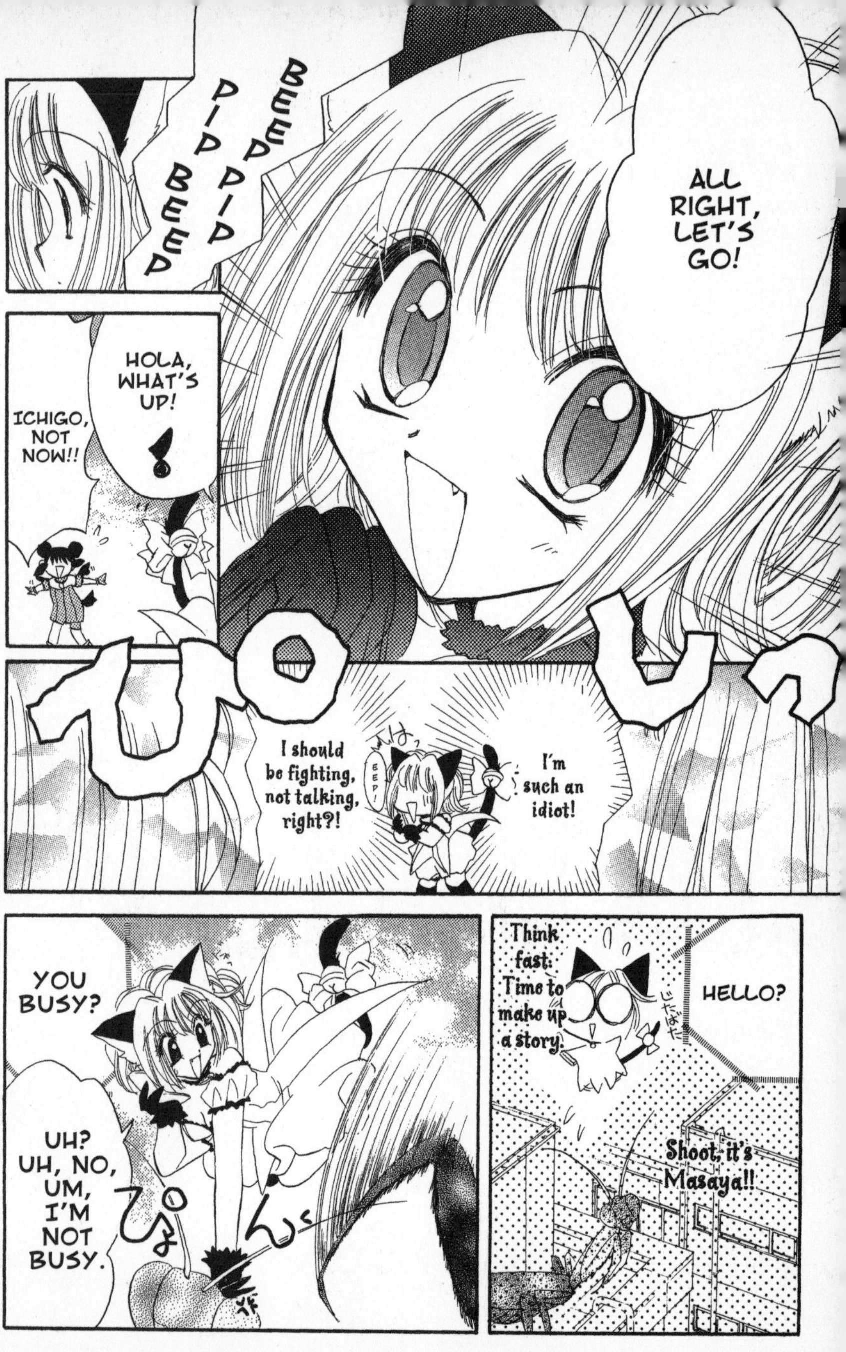
ALL RIGHT, LET'S GO!
BEEP PIP
PIP BEEP
HOLA, WHAT'S UP!
ICHIGO, NOT NOW!!
I'm such an idiot!
EEP!
I should be fighting, not talking, right?!
HELLO?
Think fast: Time to make up a story.
Shoot, it's Masaya!!
YOU BUSY?
UH? UH, NO, UM, I'M NOT BUSY.

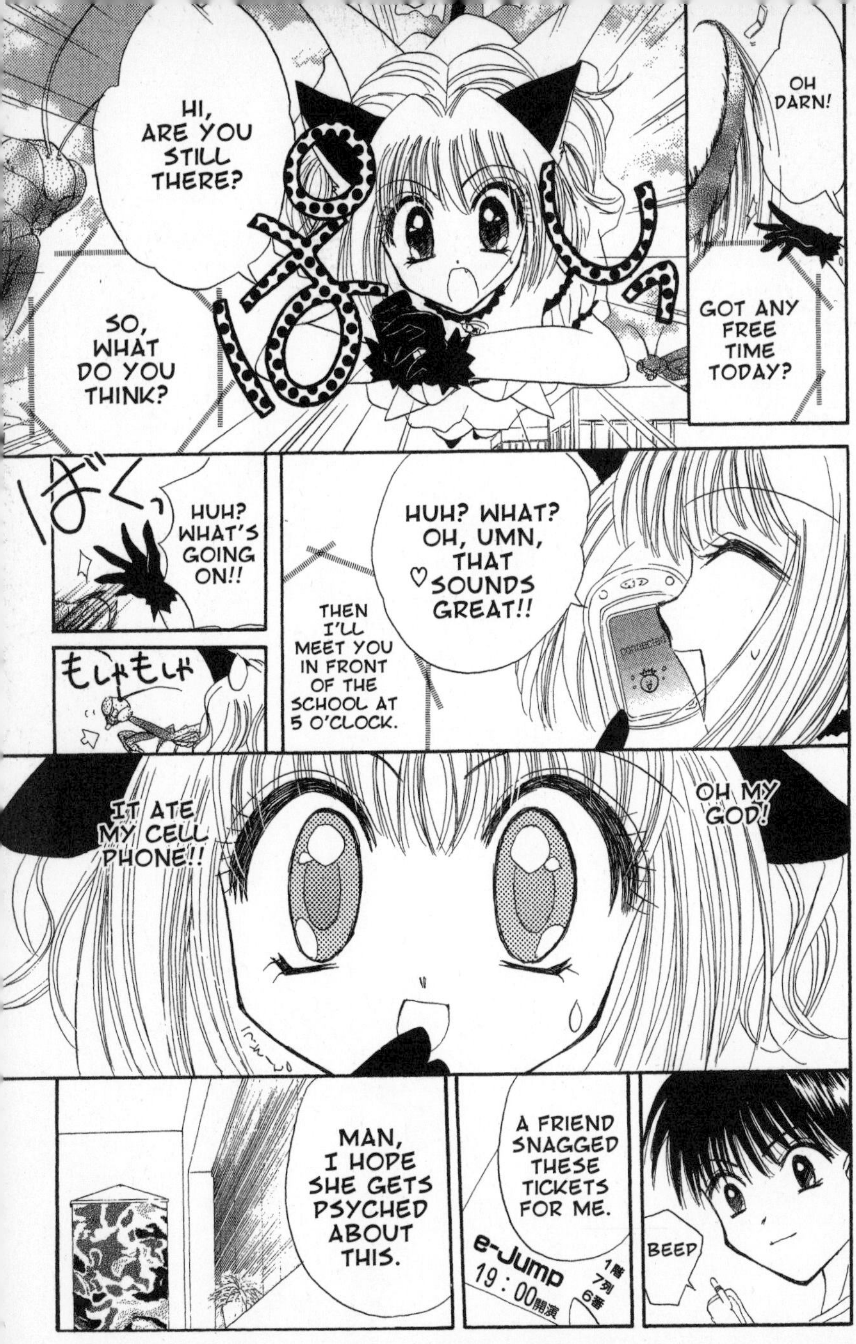
OH DARN!
GOT ANY FREE TIME TODAY?
HI, ARE YOU STILL THERE?
SO, WHAT DO YOU THINK?
HUH? WHAT? OH, UMN, ♡ THAT SOUNDS GREAT!!
THEN I'LL MEET YOU IN FRONT OF THE SCHOOL AT 5 O'CLOCK.
ぱく
HUH? WHAT'S GOING ON!!
もしゃもしゃ
OH MY GOD!
IT ATE MY CELL PHONE!!
BEEP
A FRIEND SNAGGED THESE TICKETS FOR ME.
e-Jump
19:00開演
1階 7列 6番
MAN, I HOPE SHE GETS PSYCHED ABOUT THIS.

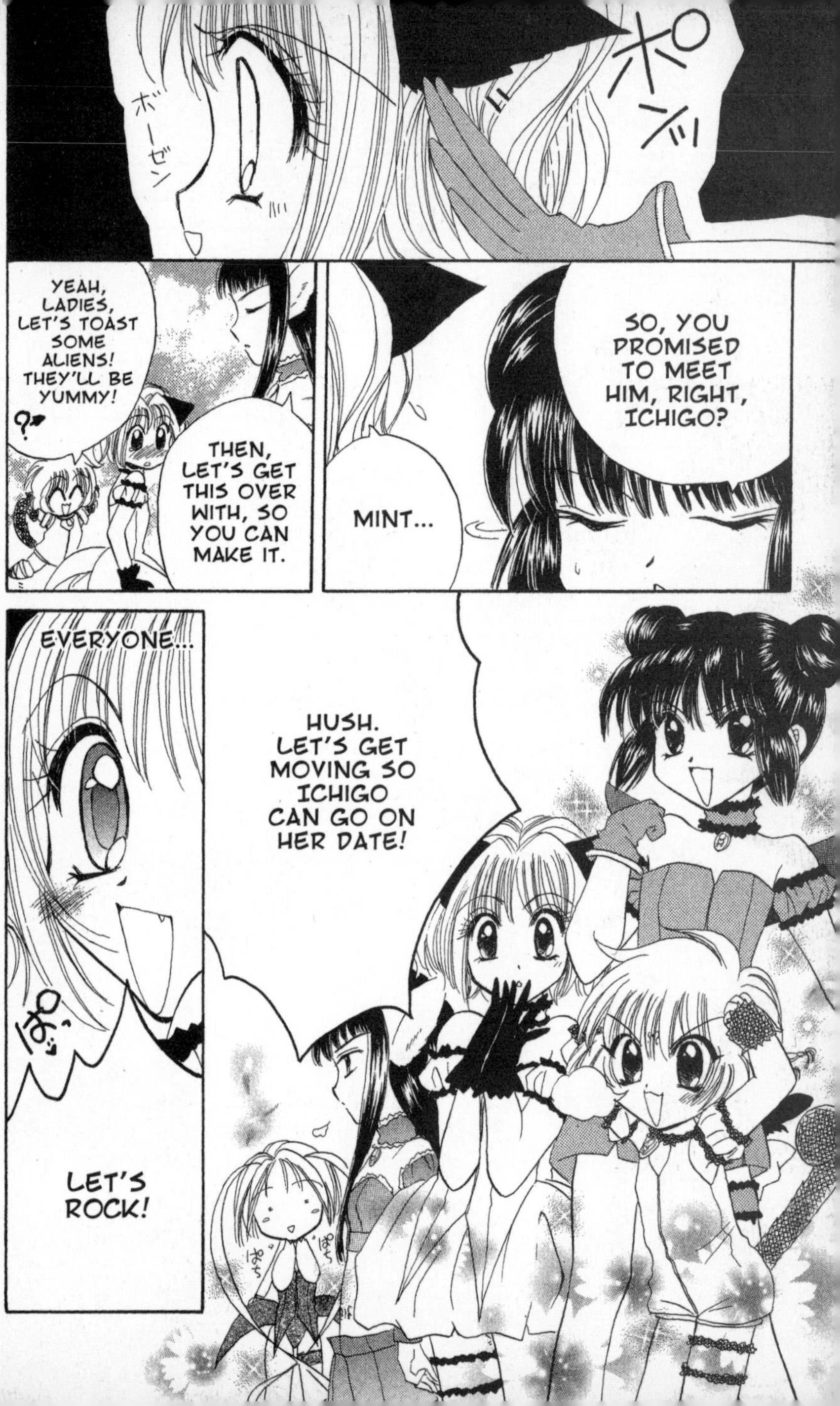
ポーンッ
ボーゼン
SO, YOU PROMISED TO MEET HIM, RIGHT, ICHIGO?
MINT...
THEN, LET'S GET THIS OVER WITH, SO YOU CAN MAKE IT.
YEAH, LADIES, LET'S TOAST SOME ALIENS! THEY'LL BE YUMMY!
HUSH. LET'S GET MOVING SO ICHIGO CAN GO ON HER DATE!
EVERYONE...
LET'S ROCK!

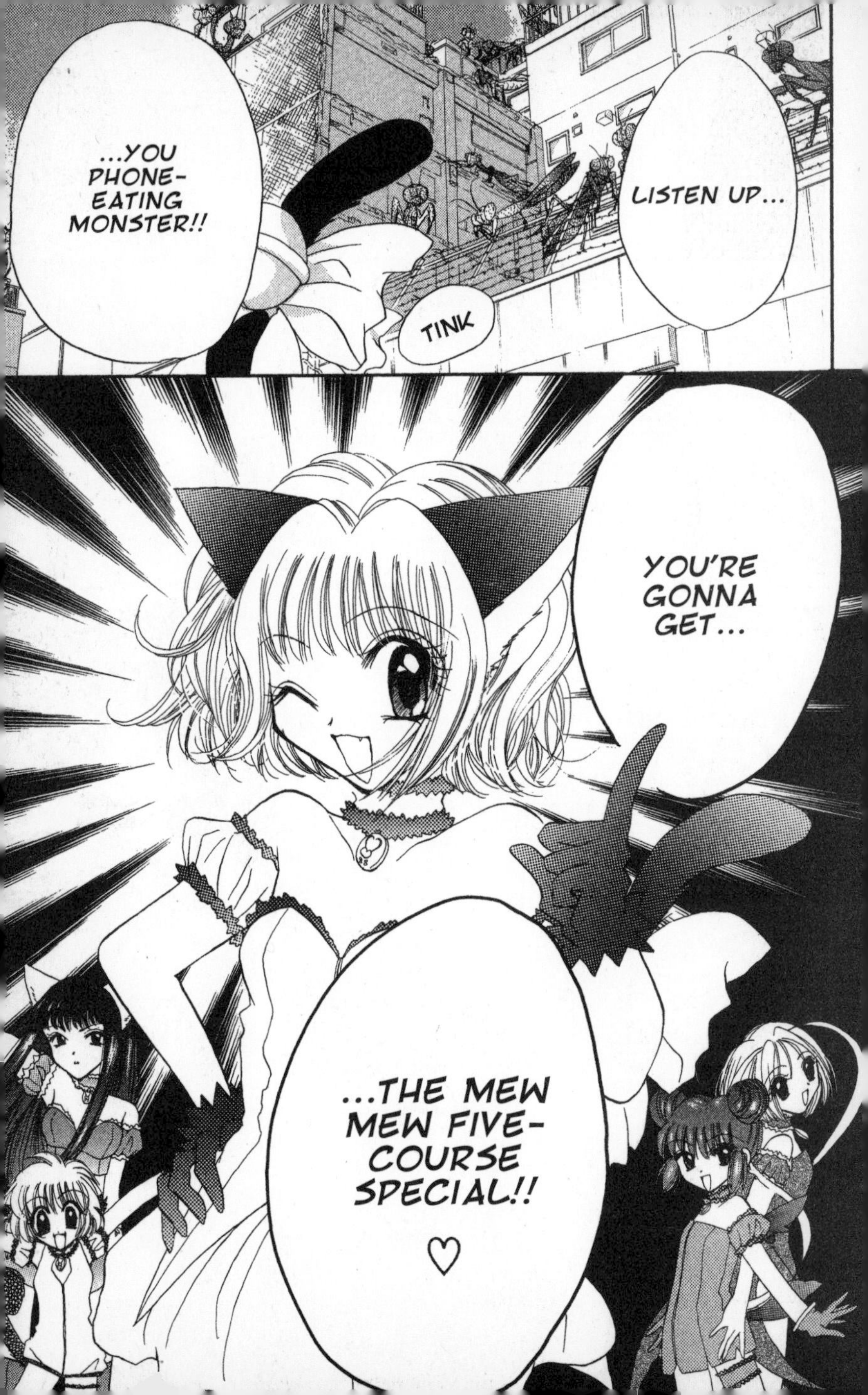
LISTEN UP...
...YOU PHONE-EATING MONSTER!!
TINK
YOU'RE GONNA GET...
...THE MEW MEW FIVE-COURSE SPECIAL!! ♡

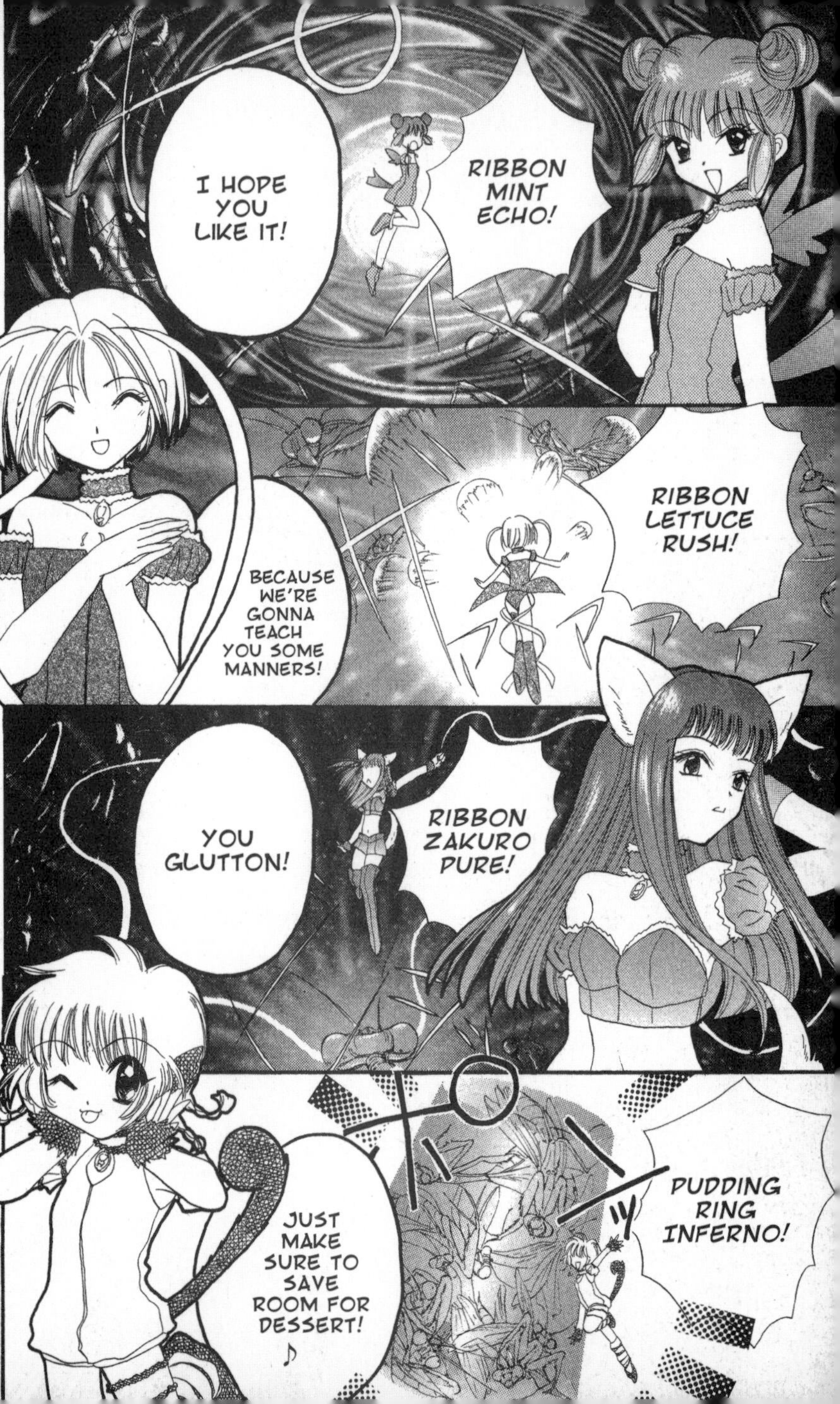
RIBBON MINT ECHO!
I HOPE YOU LIKE IT!
RIBBON LETTUCE RUSH!
BECAUSE WE'RE GONNA TEACH YOU SOME MANNERS!
RIBBON ZAKURO PURE!
YOU GLUTTON!
PUDDING RING INFERNO!
JUST MAKE SURE TO SAVE ROOM FOR DESSERT! ♪

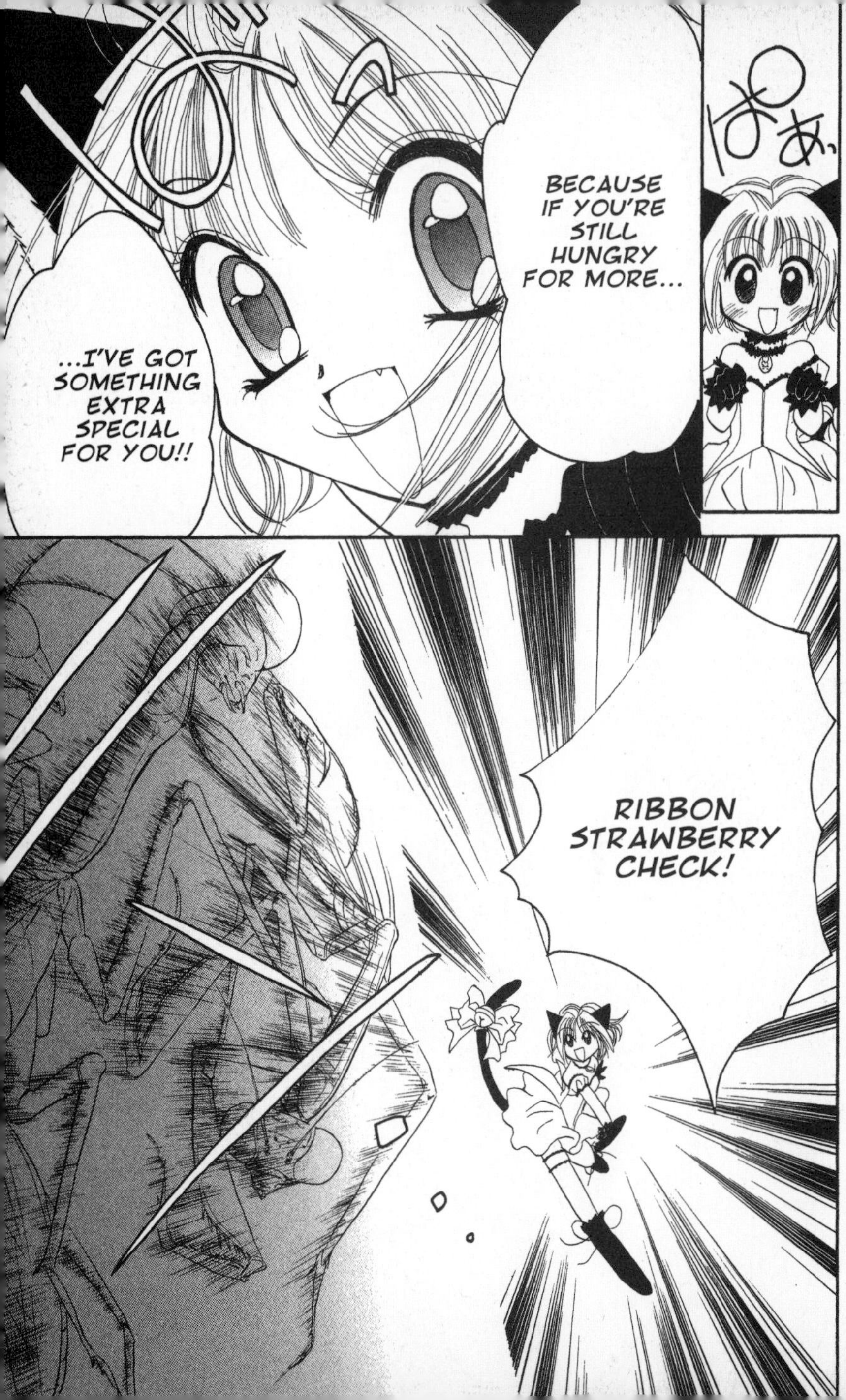
ぱあっ
BECAUSE IF YOU'RE STILL HUNGRY FOR MORE...
...I'VE GOT SOMETHING EXTRA SPECIAL FOR YOU!!
RIBBON STRAWBERRY CHECK!

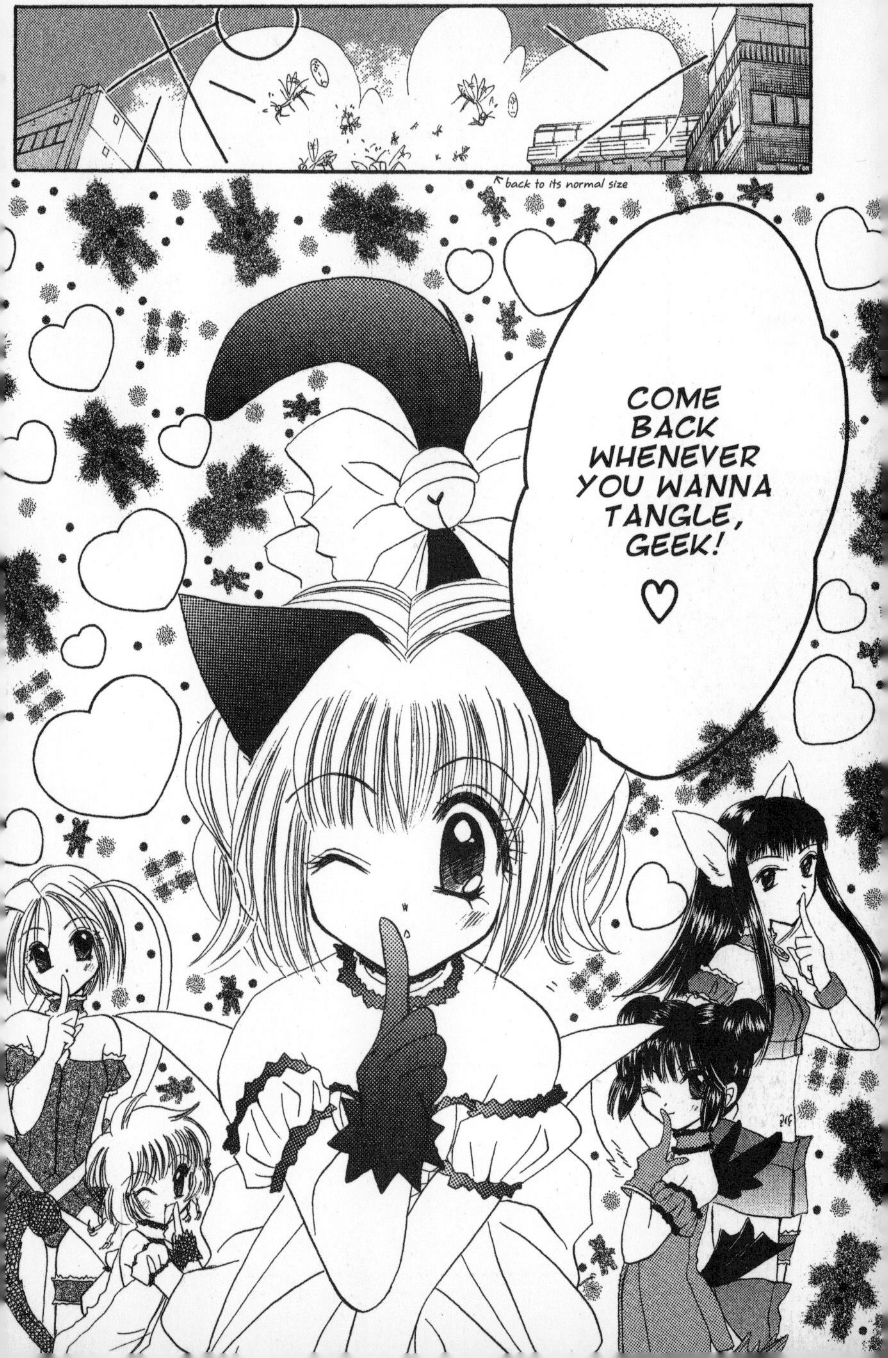
back to its normal size
COME BACK WHENEVER YOU WANNA TANGLE, GEEK! ♡

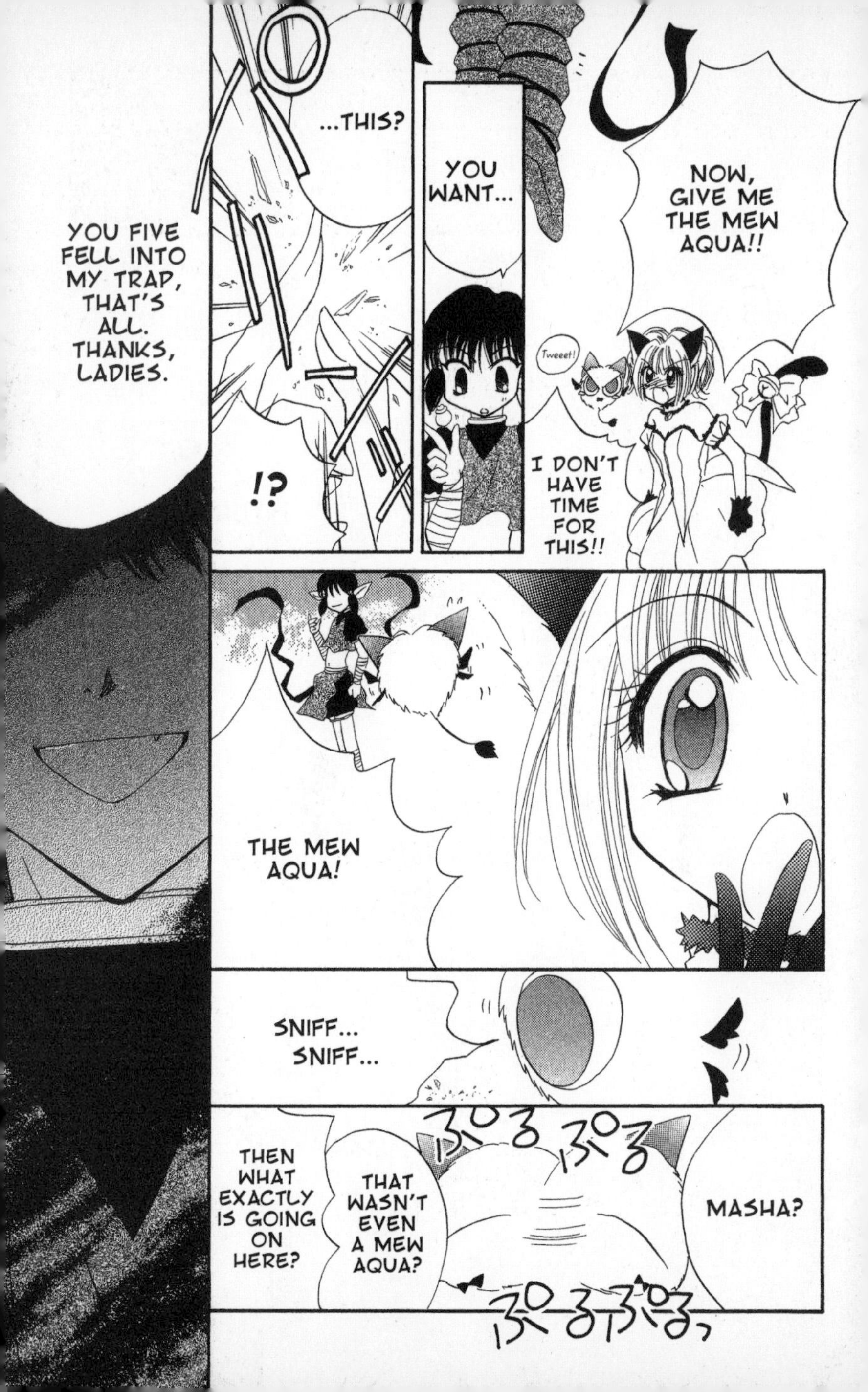
NOW, GIVE ME THE MEW AQUA!!
Tweeet!
I DON'T HAVE TIME FOR THIS!!
YOU WANT...
...THIS?
!?
THE MEW AQUA!
SNIFF... SNIFF...
MASHA?
THAT WASN'T EVEN A MEW AQUA?
THEN WHAT EXACTLY IS GOING ON HERE?
YOU FIVE FELL INTO MY TRAP, THAT'S ALL. THANKS, LADIES.

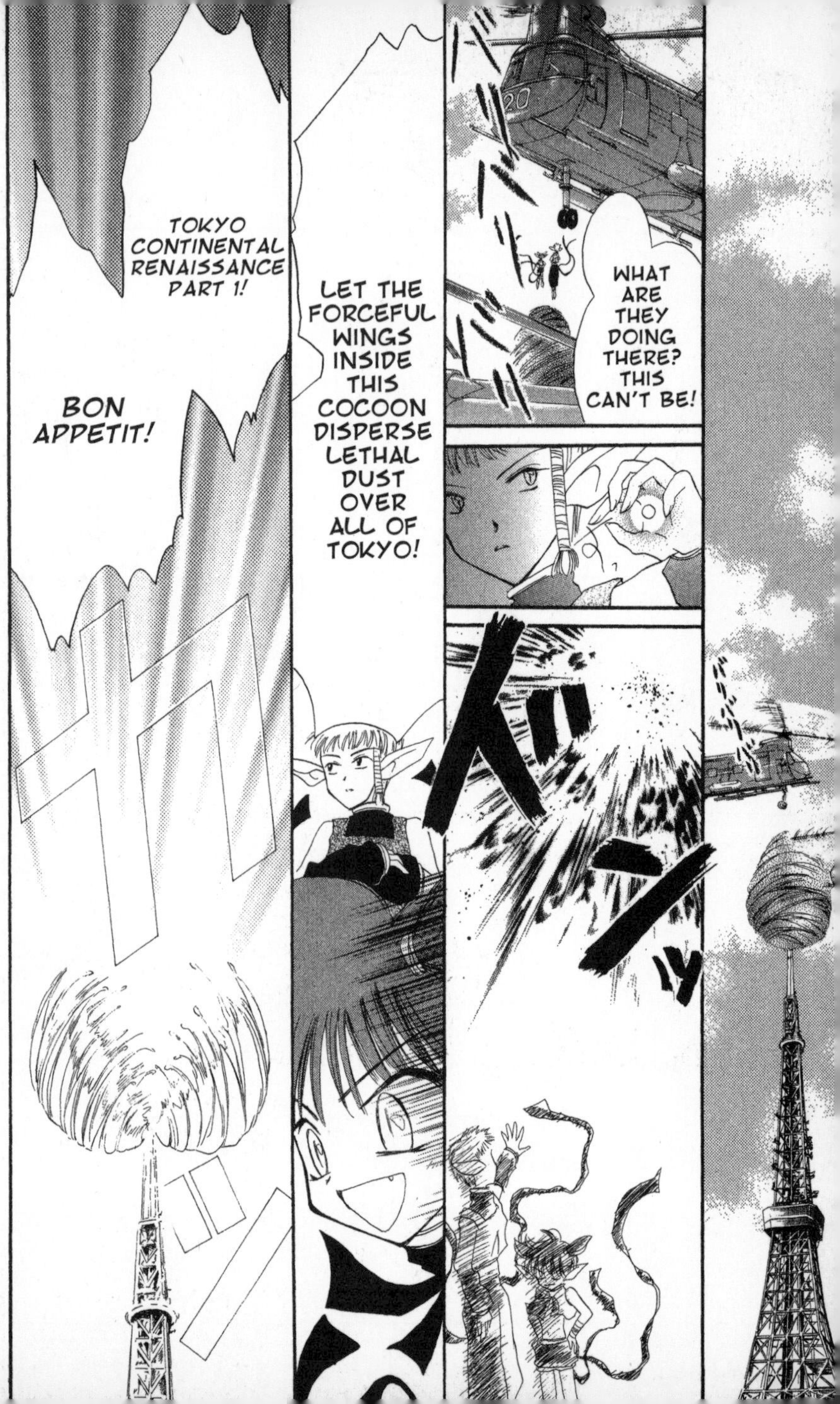
WHAT ARE THEY DOING THERE? THIS CAN'T BE!
LET THE FORCEFUL WINGS INSIDE THIS COCOON DISPERSE LETHAL DUST OVER ALL OF TOKYO!
TOKYO CONTINENTAL RENAISSANCE PART 1!
BON APPETIT!

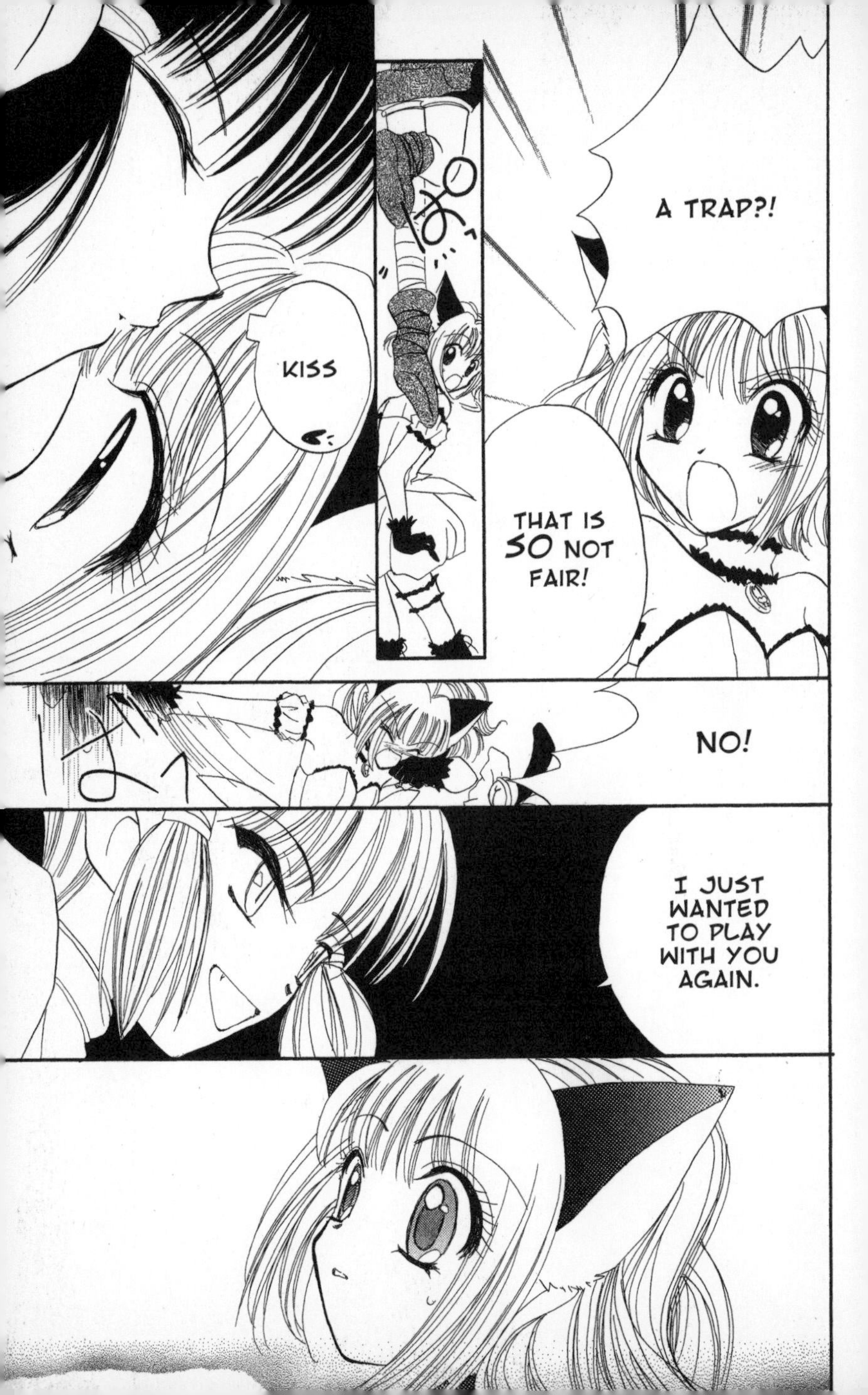
A TRAP?!
THAT IS SO NOT FAIR!
KISS
NO!
I JUST WANTED TO PLAY WITH YOU AGAIN.

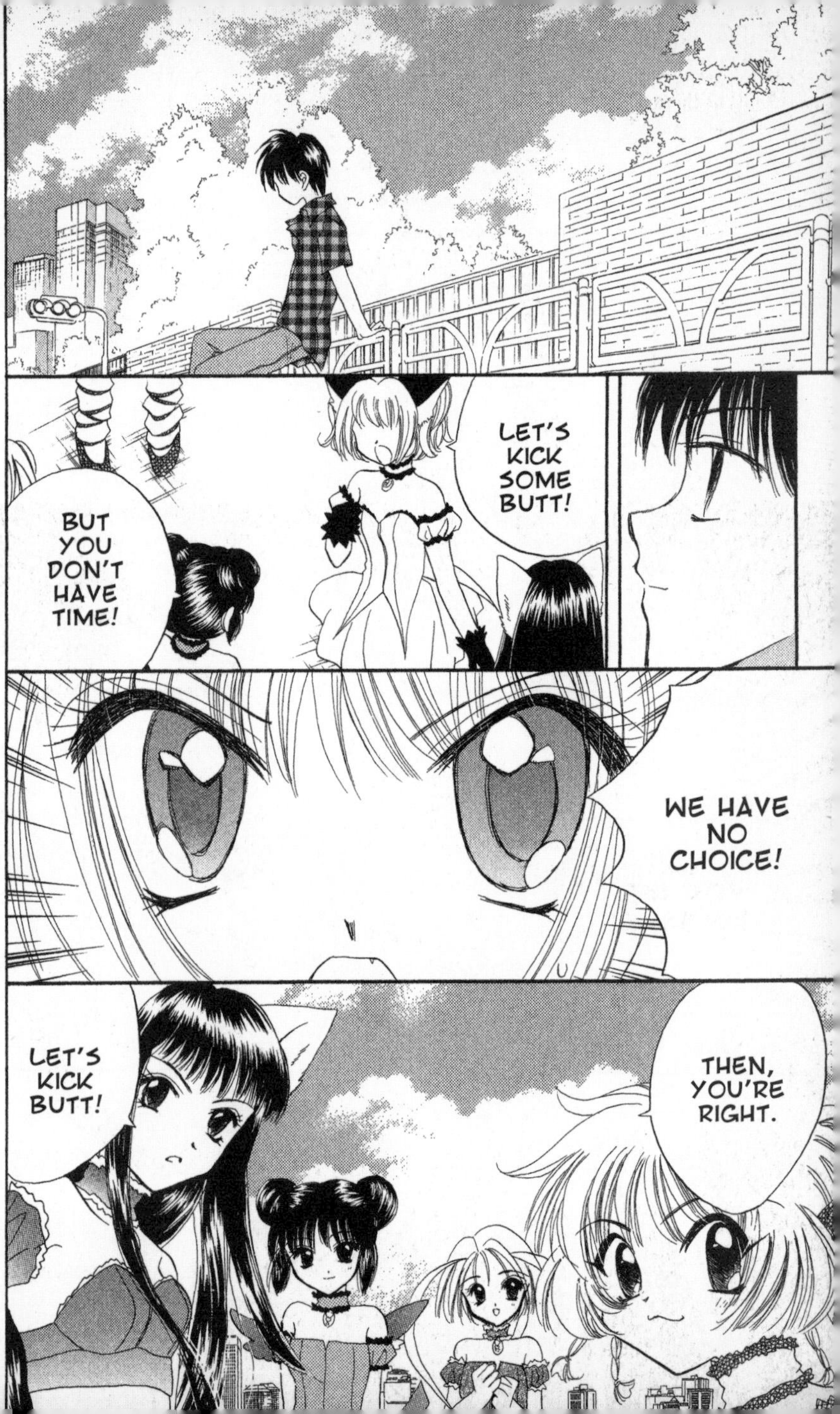
LET'S KICK SOME BUTT!
BUT YOU DON'T HAVE TIME!
WE HAVE NO CHOICE!
THEN, YOU'RE RIGHT.
LET'S KICK BUTT!

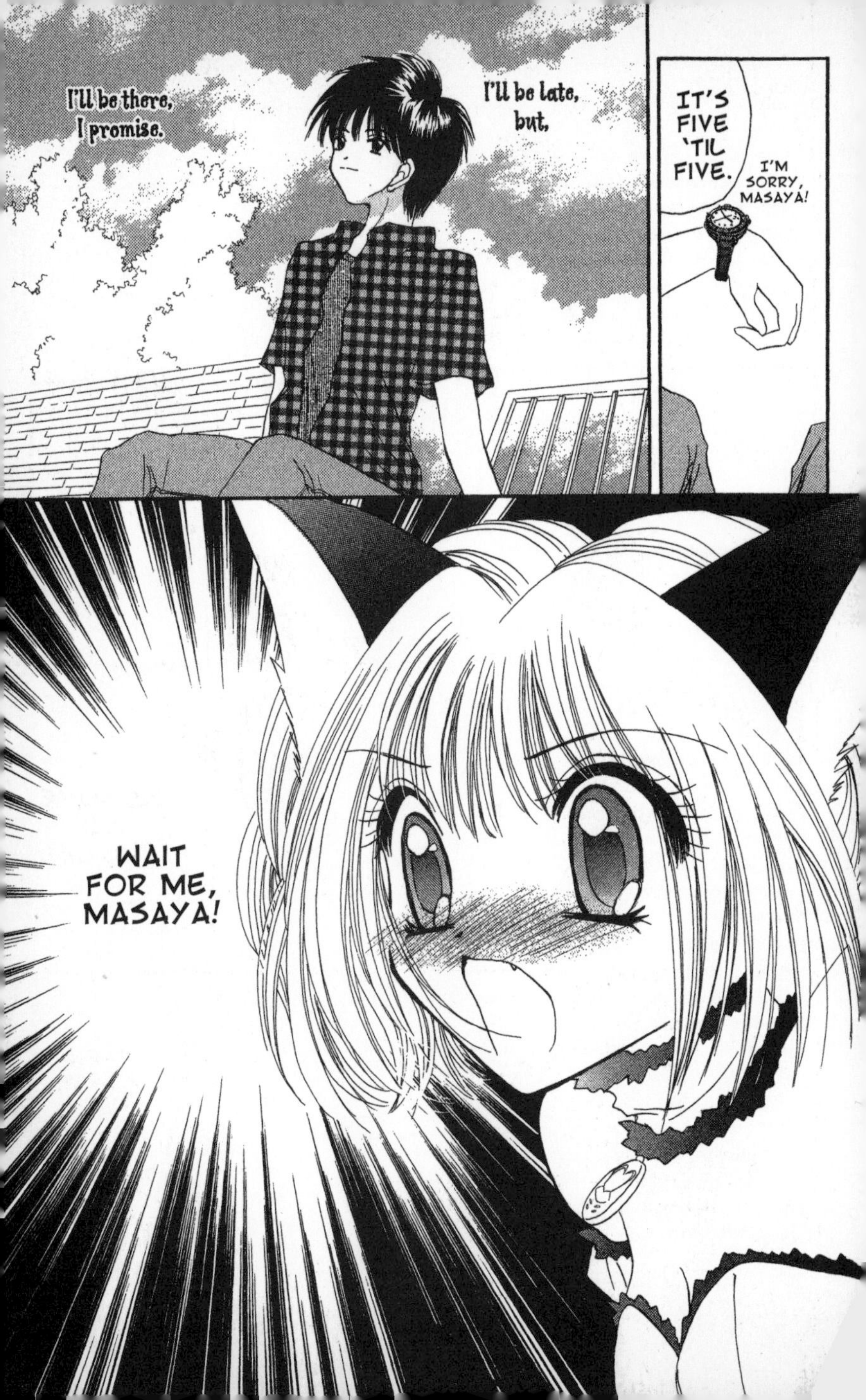
IT'S FIVE 'TIL FIVE.
I'M SORRY, MASAYA!
I'll be late, but,
I'll be there, I promise.
WAIT FOR ME, MASAYA!

Hello, it's me, Ikumi, again.

Hi! It's been a while. It's me, Mama of the Mews, Ikumi.♥ And this is the fourth volume of "Tokyo Mew Mew."
It feels like the third volume was just released, but now the fourth one's already coming out! Time flies so fast, I can't keep up anymore. Sigh.
I was wondering if you've seen my pride and joy yet? Yup, "Tokyo Mew Mew" has become an anime! Woo hoo!
I haven't had the chance to see it myself, but I've seen the drawings for the characters. The drawings are cute, and they've done a great job. I want to see Ichigo and company become the toughest girls on the planet! ♥♥
As for the voice actors, all the girls' voices are adorable. Masaya's role is acted by Ms. Megumi Ogata!! I believe it when I hear her say Masaya's romantic lines !! {I'm super excited!!}
And I can't believe the cast is so full of actors I admire!
Originally, these lines were created while I talked and joked around with business buds. Now, famous voice actors are breathing life into those same lines. I can't help but feel a bit nervous about that sometimes.
As you watch the anime series, just remember I'll be writhing around anxiously in front of the TV as I listen to the characters (especially the male characters) say their lines (laugh).
All right, I hope you enjoy the rest of "Tokyo Mew Mew 4"!♥♥

02-21-2001 Mia Ikumi

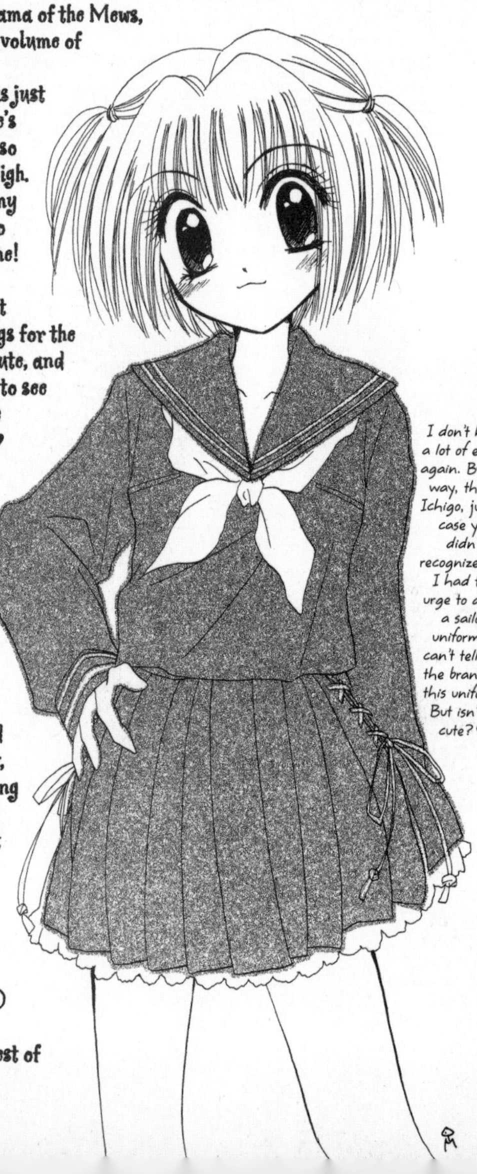

I don't have a lot of extras again. By the way, this is Ichigo, just in case you didn't recognize her. I had the urge to draw a sailor uniform. I can't tell you the brand of this uniform. But isn't it cute?♥

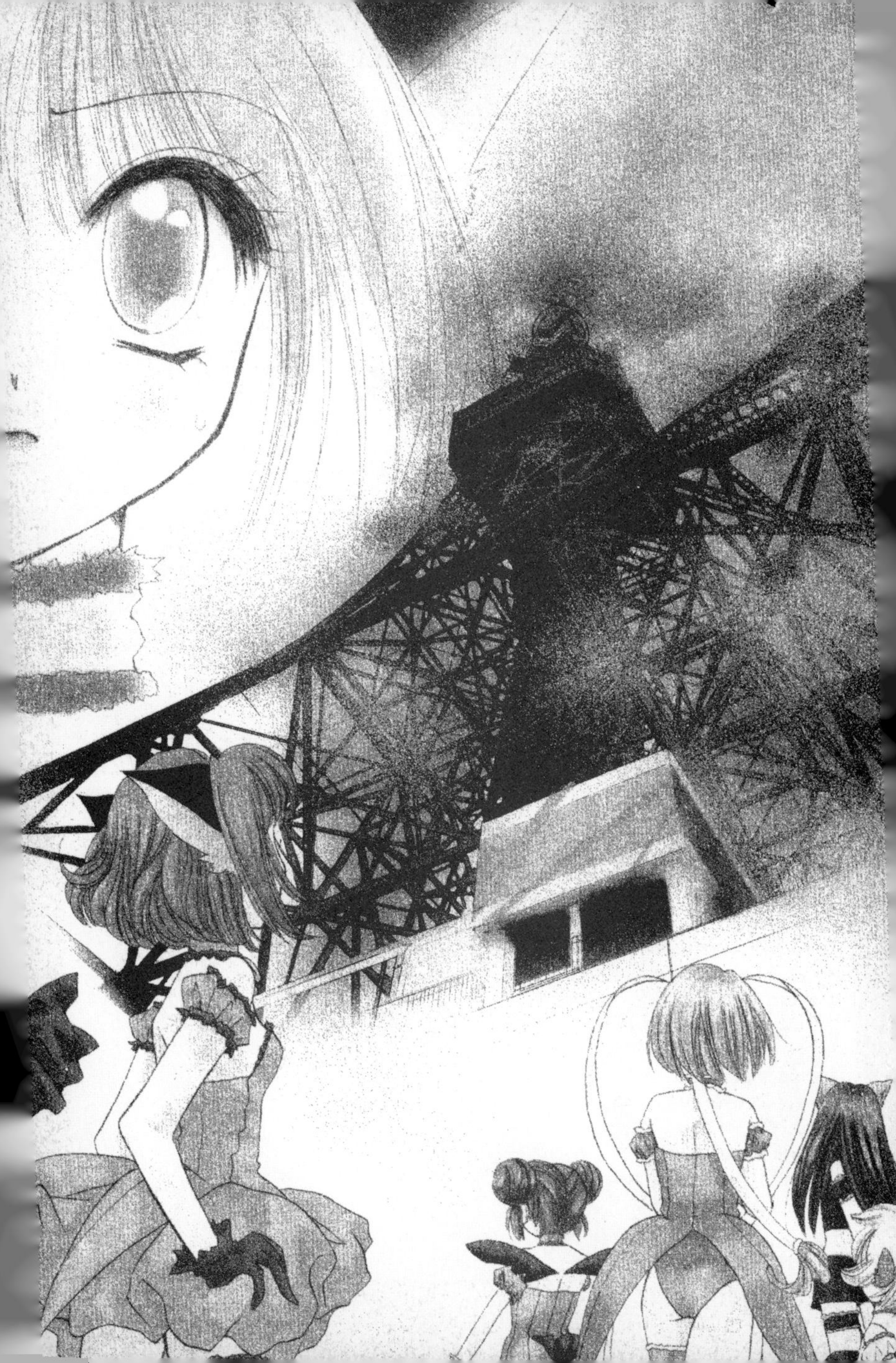

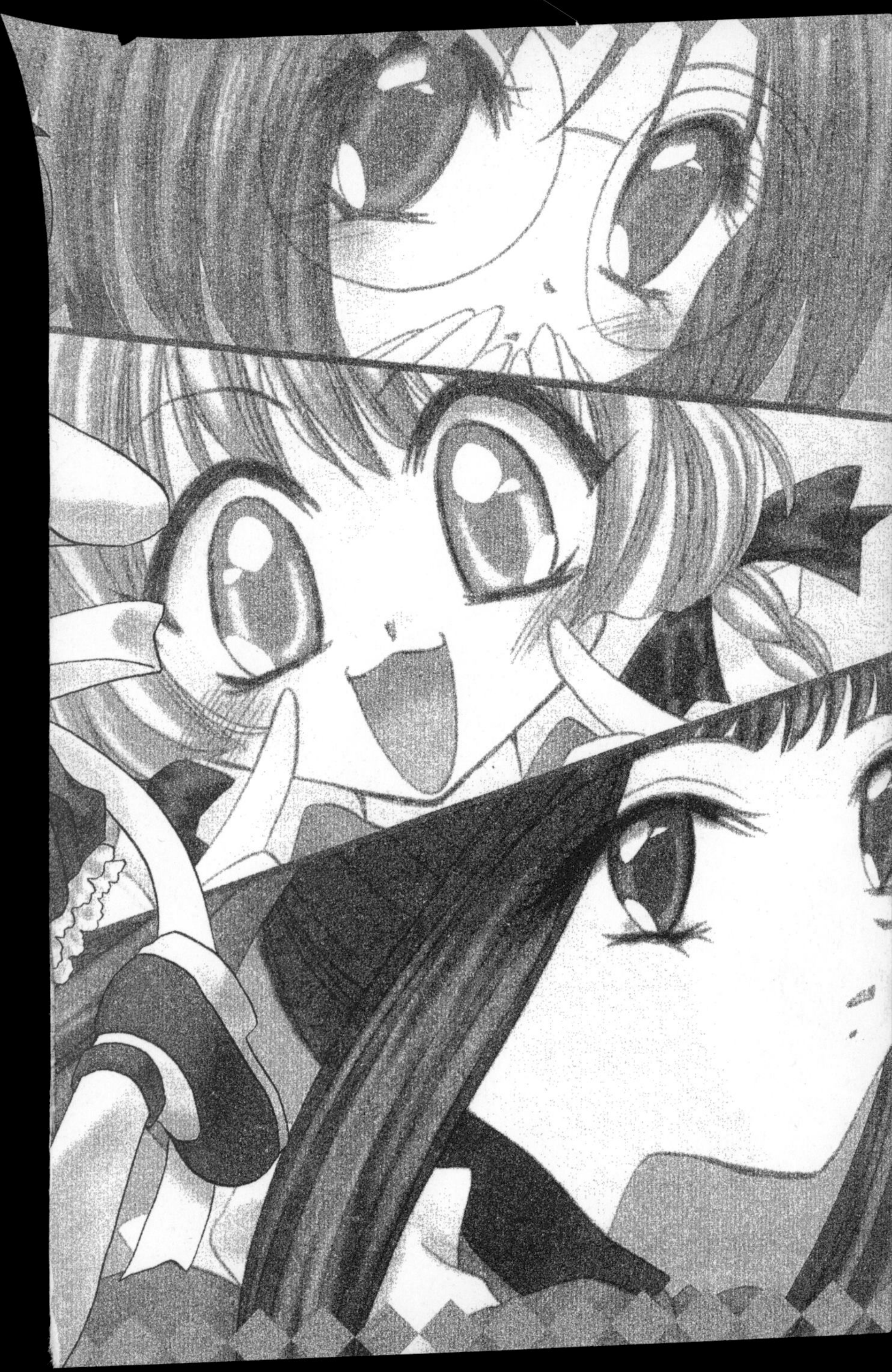

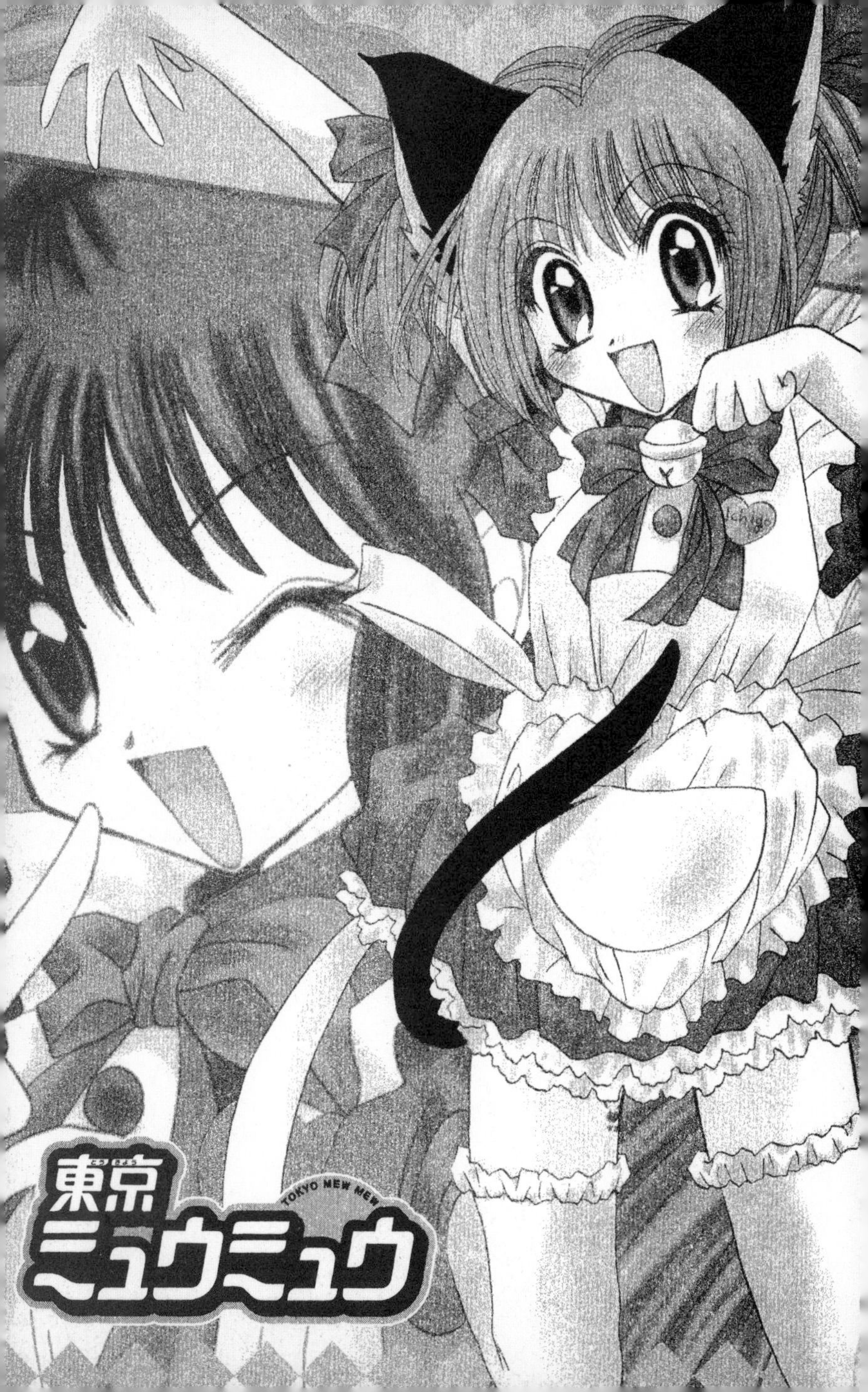
東京ミュウミュウ
TOKYO MEW MEW

Rika-chan by Takara

This is great news! (And yes, I know this has nothing to do with Rika-chan). I was already super psyched to hear that this series was going to be animated, but then I received even more big news. I heard that dolls based on my characters might be produced by Takara Inc., the company that made the Rika-chan dolls! At first I thought it was just a possibility, but guess what? It really happened! Thank you, Takara Inc.! I think they might be showing up in toy stores by now. I've received a doll for each of the characters. The first collection is called "Elegant Collection." The dolls are absolutely adorable! And it's not just because they're dolls based on my work. They're really worth it! I was thrilled because Takara Inc. listened to most of my little requests. The faces were based on my designs! (At least I think so!!!) Also, check out the hair!! Especially Mint's! Two perfect buns on either side of her head, just like it's supposed to be!
I was able to direct a lot of details on this project. I think they let me speak my opinions on everything but the voices. There will be more toys produced based on this series, so keep looking for them! I'm way beyond excited!
The picture to the right is based on a Rika-chan doll that I received from Takara Inc. as a gift. They made it especially for me, after seeing one of my drawings. I was so touched! It's too bad I can't show you the real thing. I hope they end up mass-producing this doll, too.

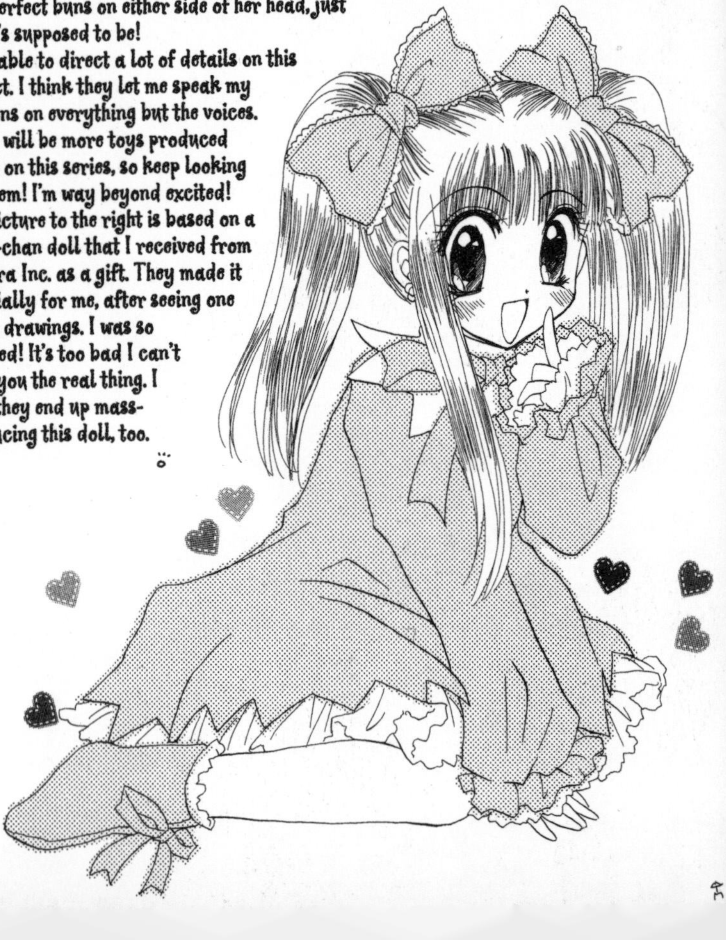

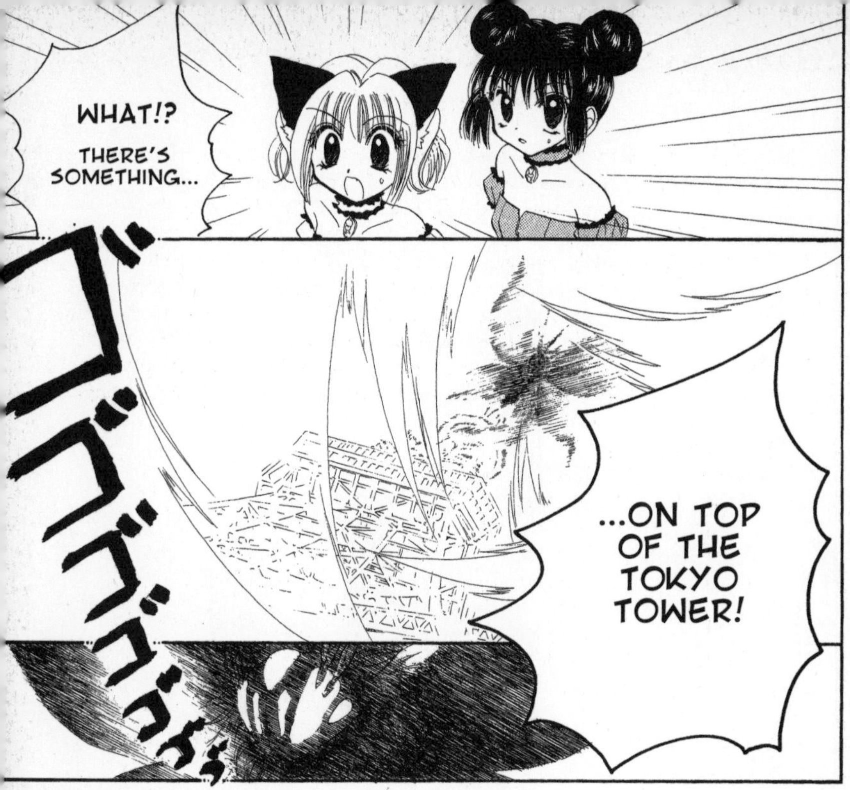
WHAT!? THERE'S SOMETHING...
...ON TOP OF THE TOKYO TOWER!
ゴゴゴゴゴ

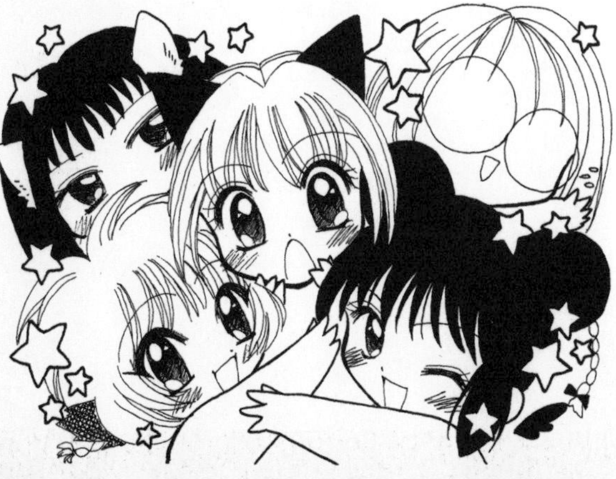

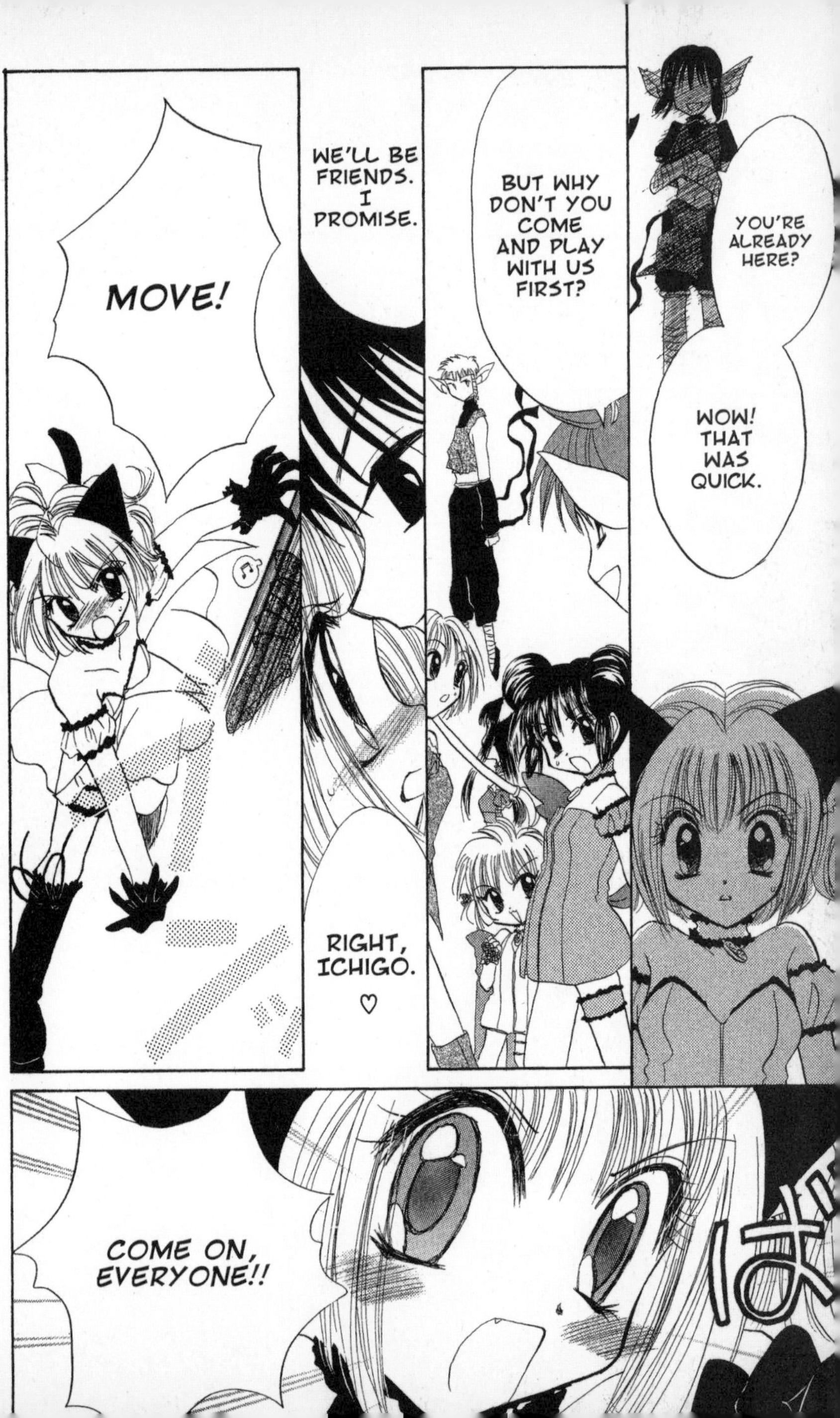

YOU'RE ALREADY HERE?
WOW! THAT WAS QUICK.
BUT WHY DON'T YOU COME AND PLAY WITH US FIRST?
RIGHT, ICHIGO. ♡
WE'LL BE FRIENDS. I PROMISE.
MOVE!
COME ON, EVERYONE!!

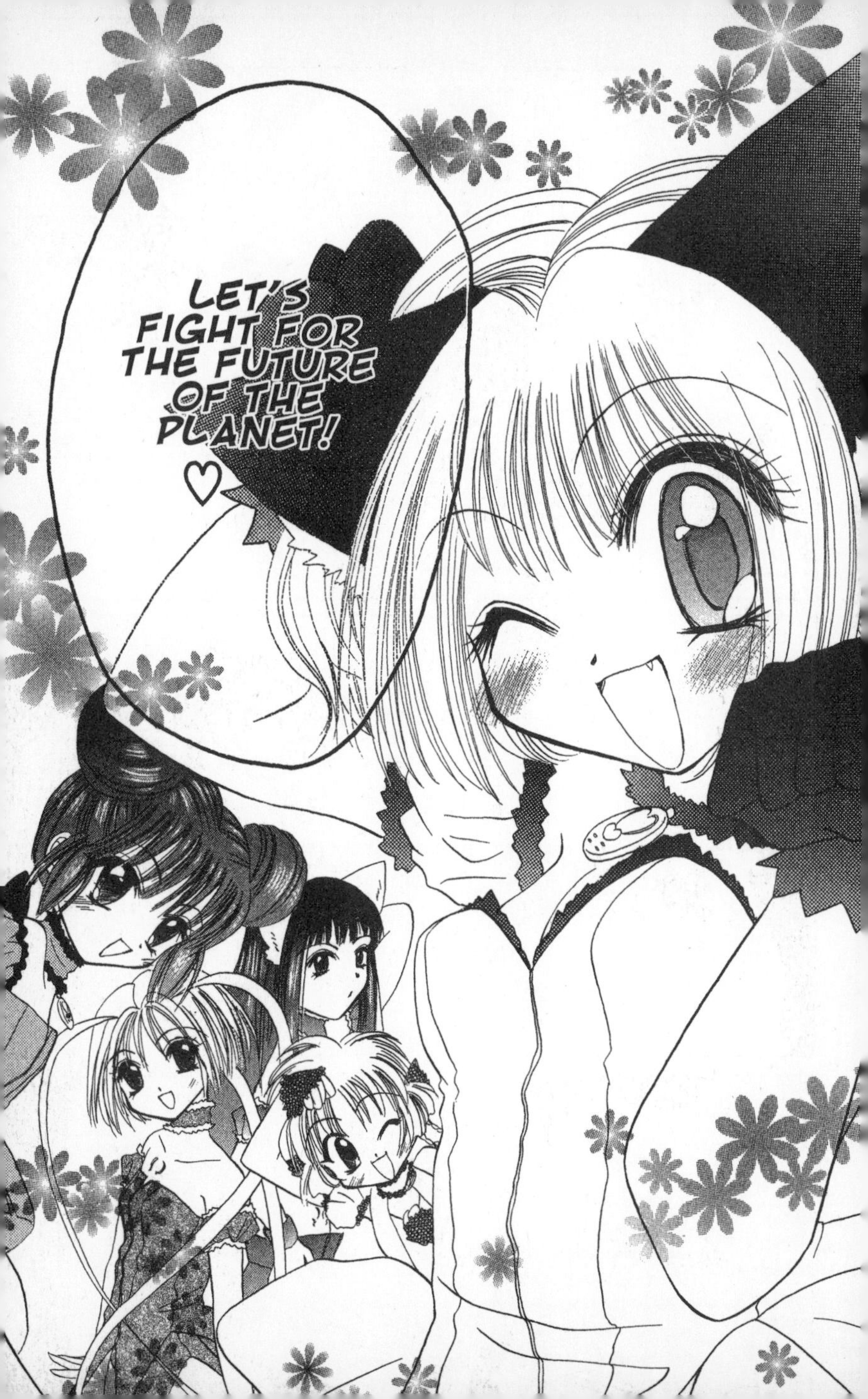
LET'S FIGHT FOR THE FUTURE OF THE PLANET! ♡

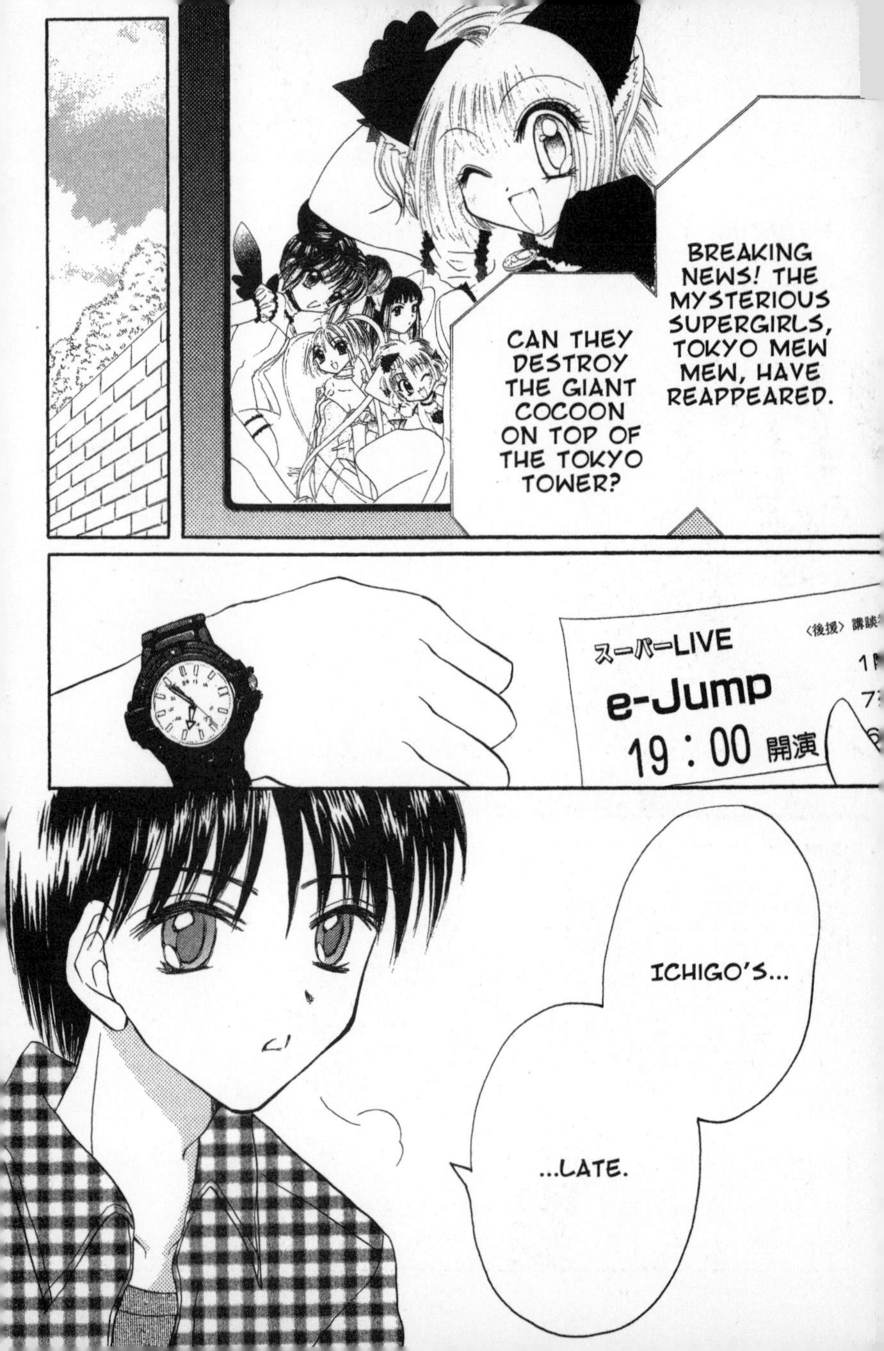
BREAKING NEWS! THE MYSTERIOUS SUPERGIRLS, TOKYO MEW MEW, HAVE REAPPEARED.
CAN THEY DESTROY THE GIANT COCOON ON TOP OF THE TOKYO TOWER?
〈後援〉講談
スーパーLIVE
e-Jump
19：00 開演
ICHIGO'S...
...LATE.

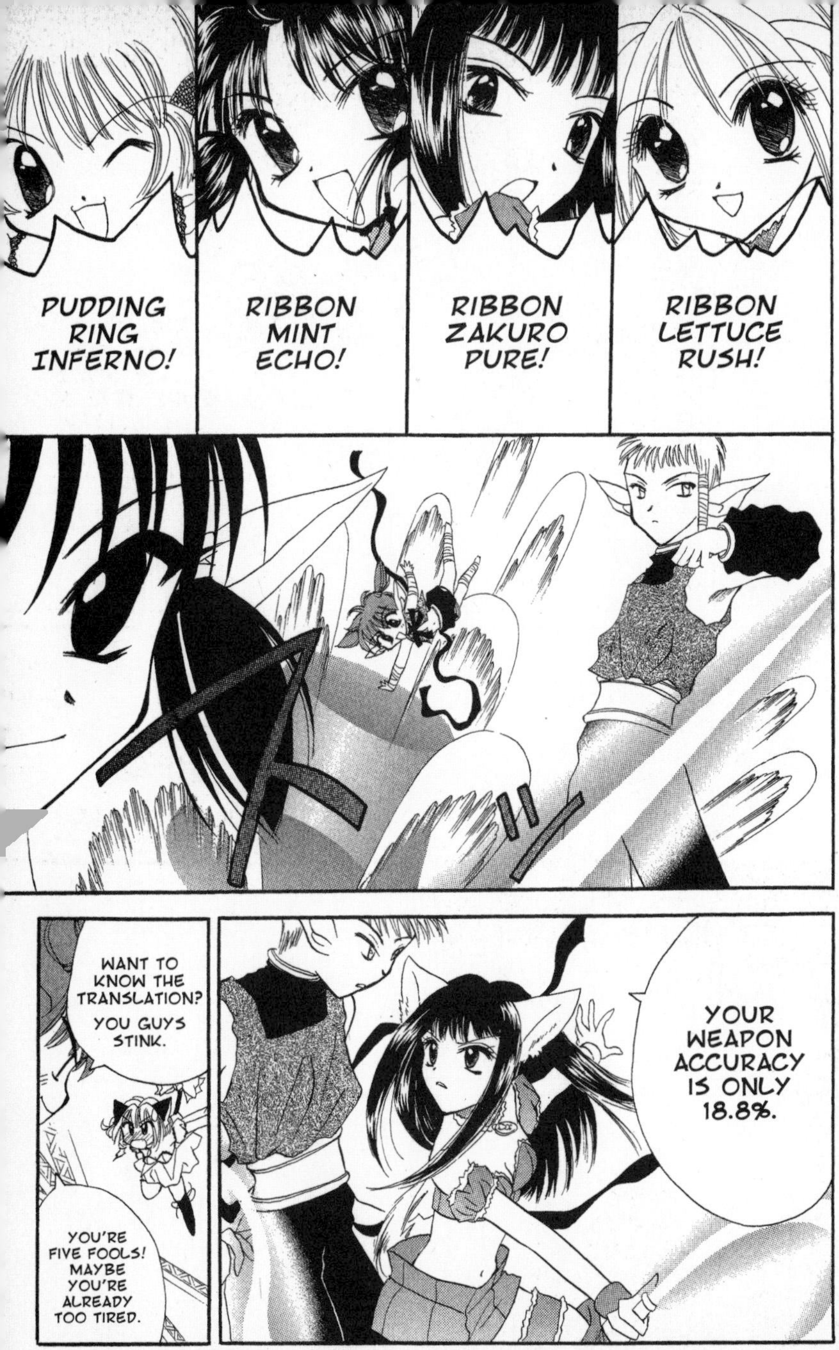
RIBBON LETTUCE RUSH!
RIBBON ZAKURO PURE!
RIBBON MINT ECHO!
PUDDING RING INFERNO!
YOUR WEAPON ACCURACY IS ONLY 18.8%.
WANT TO KNOW THE TRANSLATION? YOU GUYS STINK.
YOU'RE FIVE FOOLS! MAYBE YOU'RE ALREADY TOO TIRED.

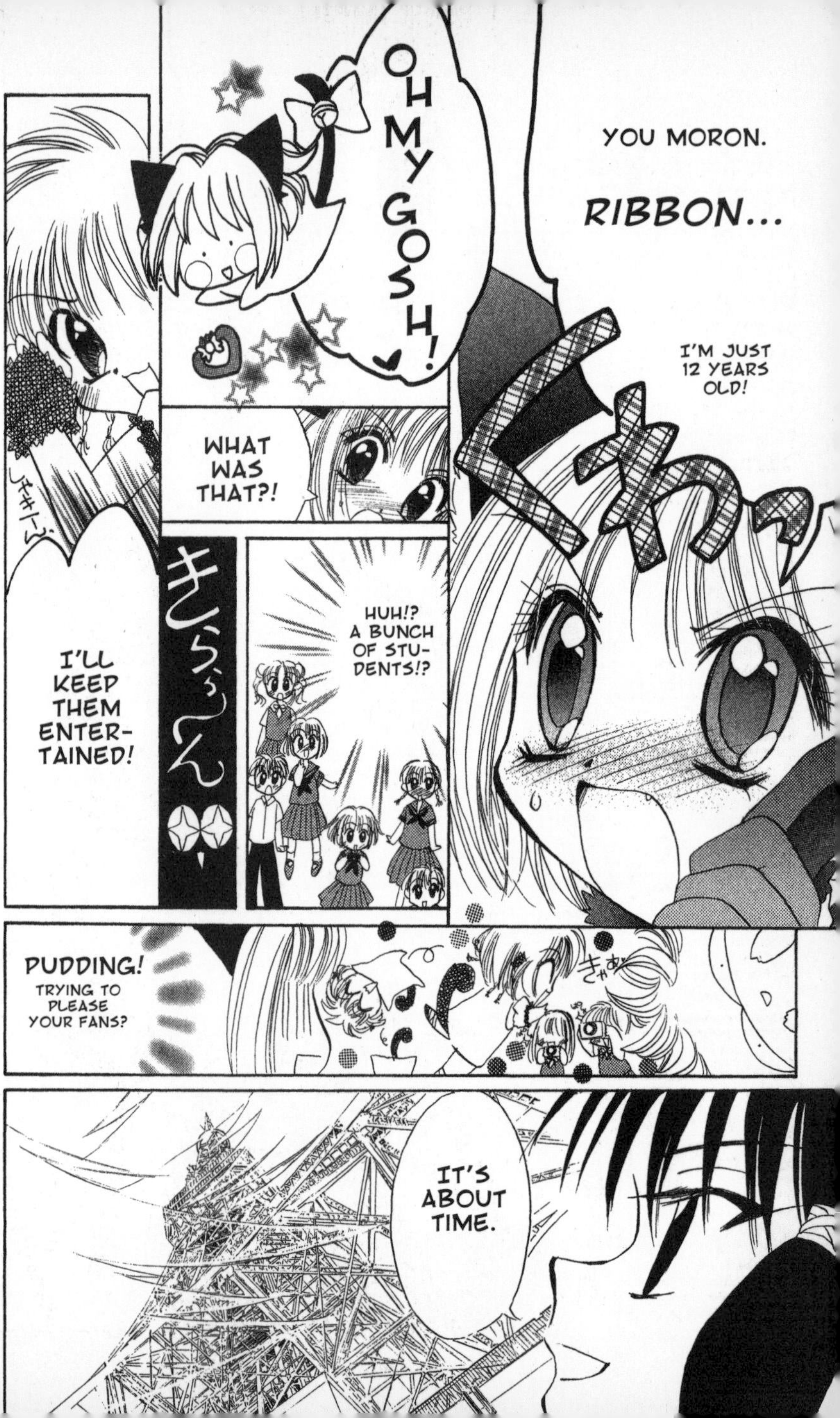
YOU MORON.
RIBBON...
I'M JUST 12 YEARS OLD!
OH MY GOSH!
WHAT WAS THAT?!
HUH!? A BUNCH OF STU-DENTS!?
I'LL KEEP THEM ENTER-TAINED!
PUDDING! TRYING TO PLEASE YOUR FANS?
IT'S ABOUT TIME.

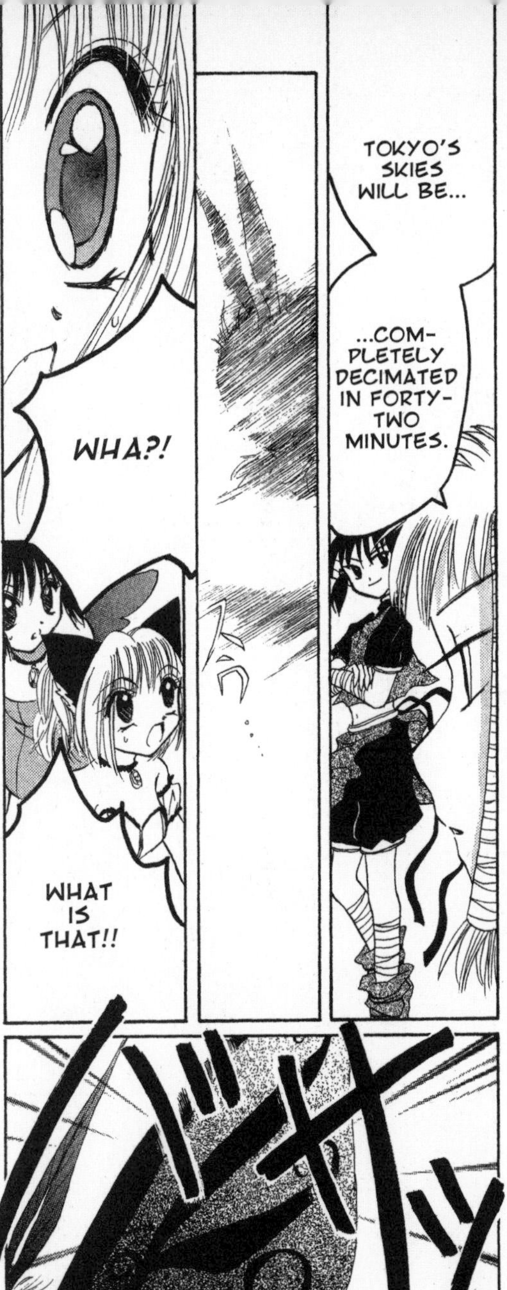
TOKYO'S SKIES WILL BE...
...COMPLETELY DECIMATED IN FORTY-TWO MINUTES.
WHA?!
WHAT IS THAT!!

Business Meeting

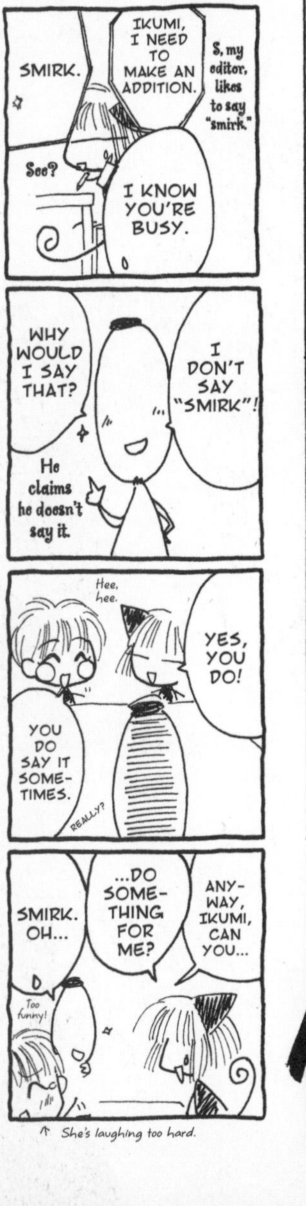
S, my editor, likes to say "smirk."
IKUMI, I NEED TO MAKE AN ADDITION.
SMIRK.
I KNOW YOU'RE BUSY.
See?
I DON'T SAY "SMIRK"!
WHY WOULD I SAY THAT?
He claims he doesn't say it.
YES, YOU DO!
Hee, hee.
YOU DO SAY IT SOMETIMES.
REALLY?
ANYWAY, IKUMI, CAN YOU...
...DO SOMETHING FOR ME?
SMIRK. OH...
Too funny!

↑ She's laughing too hard.

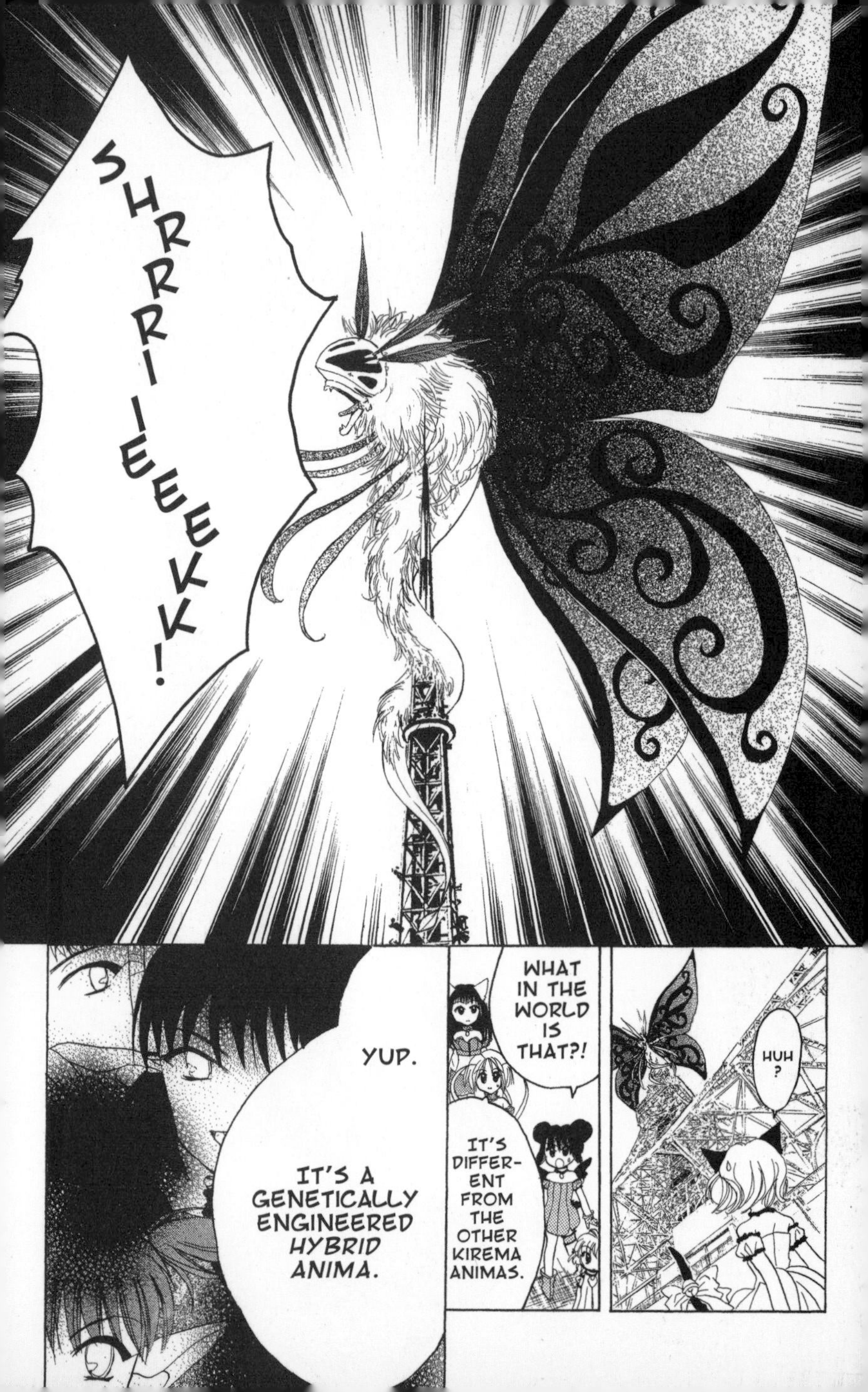
SHRRRIIEEEKK!
HUH?
WHAT IN THE WORLD IS THAT?!
IT'S DIFFERENT FROM THE OTHER KIREMA ANIMAS.
YUP.
IT'S A GENETICALLY ENGINEERED HYBRID ANIMA.

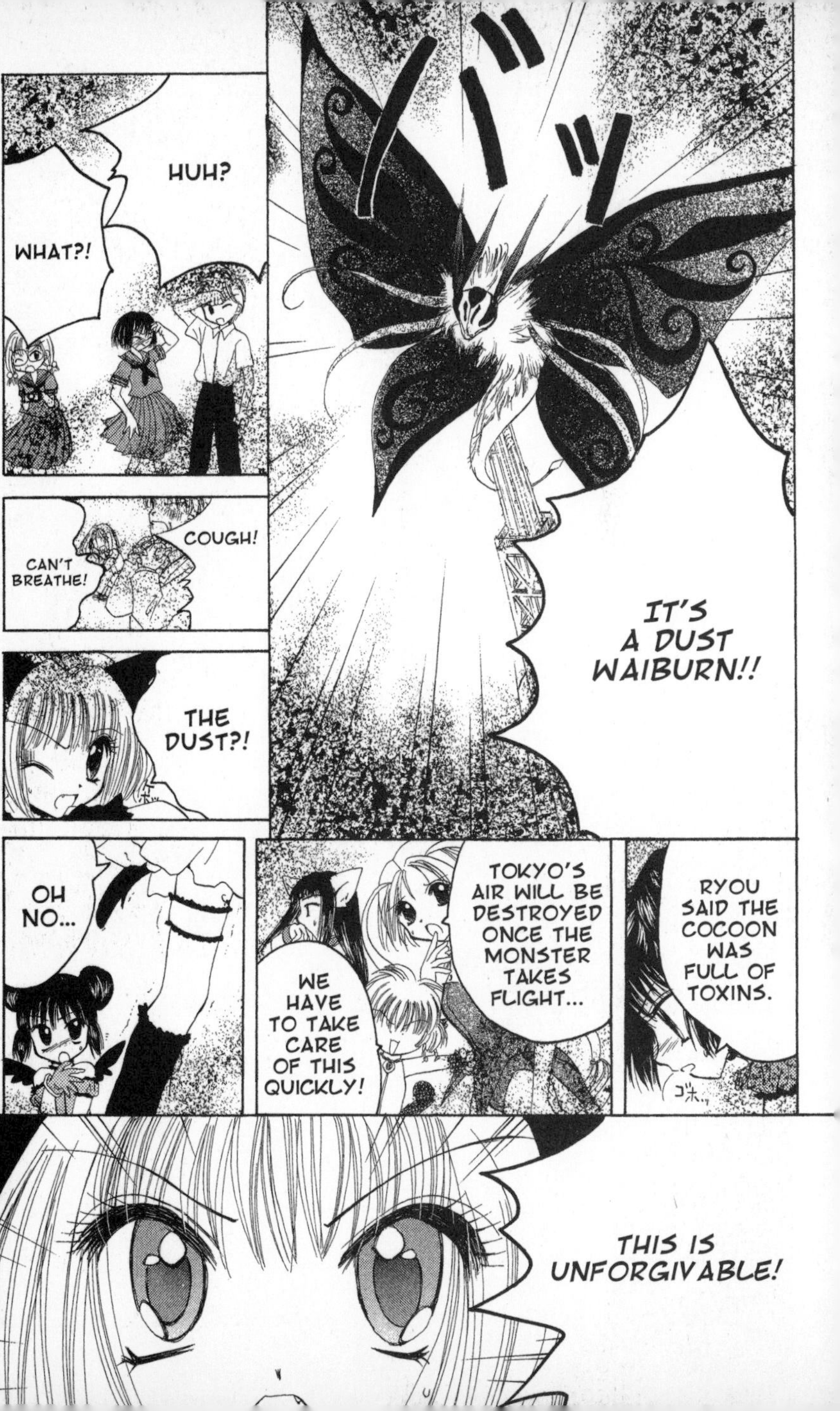
IT'S A DUST WAIBURN!!
HUH?
WHAT?!
COUGH!
CAN'T BREATHE!
THE DUST?!
RYOU SAID THE COCOON WAS FULL OF TOXINS.
TOKYO'S AIR WILL BE DESTROYED ONCE THE MONSTER TAKES FLIGHT...
WE HAVE TO TAKE CARE OF THIS QUICKLY!
OH NO...
THIS IS UNFORGIVABLE!

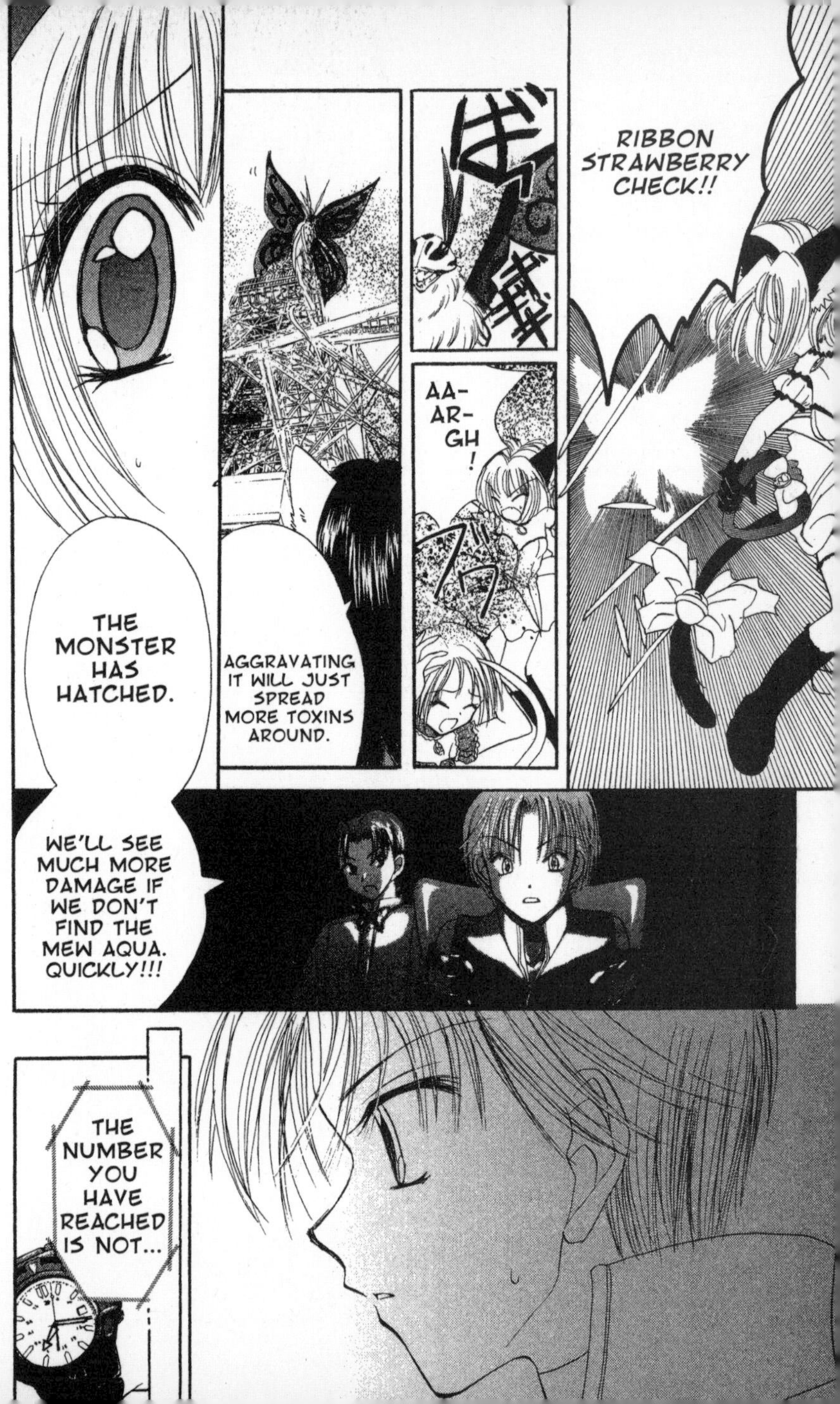
RIBBON STRAWBERRY CHECK!!
AA-AR-GH!
AGGRAVATING IT WILL JUST SPREAD MORE TOXINS AROUND.
THE MONSTER HAS HATCHED.
WE'LL SEE MUCH MORE DAMAGE IF WE DON'T FIND THE MEW AQUA. QUICKLY!!!
THE NUMBER YOU HAVE REACHED IS NOT...

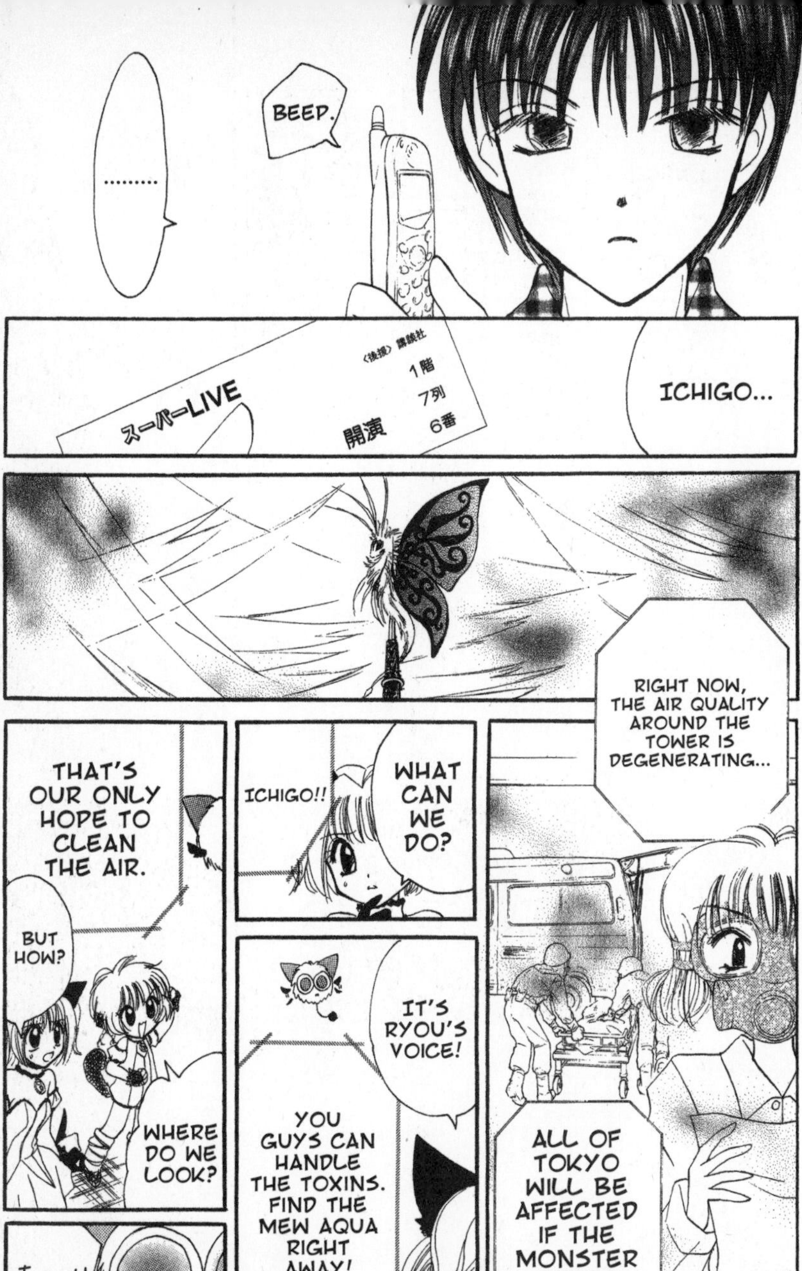
BEEP.
....
ICHIGO...
〈後援〉講談社
1階
7列
6番
開演
スーパーLIVE
RIGHT NOW, THE AIR QUALITY AROUND THE TOWER IS DEGENERATING...
ALL OF TOKYO WILL BE AFFECTED IF THE MONSTER TAKES FLIGHT!!
WHAT CAN WE DO?
ICHIGO!!
IT'S RYOU'S VOICE!
YOU GUYS CAN HANDLE THE TOXINS. FIND THE MEW AQUA RIGHT AWAY!
THAT'S OUR ONLY HOPE TO CLEAN THE AIR.
BUT HOW?
WHERE DO WE LOOK?
Tweet!

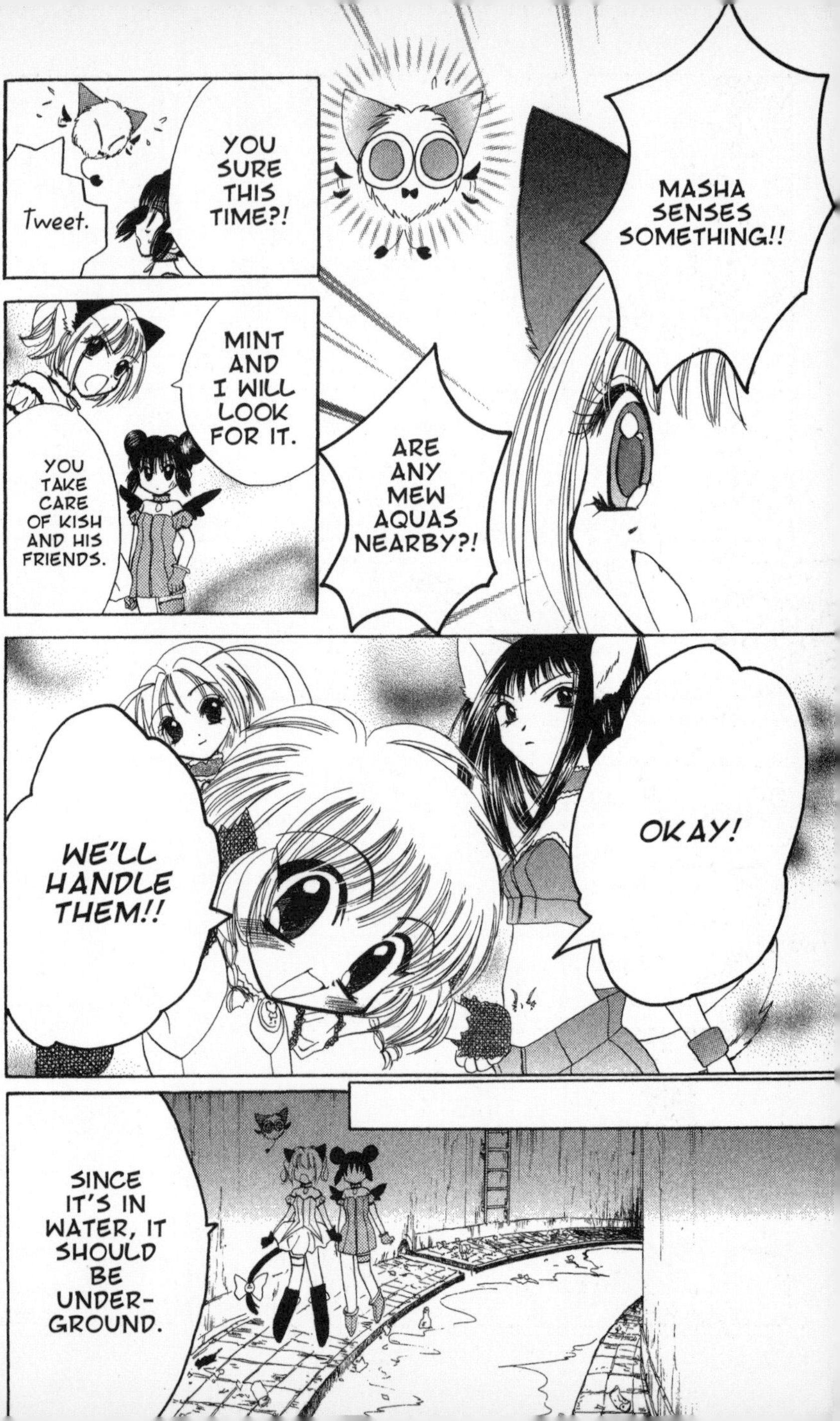
MASHA SENSES SOMETHING!!
ARE ANY MEW AQUAS NEARBY?!
YOU SURE THIS TIME?!
Tweet.
MINT AND I WILL LOOK FOR IT.
YOU TAKE CARE OF KISH AND HIS FRIENDS.
OKAY!
WE'LL HANDLE THEM!!
SINCE IT'S IN WATER, IT SHOULD BE UNDER-GROUND.

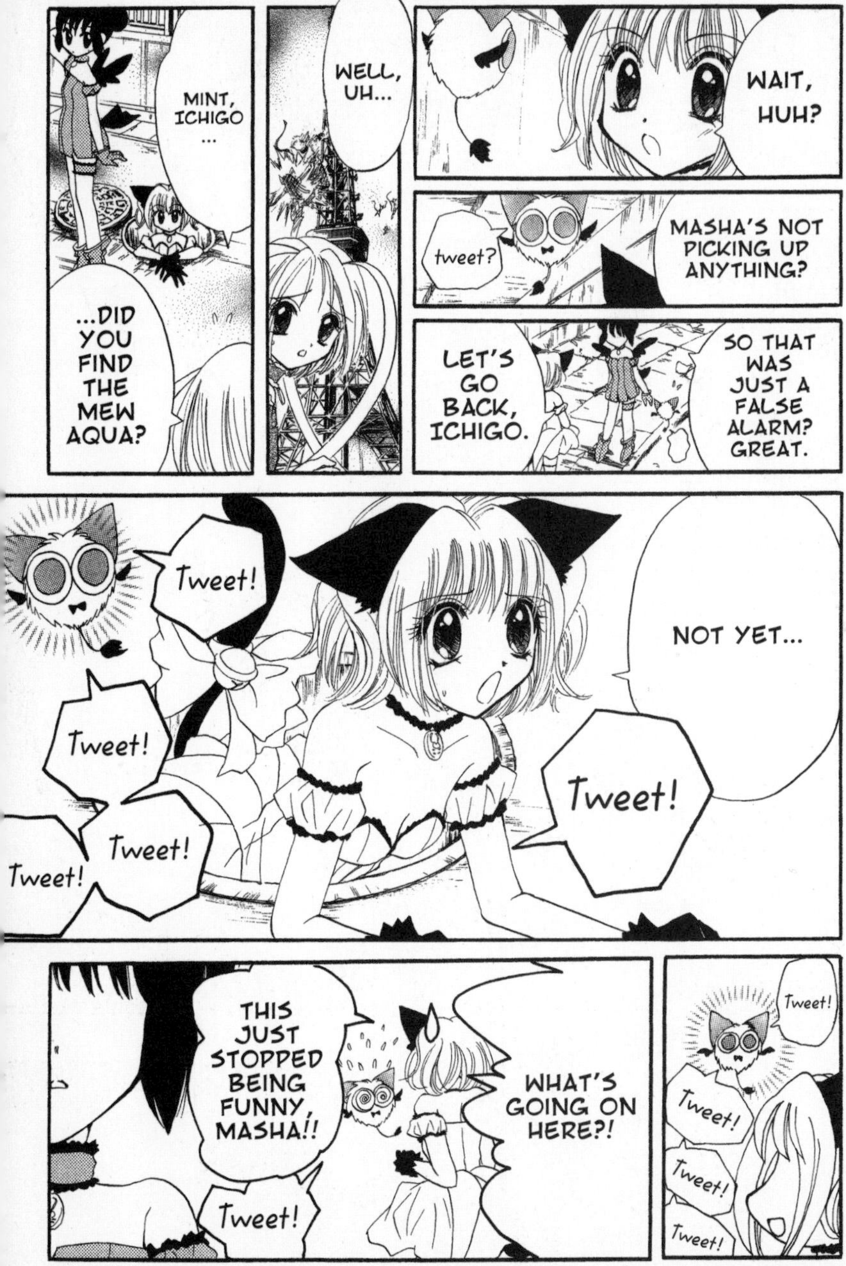
MINT, ICHIGO ...
...DID YOU FIND THE MEW AQUA?
WELL, UH...
WAIT, HUH?
tweet?
MASHA'S NOT PICKING UP ANYTHING?
LET'S GO BACK, ICHIGO.
SO THAT WAS JUST A FALSE ALARM? GREAT.
Tweet!
NOT YET...
Tweet!
Tweet!
Tweet!
Tweet!
Tweet!
THIS JUST STOPPED BEING FUNNY, MASHA!!
WHAT'S GOING ON HERE?!
Tweet!
Tweet!
Tweet!
Tweet!
Tweet!

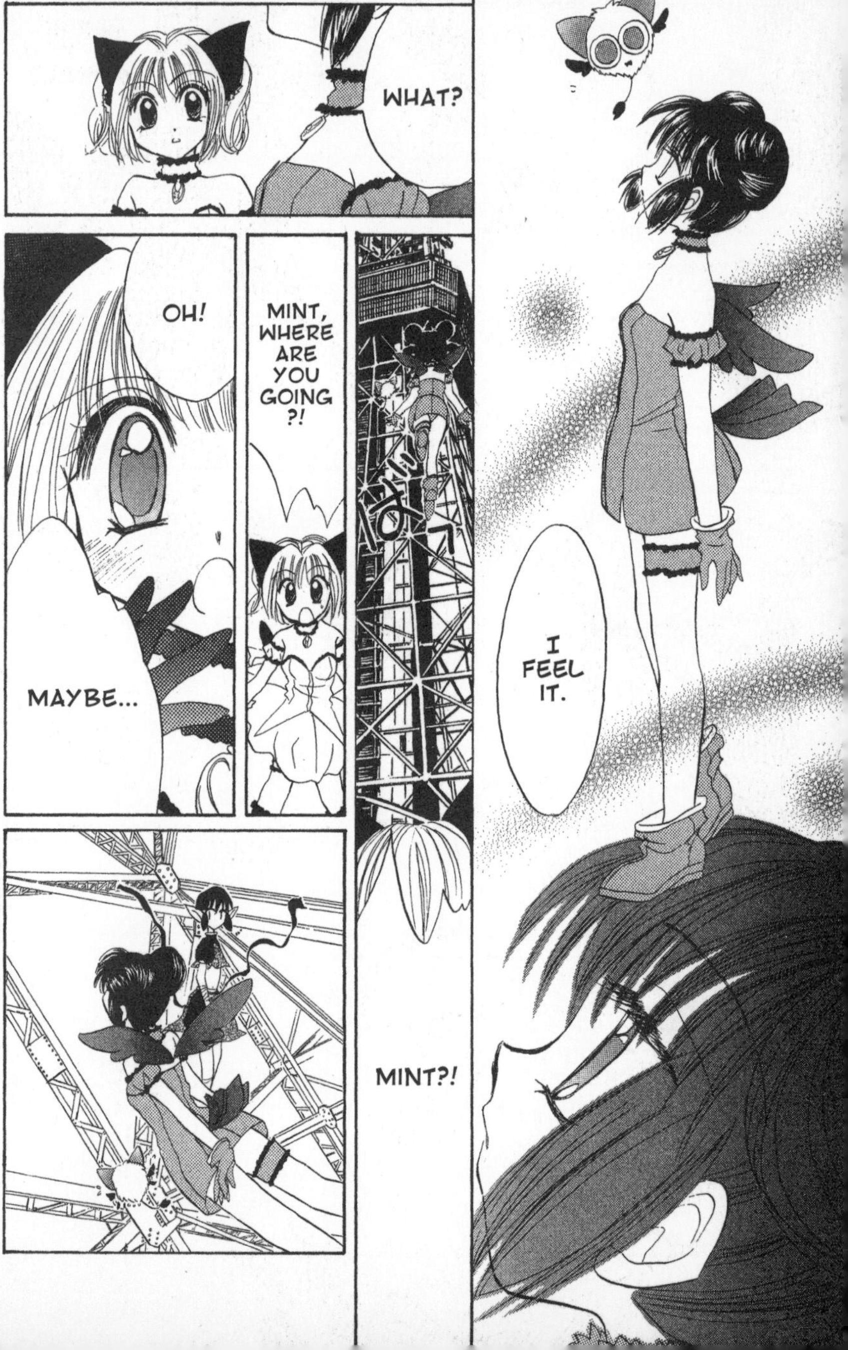
I FEEL IT.
WHAT?
MINT, WHERE ARE YOU GOING?!
OH!
MAYBE...
MINT?!

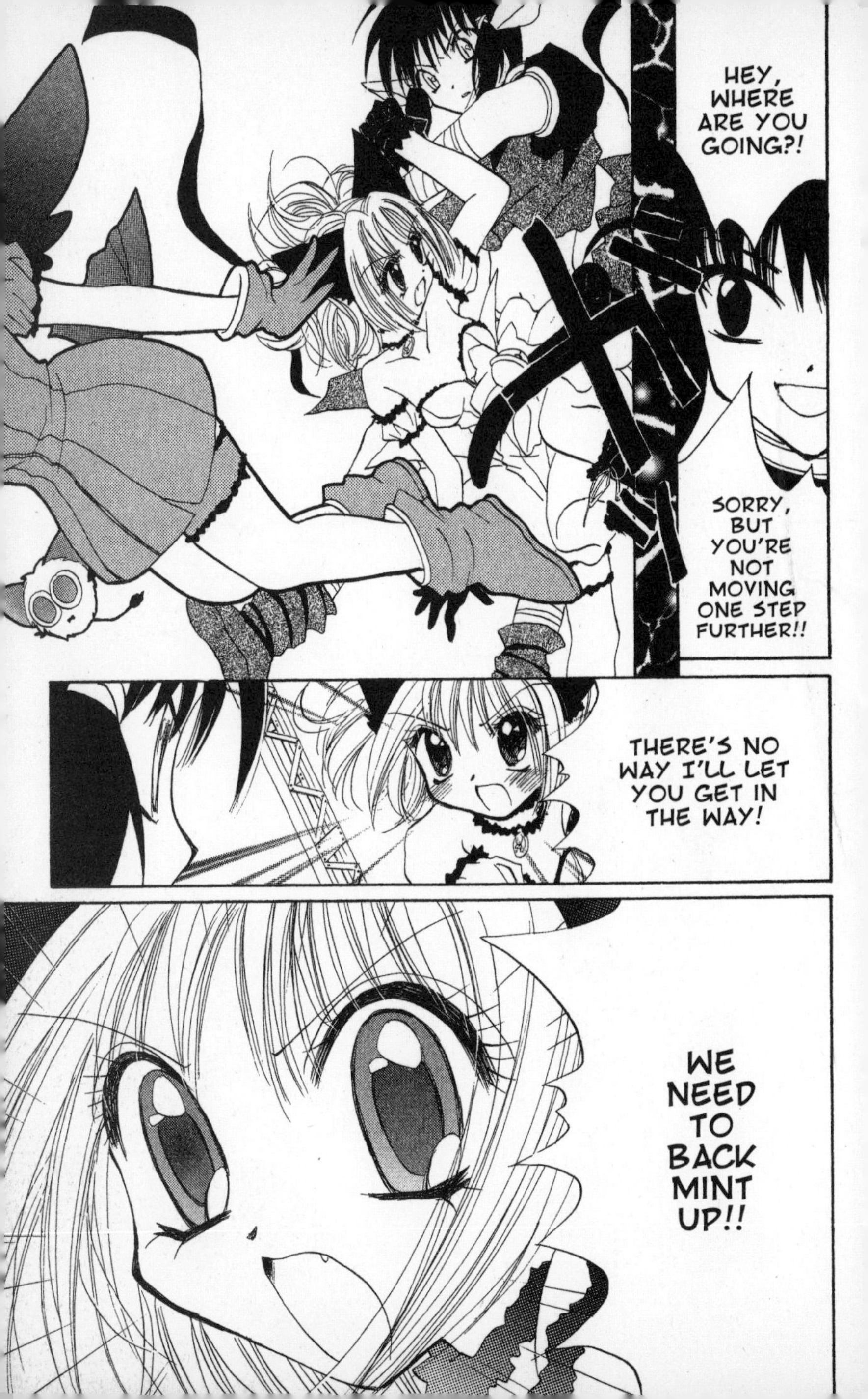
HEY, WHERE ARE YOU GOING?!
SORRY, BUT YOU'RE NOT MOVING ONE STEP FURTHER!!
THERE'S NO WAY I'LL LET YOU GET IN THE WAY!
WE NEED TO BACK MINT UP!!

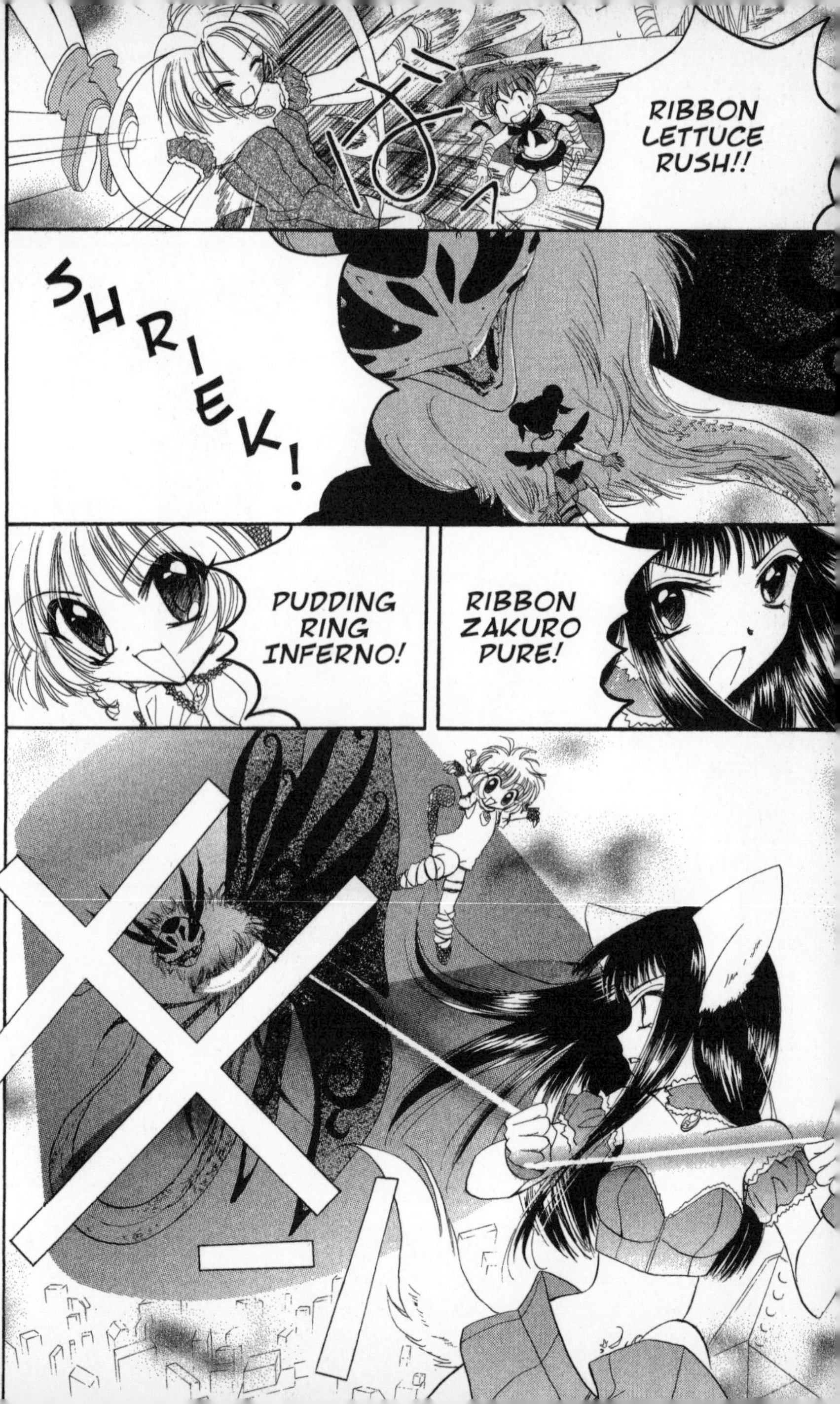
RIBBON LETTUCE RUSH!!
SHRIEK!
RIBBON ZAKURO PURE!
PUDDING RING INFERNO!

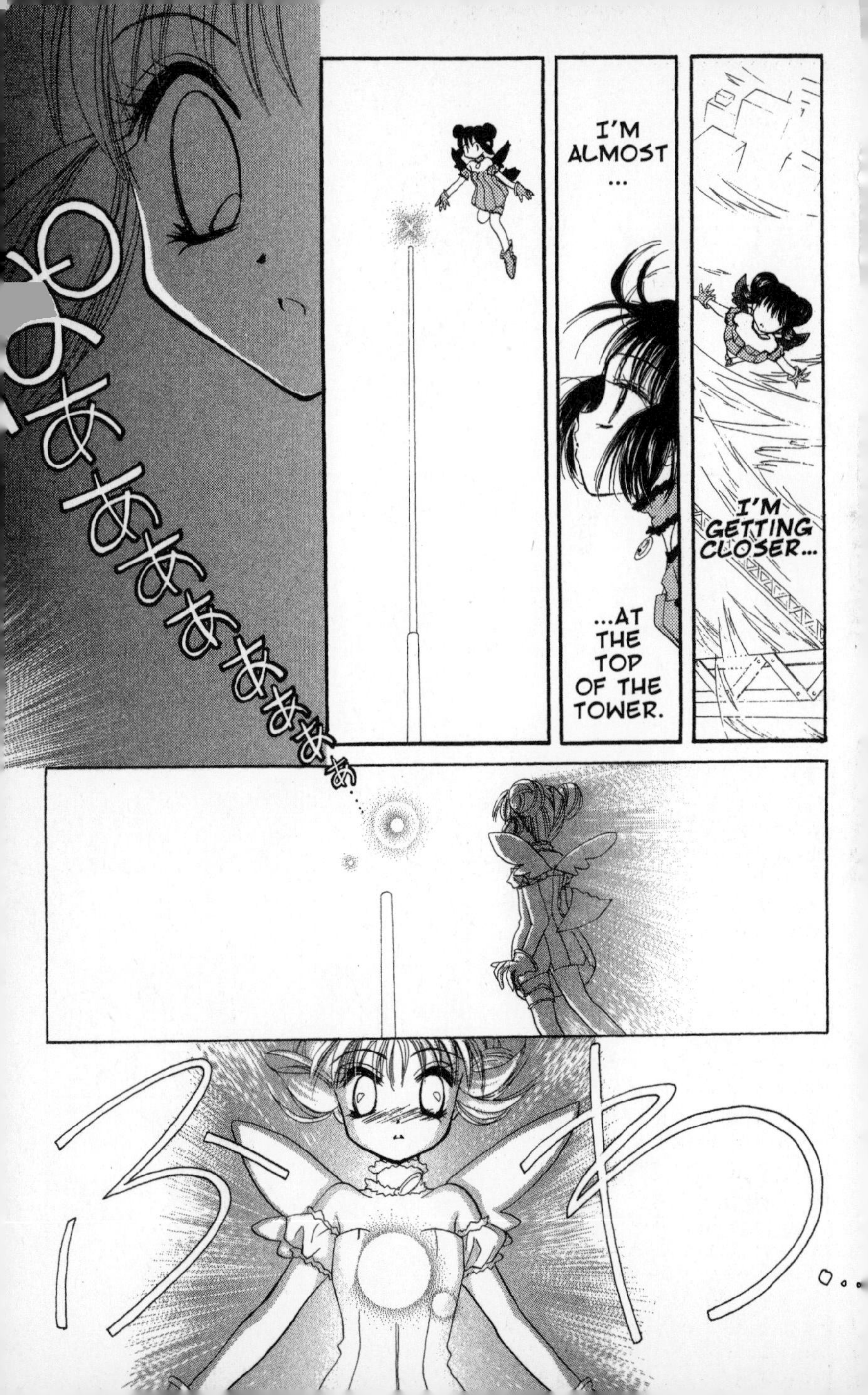

I'M GETTING CLOSER...
I'M ALMOST ...
...AT THE TOP OF THE TOWER.
ふわ

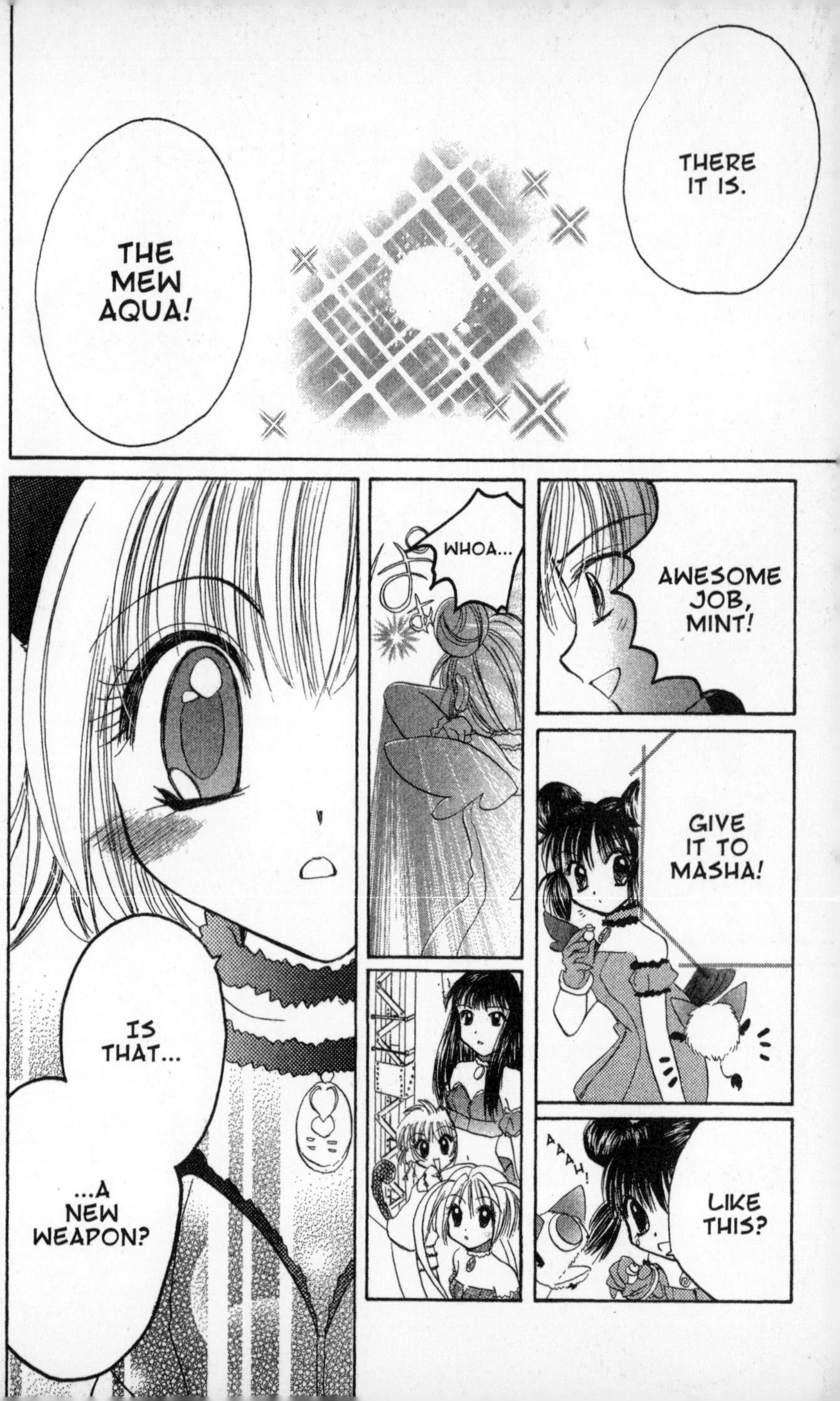
THERE IT IS.
THE MEW AQUA!
AWESOME JOB, MINT!
GIVE IT TO MASHA!
AAAH!
LIKE THIS?
WHOA...
IS THAT...
...A NEW WEAPON?

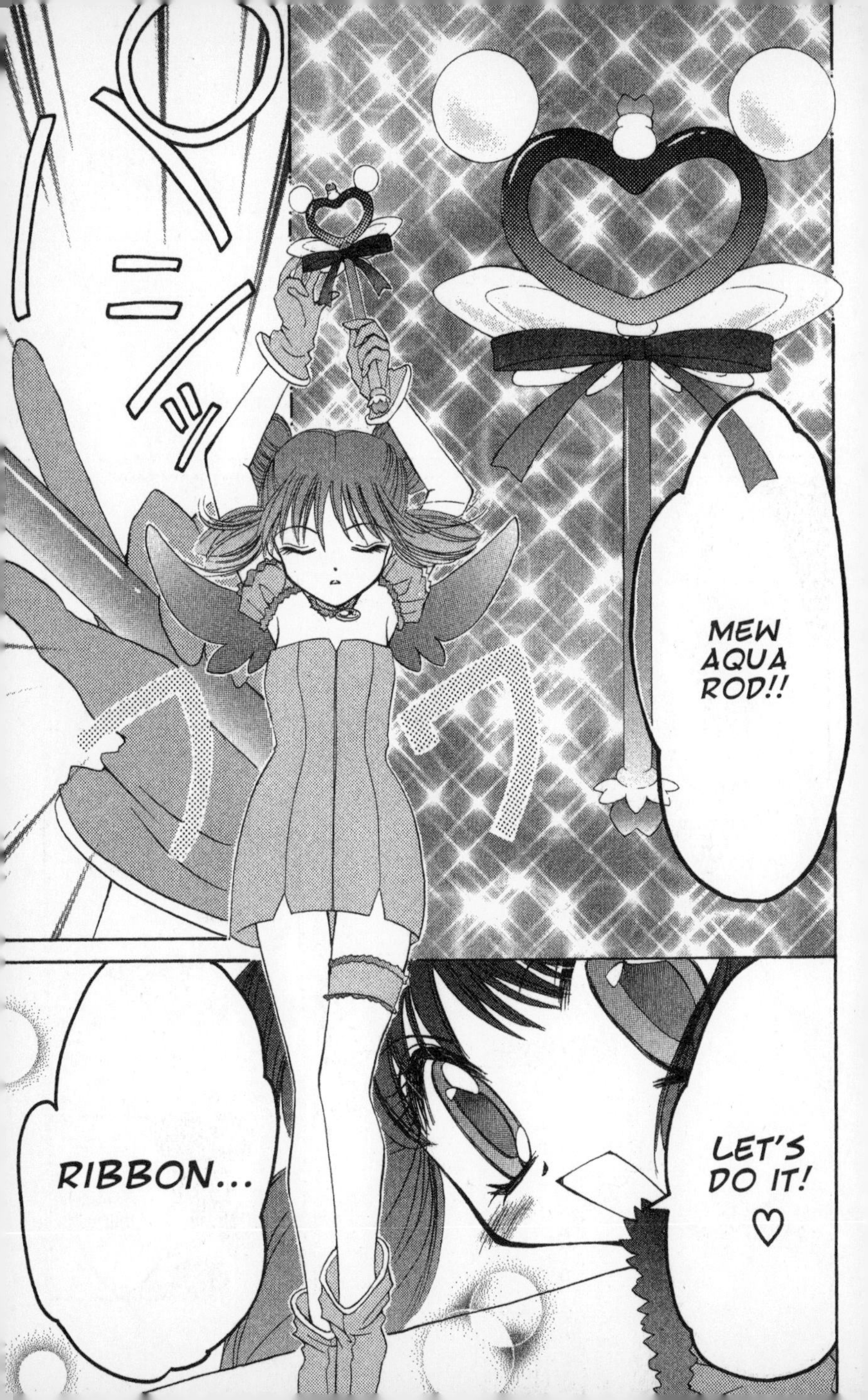
MEW AQUA ROD!!
LET'S DO IT! ♡
RIBBON...

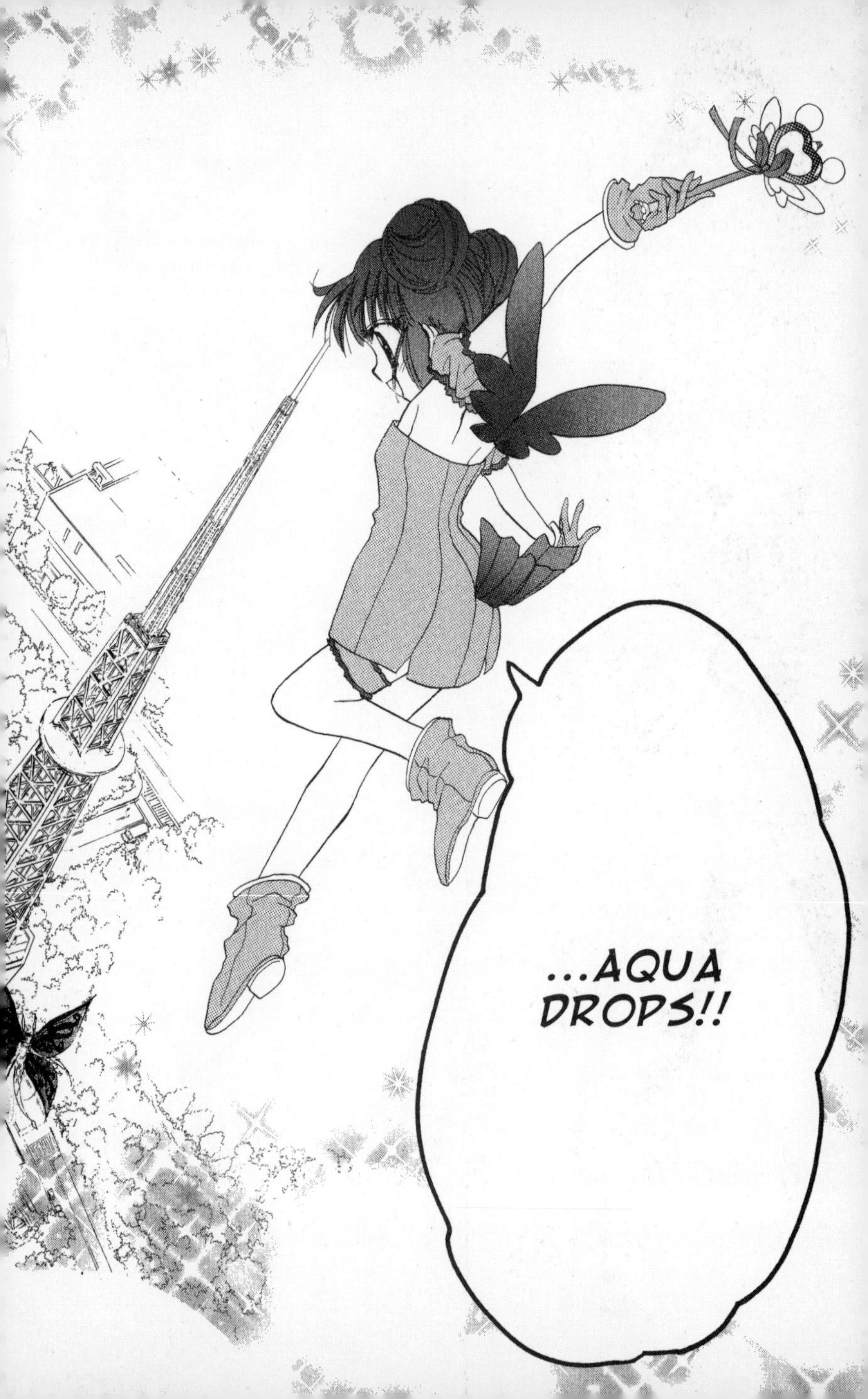
...AQUA DROPS!!

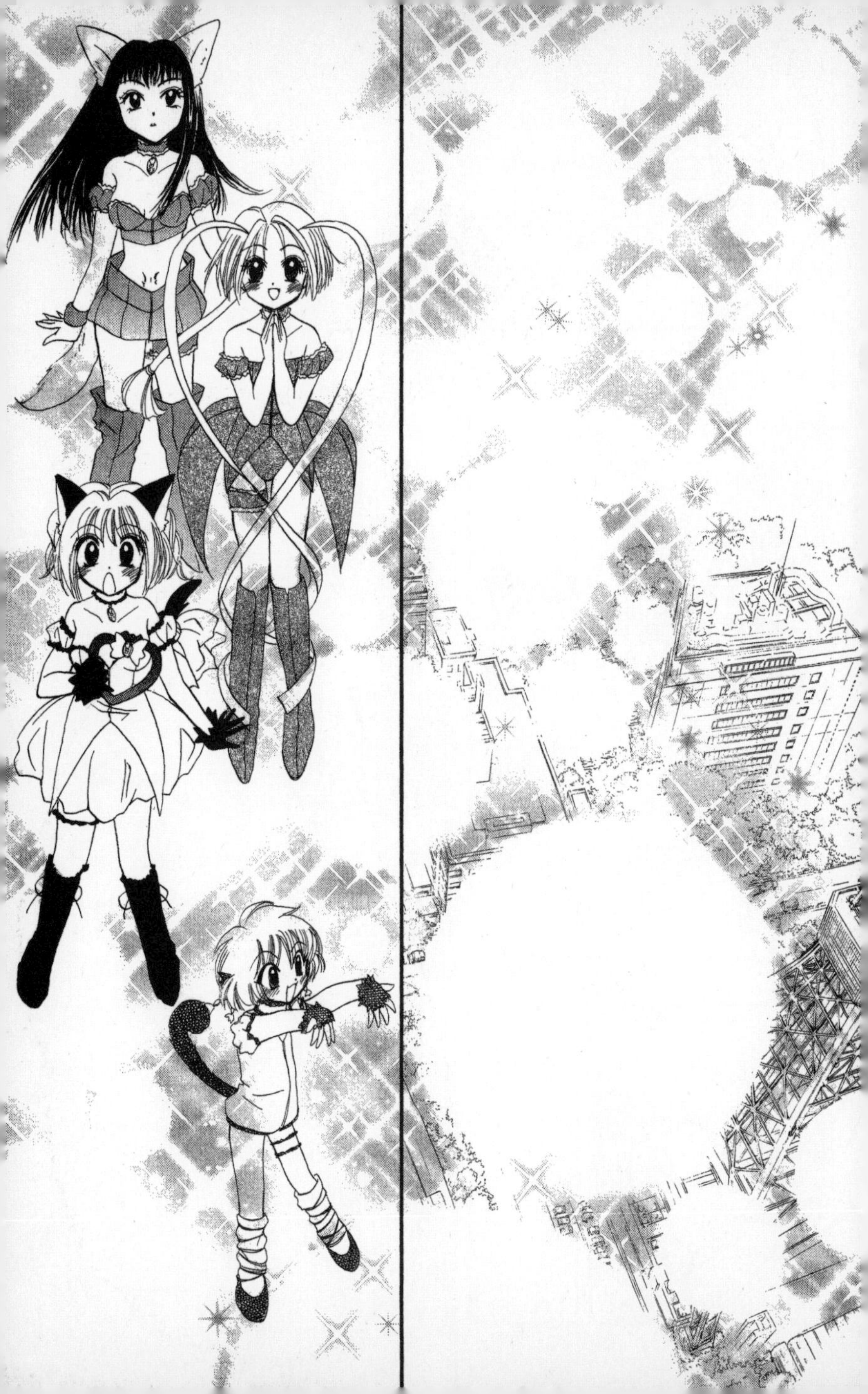

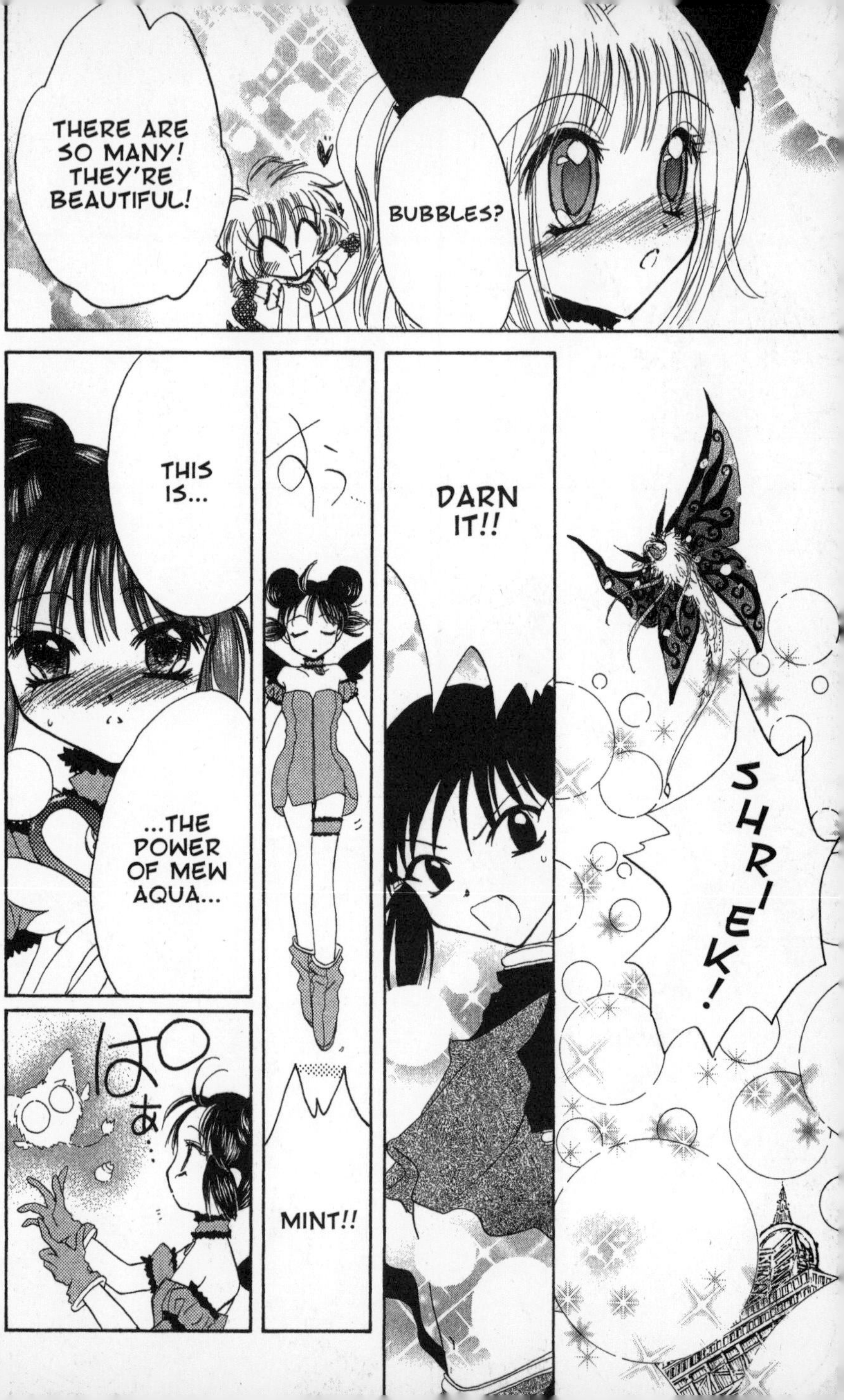
BUBBLES?
THERE ARE SO MANY! THEY'RE BEAUTIFUL!
SHRIEK!
DARN IT!!
すぅ…
MINT!!
THIS IS...
...THE POWER OF MEW AQUA...
はぁ…

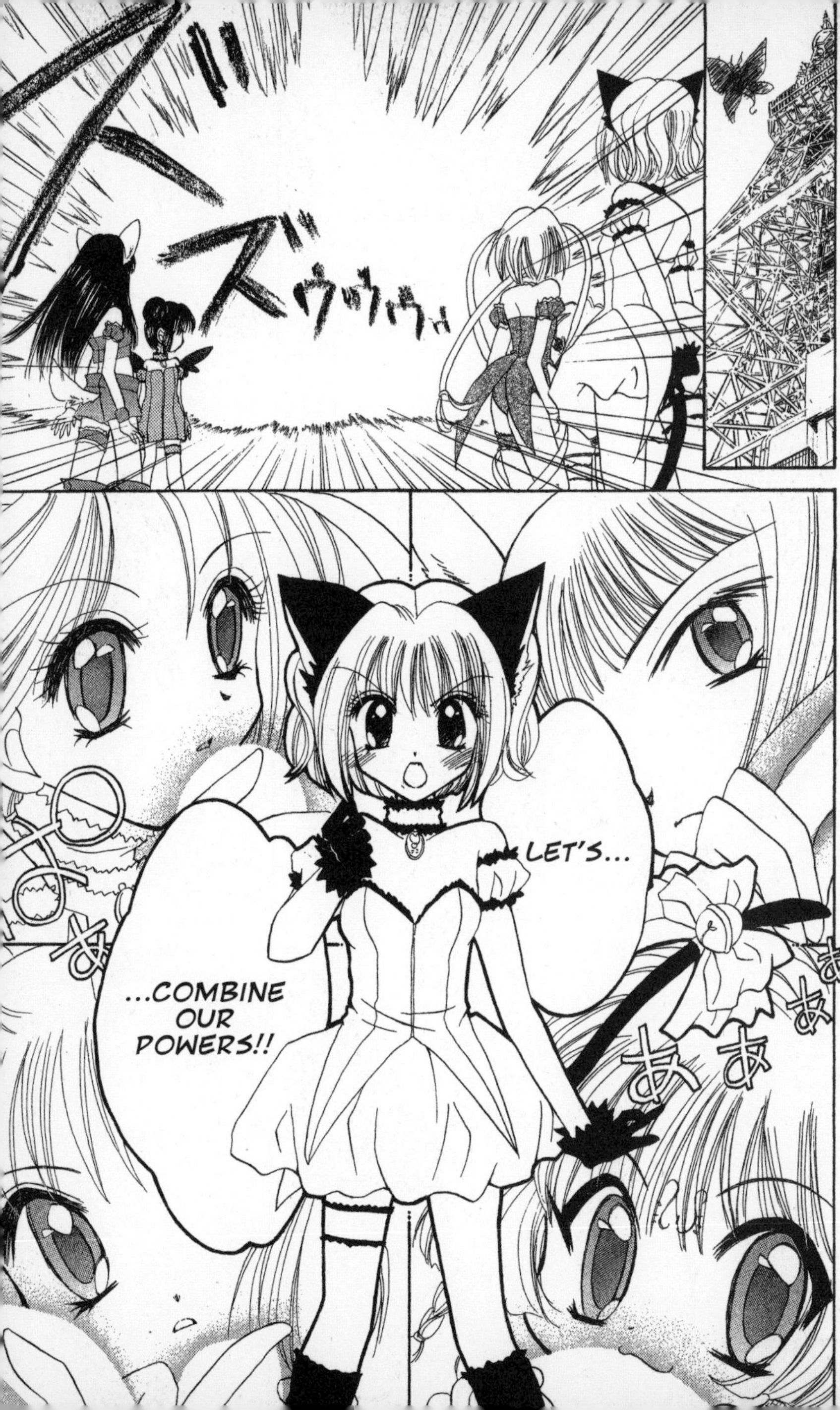
LET'S...
...COMBINE OUR POWERS!!

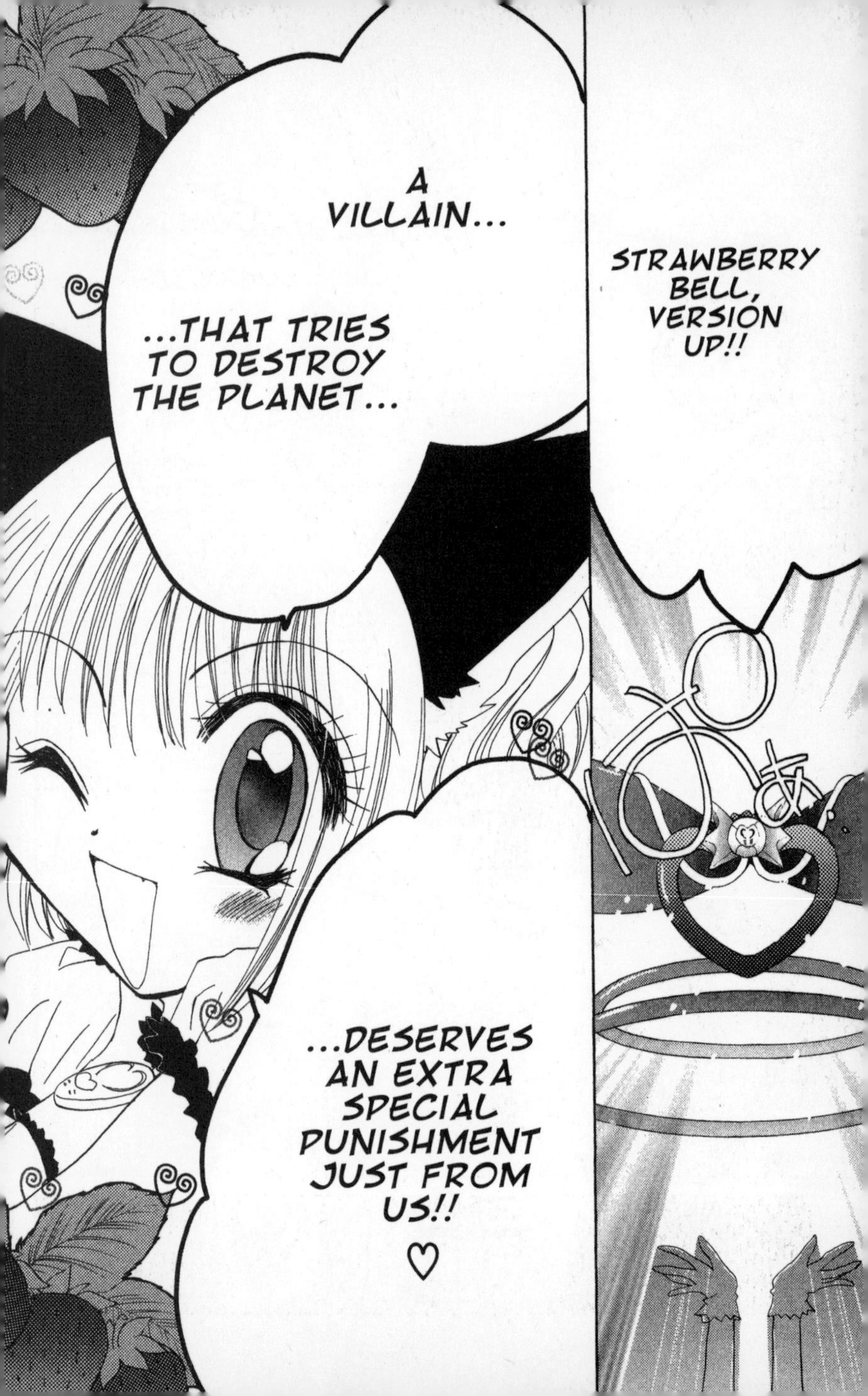
STRAWBERRY BELL, VERSION UP!!
A VILLAIN...
...THAT TRIES TO DESTROY THE PLANET...
...DESERVES AN EXTRA SPECIAL PUNISHMENT JUST FROM US!! ♡

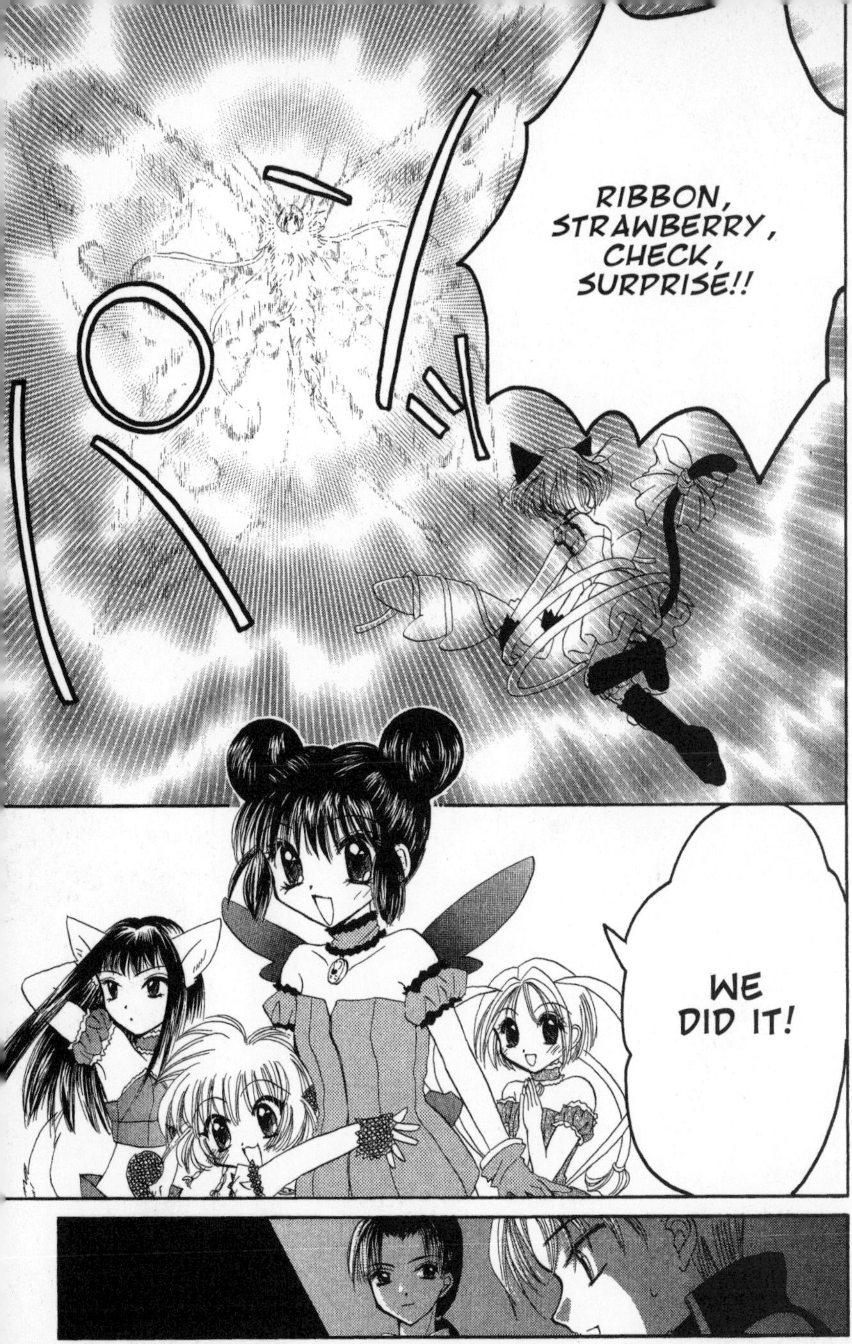
RIBBON, STRAWBERRY, CHECK, SURPRISE!!
WE DID IT!

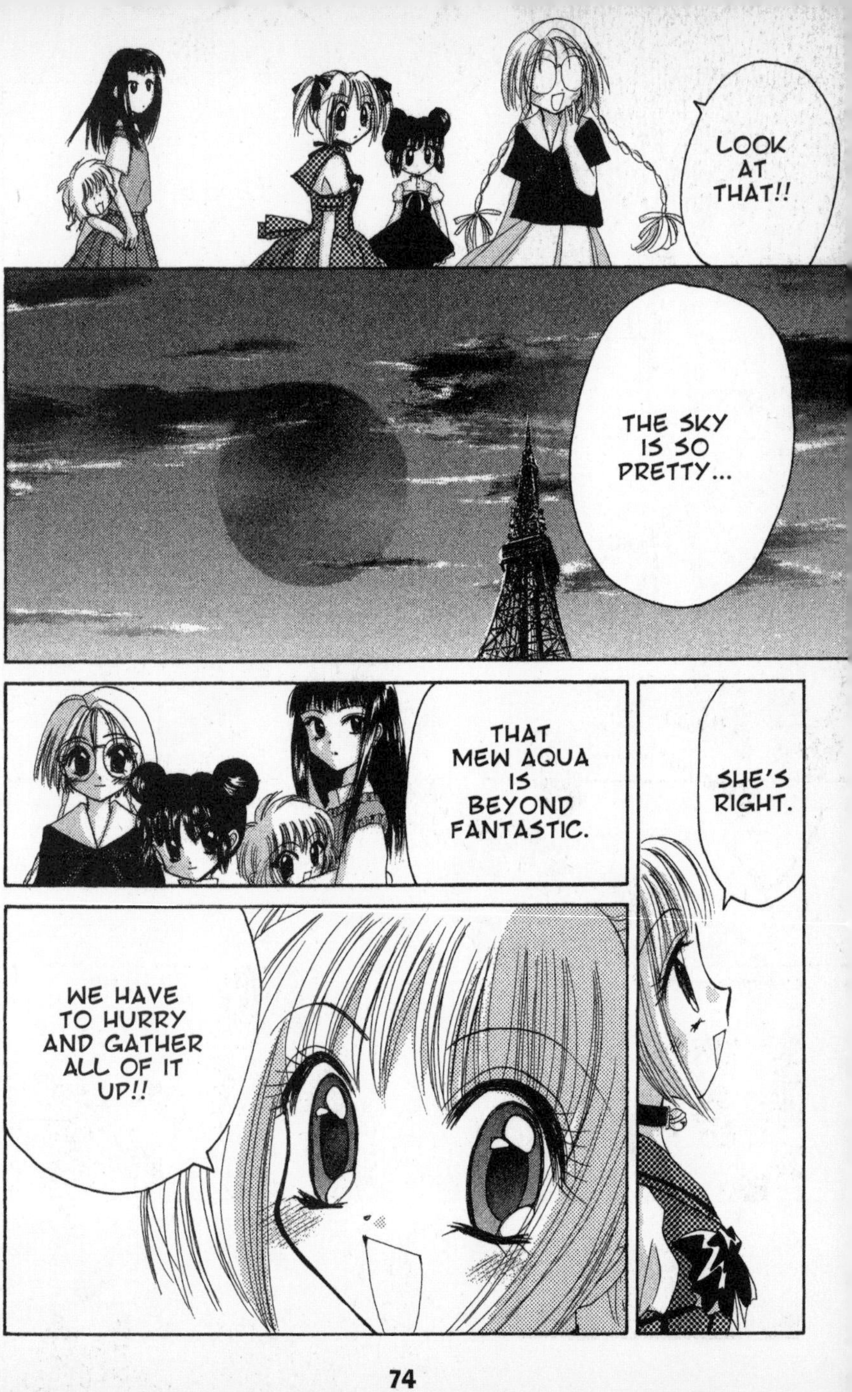
LOOK AT THAT!!
THE SKY IS SO PRETTY...
SHE'S RIGHT.
THAT MEW AQUA IS BEYOND FANTASTIC.
WE HAVE TO HURRY AND GATHER ALL OF IT UP!!

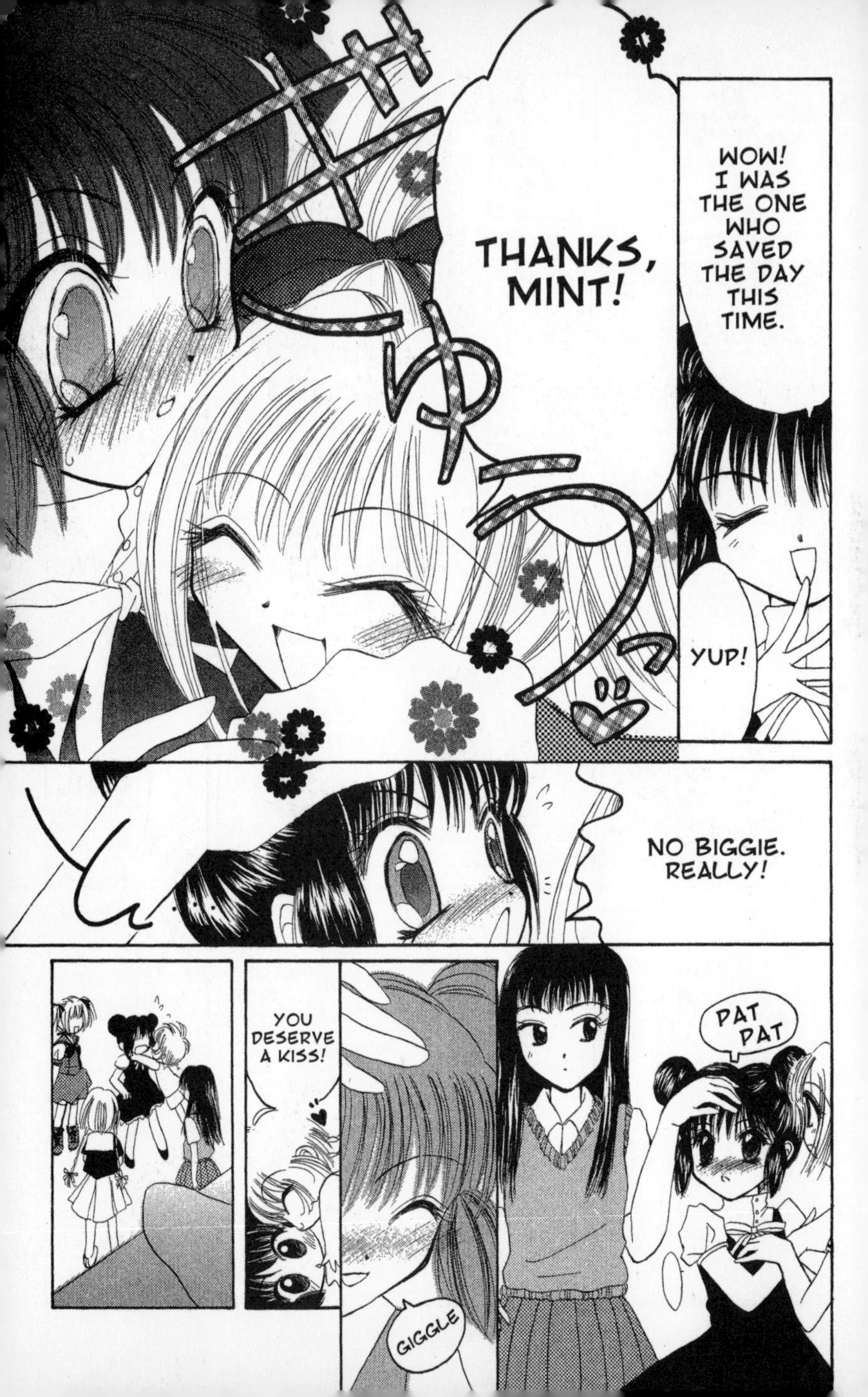
THANKS, MINT!
WOW! I WAS THE ONE WHO SAVED THE DAY THIS TIME.
YUP!
NO BIGGIE. REALLY!
PAT PAT
GIGGLE
YOU DESERVE A KISS!

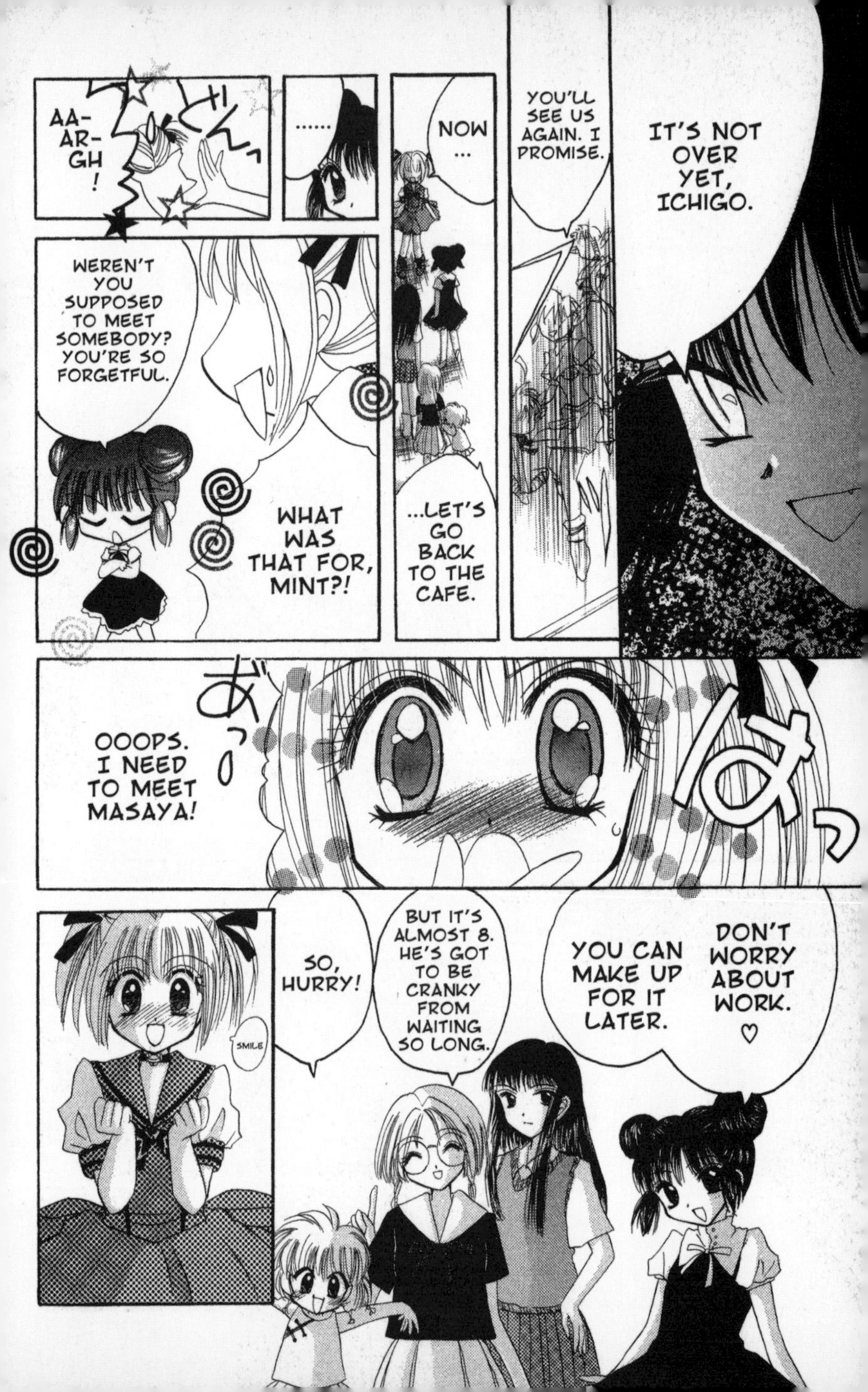
IT'S NOT OVER YET, ICHIGO.
YOU'LL SEE US AGAIN. I PROMISE.
NOW ...
...LET'S GO BACK TO THE CAFE.
......
AA-AR-GH!
WEREN'T YOU SUPPOSED TO MEET SOMEBODY? YOU'RE SO FORGETFUL.
WHAT WAS THAT FOR, MINT?!
はっ
あっ
OOOPS. I NEED TO MEET MASAYA!
DON'T WORRY ABOUT WORK. ♡
YOU CAN MAKE UP FOR IT LATER.
BUT IT'S ALMOST 8. HE'S GOT TO BE CRANKY FROM WAITING SO LONG.
SO, HURRY!
SMILE

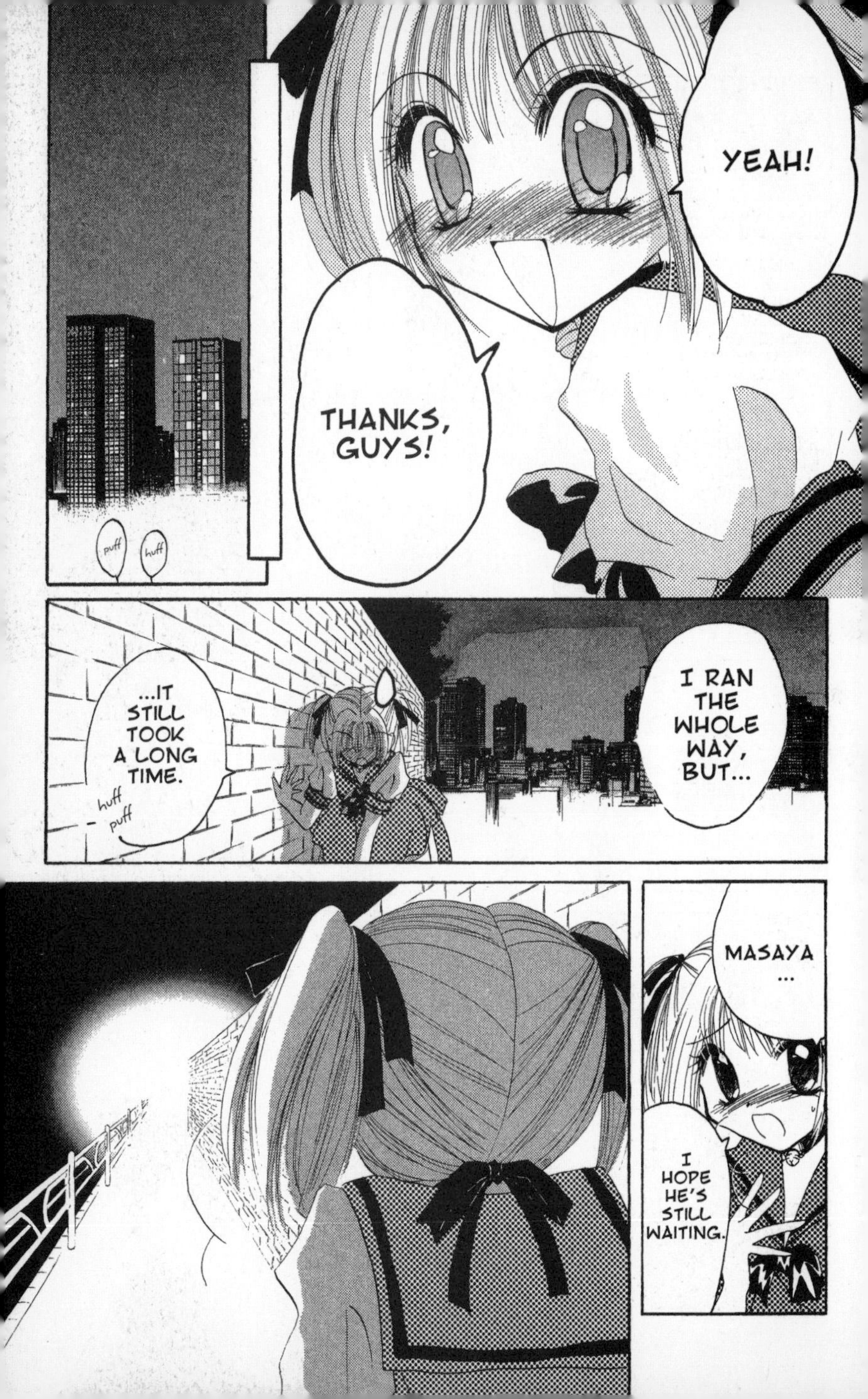
YEAH!
THANKS, GUYS!
huff
puff
I RAN THE WHOLE WAY, BUT...
...IT STILL TOOK A LONG TIME.
huff puff
MASAYA ...
I HOPE HE'S STILL WAITING.

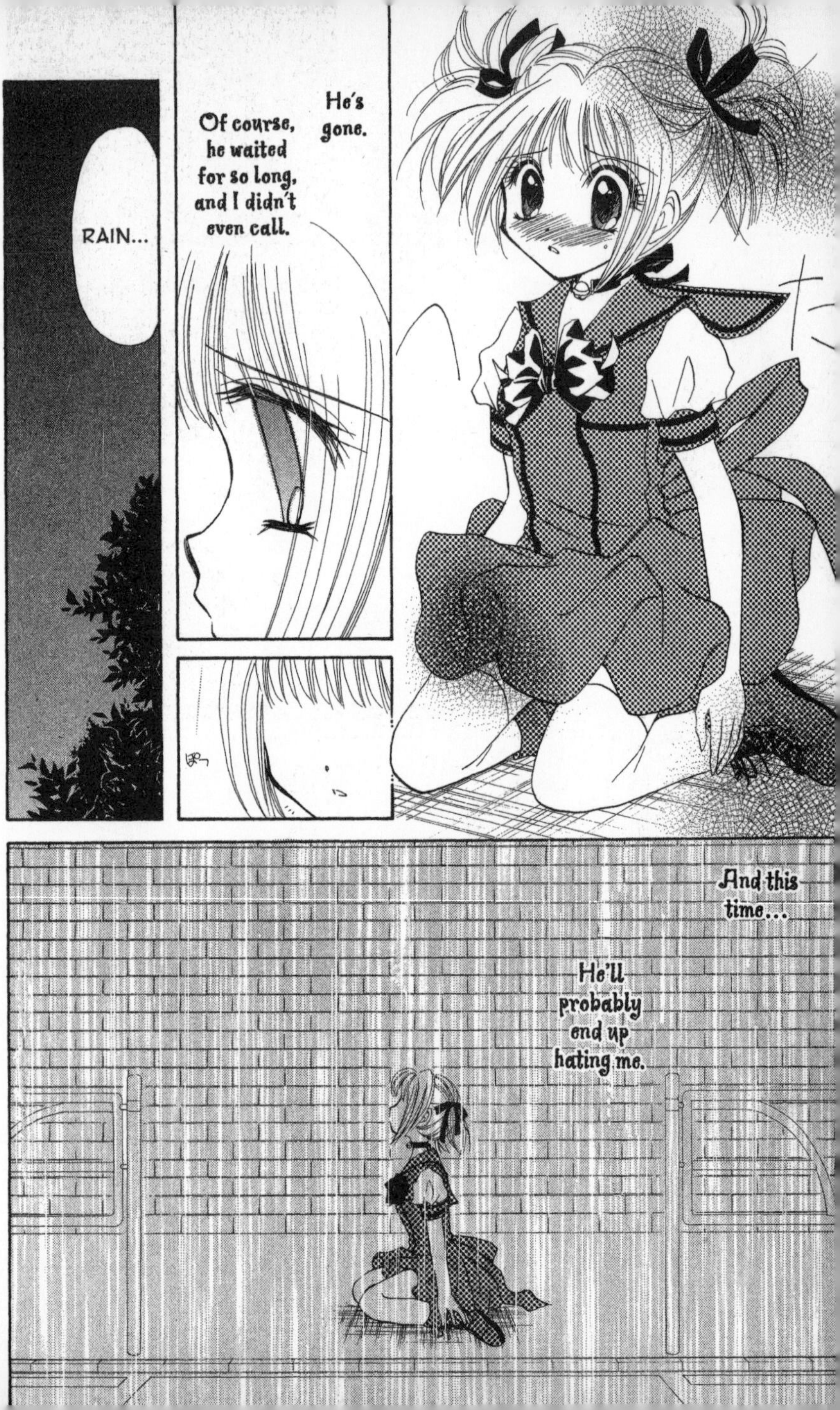
He's gone.
Of course, he waited for so long, and I didn't even call.
RAIN...
And this time...
He'll probably end up hating me.

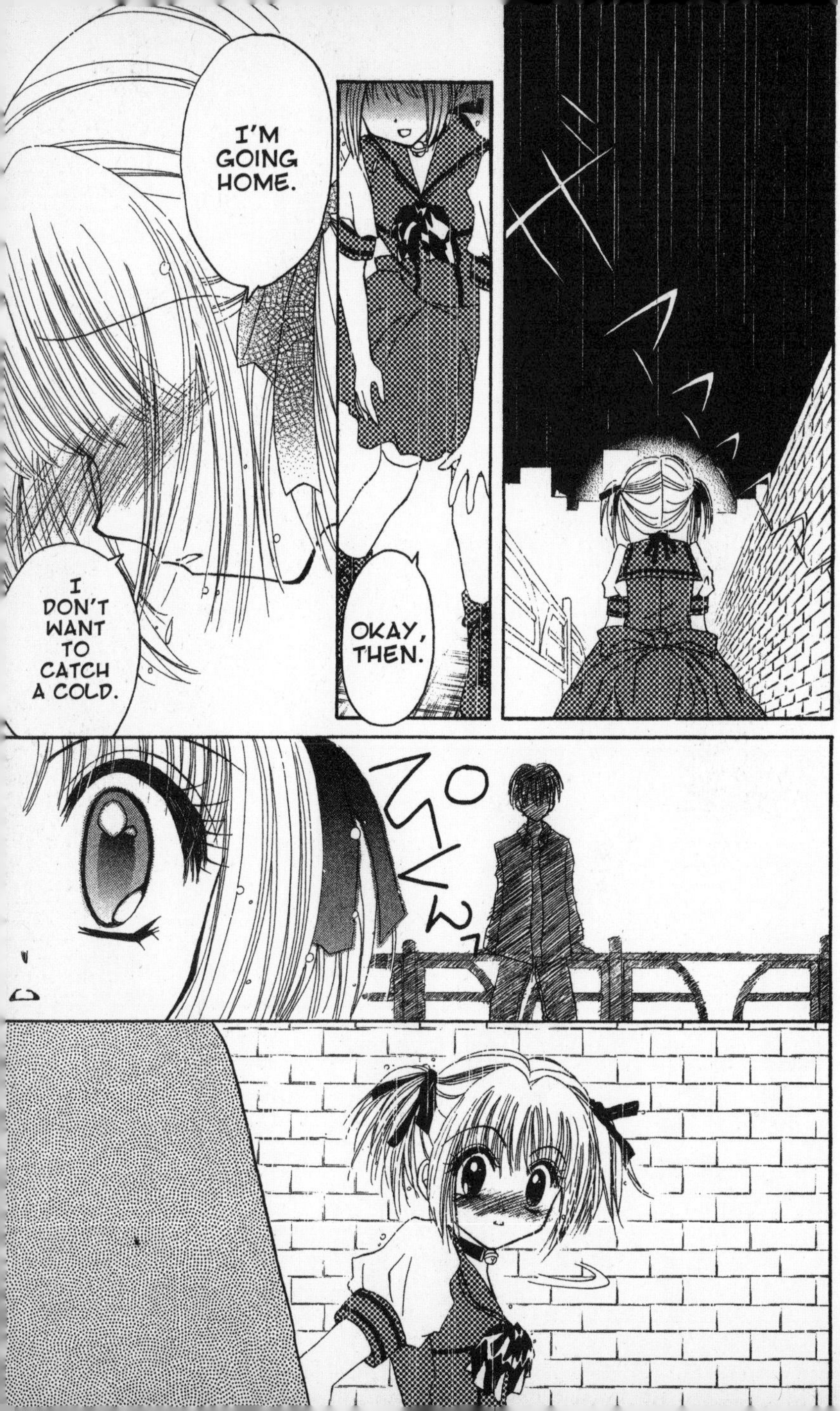
OKAY, THEN.
I'M GOING HOME.
I DON'T WANT TO CATCH A COLD.

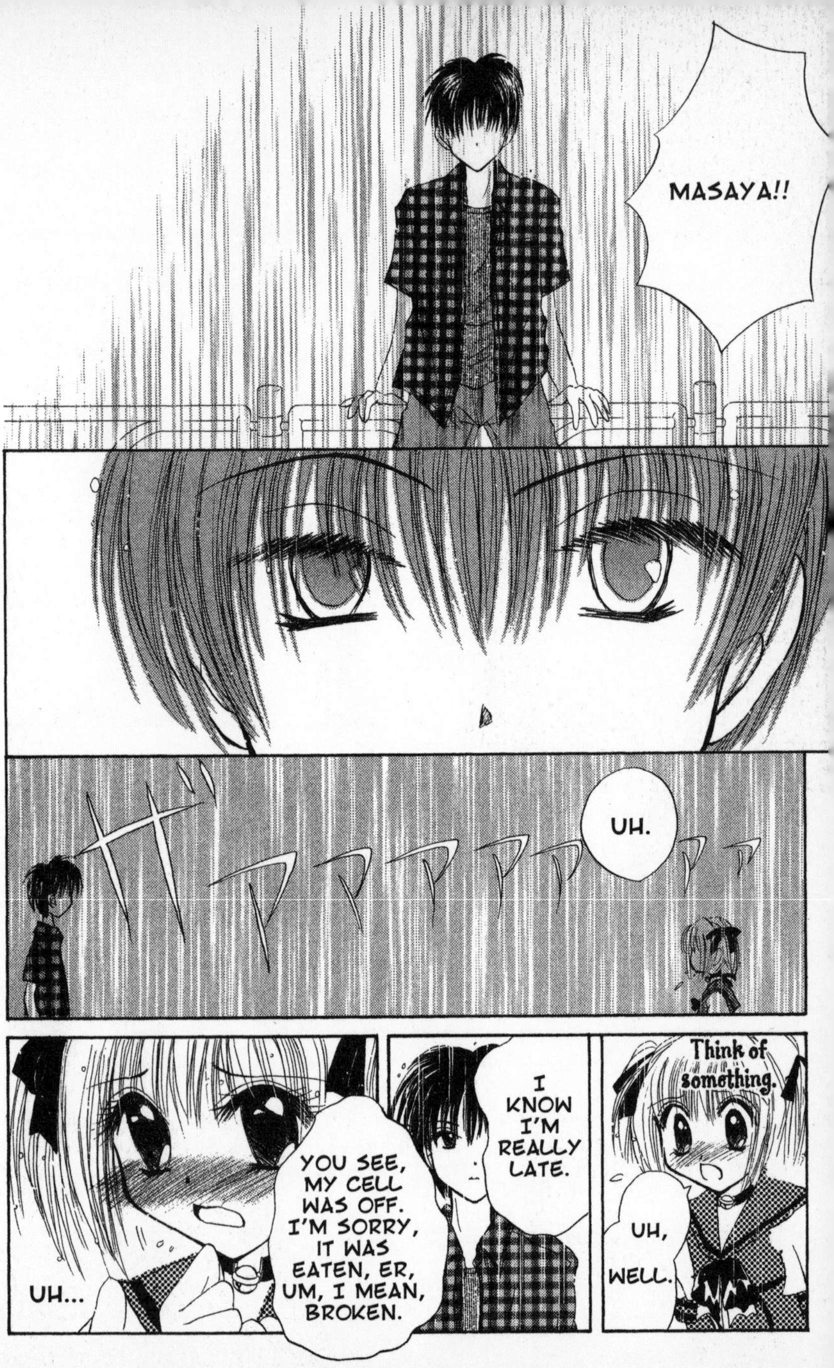
MASAYA!!
ザァァァァァァ
UH.
Think of something.
UH, WELL.
I KNOW I'M REALLY LATE.
YOU SEE, MY CELL WAS OFF. I'M SORRY, IT WAS EATEN, ER, UM, I MEAN, BROKEN.
UH...

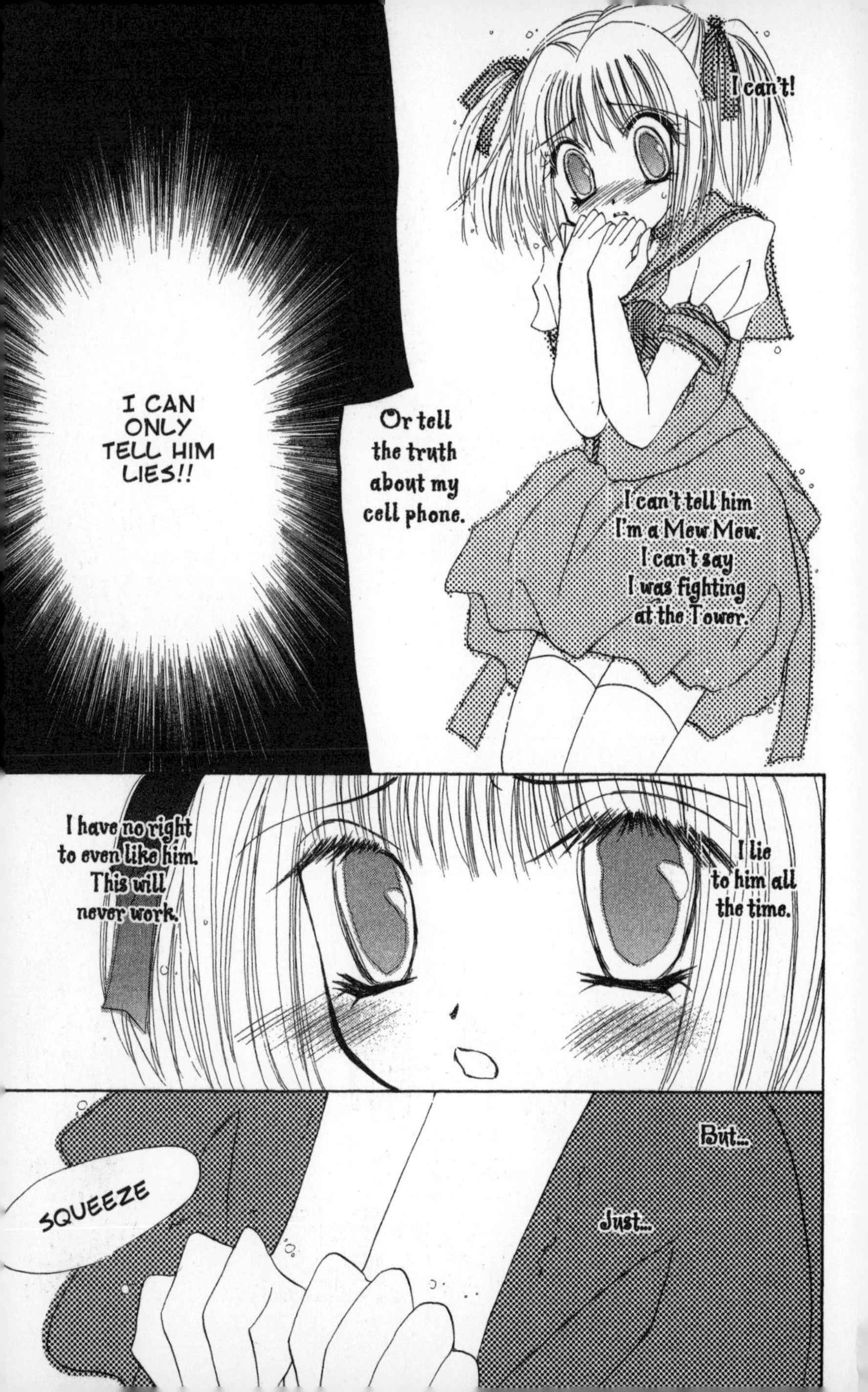
I can't!
I can't tell him I'm a Mew Mew. I can't say I was fighting at the Tower.
Or tell the truth about my cell phone.
I CAN ONLY TELL HIM LIES!!
I lie to him all the time.
I have no right to even like him. This will never work.
But...
Just...
SQUEEZE

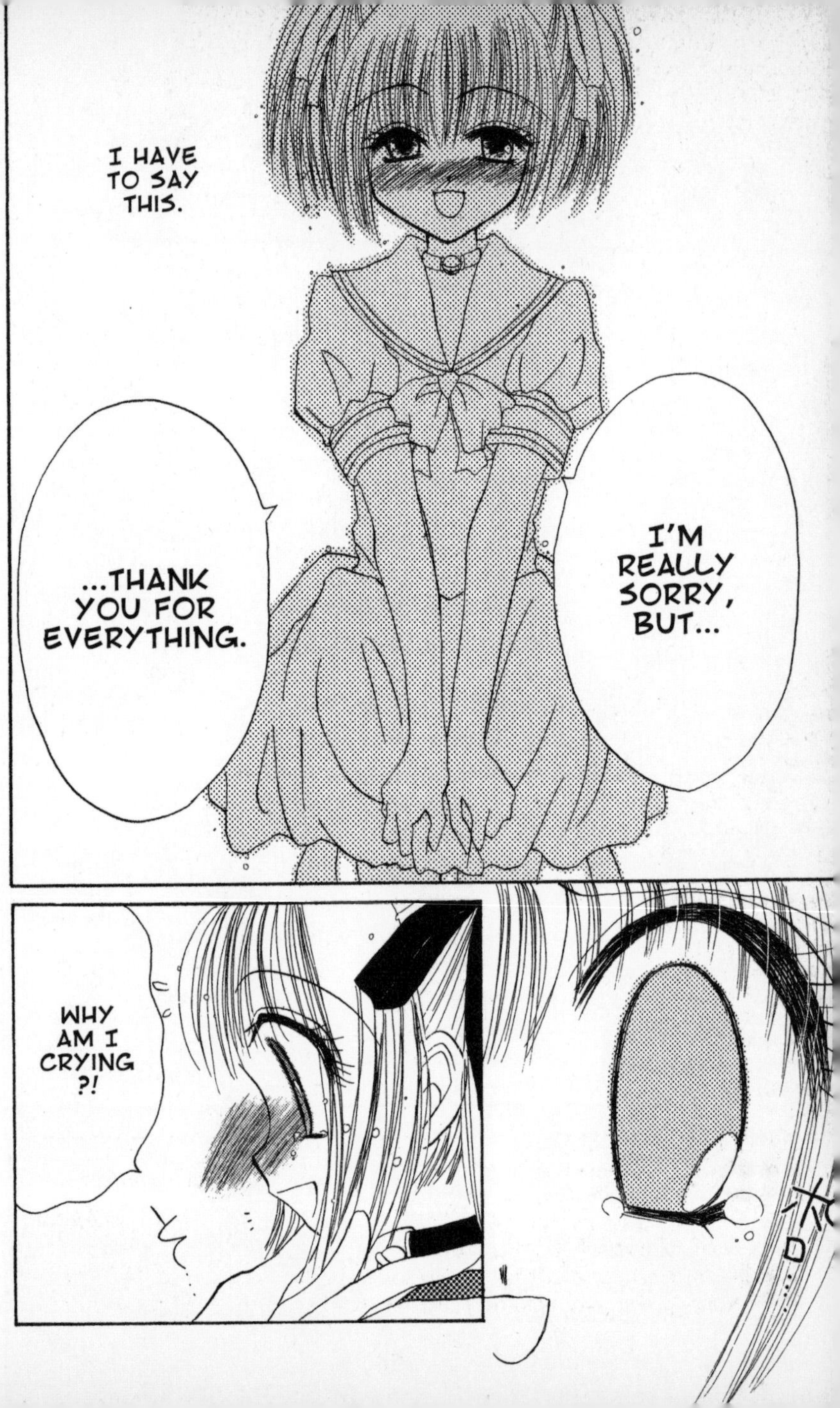
I HAVE TO SAY THIS.
I'M REALLY SORRY, BUT...
...THANK YOU FOR EVERYTHING.
WHY AM I CRYING ?!

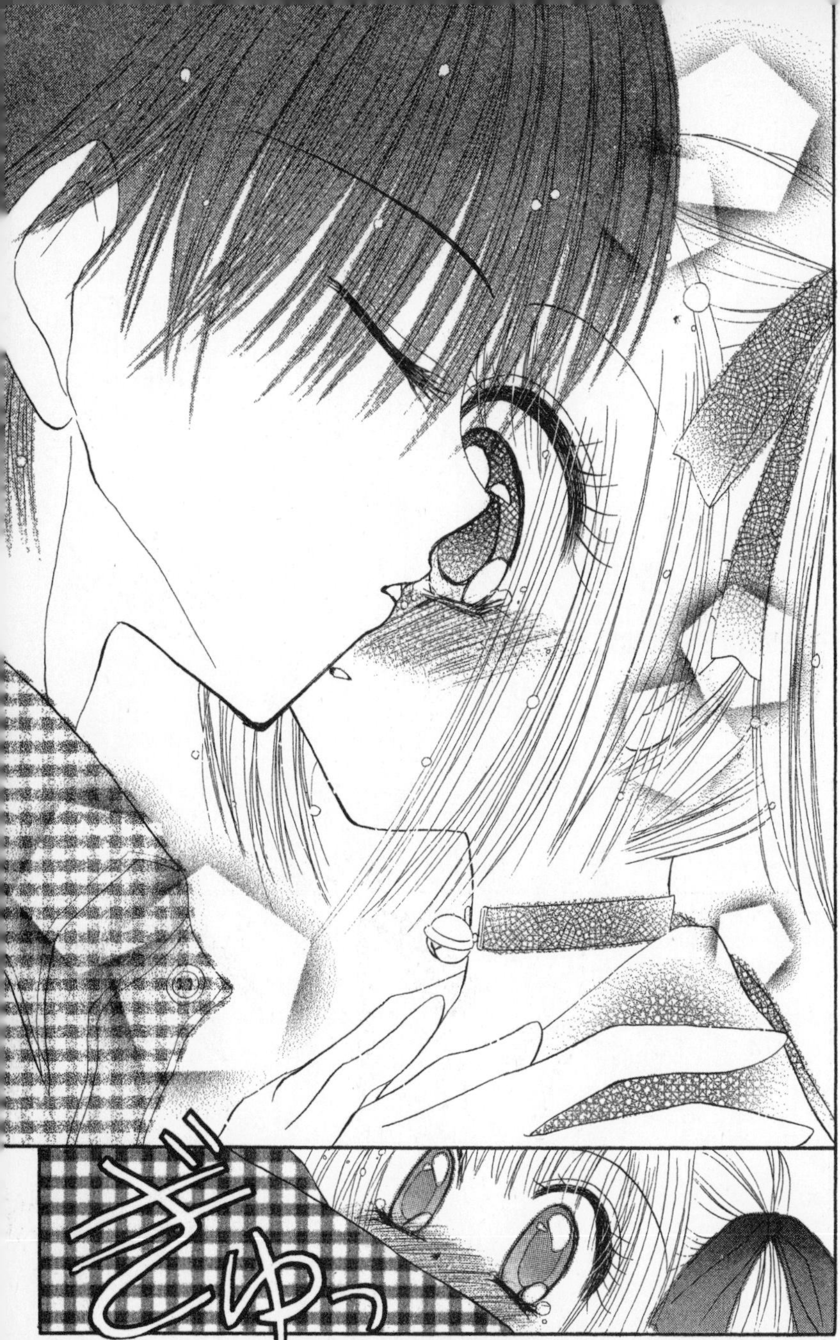
ぎゅっ

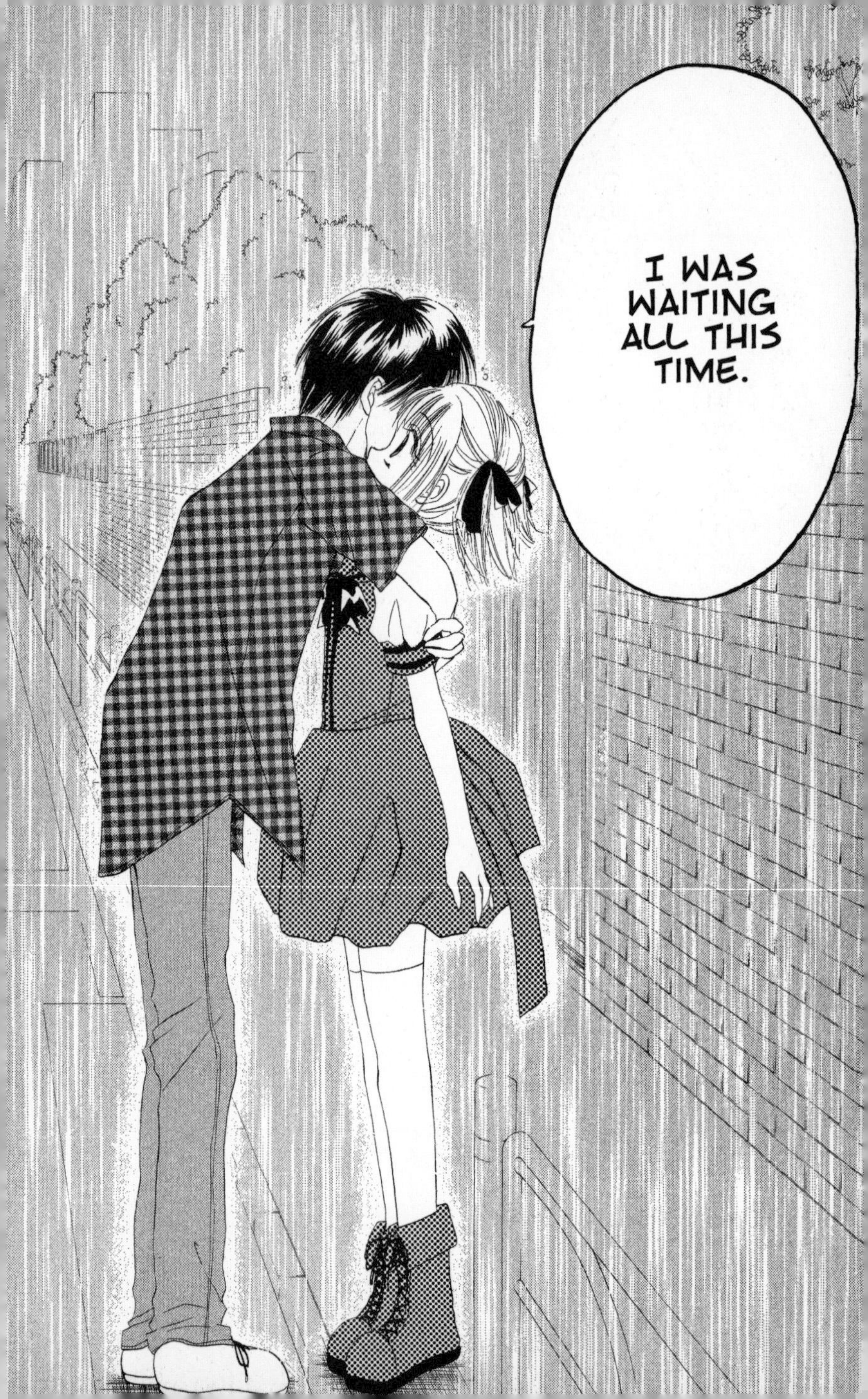
I WAS WAITING ALL THIS TIME.

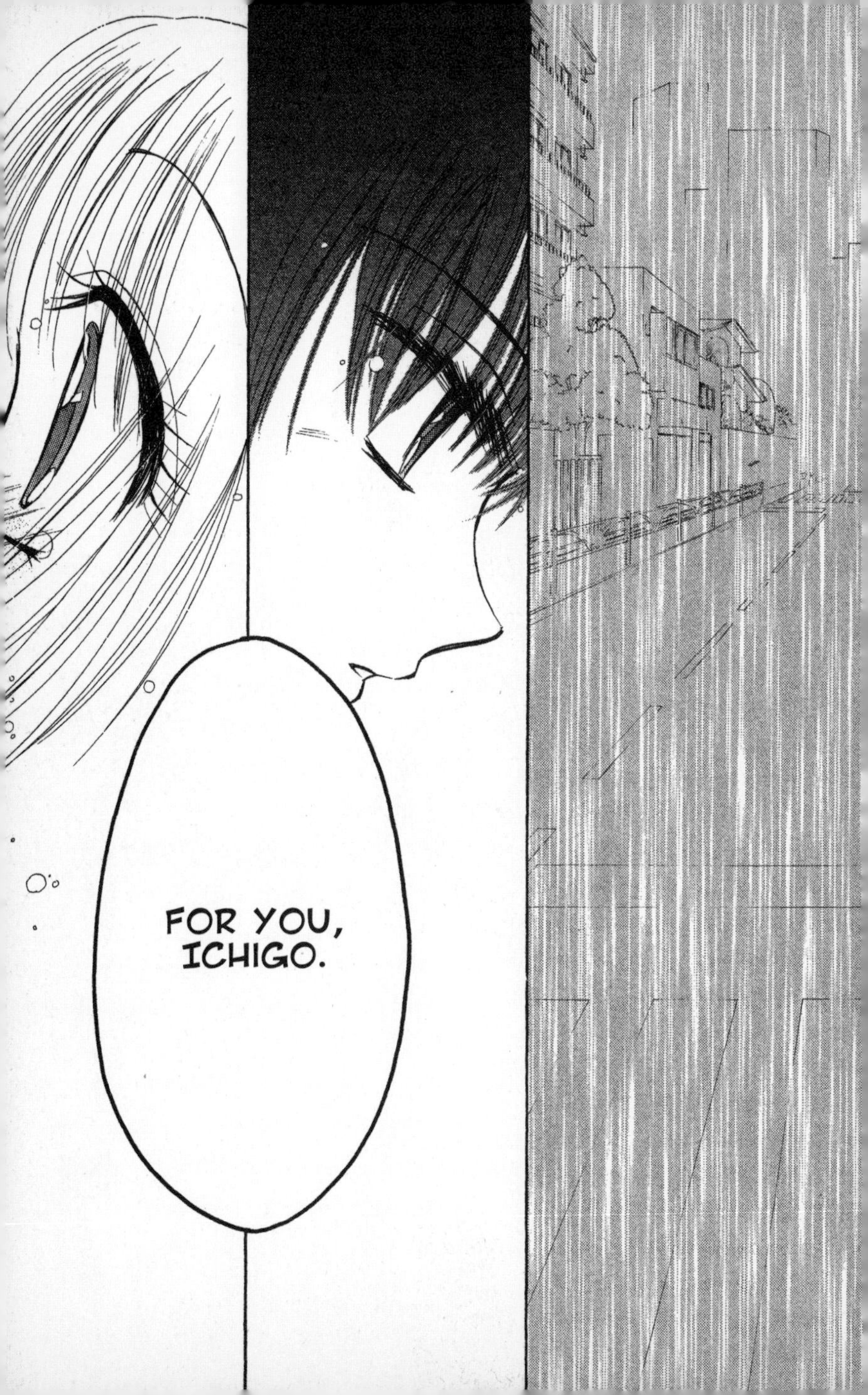
FOR YOU, ICHIGO.

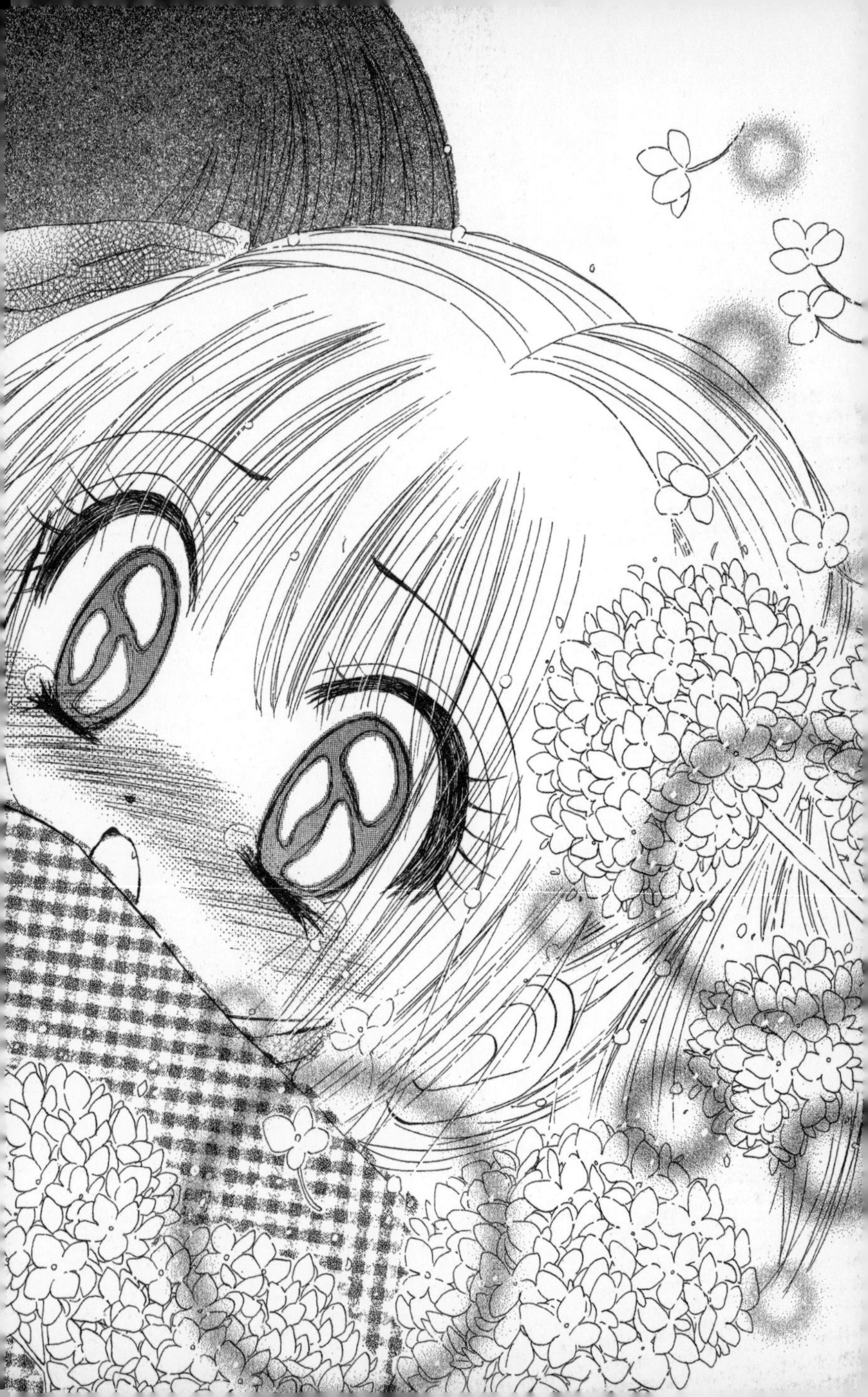

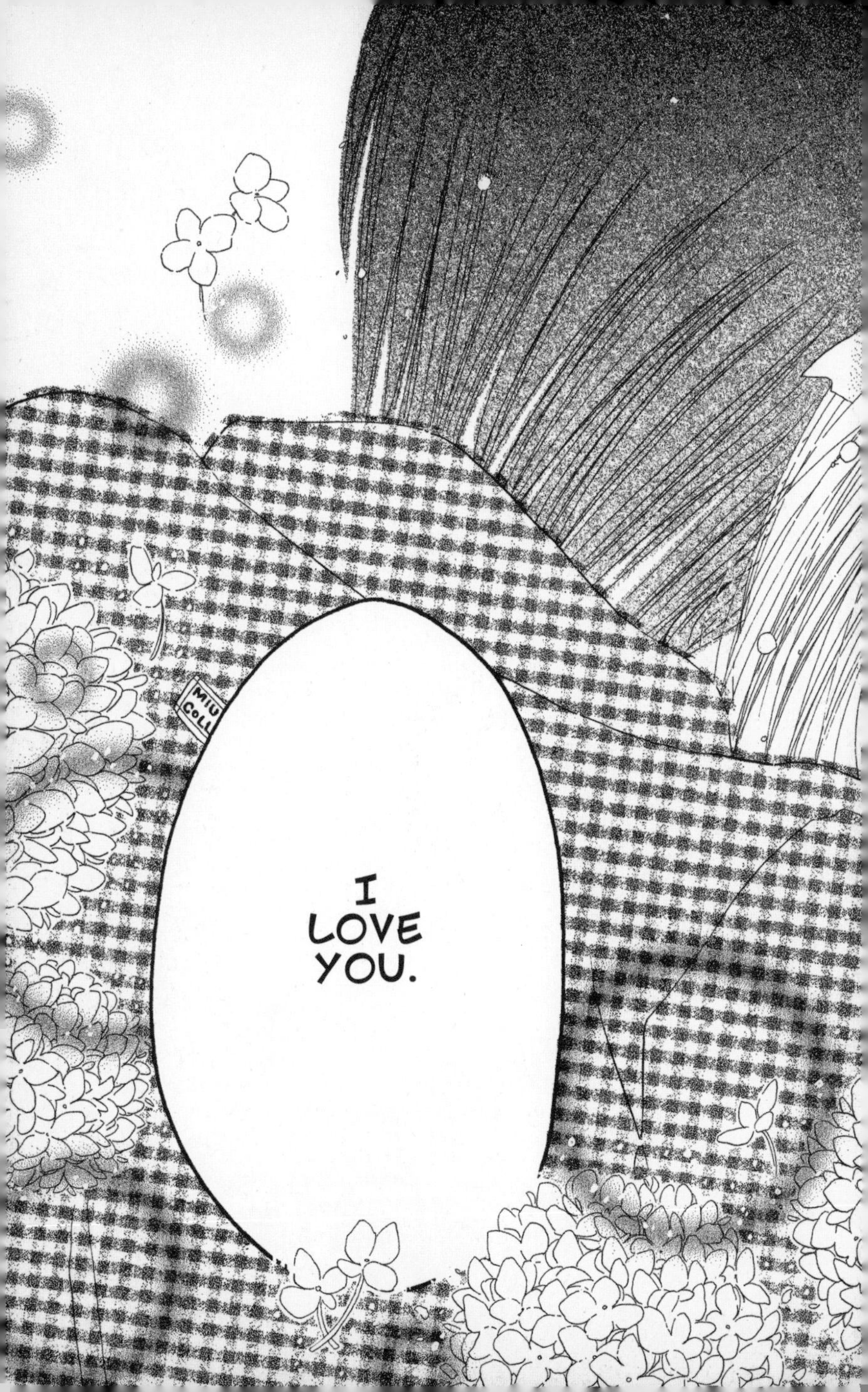
I LOVE YOU.

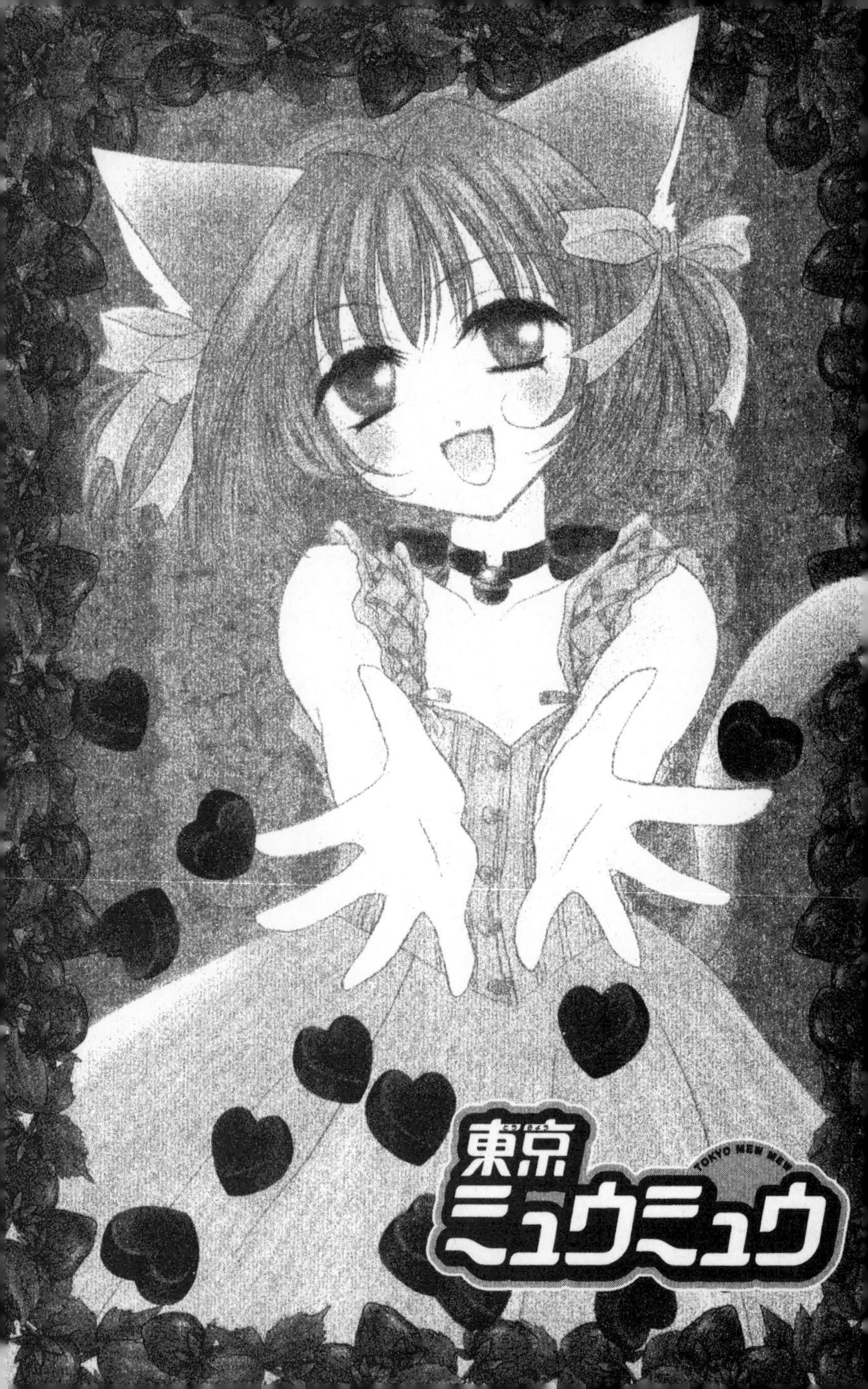
東京
ミュウミュウ
TOKYO MEW MEW

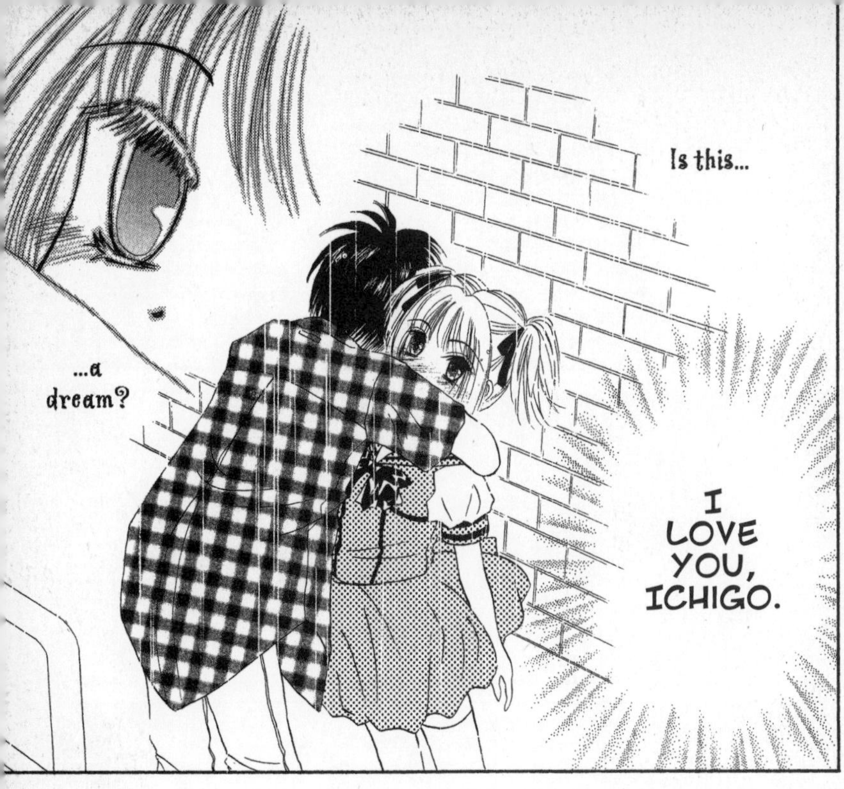
Is this...
I LOVE YOU, ICHIGO.
...a dream?

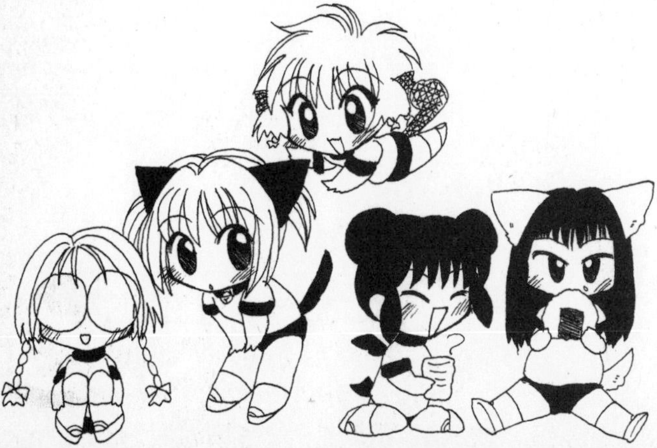

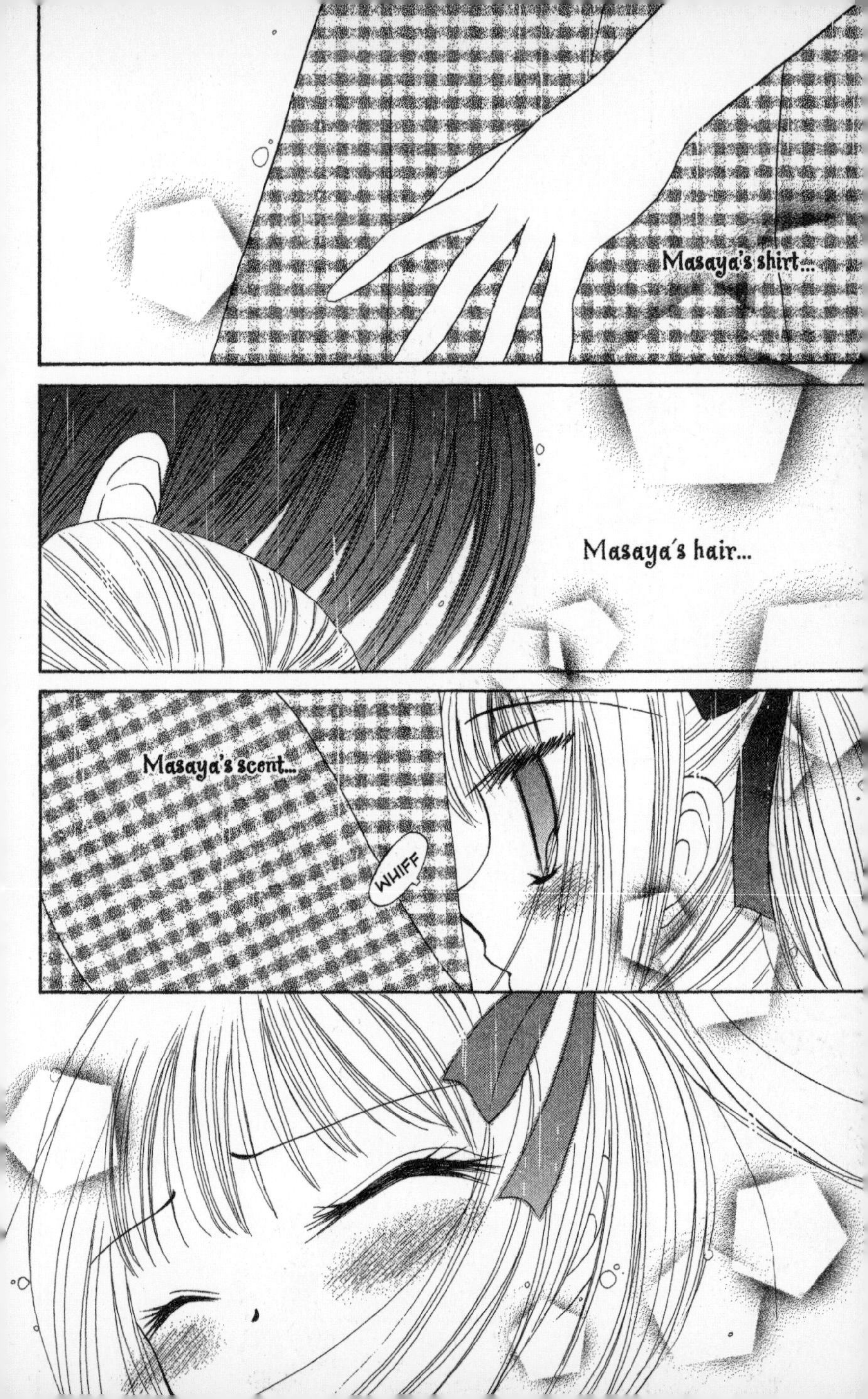
Masaya's shirt...
Masaya's hair...
Masaya's scent...
WHIFF

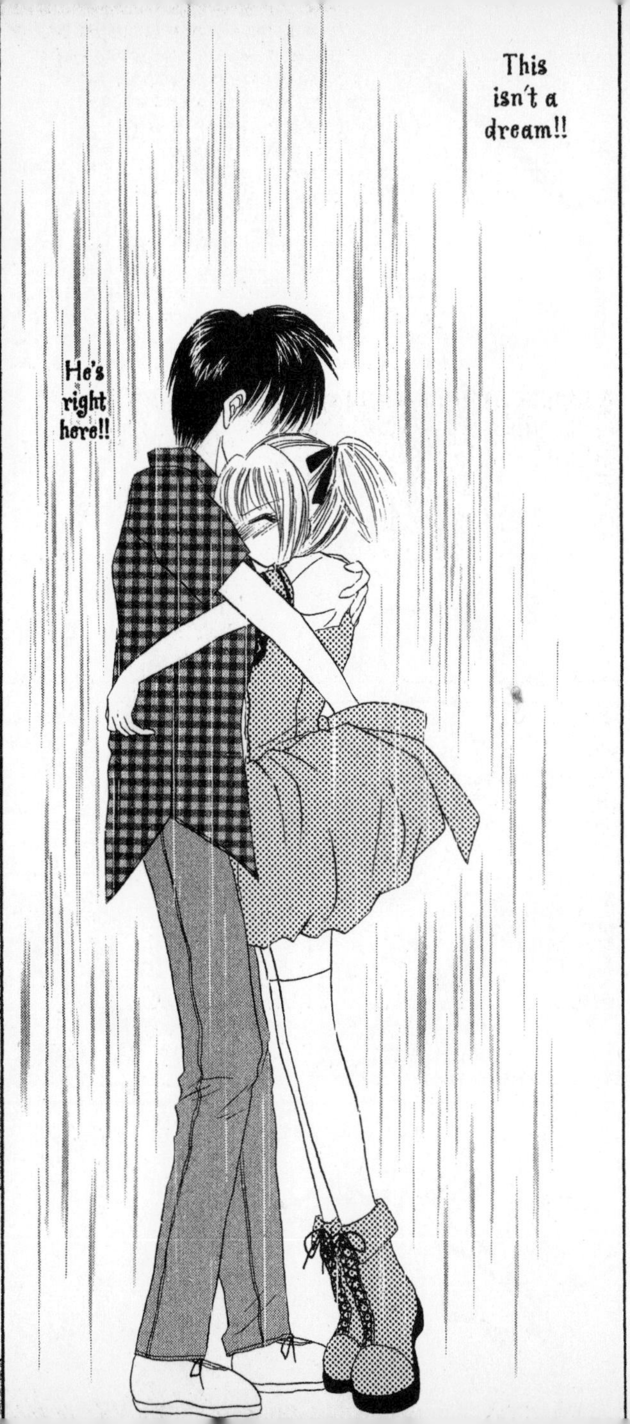
This isn't a dream!!
He's right here!!
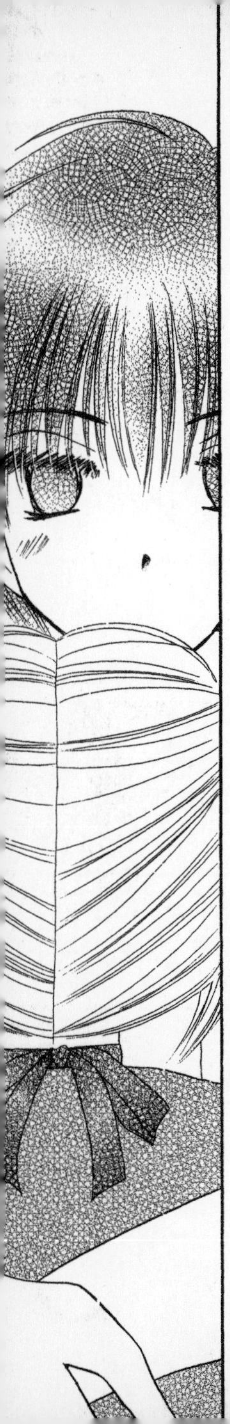

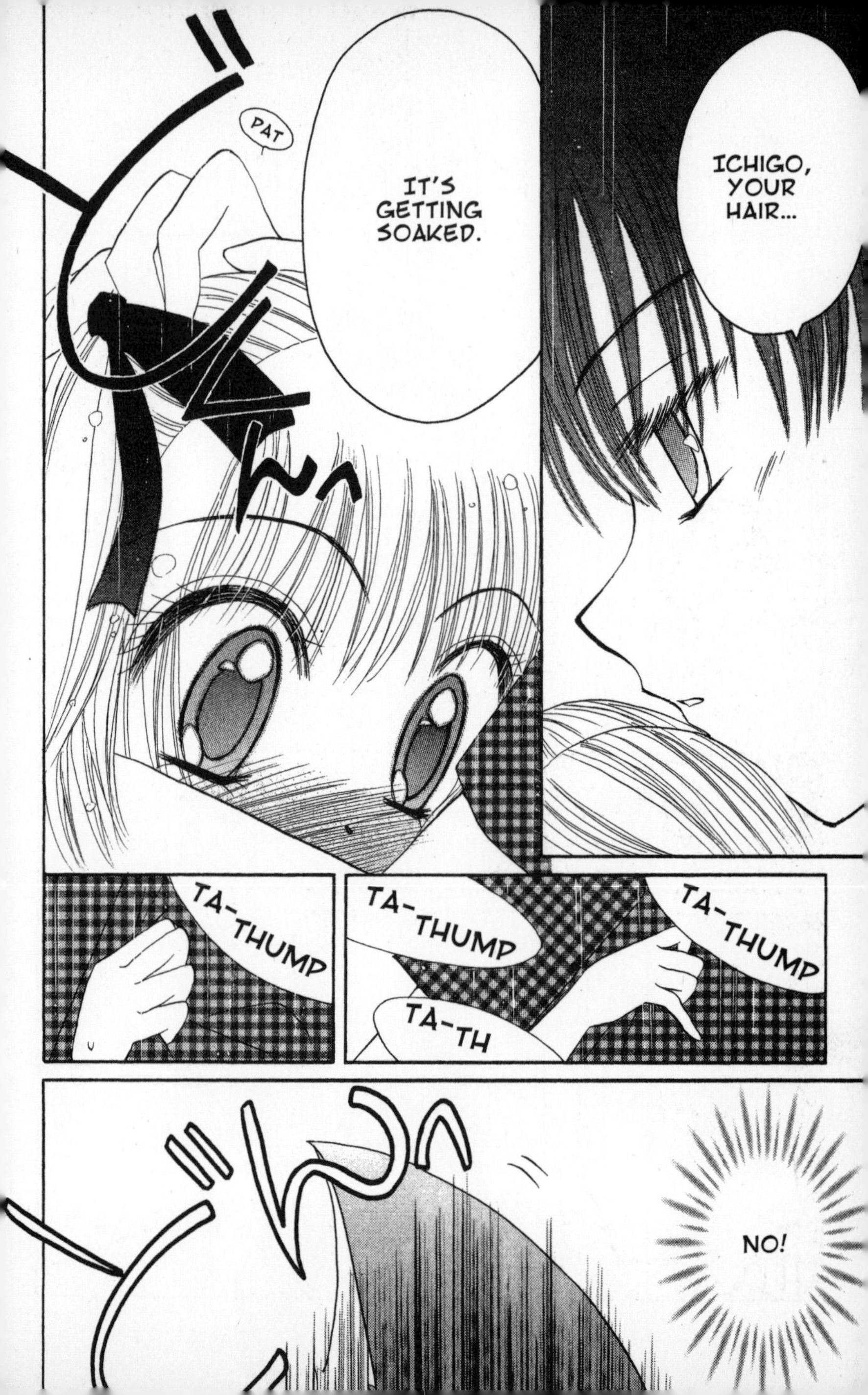
ICHIGO, YOUR HAIR...
IT'S GETTING SOAKED.
PAT
TA-THUMP
TA-THUMP
TA-TH
TA-THUMP
NO!

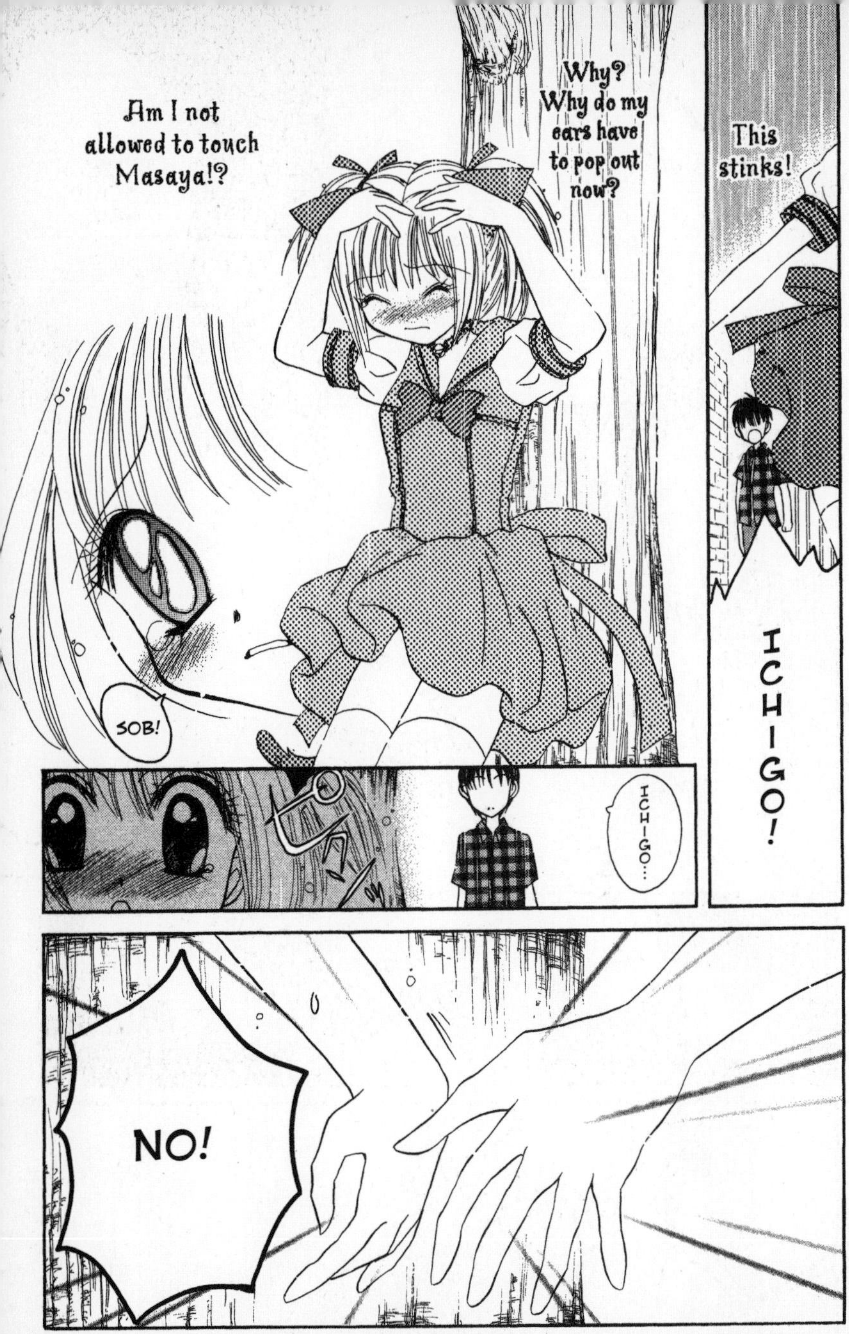
This stinks!
ICHIGO!
Why? Why do my ears have to pop out now?
Am I not allowed to touch Masaya!?
SOB!
ICHIGO...
NO!

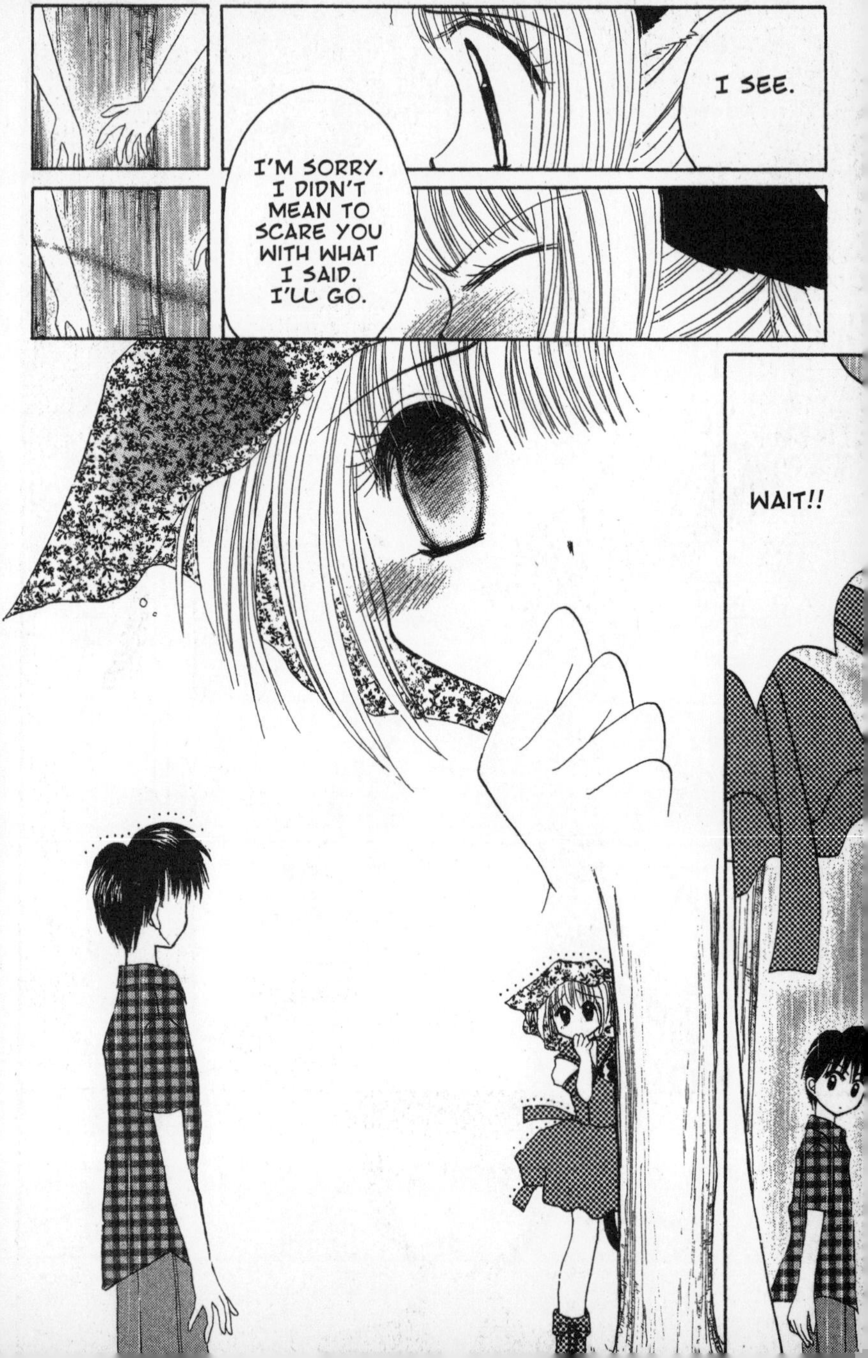
I SEE.
I'M SORRY. I DIDN'T MEAN TO SCARE YOU WITH WHAT I SAID. I'LL GO.
WAIT!!

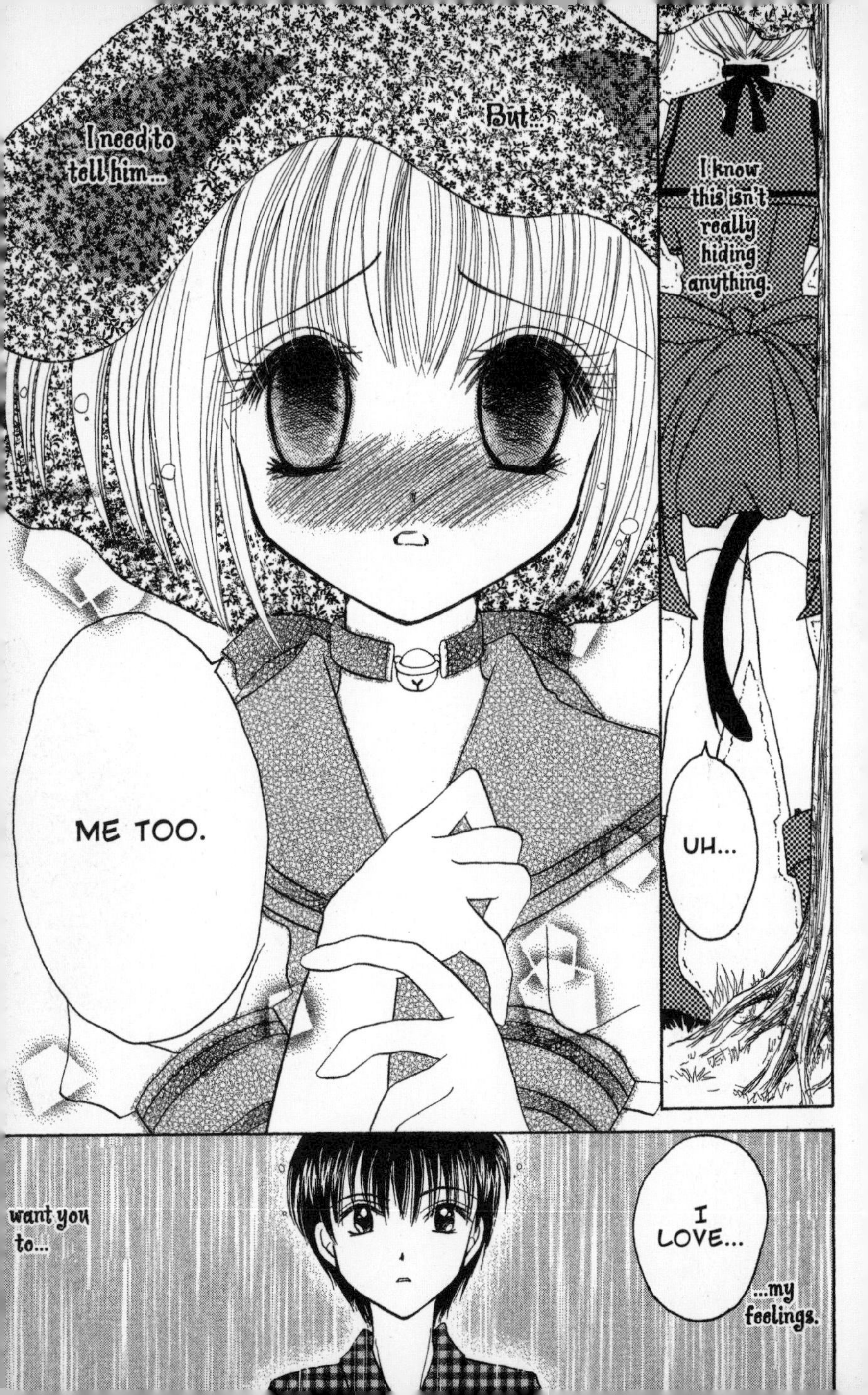
I know this isn't really hiding anything.
UH...
But...
I need to tell him...
ME TOO.
I LOVE...
want you to...
...my feelings.

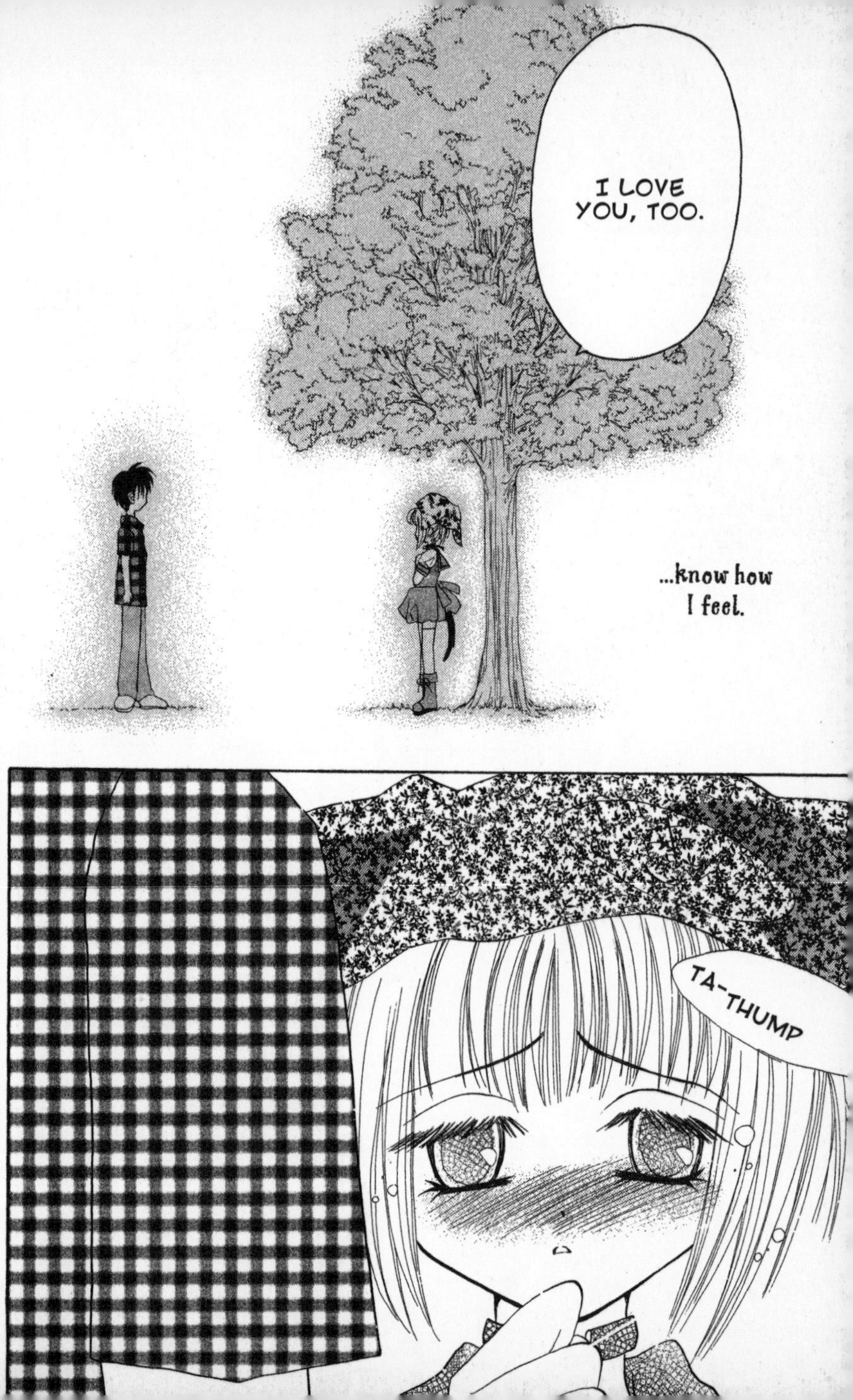
I LOVE YOU, TOO.
...know how I feel.
TA-THUMP

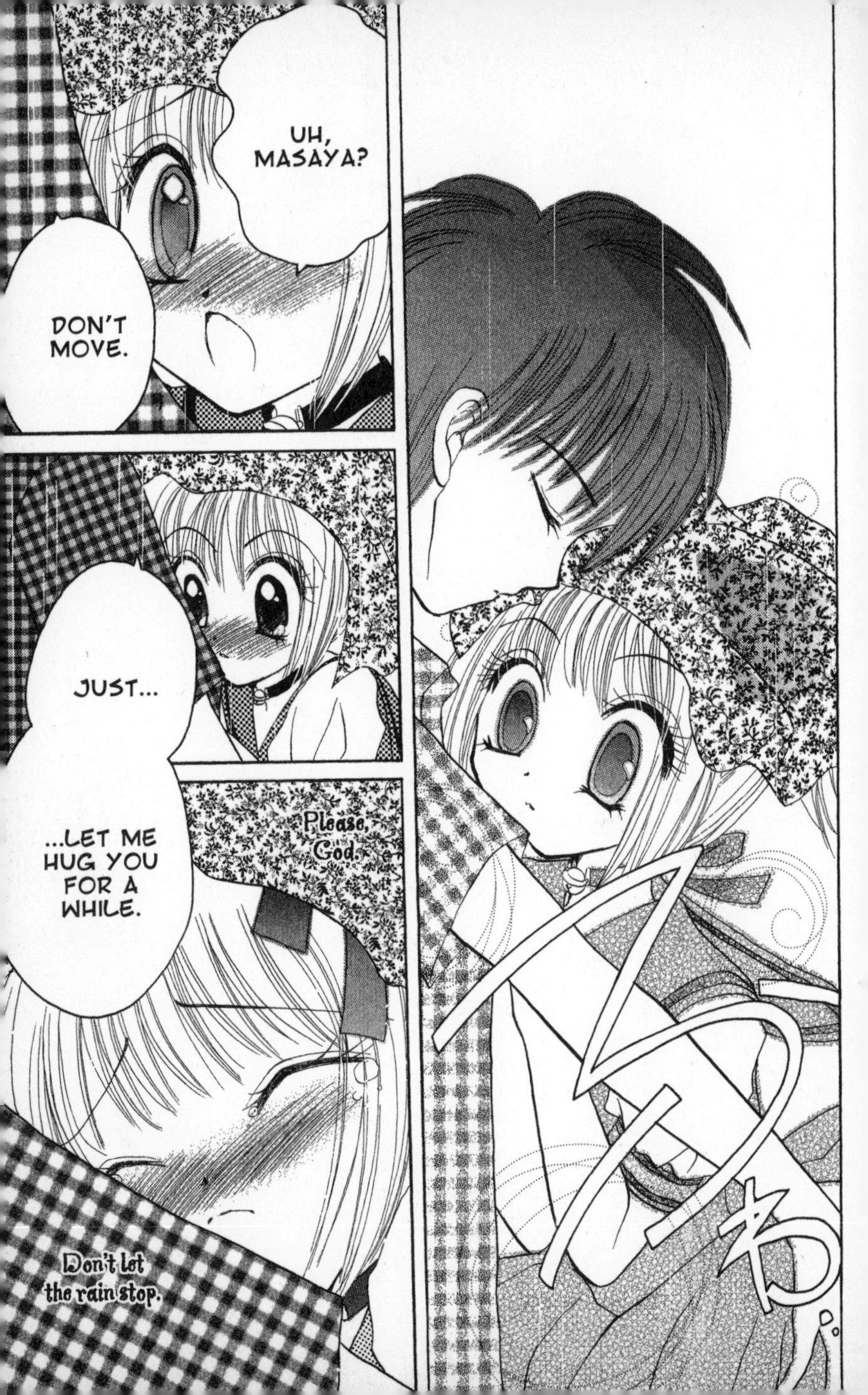
UH, MASAYA?
DON'T MOVE.
JUST...
...LET ME HUG YOU FOR A WHILE.
Please, God.
Don't let the rain stop.

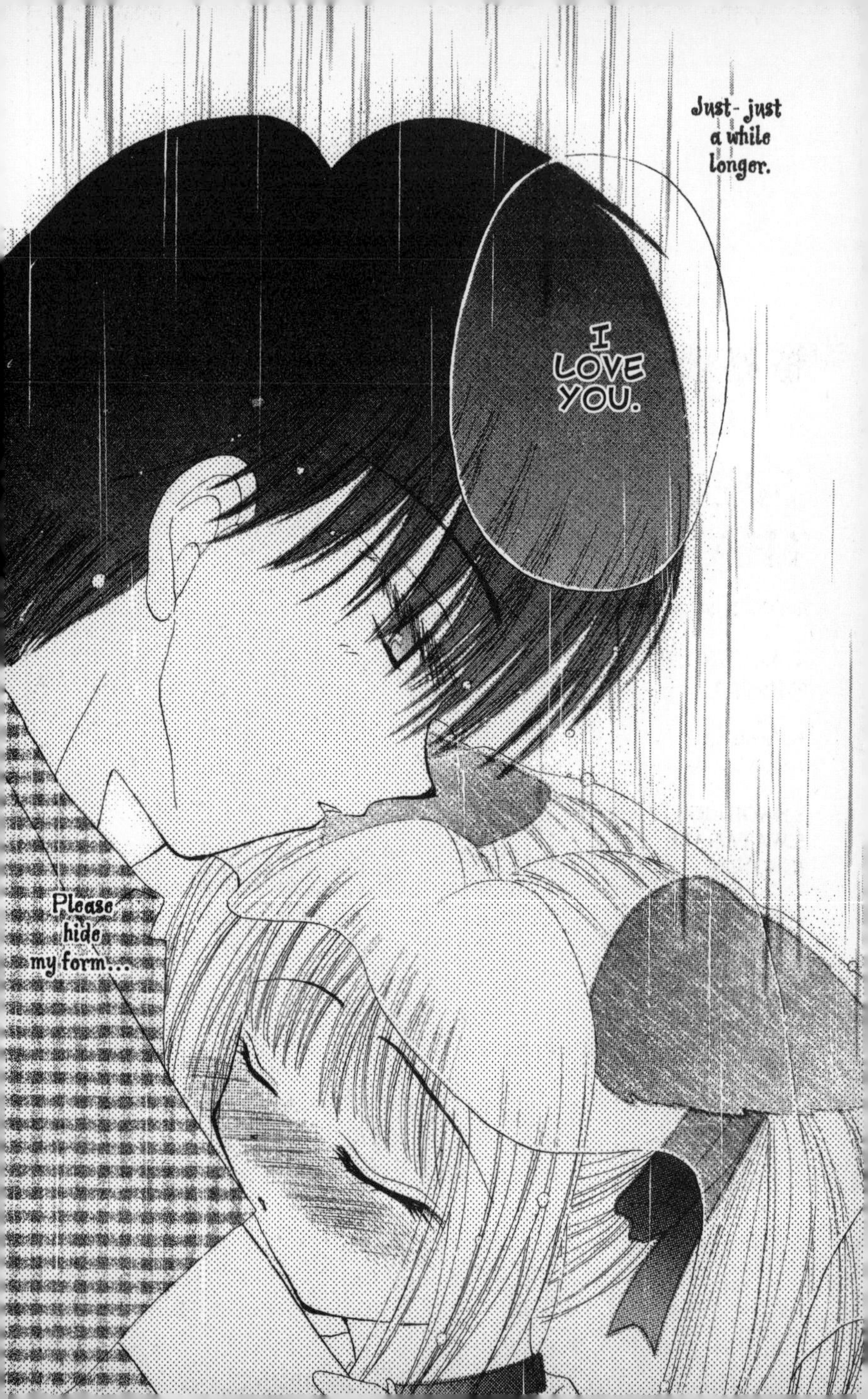
Just- just a while longer.
I LOVE YOU.
Please hide my form...

SPECIAL THANKS!!

R.YOSHIDA

H.MATSUMOTO
M.OMORI

A.SUZUKI
S.SHIMADA

S.NAOHARA
S.WATANABE
K.HONDA

H.OIKAWA

M.SEKIYA
S.SUDA

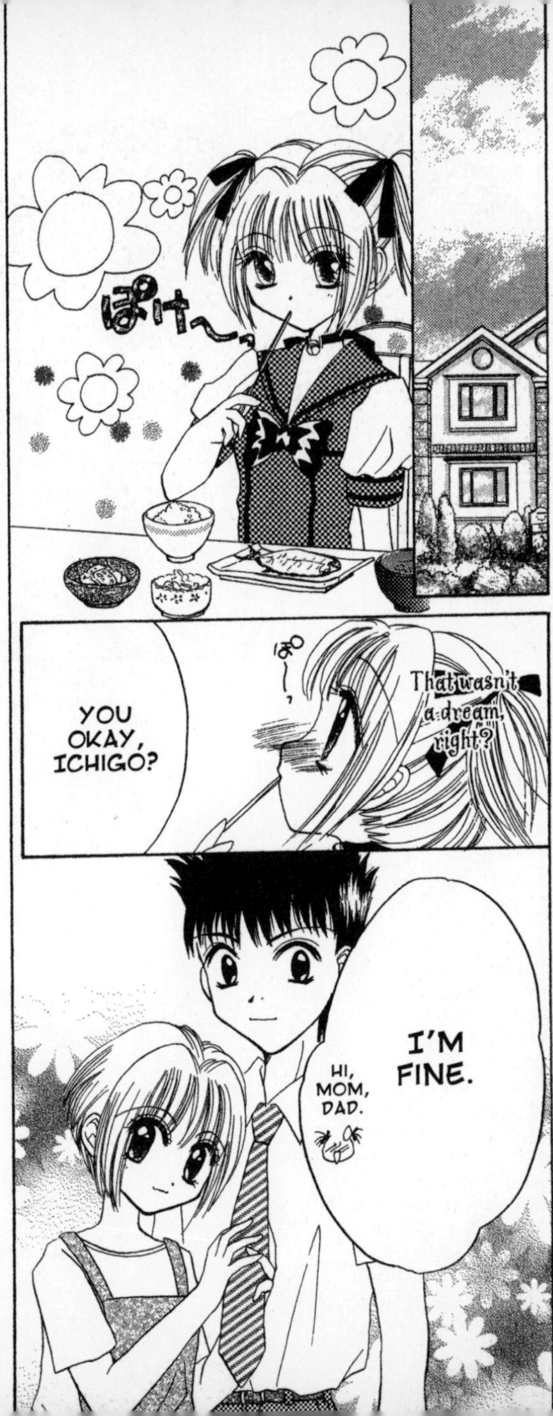

ぽけ〜
That wasn't a dream, right?
ぽ〜
YOU OKAY, ICHIGO?
I'M FINE.
HI, MOM, DAD.

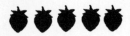

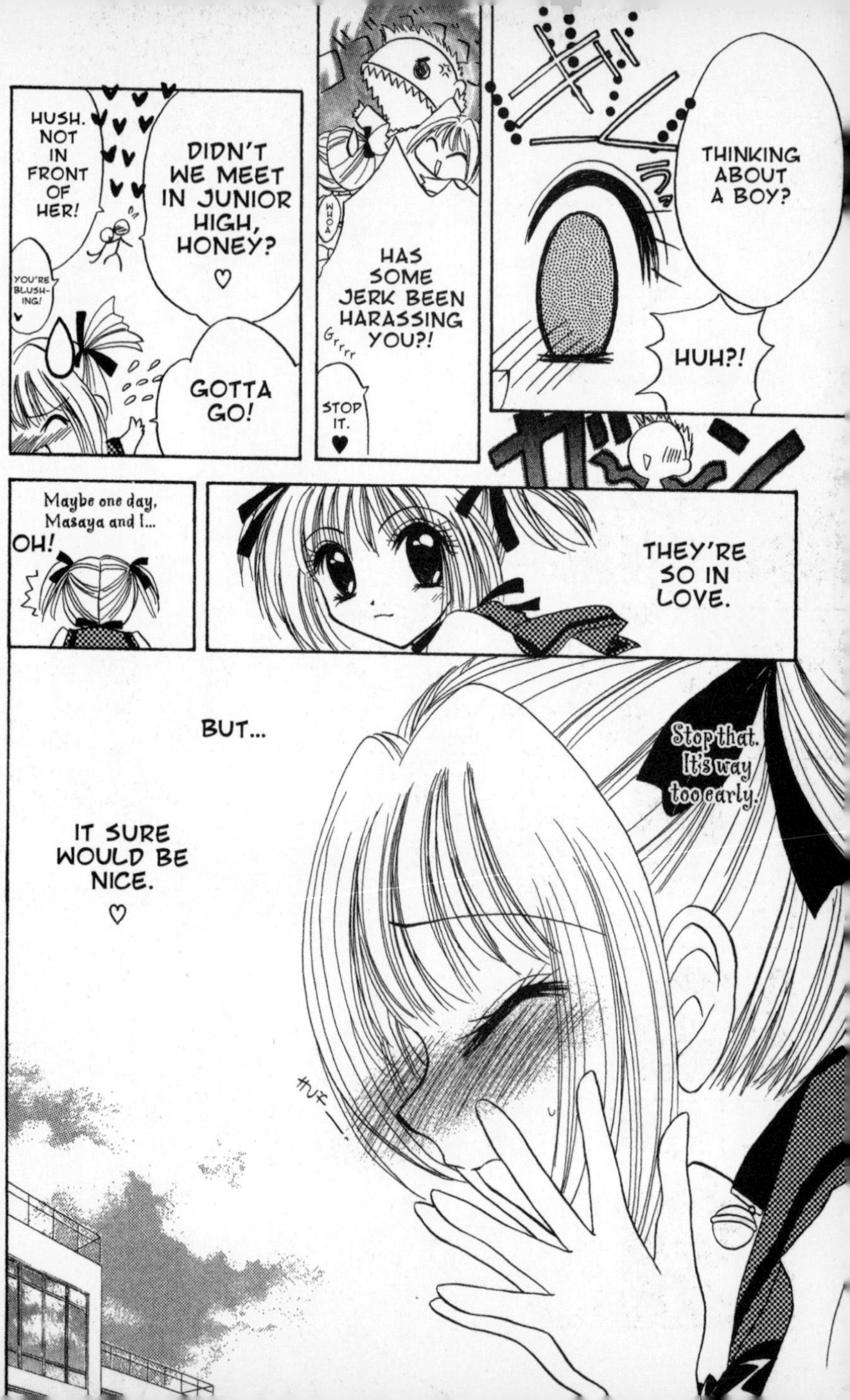
THINKING ABOUT A BOY?
HUH?!
WHOA
HAS SOME JERK BEEN HARASSING YOU?!
Grrrr
STOP IT. ♥
DIDN'T WE MEET IN JUNIOR HIGH, HONEY? ♡
HUSH. NOT IN FRONT OF HER!
YOU'RE BLUSHING! ♥
GOTTA GO!
THEY'RE SO IN LOVE.
Maybe one day, Masaya and I...
OH!
Stop that. It's way too early.
BUT...
IT SURE WOULD BE NICE. ♡

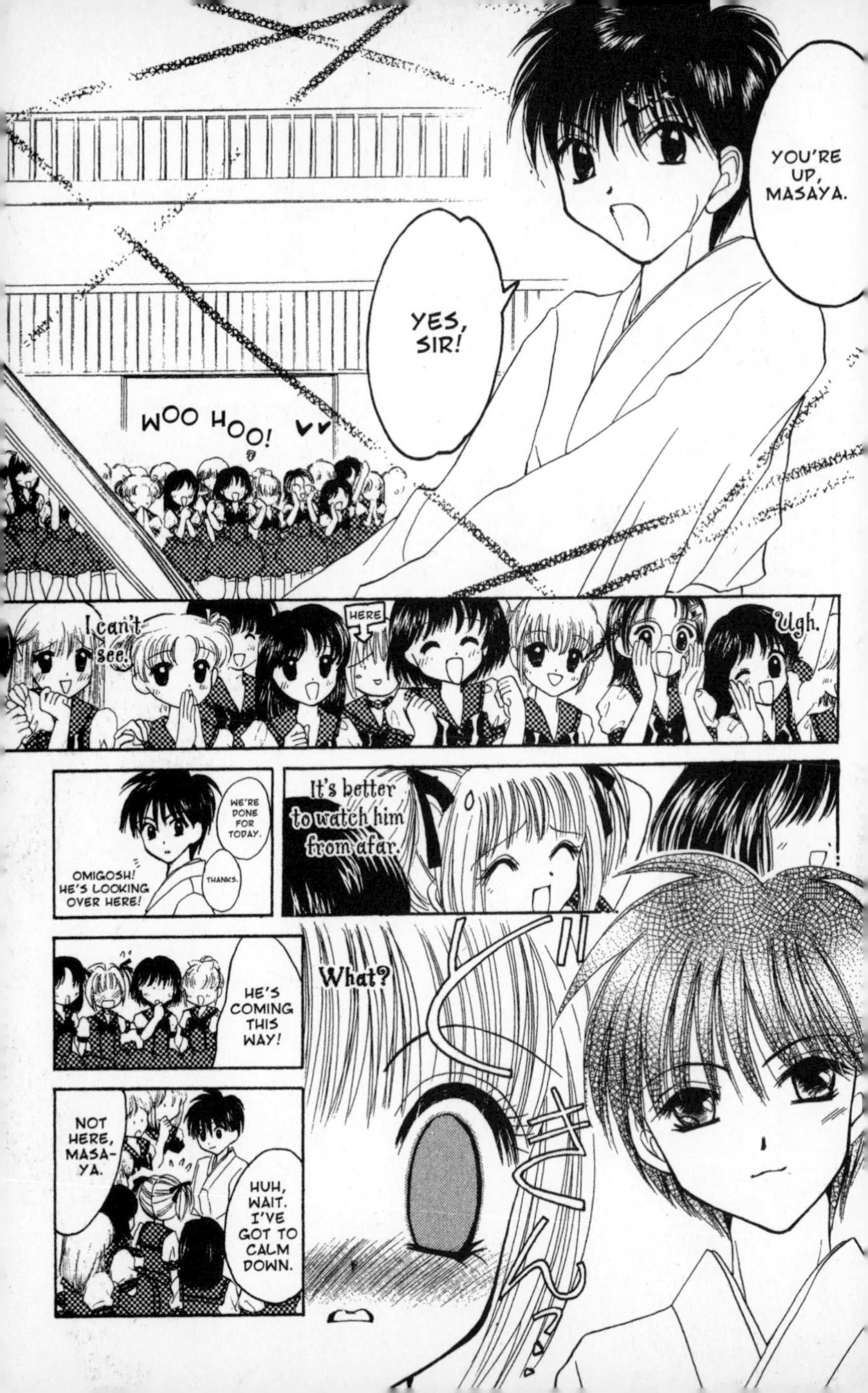
YOU'RE UP, MASAYA.
YES, SIR!
WOO HOO!
Ugh.
HERE
I can't see!
It's better to watch him from afar.
WE'RE DONE FOR TODAY.
THANKS.
OMIGOSH! HE'S LOOKING OVER HERE!
What?
HE'S COMING THIS WAY!
NOT HERE, MASAYA.
HUH, WAIT. I'VE GOT TO CALM DOWN.

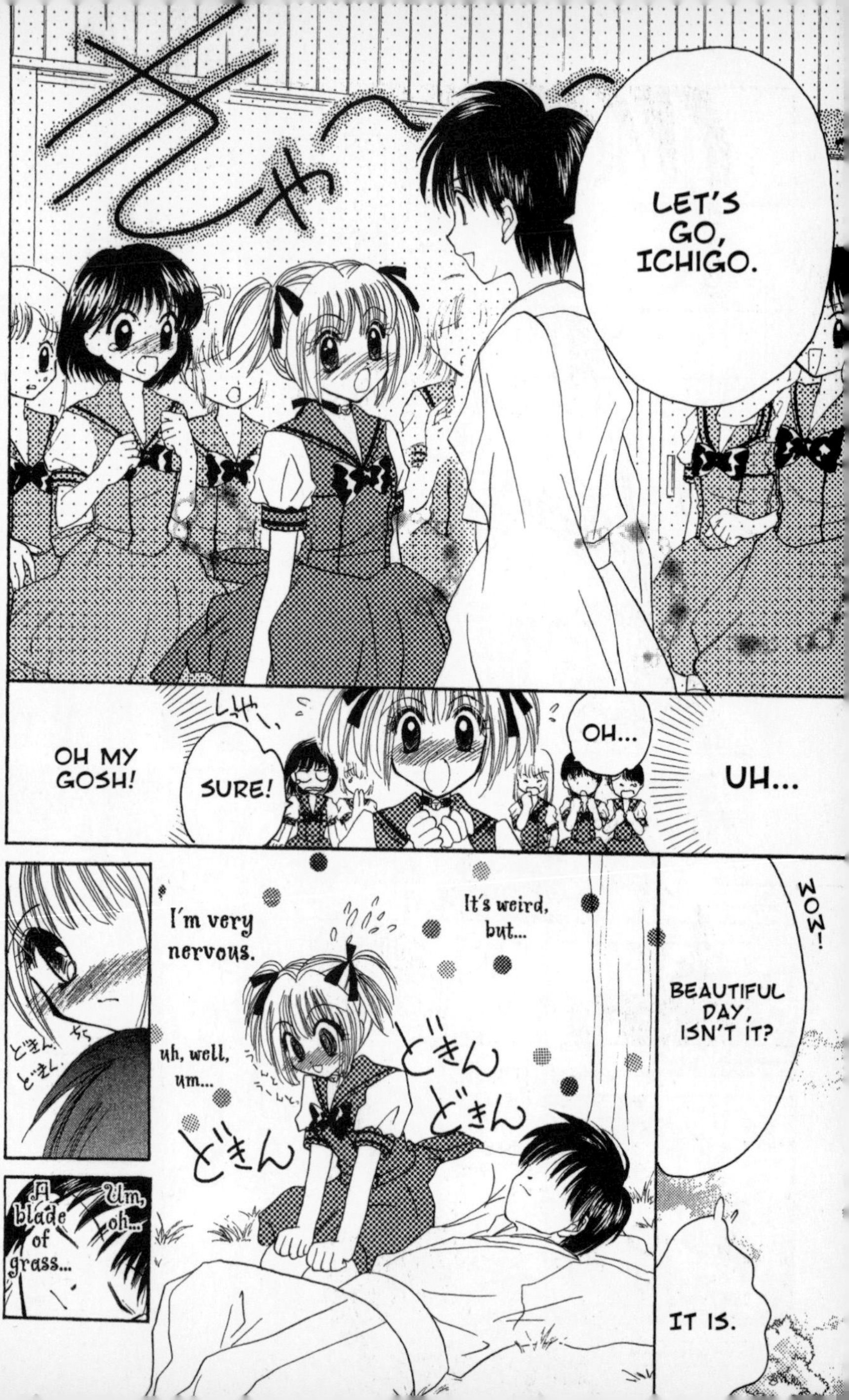
LET'S GO, ICHIGO.
UH...
OH...
SURE!
OH MY GOSH!
WOW!
BEAUTIFUL DAY, ISN'T IT?
IT IS.
It's weird, but...
I'm very nervous.
uh, well, um...
どきん どきん
どきん
Um, oh...
A blade of grass...

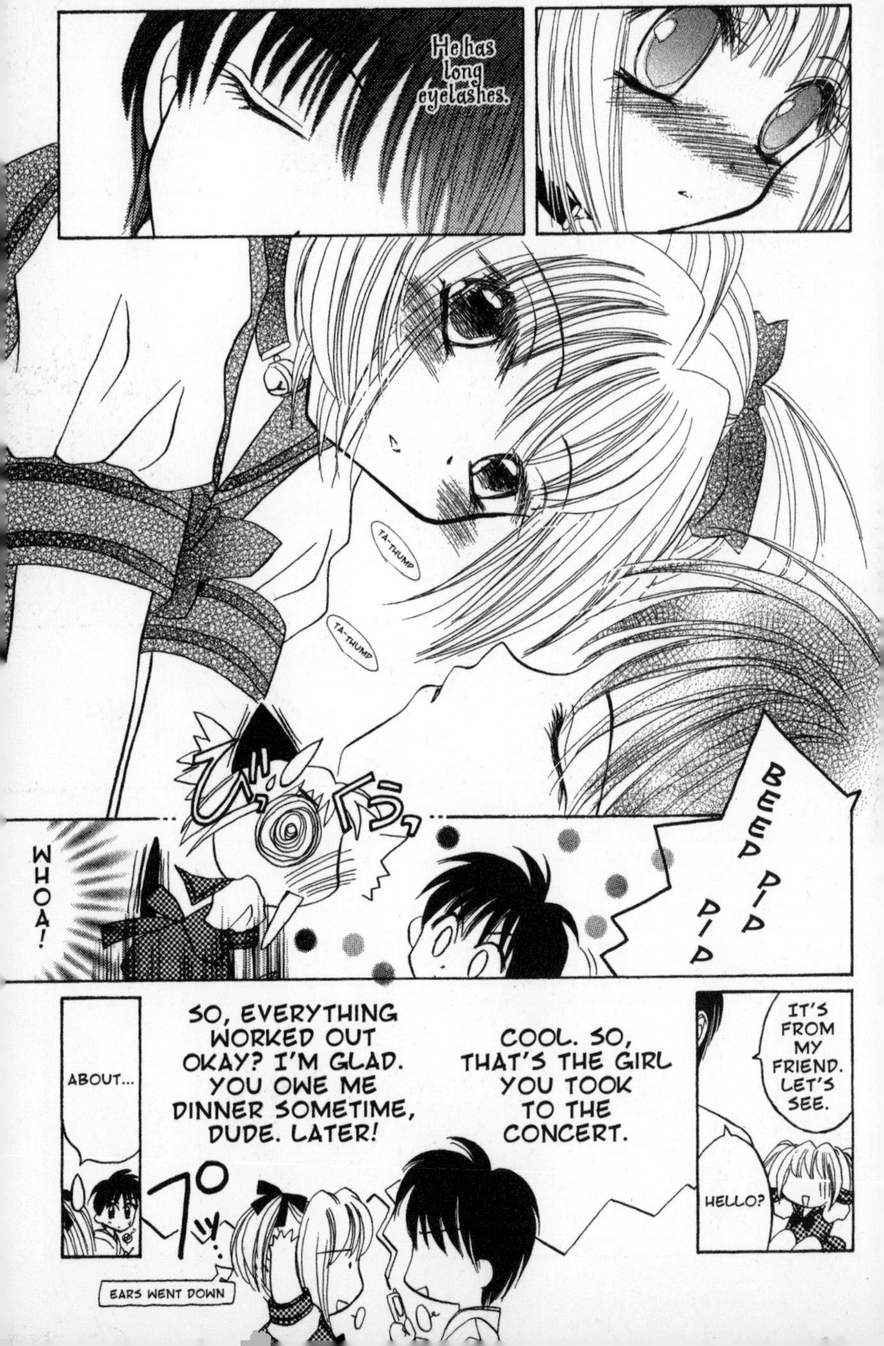
He has long eyelashes.
TA-THUMP
TA-THUMP
BEEP PIP PIP
WHOA!
IT'S FROM MY FRIEND. LET'S SEE.
HELLO?
COOL. SO, THAT'S THE GIRL YOU TOOK TO THE CONCERT.
SO, EVERYTHING WORKED OUT OKAY? I'M GLAD. YOU OWE ME DINNER SOMETIME, DUDE. LATER!
ABOUT...
EARS WENT DOWN

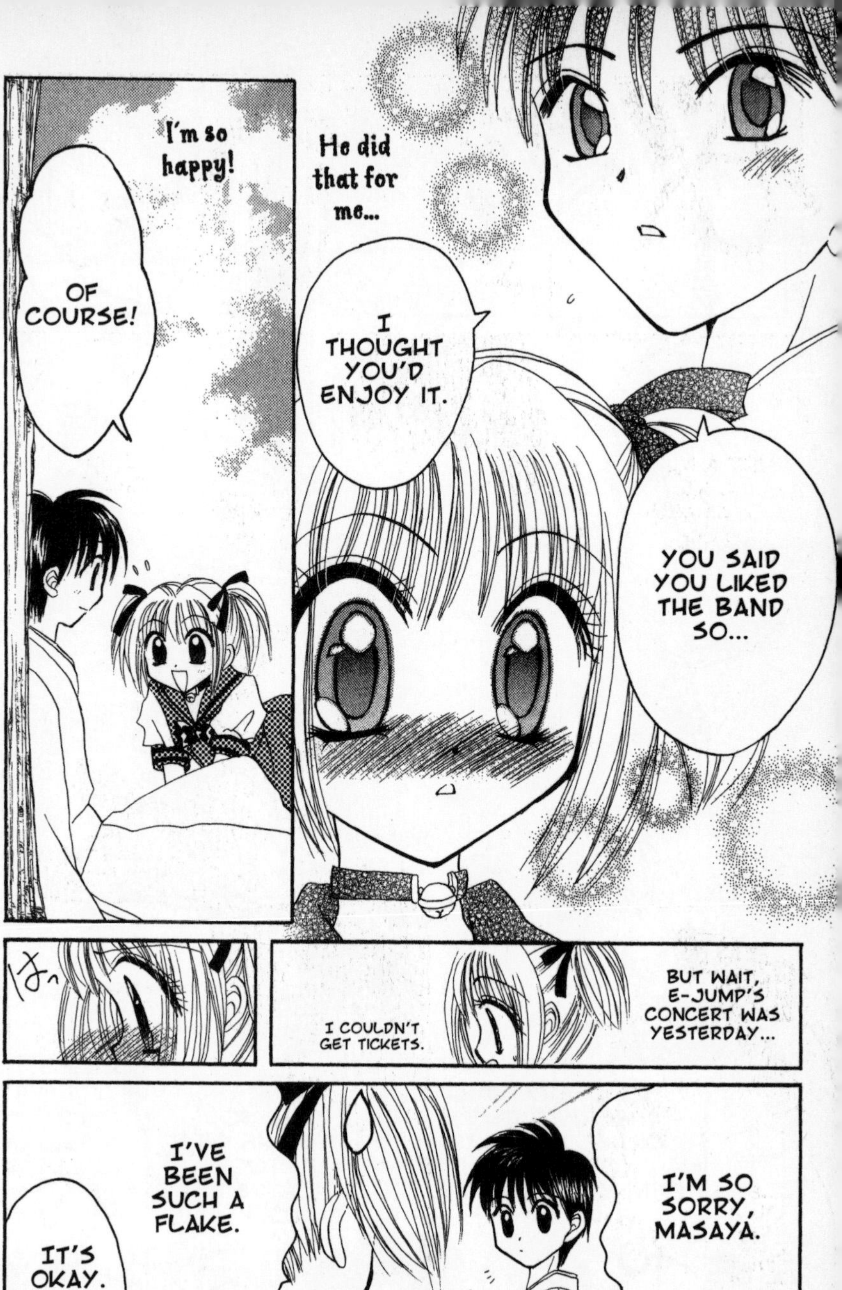
YOU SAID YOU LIKED THE BAND SO...
I THOUGHT YOU'D ENJOY IT.
He did that for me...
OF COURSE!
I'm so happy!
BUT WAIT, E-JUMP'S CONCERT WAS YESTERDAY...
I COULDN'T GET TICKETS.
は
I'M SO SORRY, MASAYA.
I'VE BEEN SUCH A FLAKE.
IT'S OKAY.

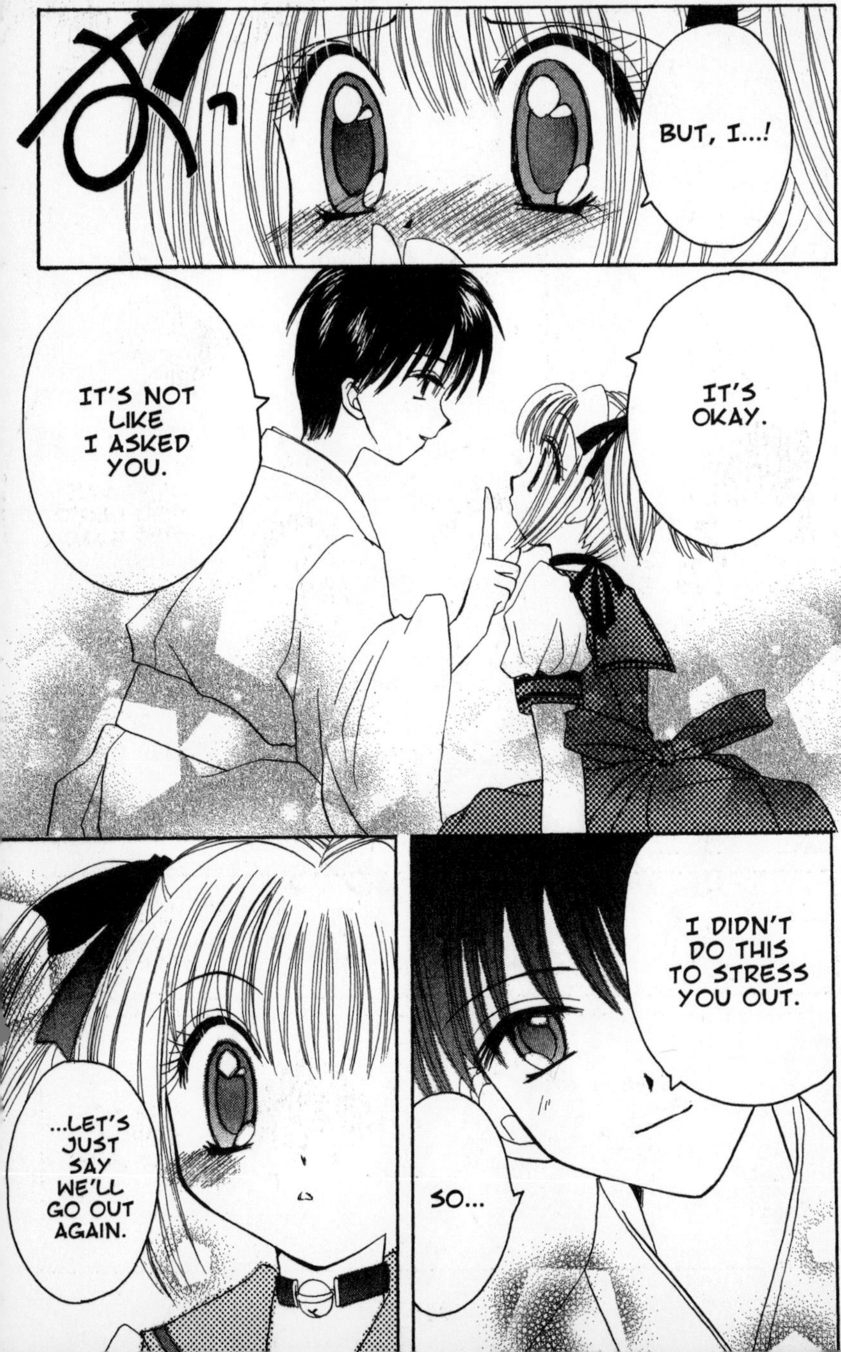
BUT, I...!
IT'S OKAY.
IT'S NOT LIKE I ASKED YOU.
I DIDN'T DO THIS TO STRESS YOU OUT.
SO...
...LET'S JUST SAY WE'LL GO OUT AGAIN.

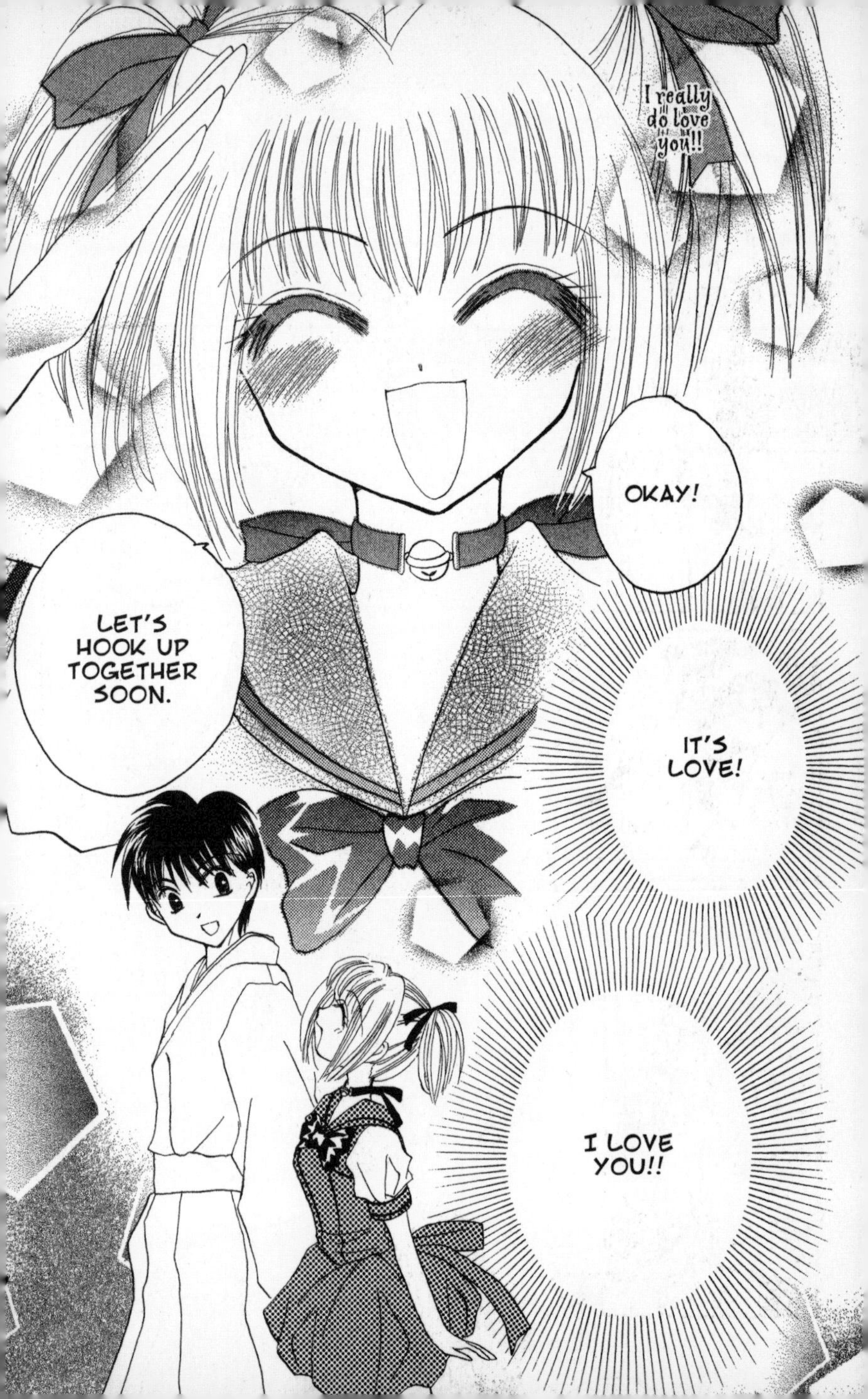
I really do love you!!
OKAY!
LET'S HOOK UP TOGETHER SOON.
IT'S LOVE!
I LOVE YOU!!

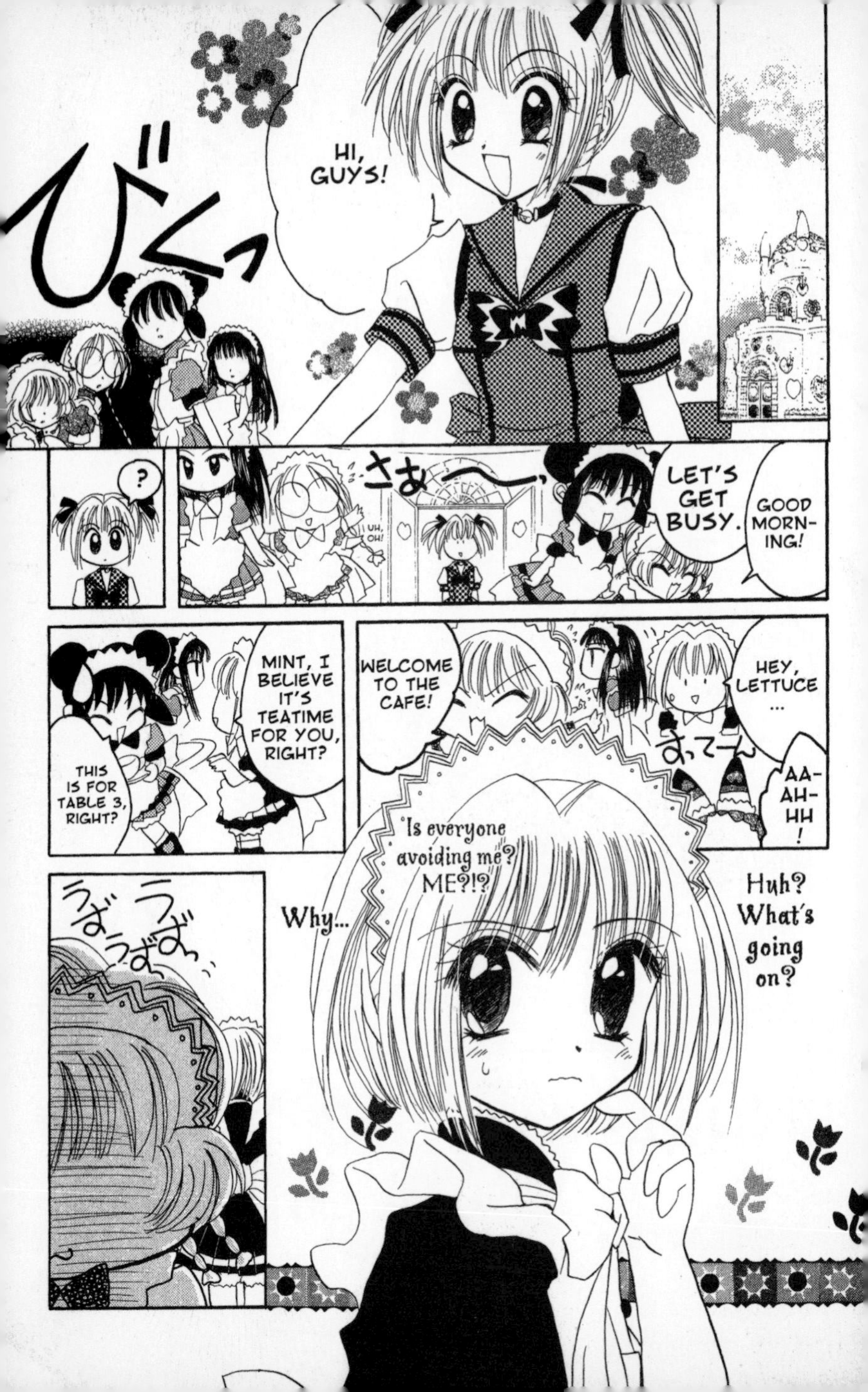
HI, GUYS!
びくっ
GOOD MORNING!
LET'S GET BUSY.
さあ〜〜
UH, OH!
?
HEY, LETTUCE ...
AA-AH-HH!
すてーん
WELCOME TO THE CAFE!
MINT, I BELIEVE IT'S TEATIME FOR YOU, RIGHT?
THIS IS FOR TABLE 3, RIGHT?
Huh? What's going on?
Is everyone avoiding me? ME?!?
Why...
うずうずうず

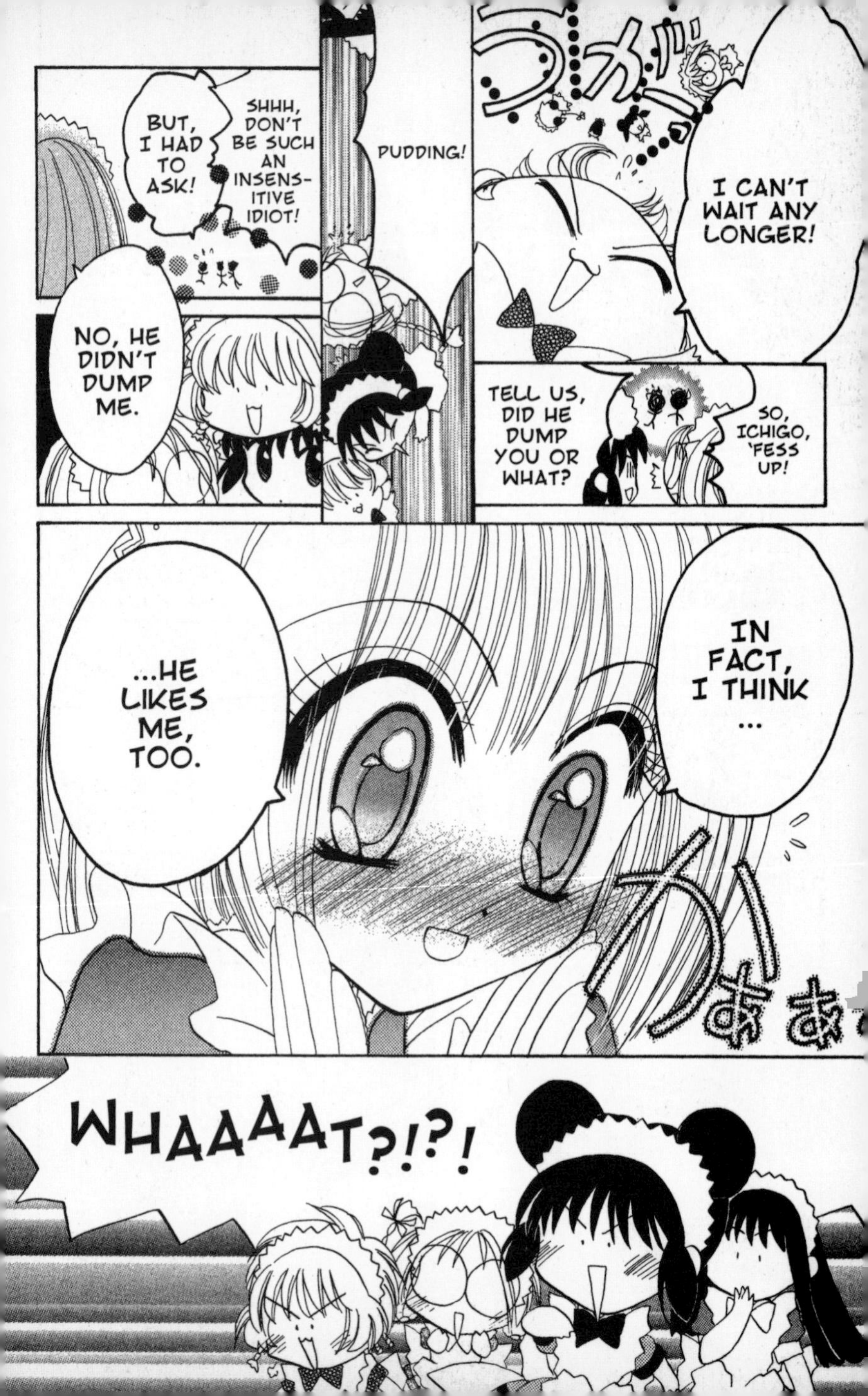
I CAN'T WAIT ANY LONGER!
SO, ICHIGO, 'FESS UP!
TELL US, DID HE DUMP YOU OR WHAT?
PUDDING!
SHHH, DON'T BE SUCH AN INSENS-ITIVE IDIOT!
BUT, I HAD TO ASK!
NO, HE DIDN'T DUMP ME.
IN FACT, I THINK ...
...HE LIKES ME, TOO.
WHAAAAT?!?!

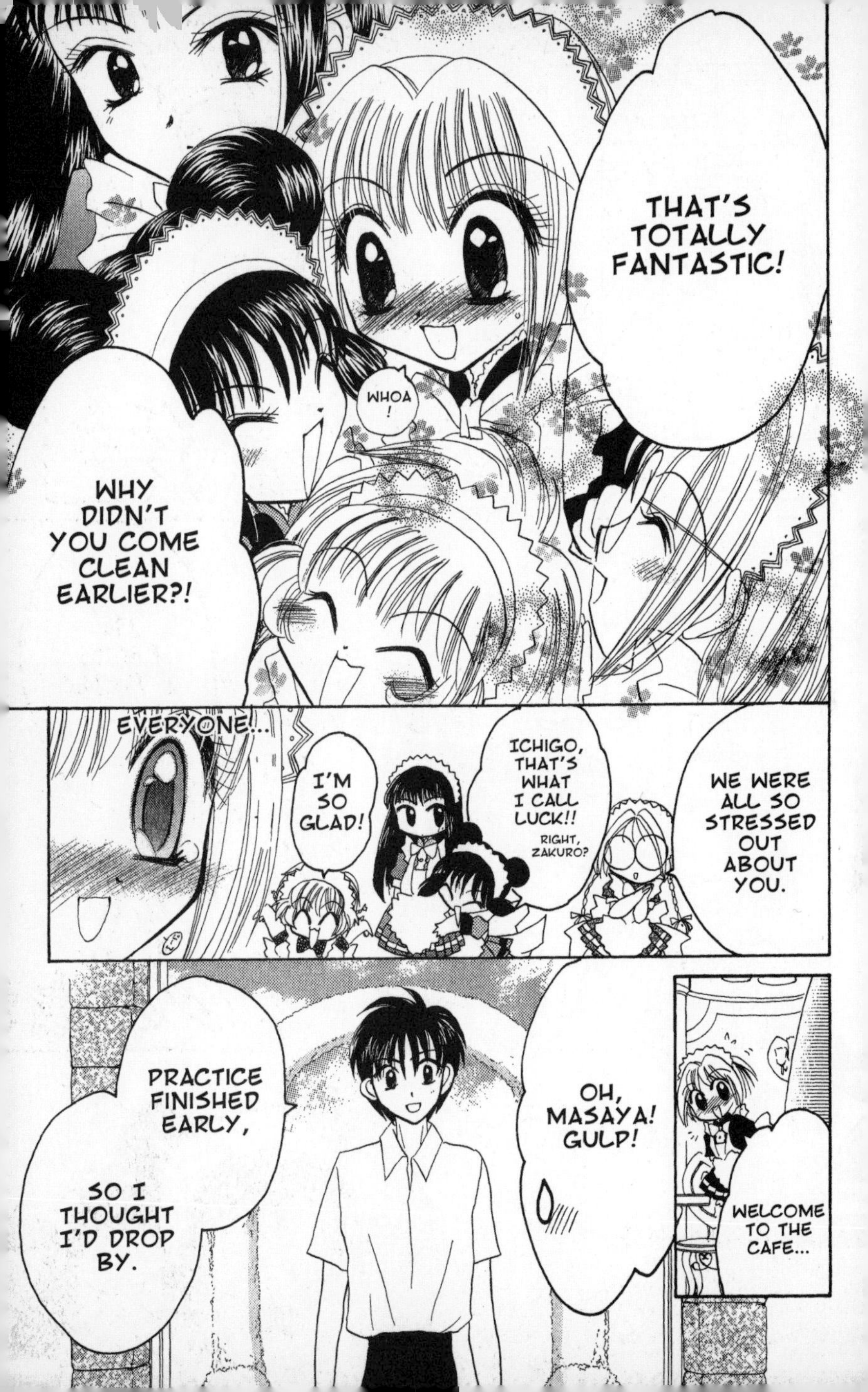
THAT'S TOTALLY FANTASTIC!
WHOA!
WHY DIDN'T YOU COME CLEAN EARLIER?!
WE WERE ALL SO STRESSED OUT ABOUT YOU.
ICHIGO, THAT'S WHAT I CALL LUCK!!
RIGHT, ZAKURO?
I'M SO GLAD!
EVERYONE...
WELCOME TO THE CAFE...
OH, MASAYA! GULP!
PRACTICE FINISHED EARLY,
SO I THOUGHT I'D DROP BY.

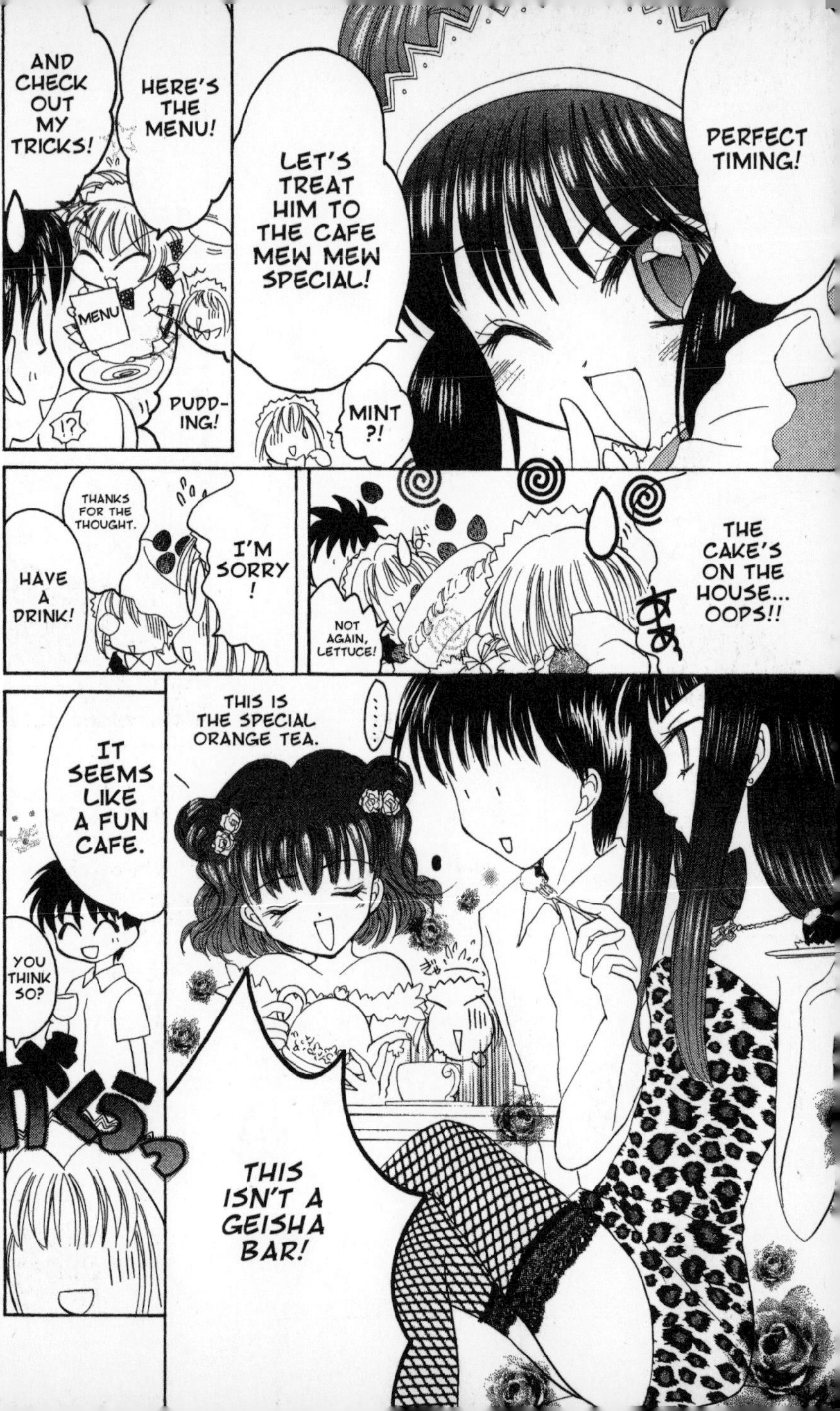
PERFECT TIMING!
LET'S TREAT HIM TO THE CAFE MEW MEW SPECIAL!
MINT ?!
HERE'S THE MENU!
AND CHECK OUT MY TRICKS!
MENU
PUDDING!
!?
THE CAKE'S ON THE HOUSE... OOPS!!
NOT AGAIN, LETTUCE!
I'M SORRY!
THANKS FOR THE THOUGHT.
HAVE A DRINK!
THIS IS THE SPECIAL ORANGE TEA.
......
THIS ISN'T A GEISHA BAR!
IT SEEMS LIKE A FUN CAFE.
YOU THINK SO?

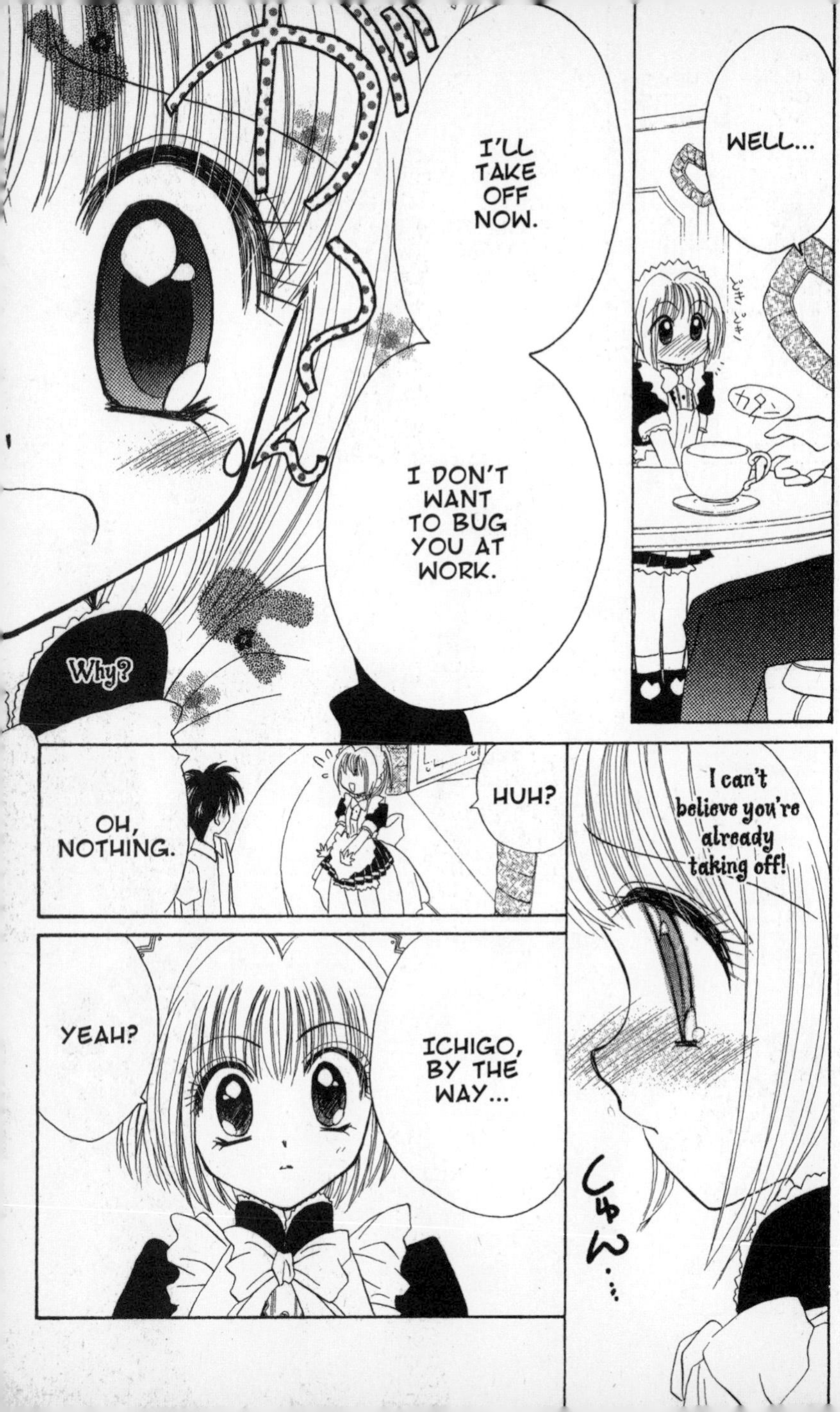
WELL...
カタン
I'LL TAKE OFF NOW.
I DON'T WANT TO BUG YOU AT WORK.
Why?
I can't believe you're already taking off!
じゅん...
HUH?
OH, NOTHING.
ICHIGO, BY THE WAY...
YEAH?

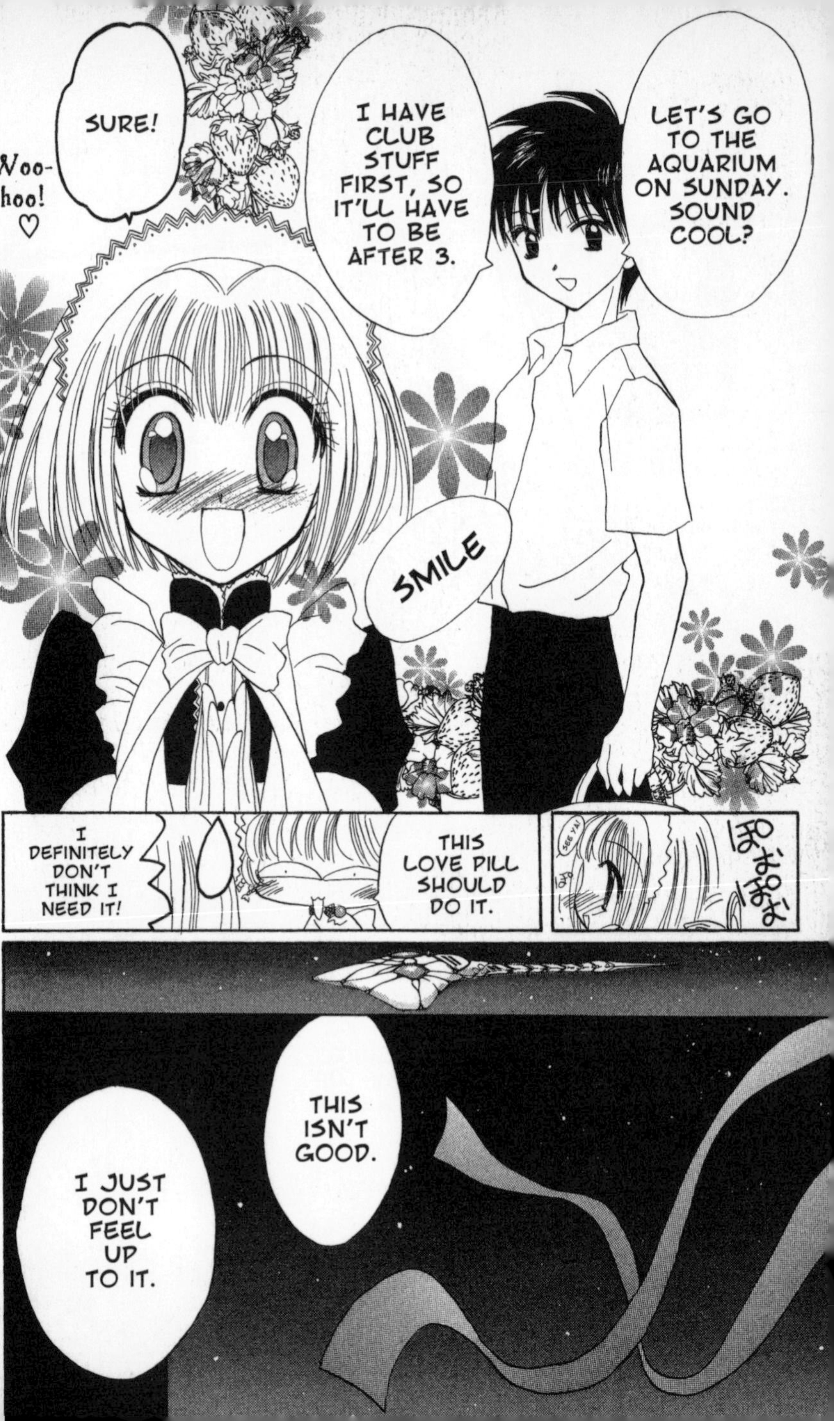
LET'S GO TO THE AQUARIUM ON SUNDAY. SOUND COOL?
I HAVE CLUB STUFF FIRST, SO IT'LL HAVE TO BE AFTER 3.
SURE!
Woo-hoo! ♡
SMILE
SEE YA!
THIS LOVE PILL SHOULD DO IT.
I DEFINITELY DON'T THINK I NEED IT!
THIS ISN'T GOOD.
I JUST DON'T FEEL UP TO IT.

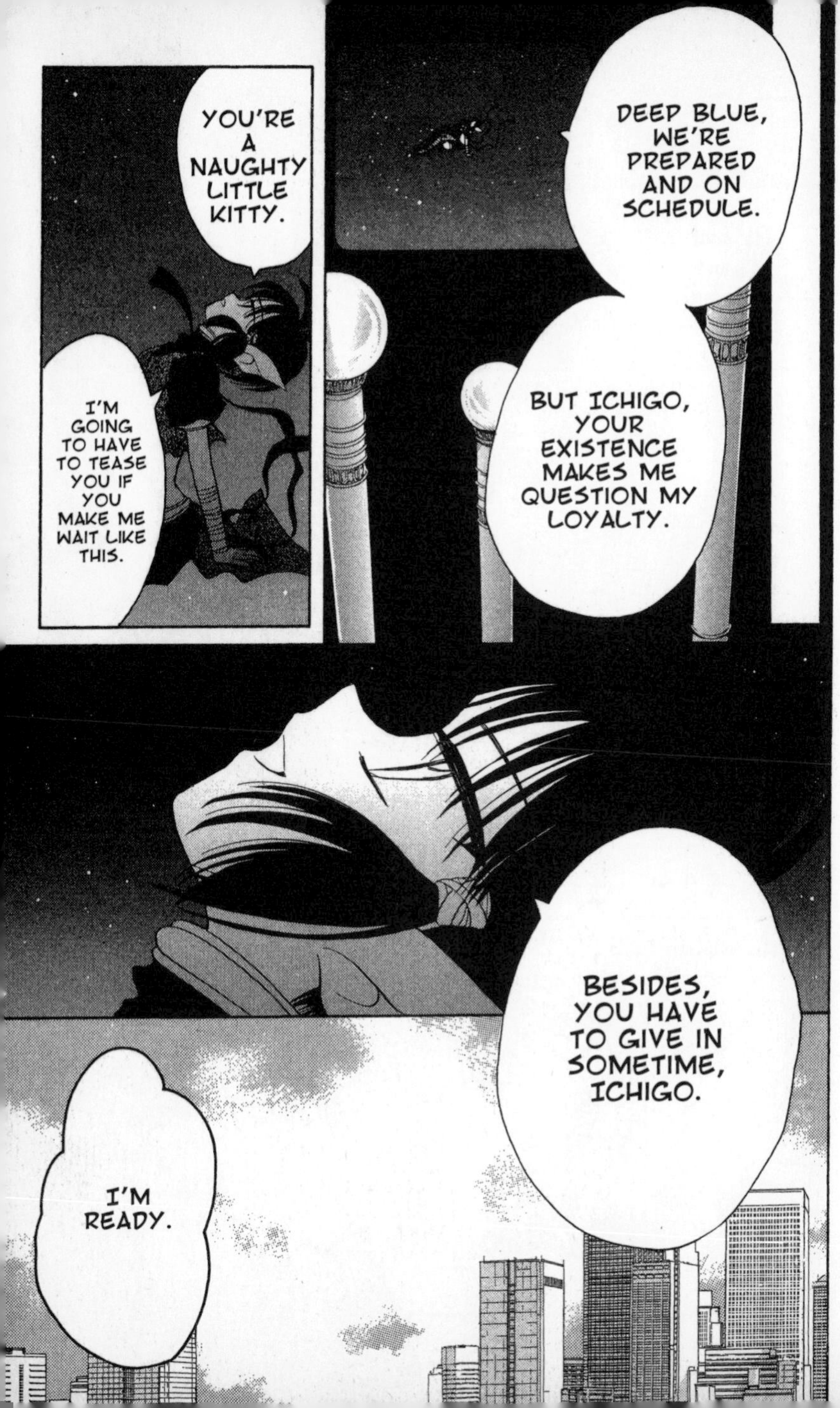
DEEP BLUE, WE'RE PREPARED AND ON SCHEDULE.
BUT ICHIGO, YOUR EXISTENCE MAKES ME QUESTION MY LOYALTY.
YOU'RE A NAUGHTY LITTLE KITTY.
I'M GOING TO HAVE TO TEASE YOU IF YOU MAKE ME WAIT LIKE THIS.
BESIDES, YOU HAVE TO GIVE IN SOMETIME, ICHIGO.
I'M READY.

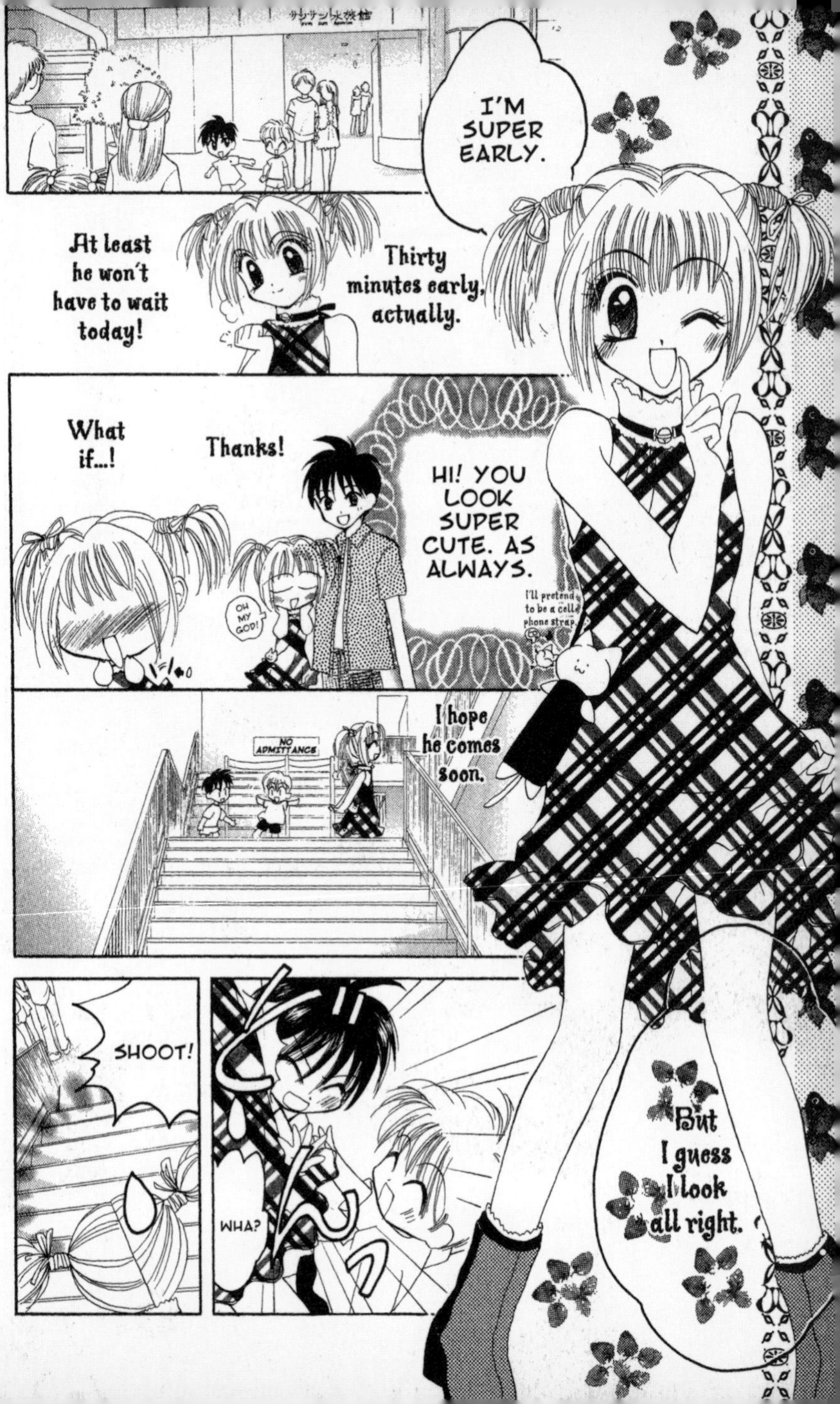

I'M SUPER EARLY.
I'll pretend to be a cell phone strap.
But I guess I look all right.
Thirty minutes early, actually.
At least he won't have to wait today!
HI! YOU LOOK SUPER CUTE. AS ALWAYS.
Thanks!
OH MY GOD!
What if...!
I hope he comes soon.
NO ADMITTANCE
WHA?
SHOOT!

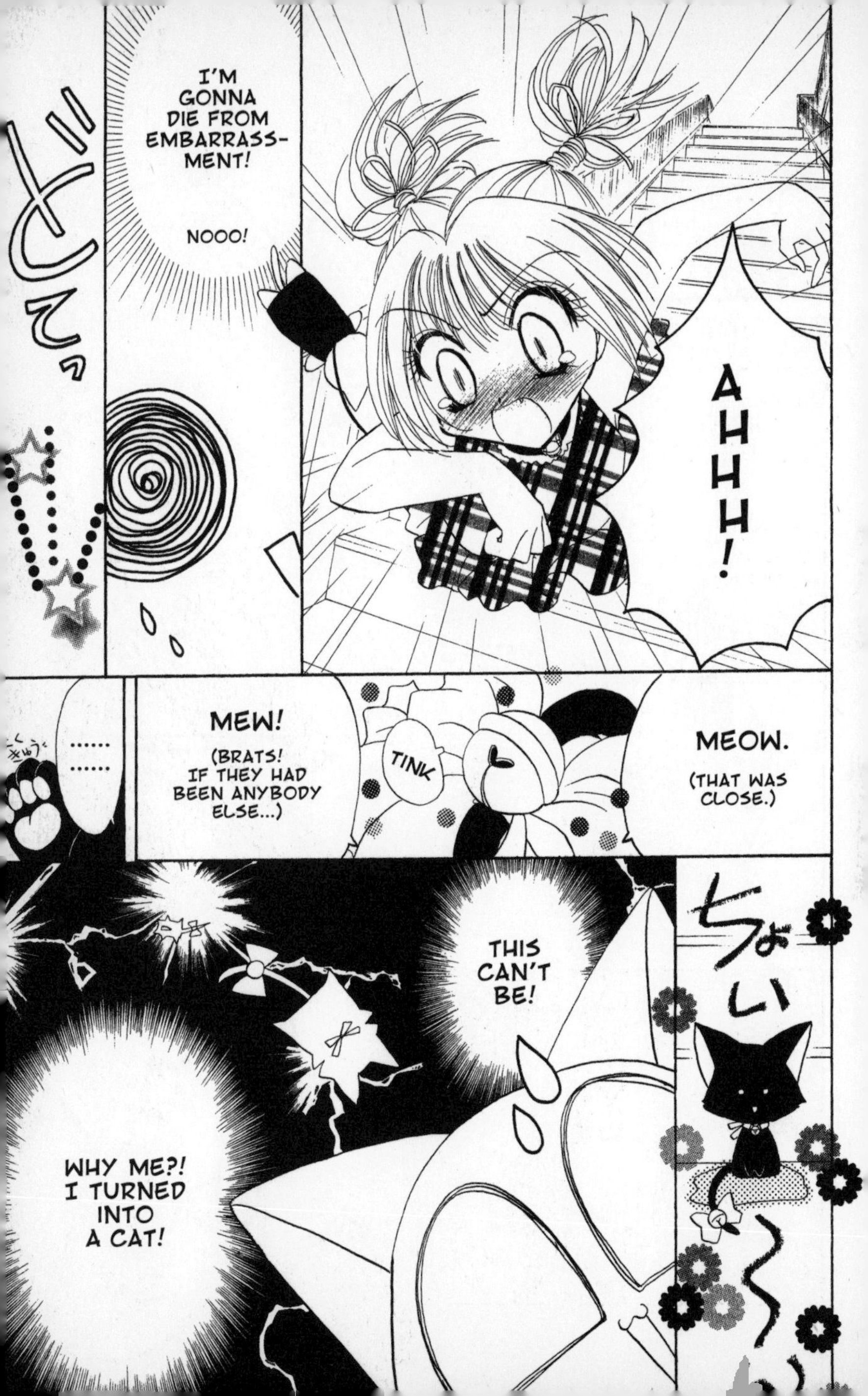
AHHH!
I'M GONNA DIE FROM EMBARRASS-MENT!
NOOO!
どてっ
MEOW.
(THAT WAS CLOSE.)
TINK
MEW!
(BRATS! IF THEY HAD BEEN ANYBODY ELSE...)
......
......
ちょい
THIS CAN'T BE!
WHY ME?! I TURNED INTO A CAT!

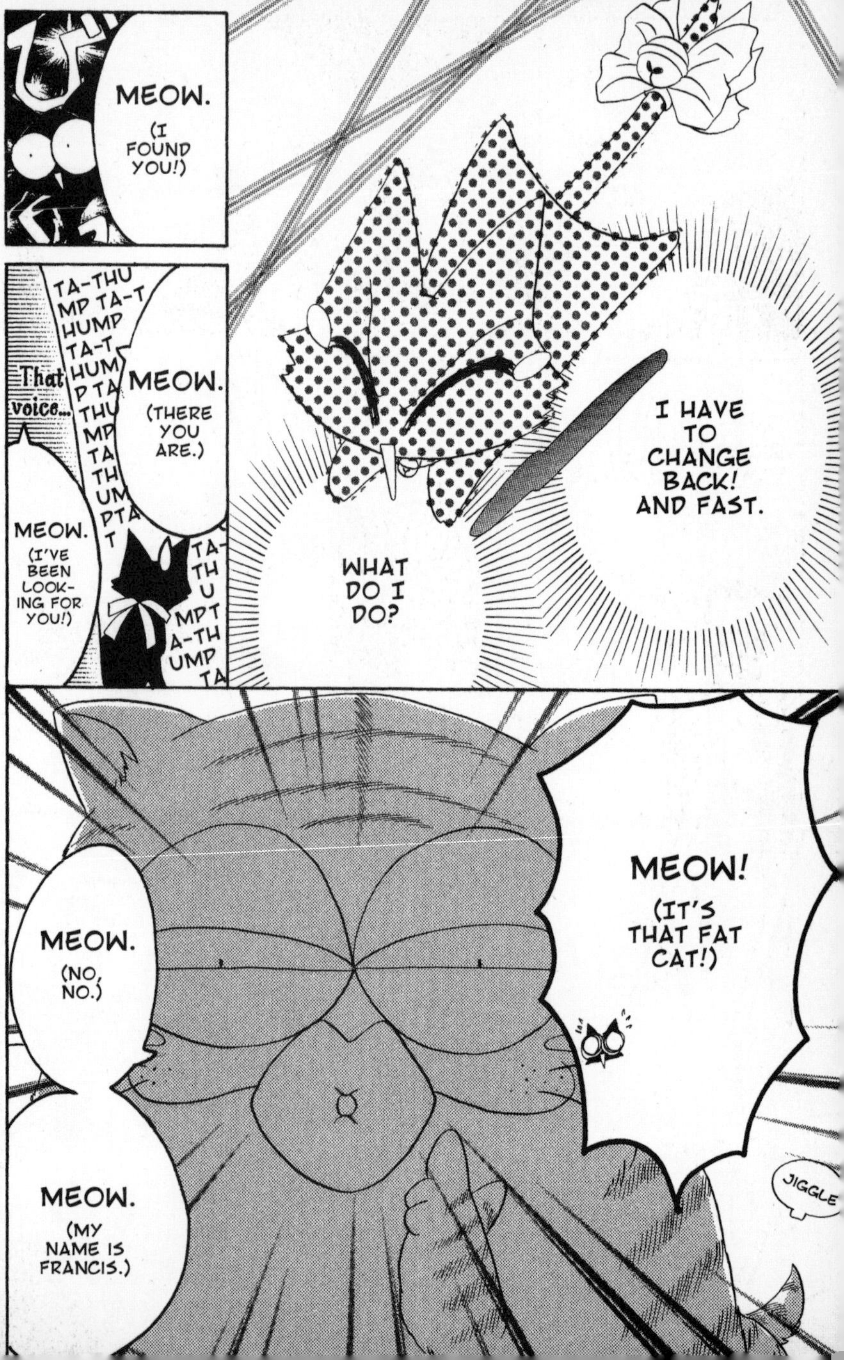

I HAVE TO CHANGE BACK! AND FAST.
WHAT DO I DO?
MEOW. (I FOUND YOU!)
TA-THUMP TA-THUMP TA-THUMP TA-THUMP TA-THUMP TA-THUMP TA-T
MEOW. (THERE YOU ARE.)
TA-THUMPTA-THUMP TA
That voice...
MEOW. (I'VE BEEN LOOKING FOR YOU!)
MEOW! (IT'S THAT FAT CAT!)
JIGGLE
MEOW. (NO, NO.)
MEOW. (MY NAME IS FRANCIS.)

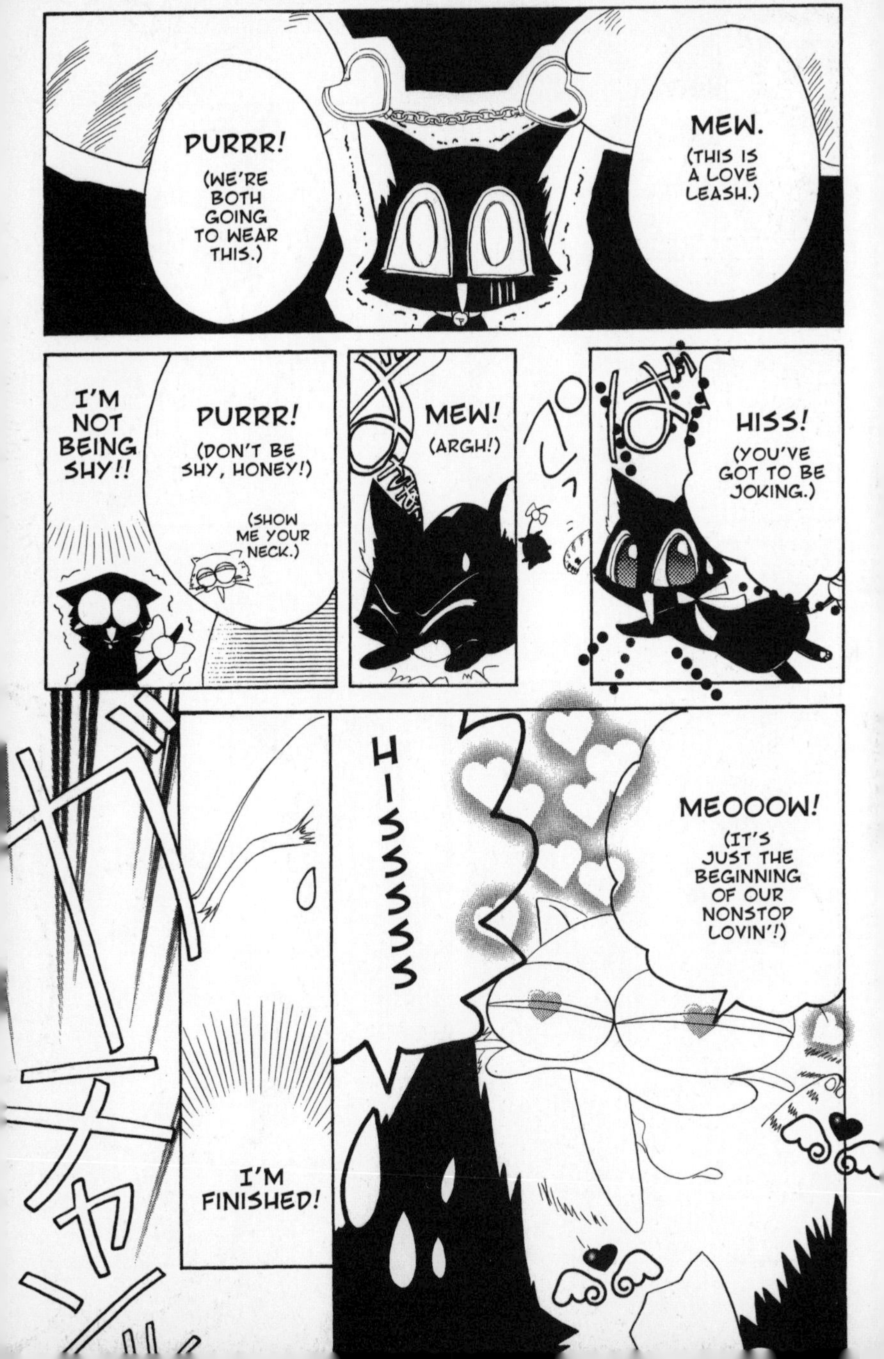
MEW.
(THIS IS A LOVE LEASH.)
PURRR!
(WE'RE BOTH GOING TO WEAR THIS.)
HISS!
(YOU'VE GOT TO BE JOKING.)
MEW!
(ARGH!)
PURRR!
(DON'T BE SHY, HONEY!)
(SHOW ME YOUR NECK.)
I'M NOT BEING SHY!!
MEOOOW!
(IT'S JUST THE BEGINNING OF OUR NONSTOP LOVIN'!)
HISSSSS
I'M FINISHED!

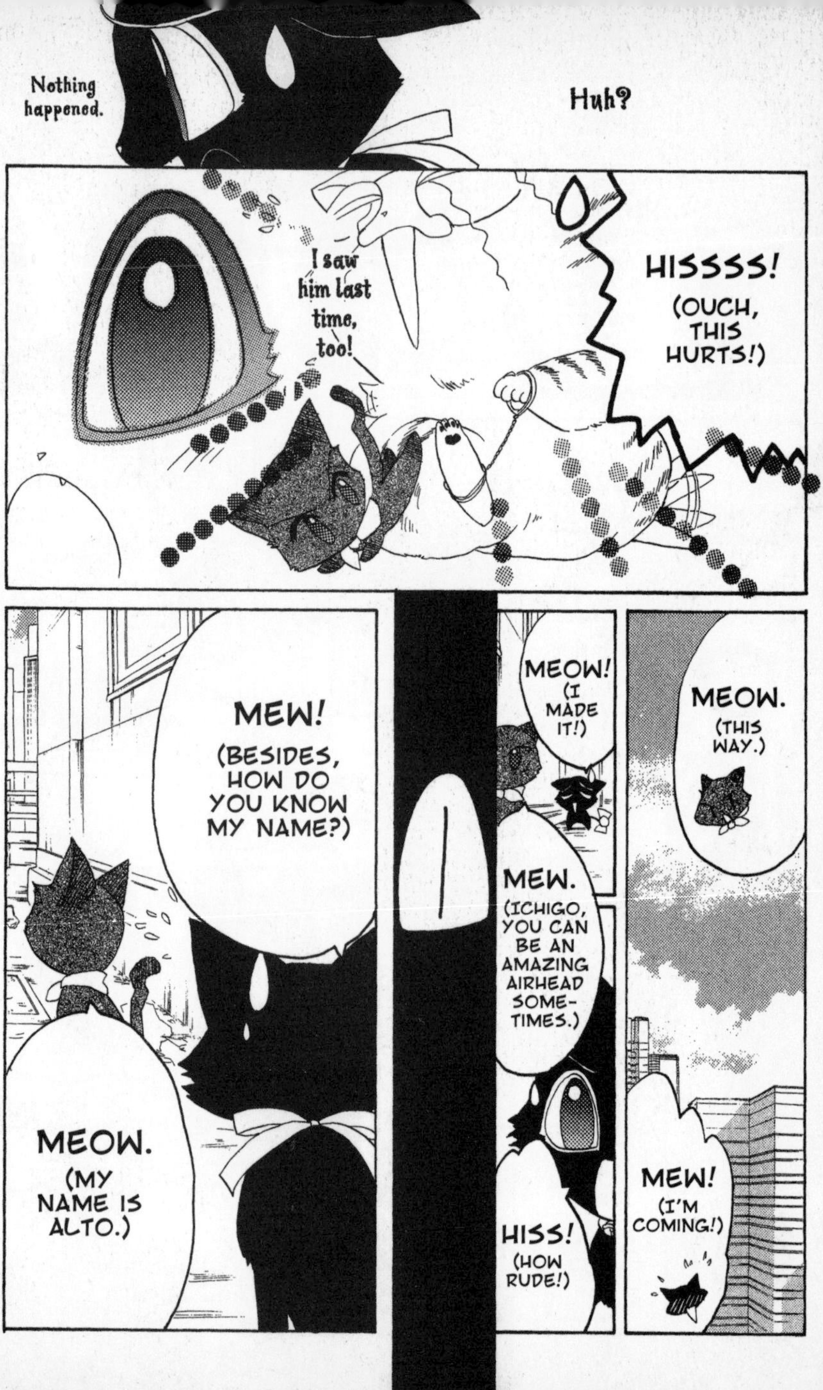
Huh?
Nothing happened.
HISSSS!
(OUCH, THIS HURTS!)
I saw him last time, too!
MEOW.
(THIS WAY.)
MEW!
(I'M COMING!)
MEOW!
(I MADE IT!)
MEW.
(ICHIGO, YOU CAN BE AN AMAZING AIRHEAD SOME-TIMES.)
HISS!
(HOW RUDE!)
MEW!
(BESIDES, HOW DO YOU KNOW MY NAME?)
MEOW.
(MY NAME IS ALTO.)

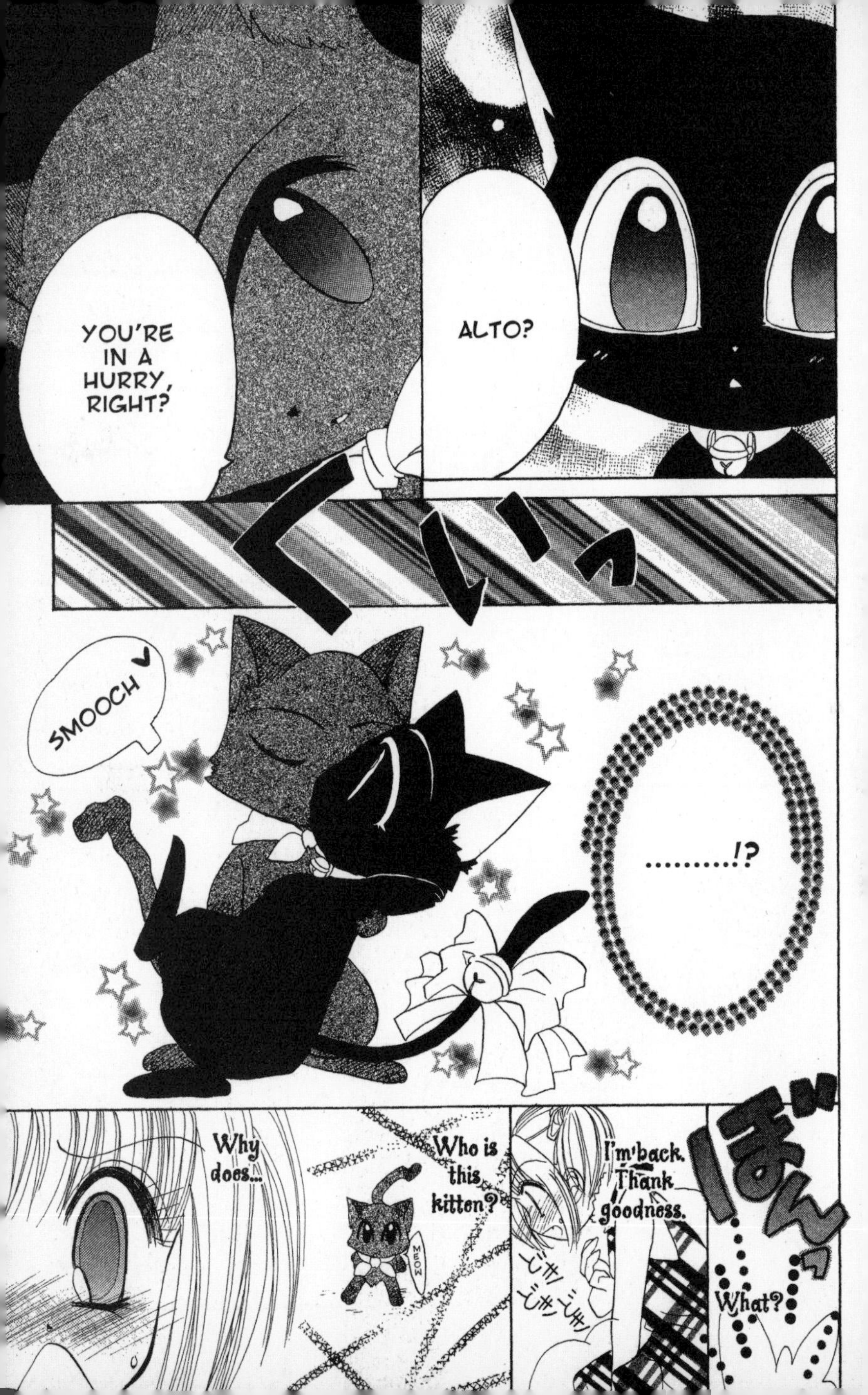
ALTO?
YOU'RE IN A HURRY, RIGHT?
くいっ
..........!?
SMOOCH
ぼんっ
What?
I'm back. Thank goodness.
どきどき
Who is this kitten?
MEOW
Why does...

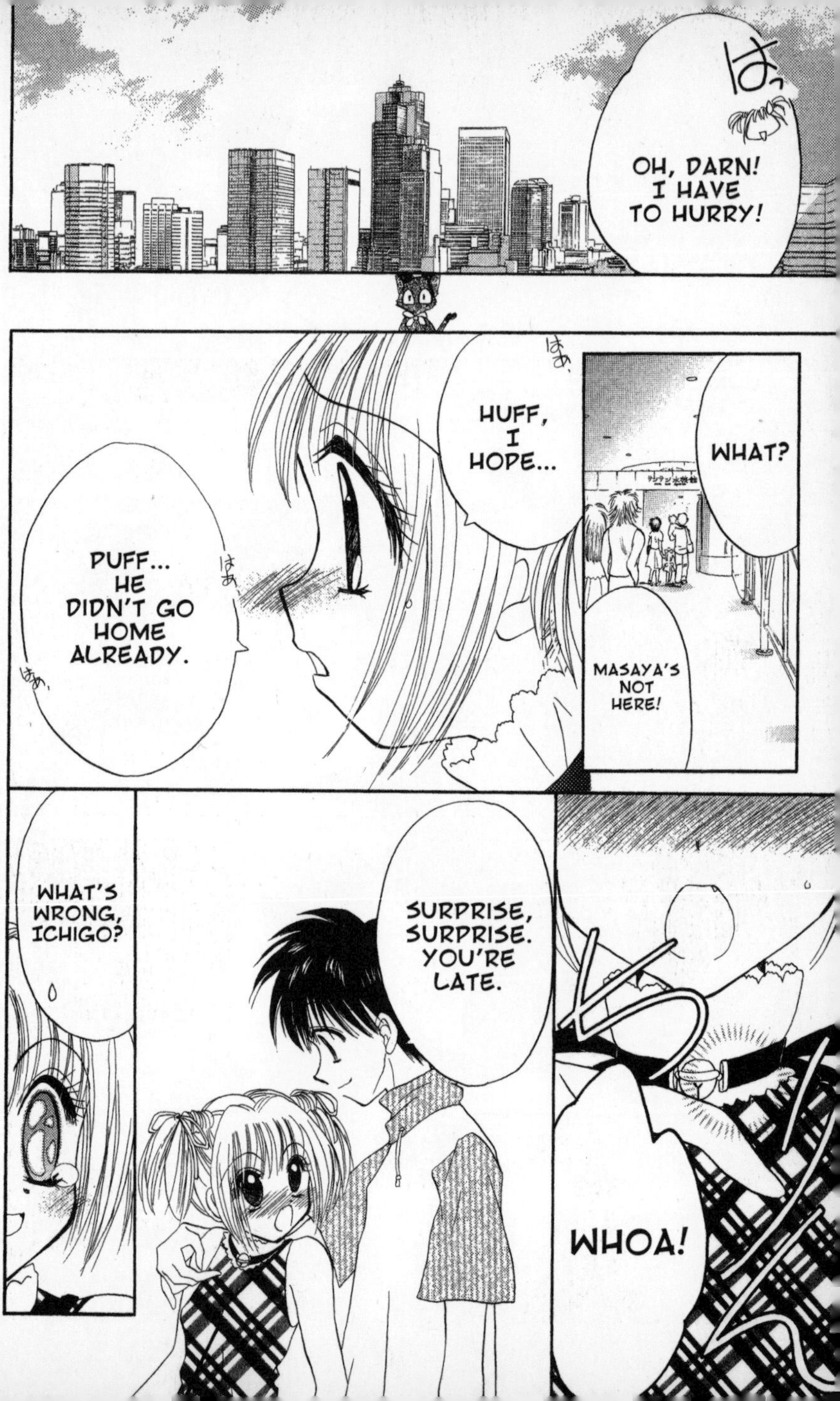
はっ
OH, DARN! I HAVE TO HURRY!
WHAT?
MASAYA'S NOT HERE!
はあ
HUFF, I HOPE...
はあ
PUFF... HE DIDN'T GO HOME ALREADY.
はあ
WHOA!
SURPRISE, SURPRISE. YOU'RE LATE.
WHAT'S WRONG, ICHIGO?

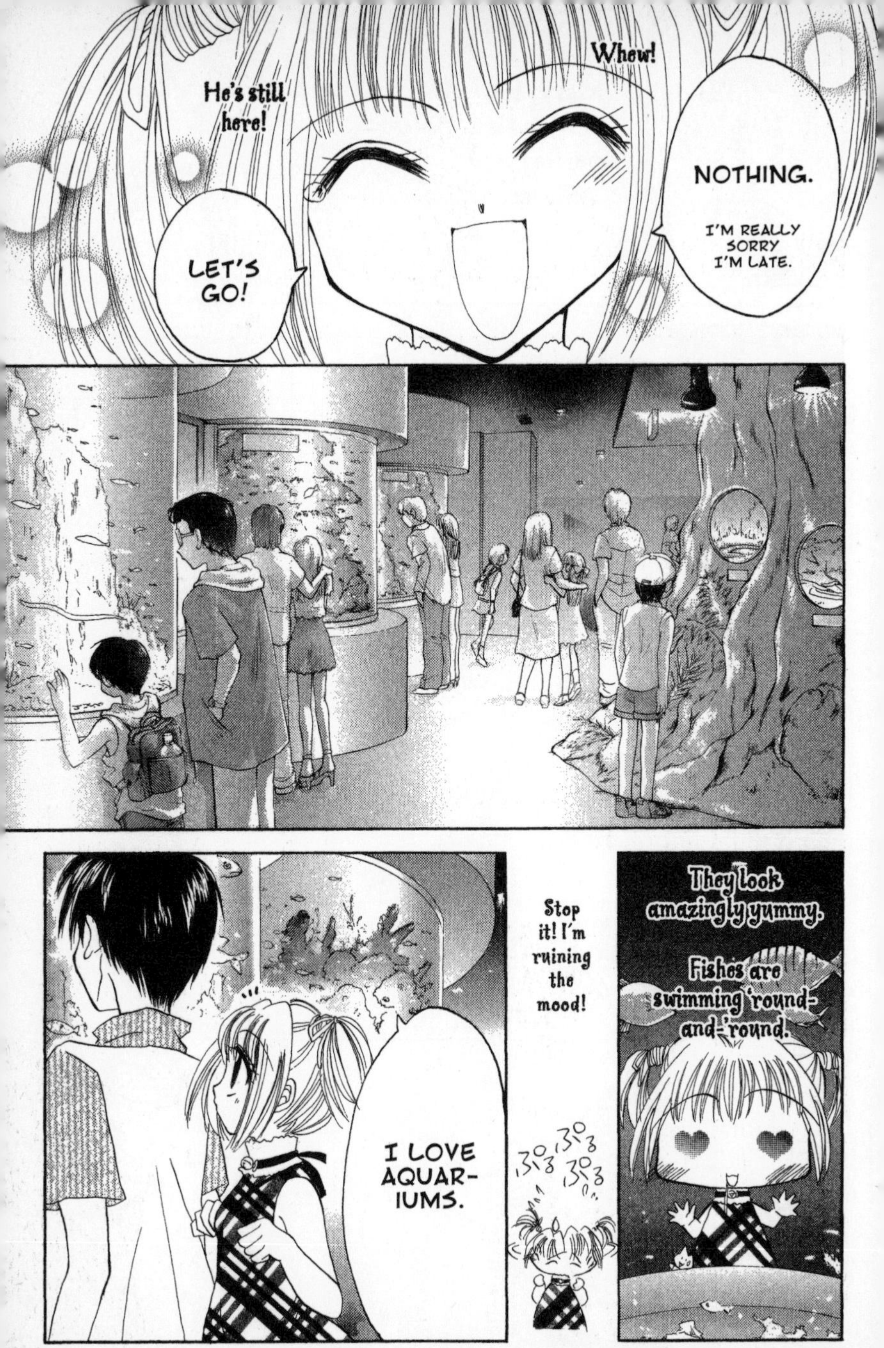
Whew!
NOTHING.
I'M REALLY SORRY I'M LATE.
He's still here!
LET'S GO!
They look amazingly yummy.
Fishes are swimming 'round-and-'round.
Stop it! I'm ruining the mood!
I LOVE AQUARIUMS.

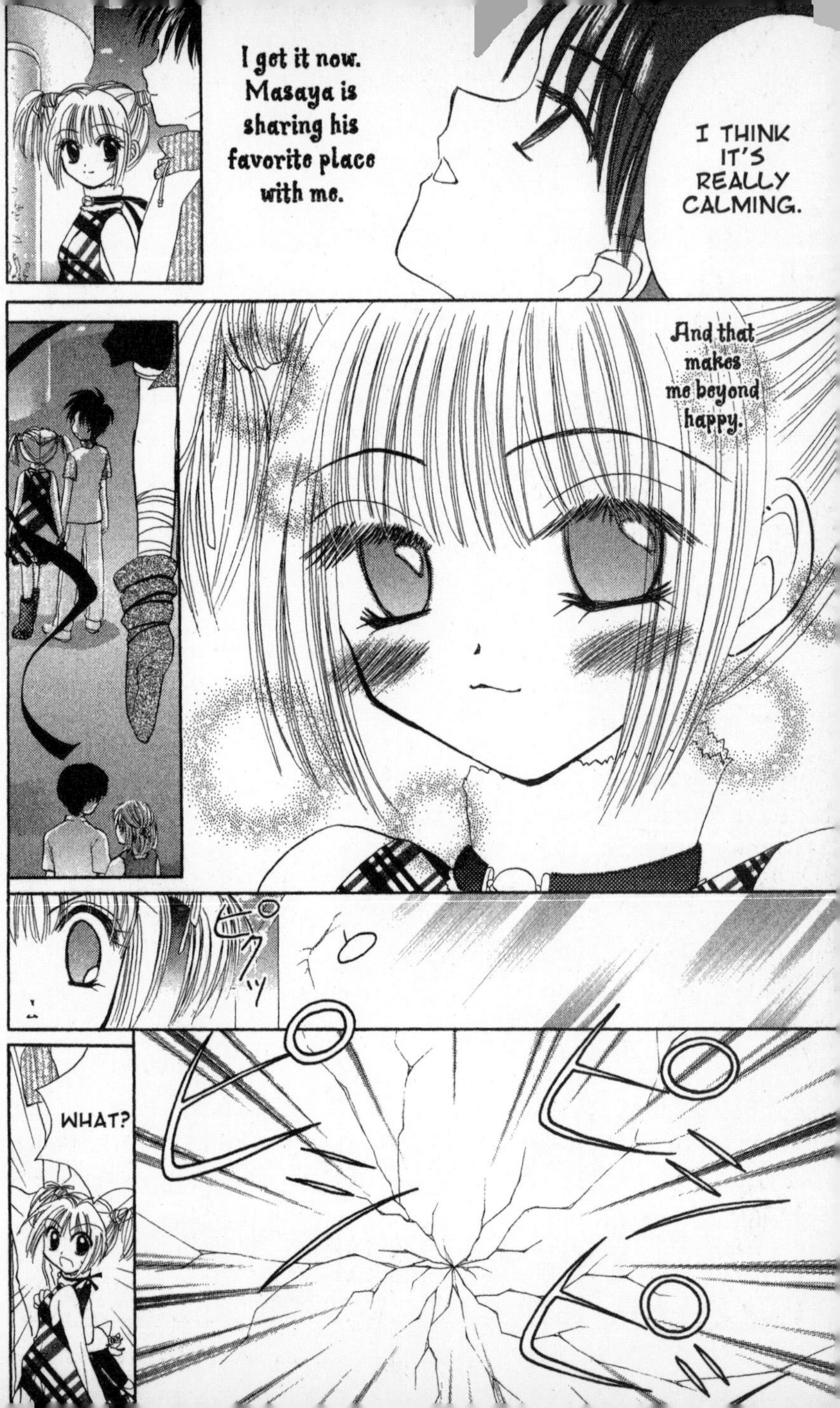
I THINK IT'S REALLY CALMING.
I get it now. Masaya is sharing his favorite place with me.
And that makes me beyond happy.
ピクッ
WHAT?

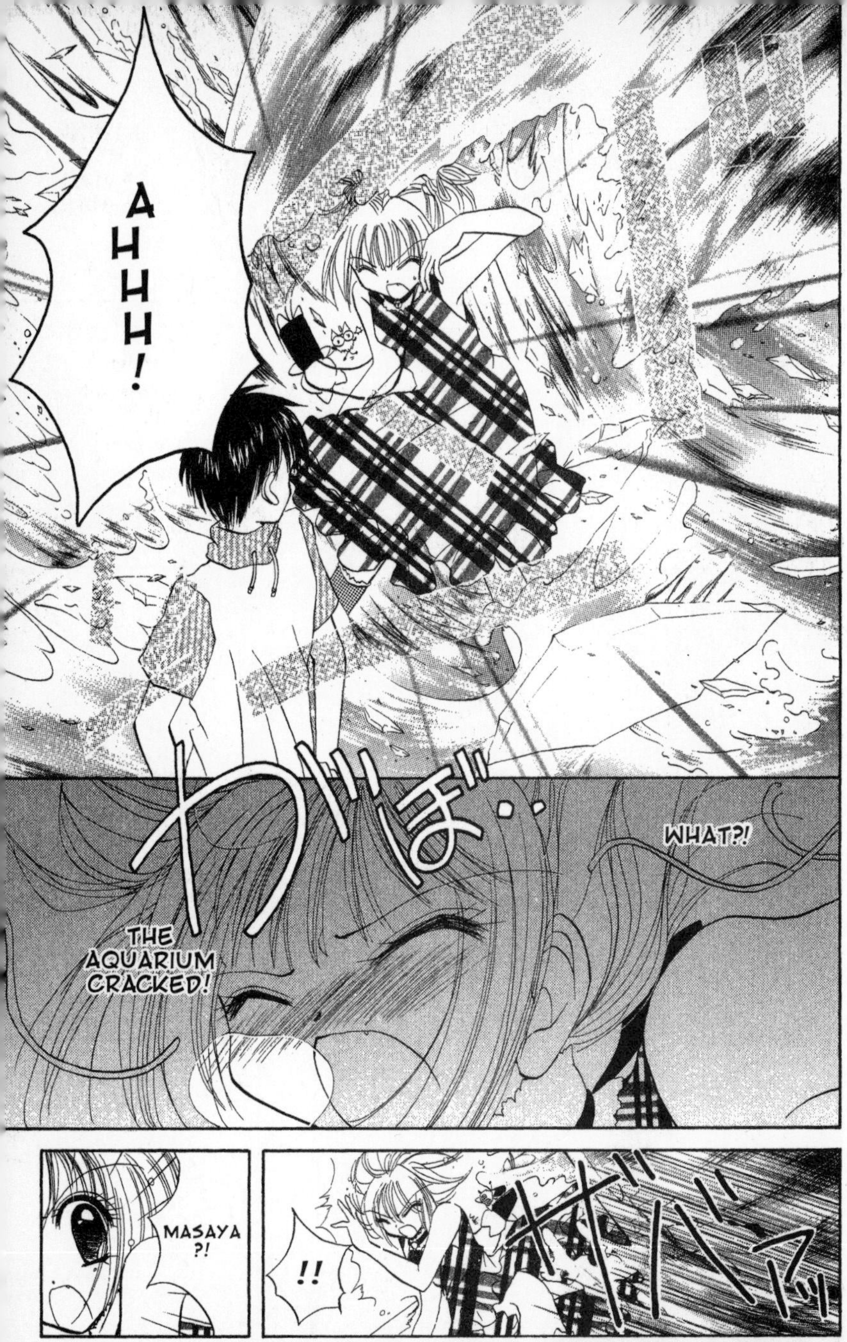
AHHHH!
WHAT?!
THE AQUARIUM CRACKED!
!!
MASAYA ?!

Appeared in *Nakayoshi* magazine
Nov 2001, Jan 2002 and Feb 2002 issues

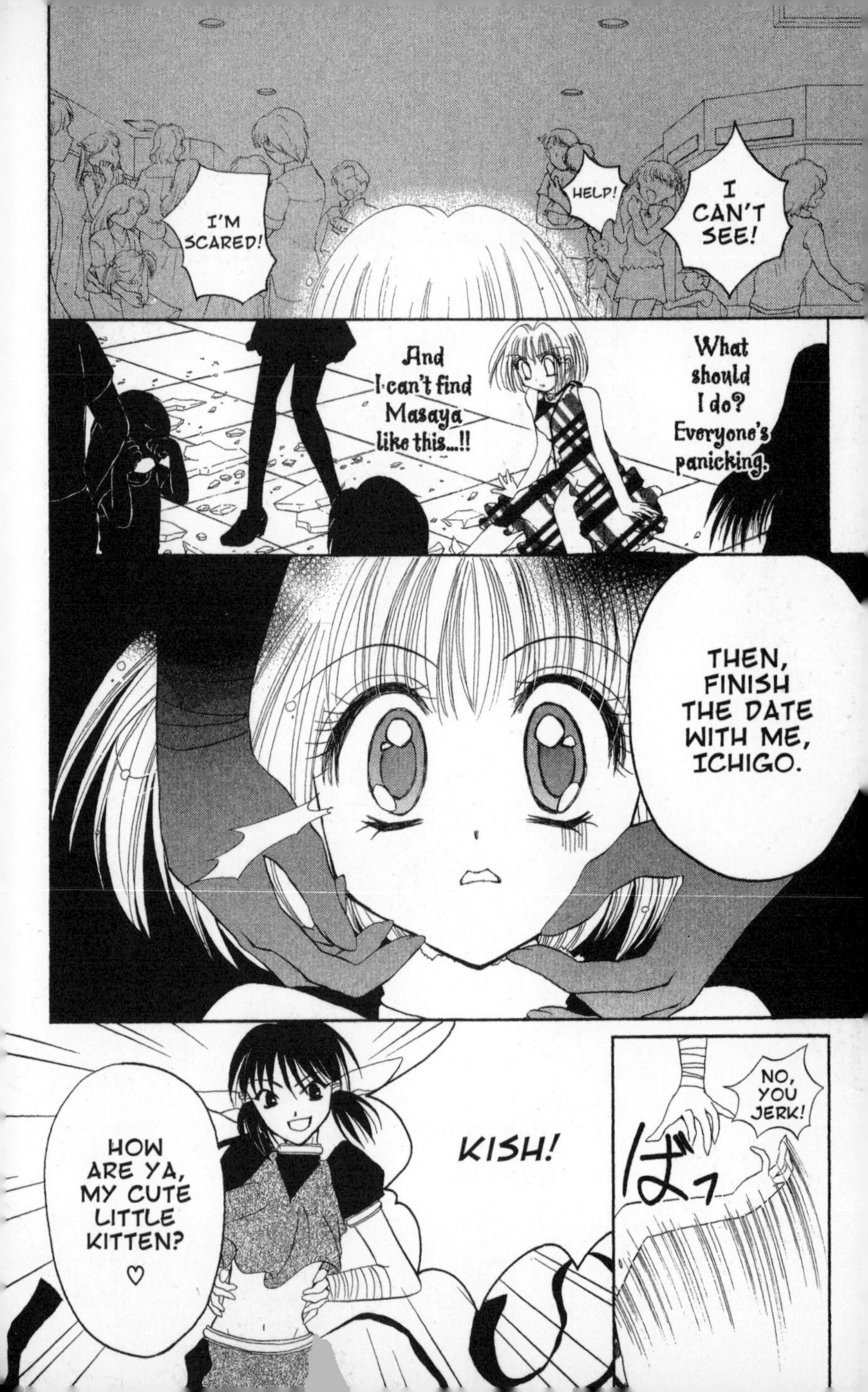
I CAN'T SEE!
HELP!
I'M SCARED!
What should I do? Everyone's panicking.
And I can't find Masaya like this...!!
THEN, FINISH THE DATE WITH ME, ICHIGO.
NO, YOU JERK!
ばっ
KISH!
HOW ARE YA, MY CUTE LITTLE KITTEN? ♡

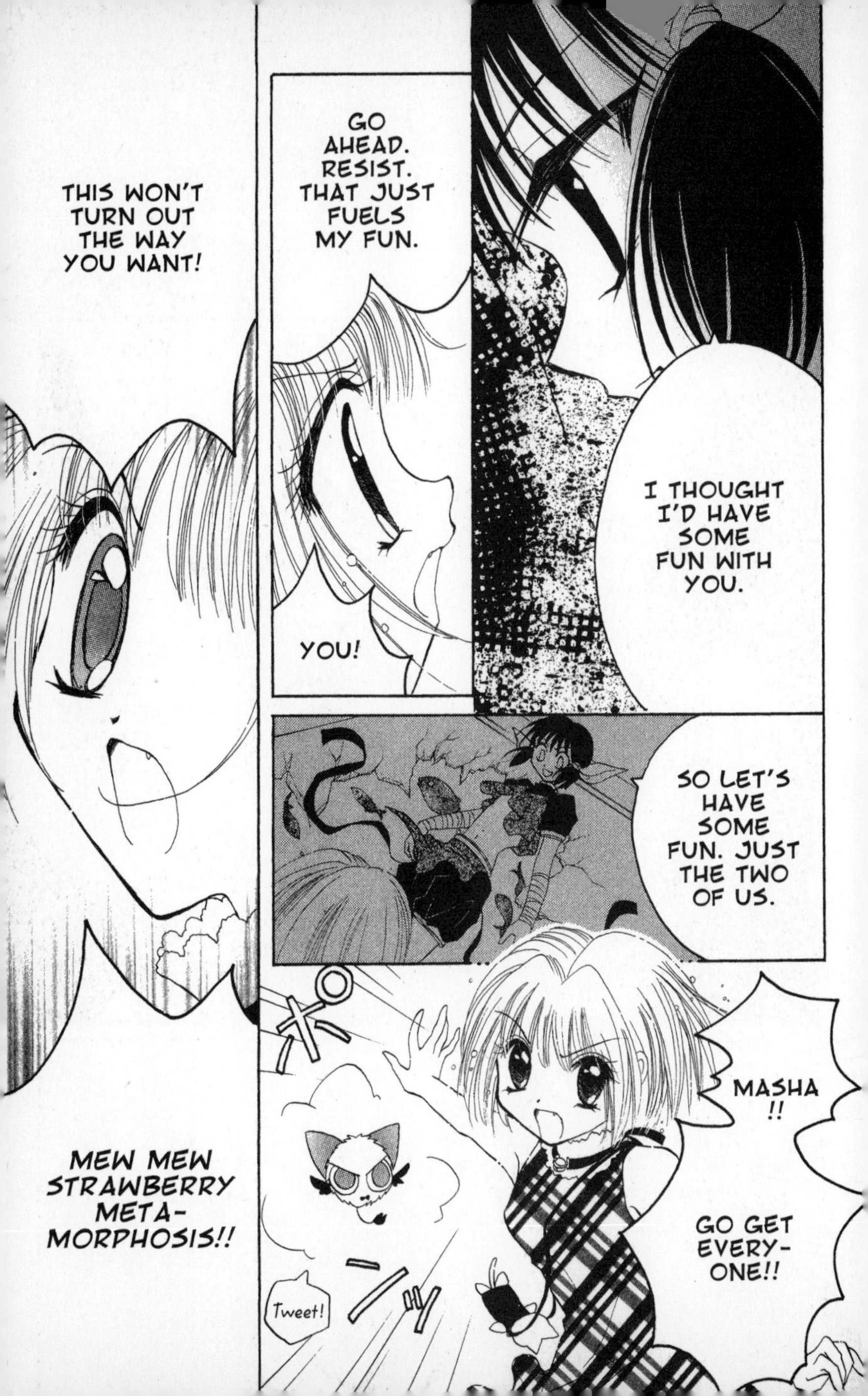
I THOUGHT I'D HAVE SOME FUN WITH YOU.
GO AHEAD. RESIST. THAT JUST FUELS MY FUN.
YOU!
SO LET'S HAVE SOME FUN. JUST THE TWO OF US.
MASHA!!
GO GET EVERY-ONE!!
Tweet!
THIS WON'T TURN OUT THE WAY YOU WANT!
MEW MEW STRAWBERRY META-MORPHOSIS!!

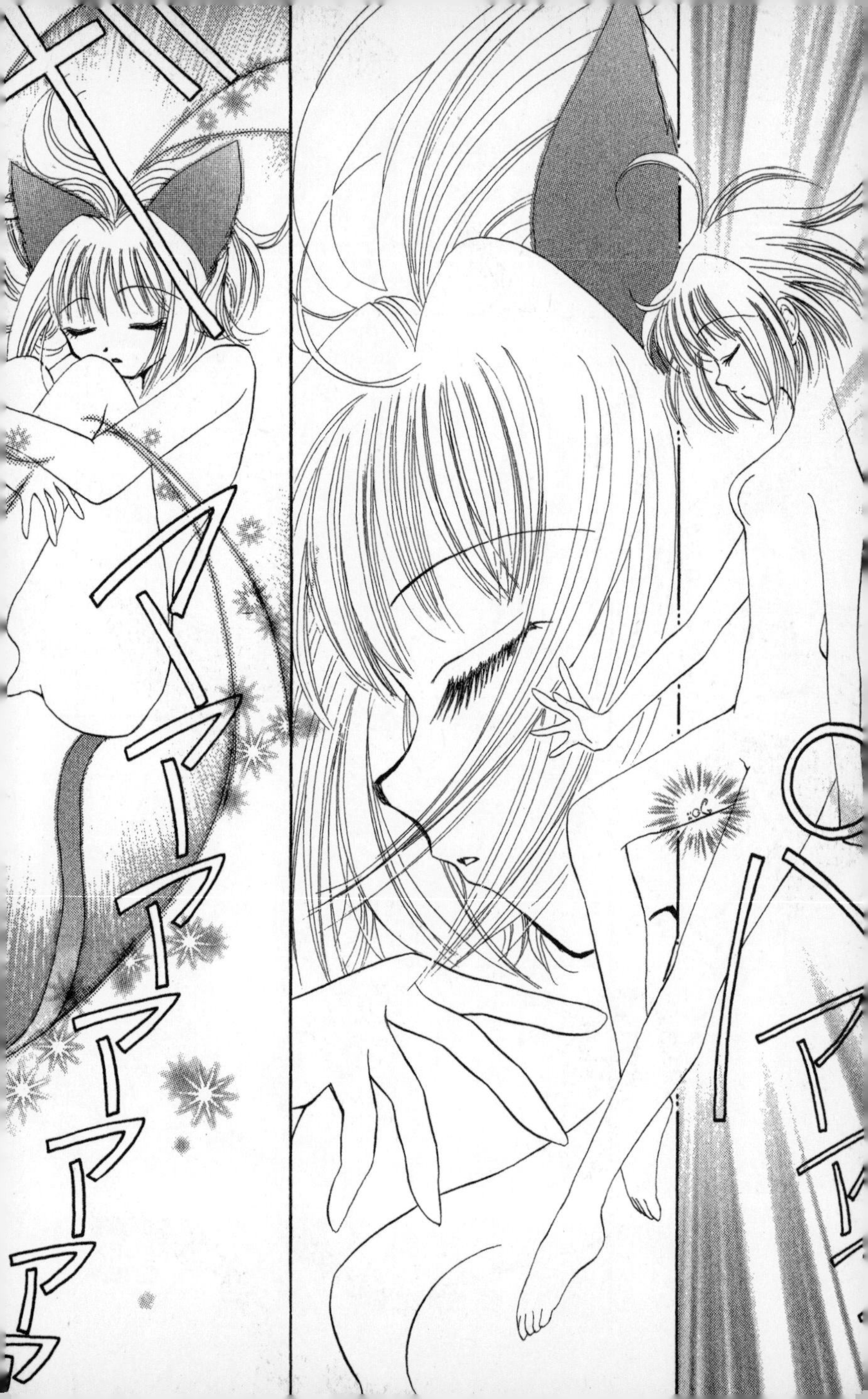
パア
キアアアアアア

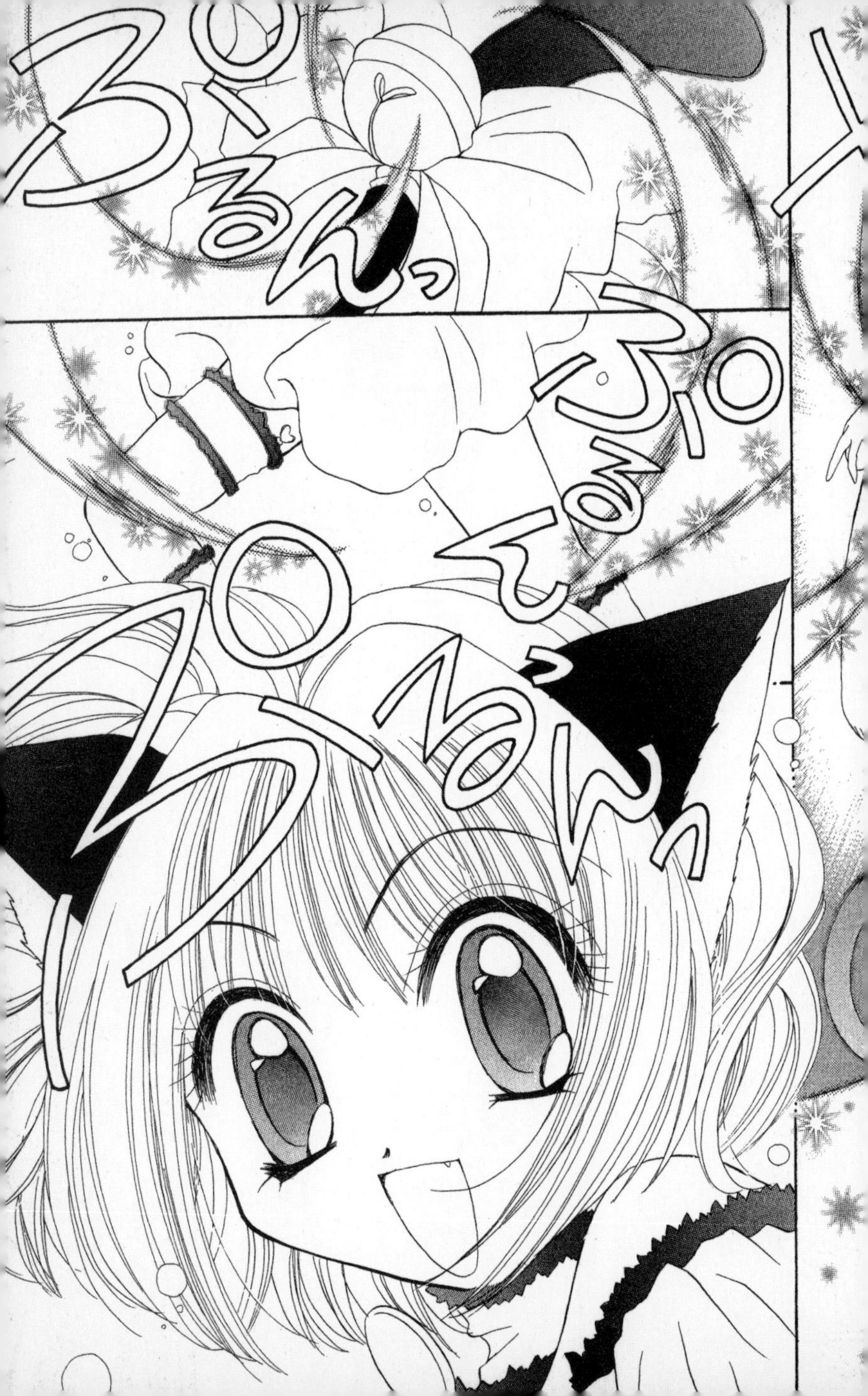
ぷぃるんっ
ぷぃるるんっ
ぷぃるるるんっ

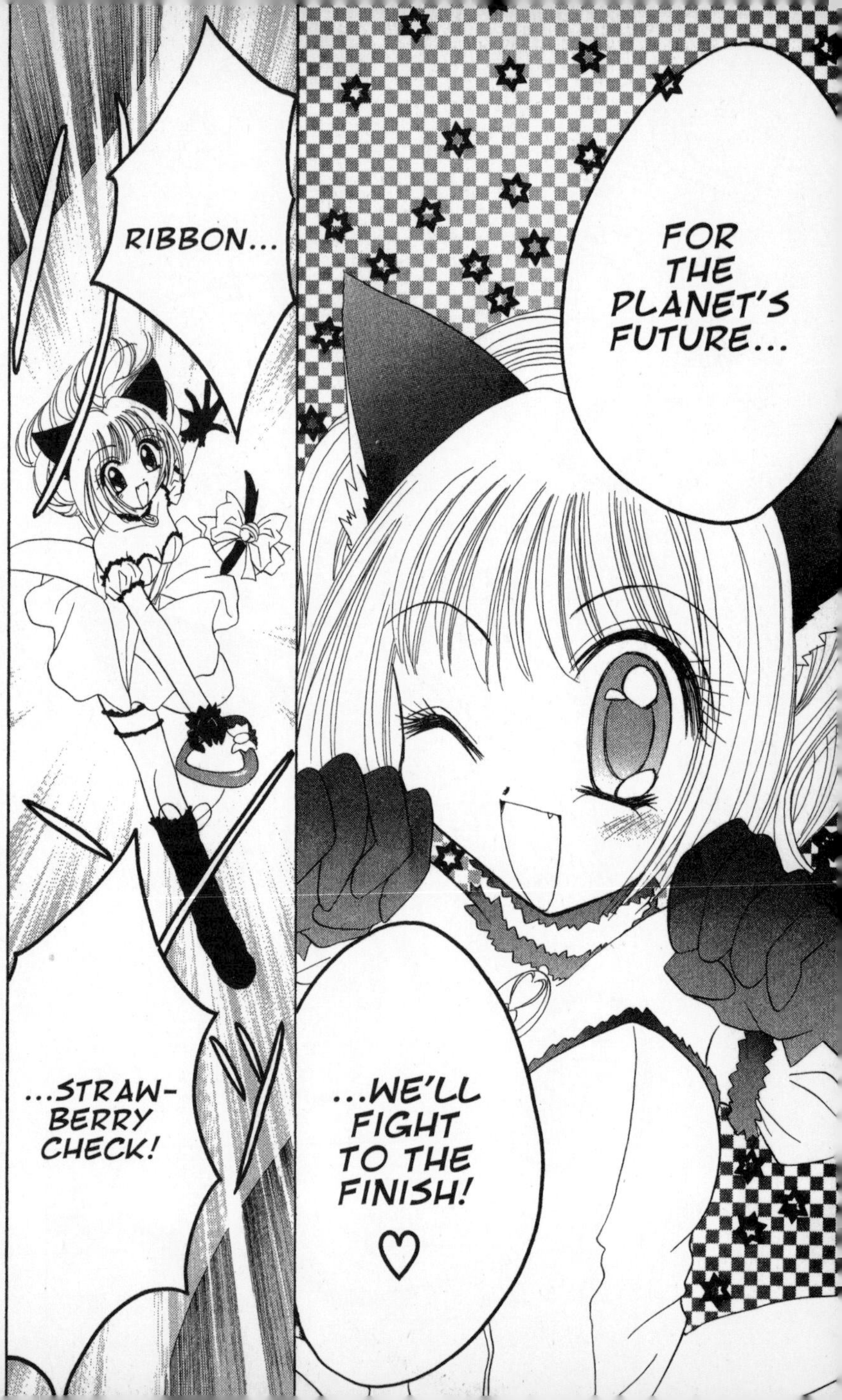
FOR THE PLANET'S FUTURE...
...WE'LL FIGHT TO THE FINISH! ♡
RIBBON...
...STRAW-BERRY CHECK!

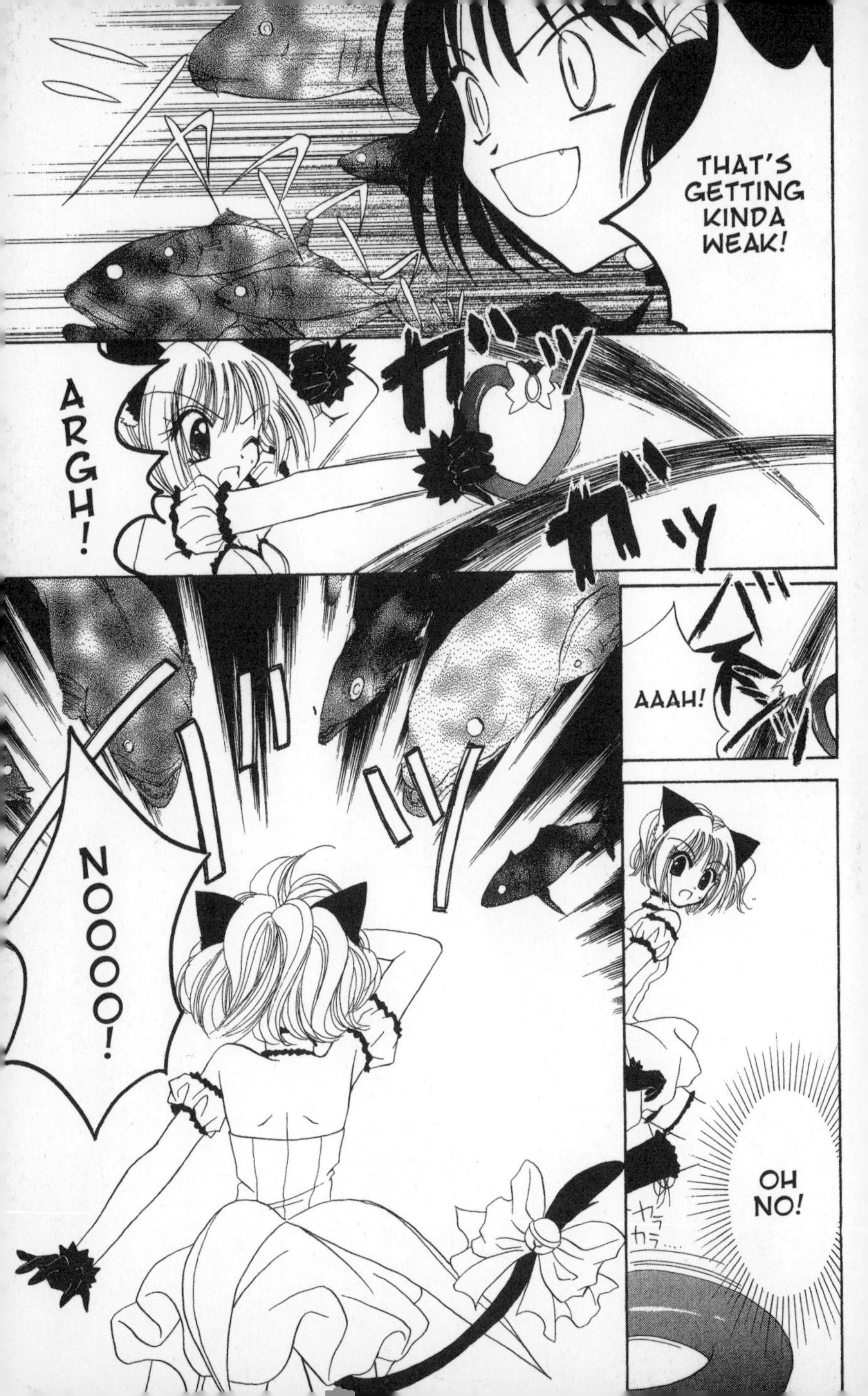
THAT'S GETTING KINDA WEAK!
ガッ
ARGH!
ガッ
AAAH!
OH NO!
NOOOOO!

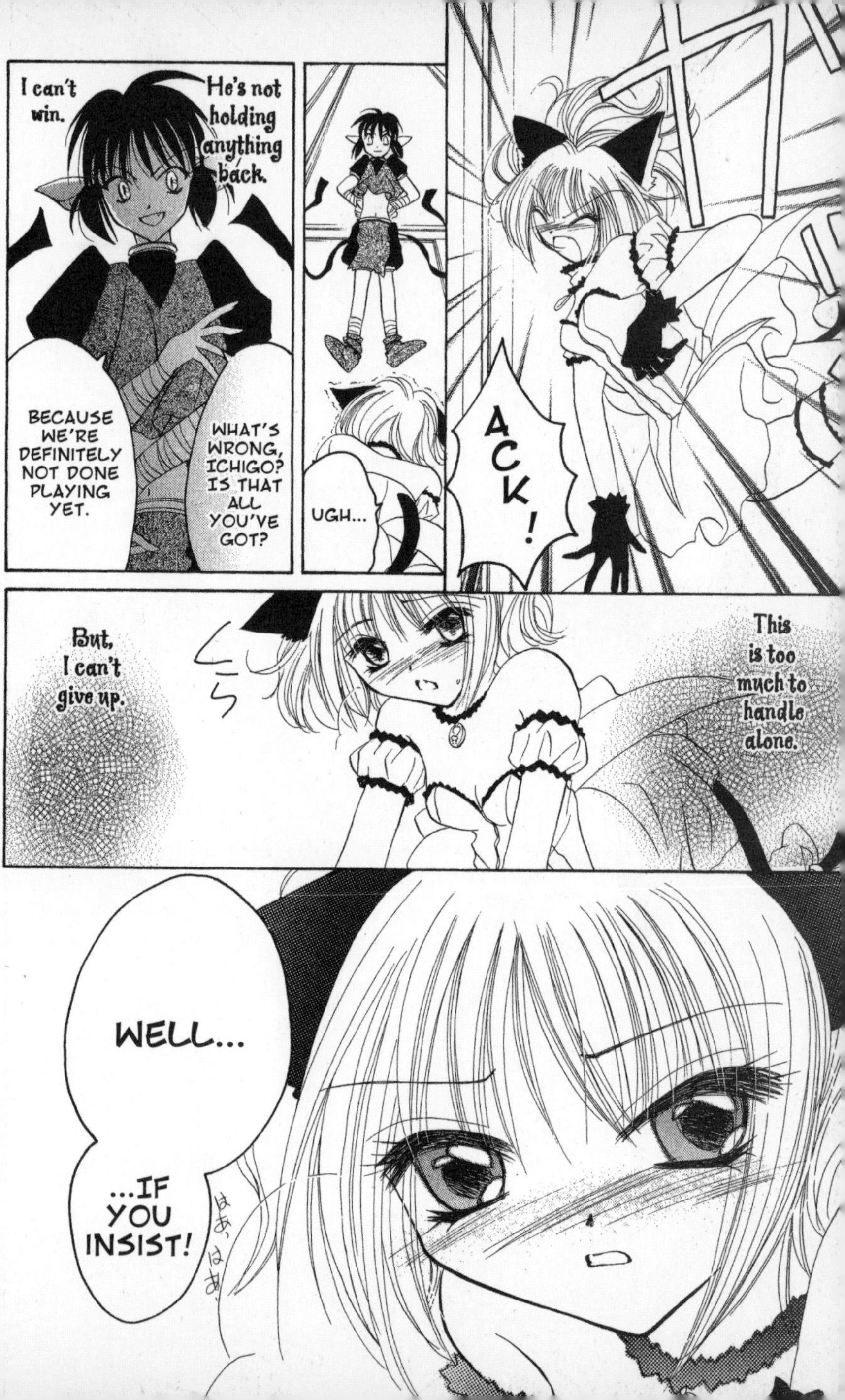
ACK!
UGH...
He's not holding anything back.
I can't win.
WHAT'S WRONG, ICHIGO? IS THAT ALL YOU'VE GOT?
BECAUSE WE'RE DEFINITELY NOT DONE PLAYING YET.
This is too much to handle alone.
くら
But, I can't give up.
はあ、はあ、
WELL...
...IF YOU INSIST!

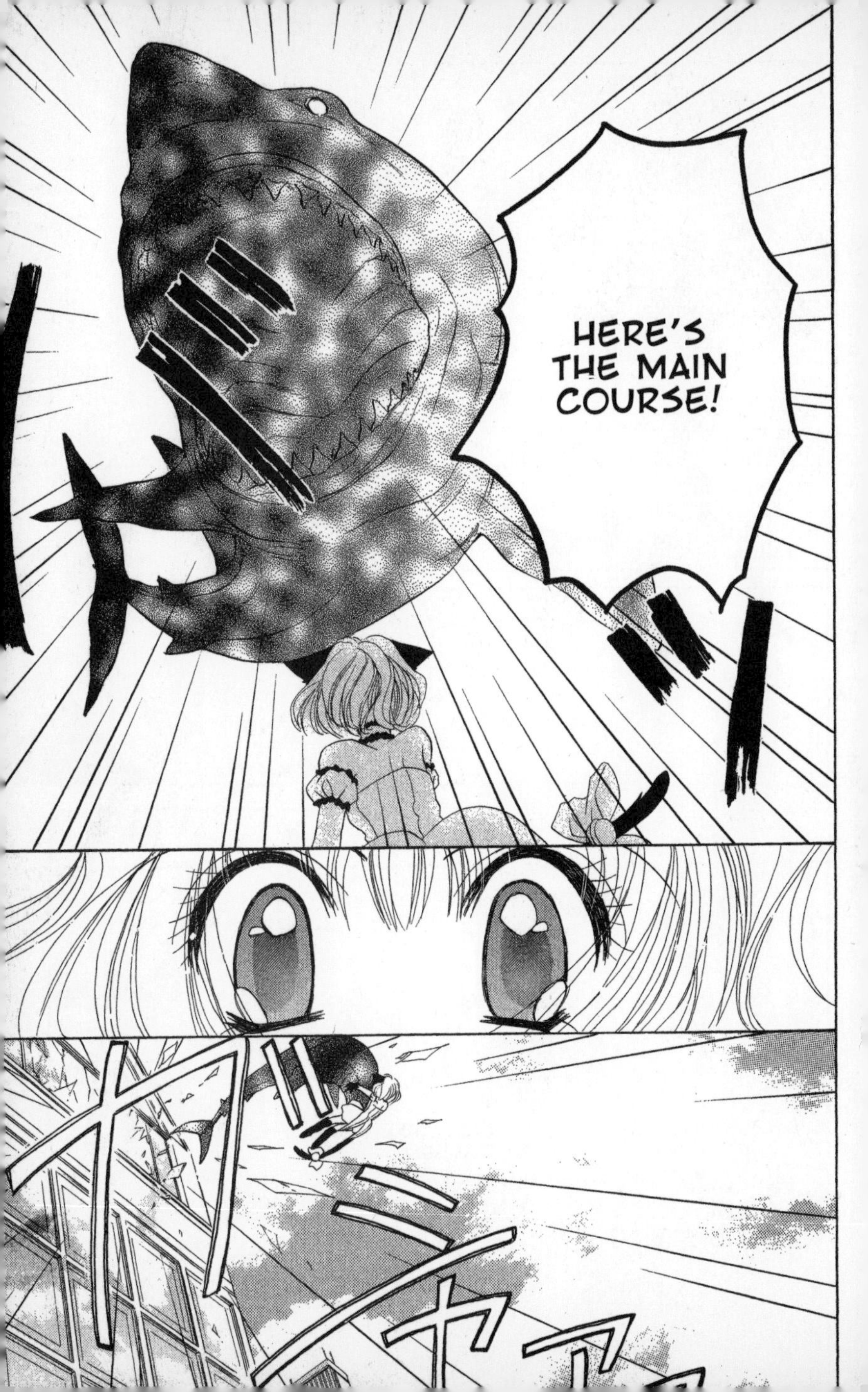
HERE'S THE MAIN COURSE!

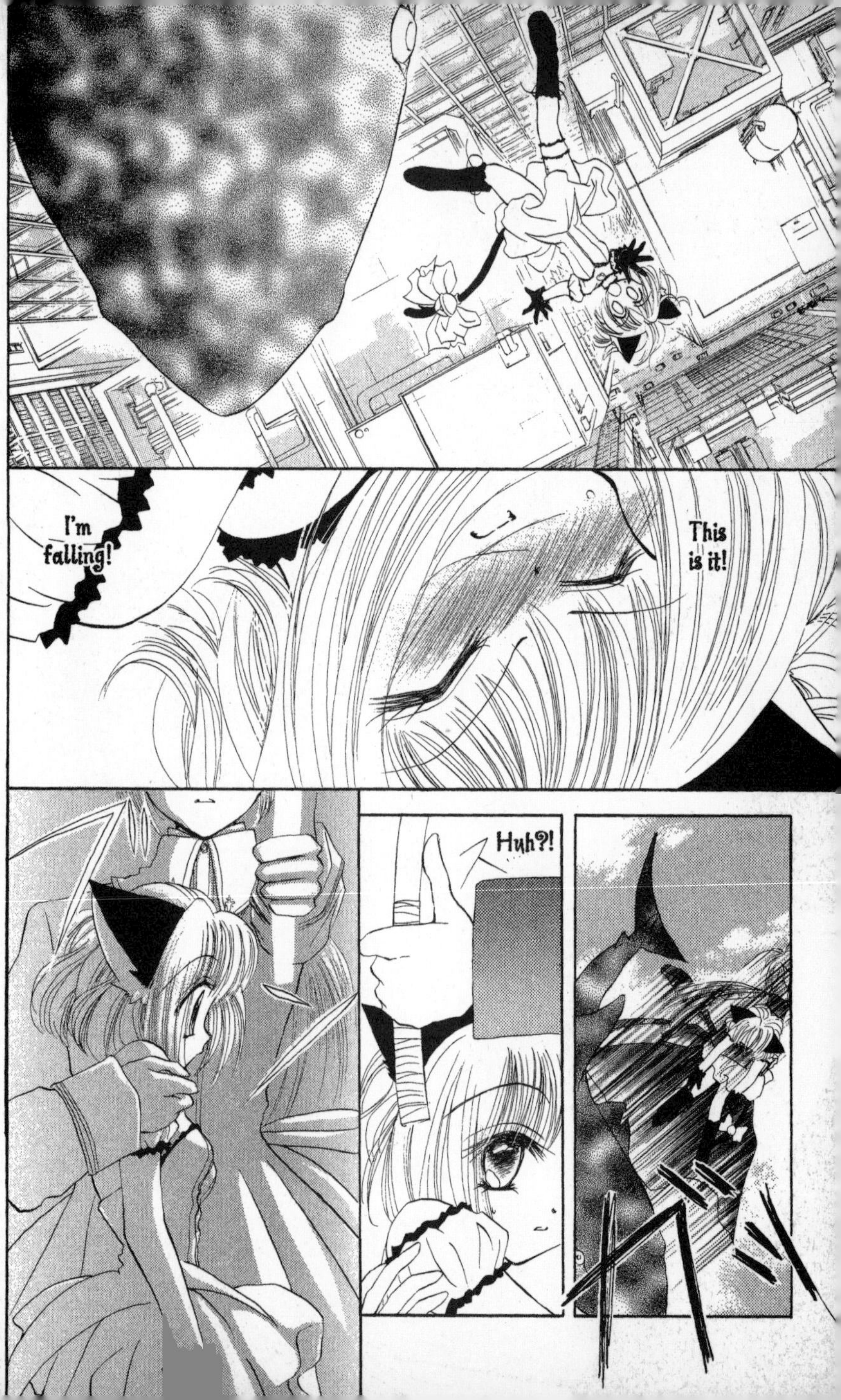
This is it!
I'm falling!
Huh?!

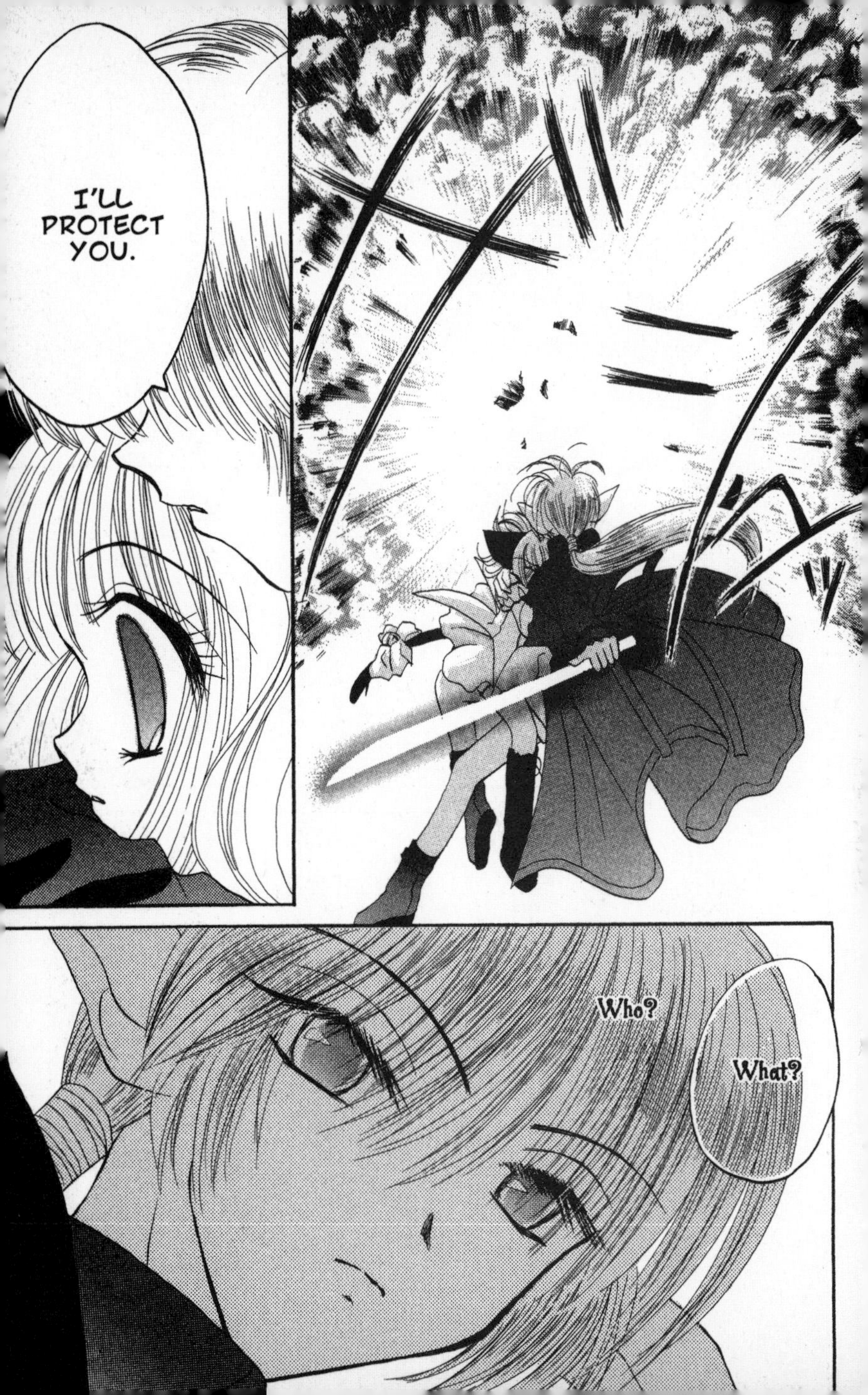
I'LL PROTECT YOU.
Who?
What?

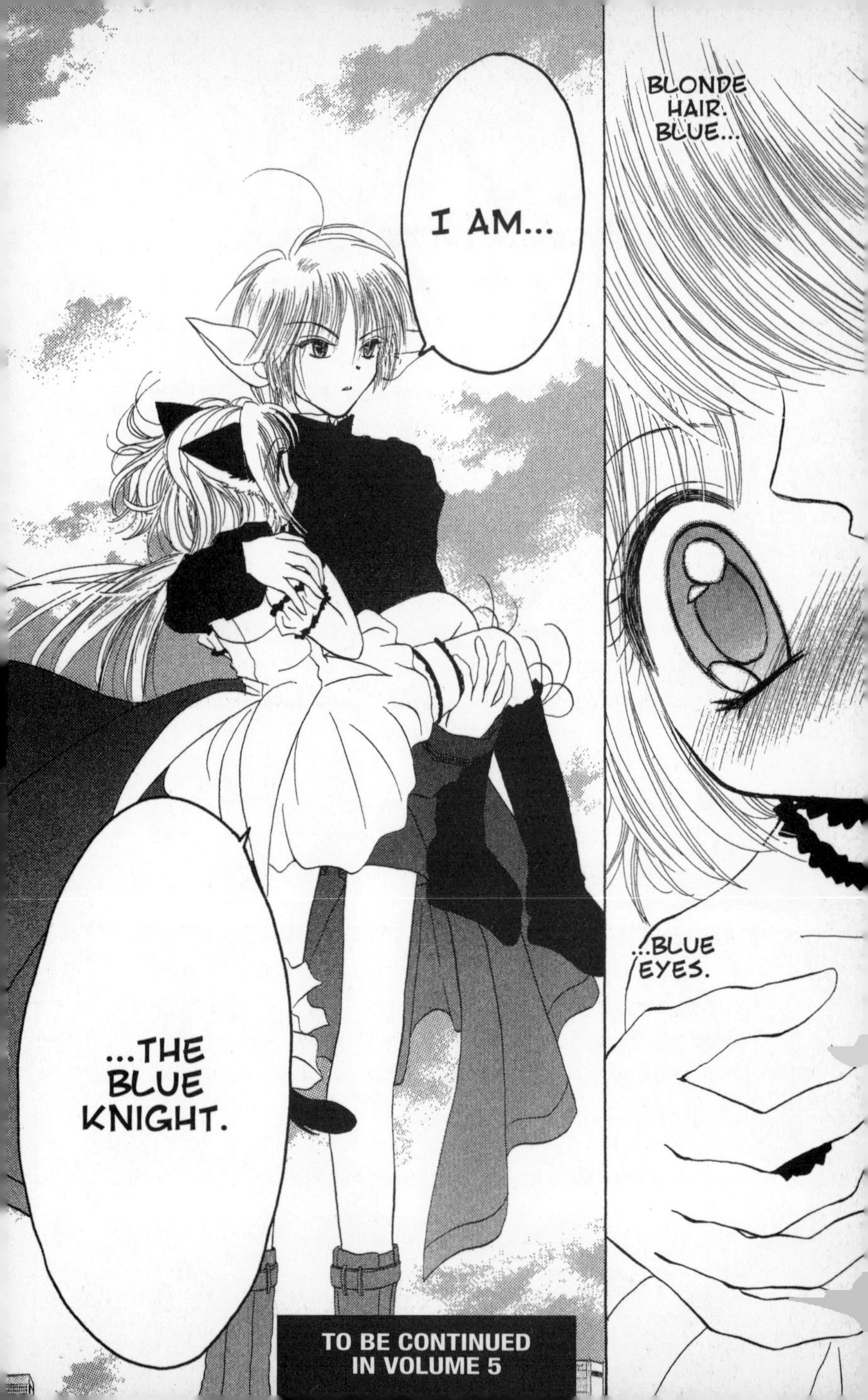
BLONDE HAIR. BLUE...
...BLUE EYES.
I AM...
...THE BLUE KNIGHT.
TO BE CONTINUED IN VOLUME 5

About the Fourth Volume
by Reiko Yoshida

The "Mew Mews" got their special powers when they were fused with genes from endangered species. Many animals have special, interesting abilities, too.

For example, certain whale species can stun their food by emitting powerful sonar waves. Snakes can taste the air with their tongue. Armadillos are protected by their armor-like skin when they curl up into a ball. Skunks and aardvarks can emit a foul odor to escape from their enemies. I'm amazed at all these adaptations that different animals have developed.

I used to have a pet hamster. I was always surprised by its ability to store a lot of food in his cheeks. However, when he stored cookies, it would turn into mush.

If you were fused with an animal, which animal would help you out the most? If you're always running late, the swift cheetah would probably make a good choice. If you get cold easily, a fluffy sheep is a great option. But if you want to be popular, an endearing animal, like the panda, would suit you well.

Animals can be amazingly interesting!

Tokyo Black Cat Girl.

This was a project I finished before I started on "Tokyo Mew Mew." I remember having fun as I worked on this. I had just moved to Tokyo around that time. Life was pretty rough for me. For example, I ate mainly cabbages and beans for an entire week straight because they were on sale. I think I spent more time looking for affordable places to shop than working on manga like I should have (laugh).

People often ask, "Why did you choose Tokyo?" I don't really have a reason. I thought "Tokyo" sounded good in the title. That's all. I promise.

By the way, this drawing matches the drawing for the intro page of the May issue.

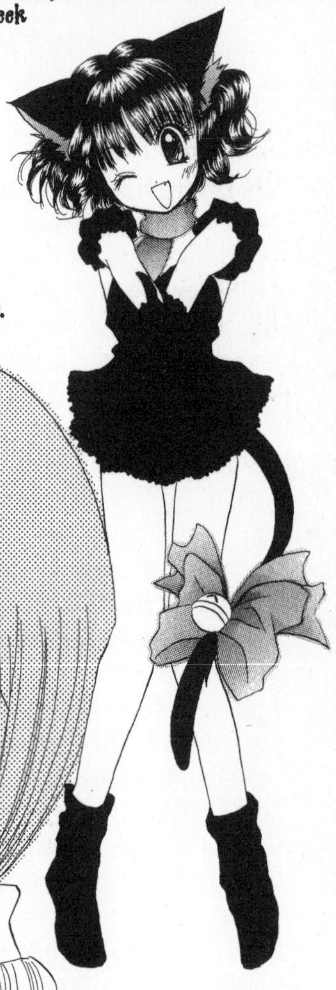

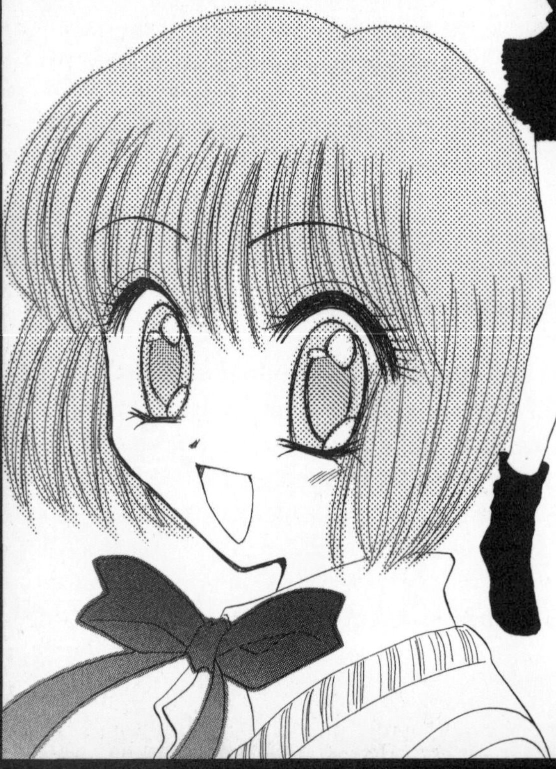

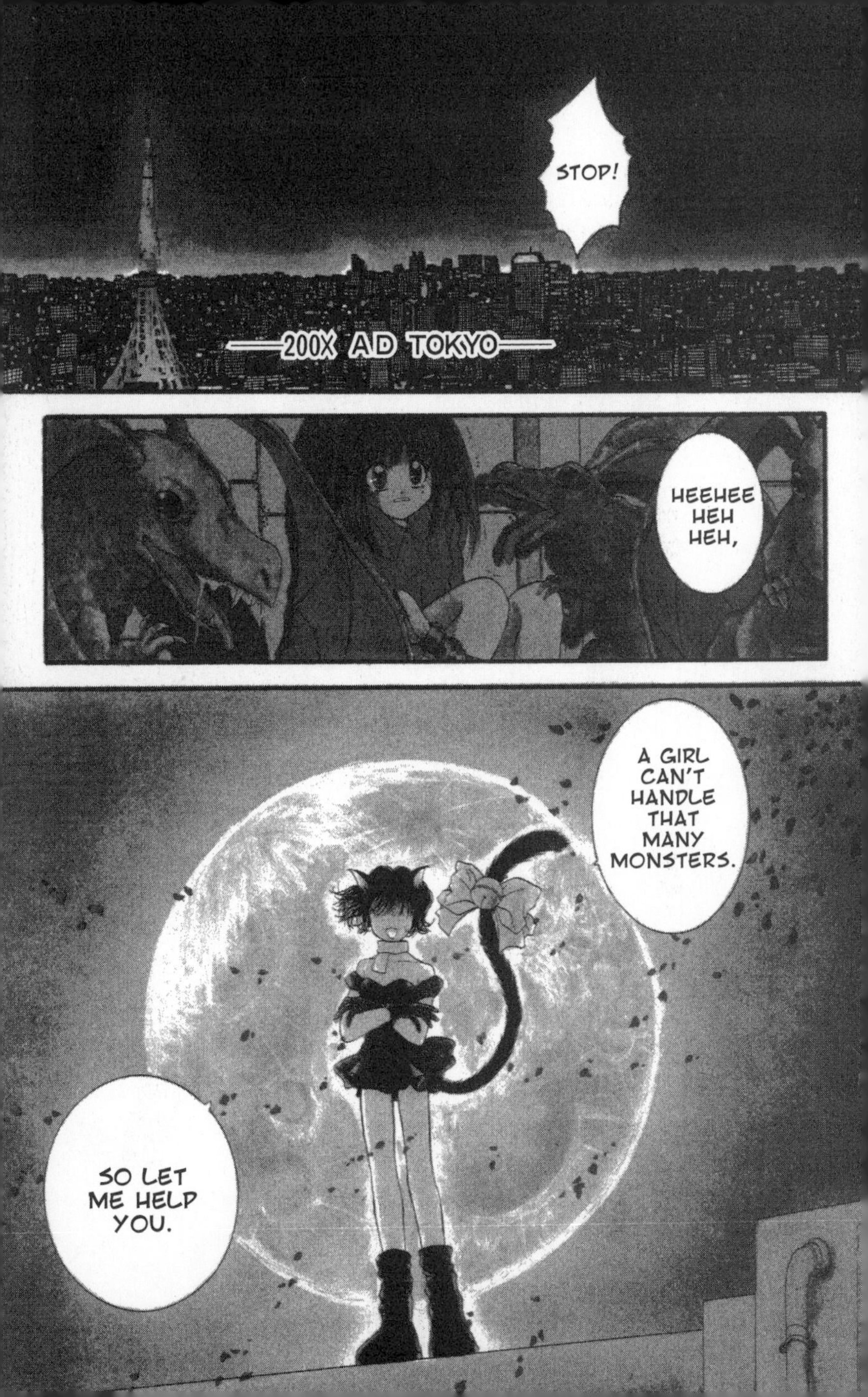
STOP!
200X AD TOKYO
HEEHEE HEH HEH,
A GIRL CAN'T HANDLE THAT MANY MONSTERS.
SO LET ME HELP YOU.

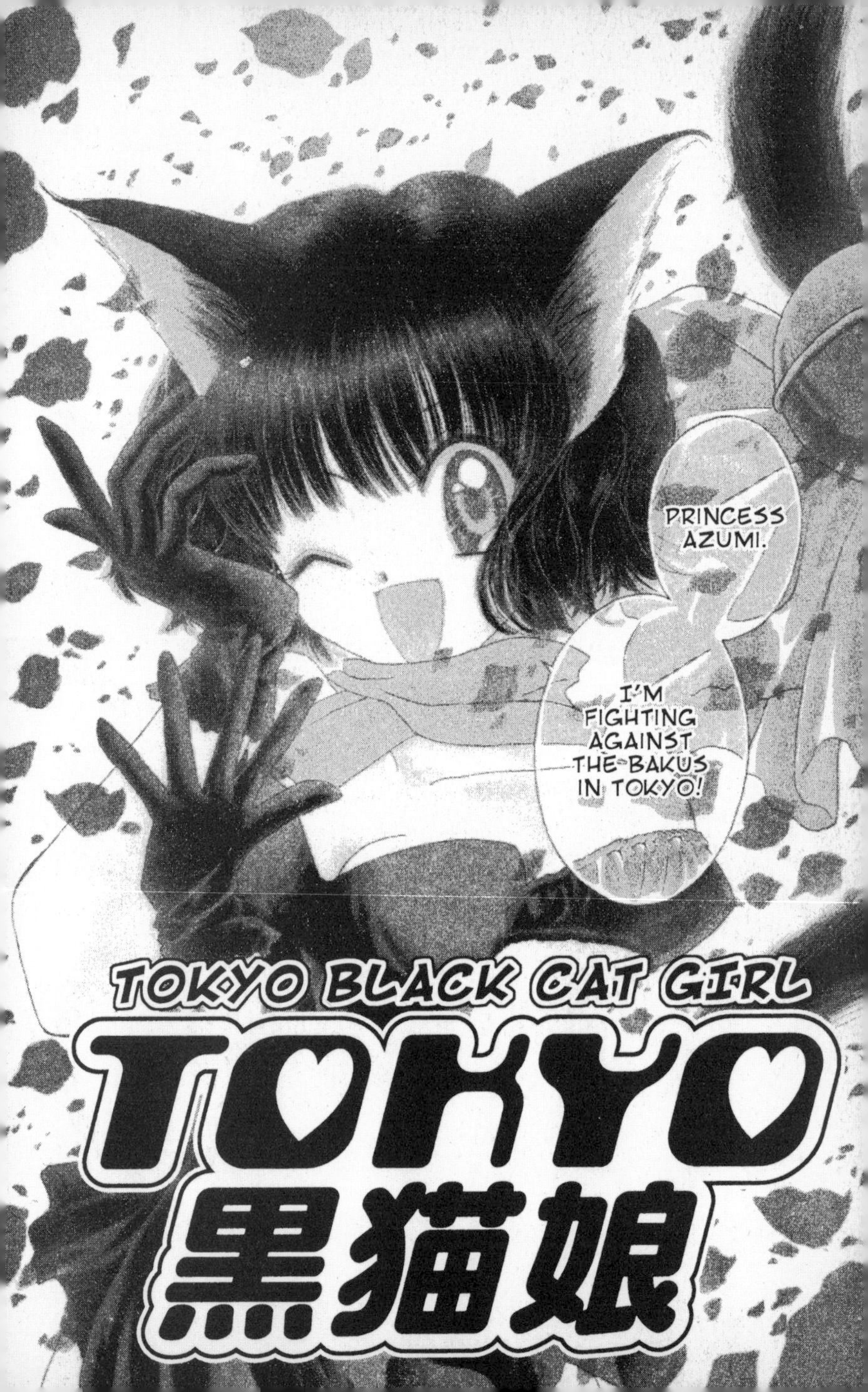
PRINCESS AZUMI.
I'M FIGHTING AGAINST THE BAKUS IN TOKYO!
TOKYO BLACK CAT GIRL
TOKYO
黒猫娘

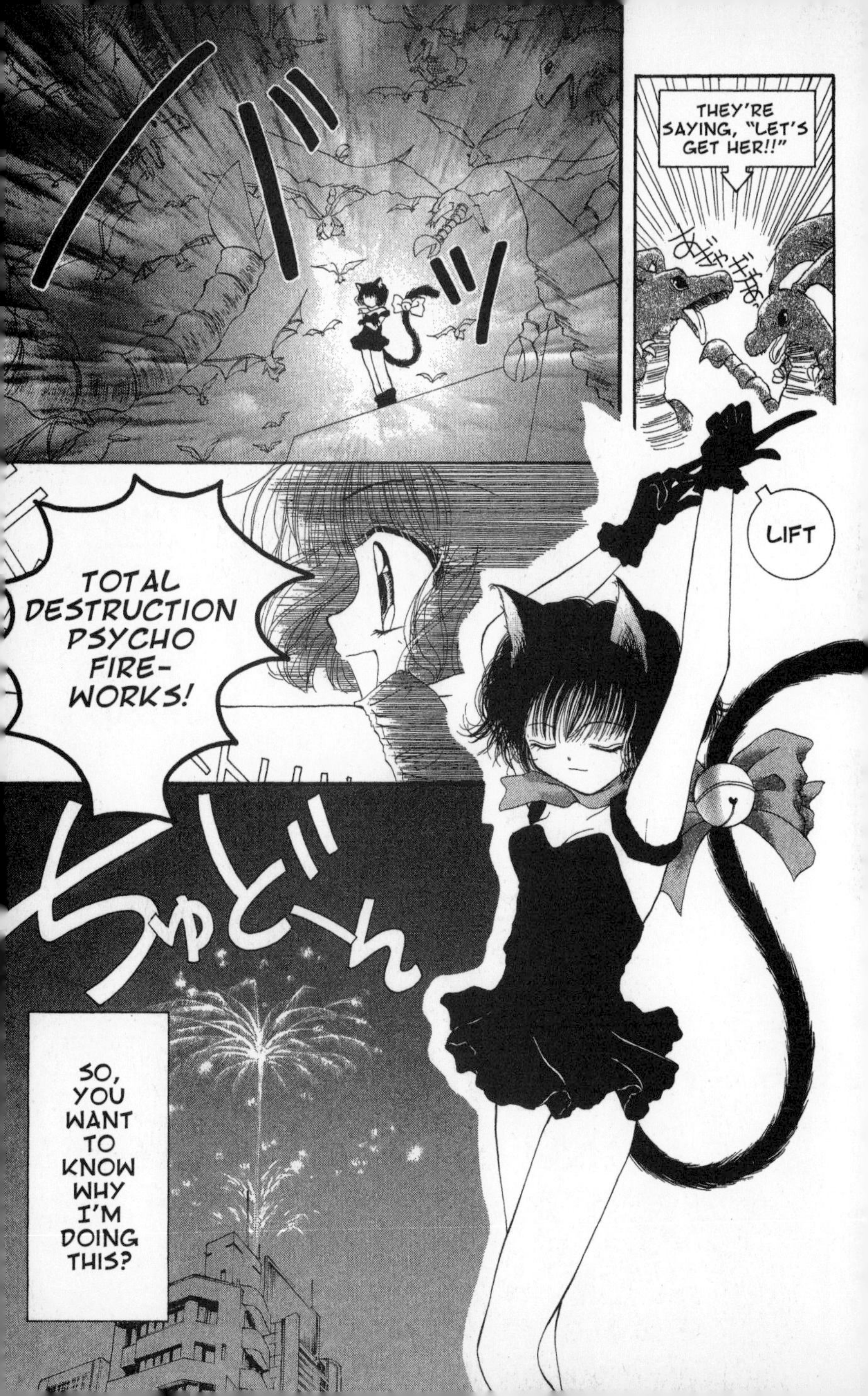
THEY'RE SAYING, "LET'S GET HER!!"
LIFT
TOTAL DESTRUCTION PSYCHO FIRE-WORKS!
ちゅどーん
SO, YOU WANT TO KNOW WHY I'M DOING THIS?

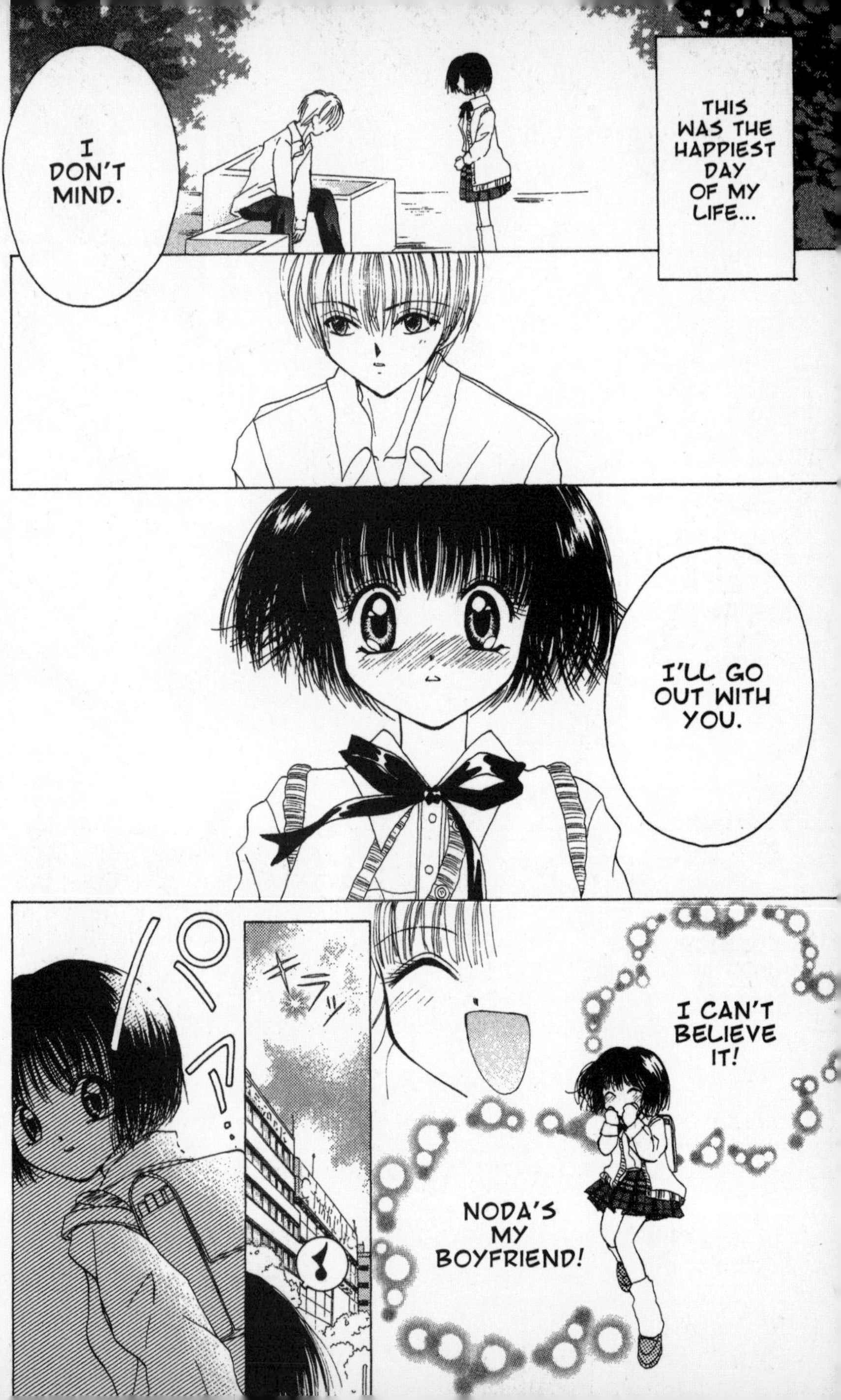
THIS WAS THE HAPPIEST DAY OF MY LIFE...
I DON'T MIND.
I'LL GO OUT WITH YOU.
I CAN'T BELIEVE IT!
NODA'S MY BOYFRIEND!
キラッ
パア…

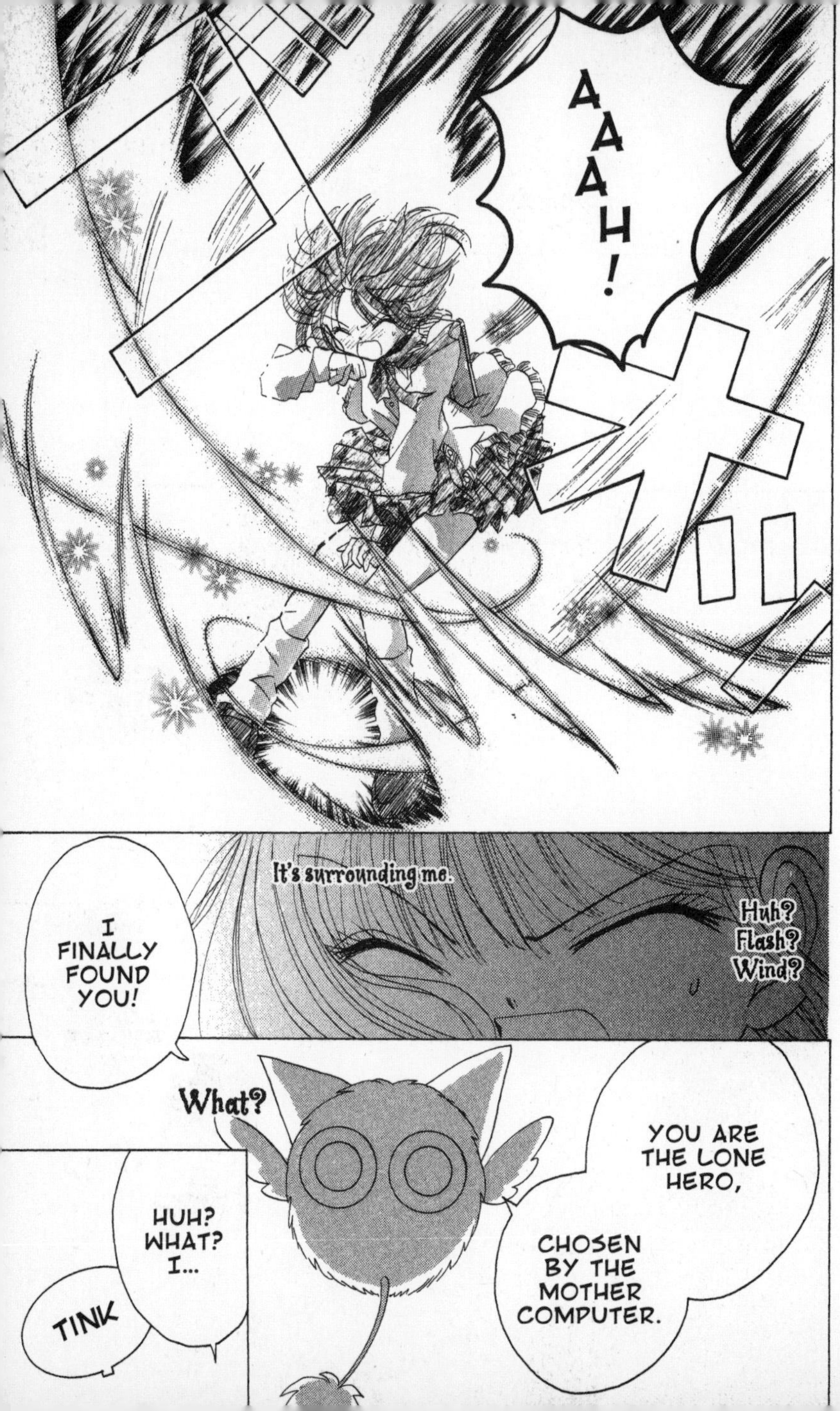
AAAAH!
Huh? Flash? Wind?
It's surrounding me.
I FINALLY FOUND YOU!
YOU ARE THE LONE HERO,
CHOSEN BY THE MOTHER COMPUTER.
What?
HUH? WHAT? I...
TINK

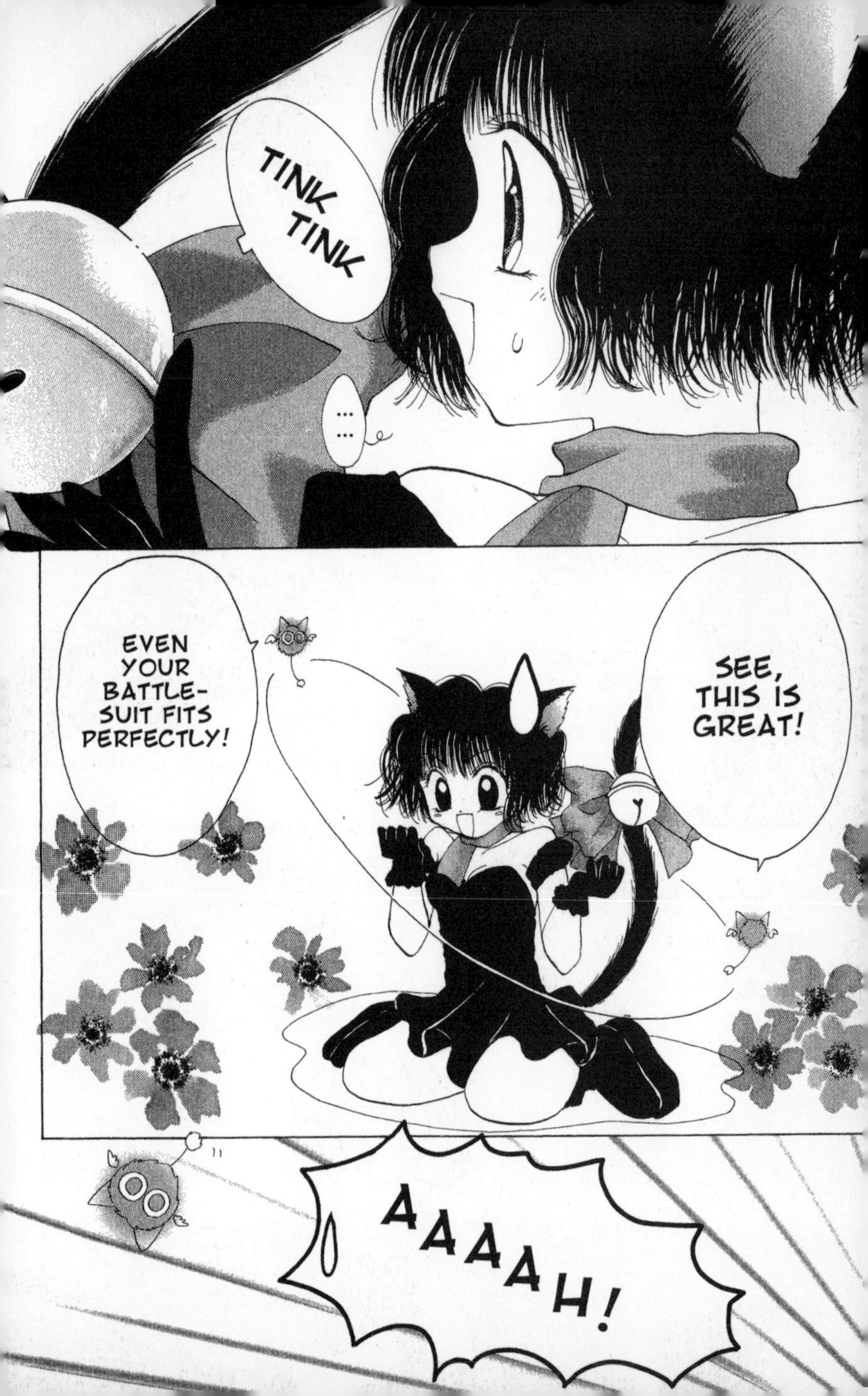
TINK TINK
......
SEE, THIS IS GREAT!
EVEN YOUR BATTLE-SUIT FITS PERFECTLY!
AAAAAH!

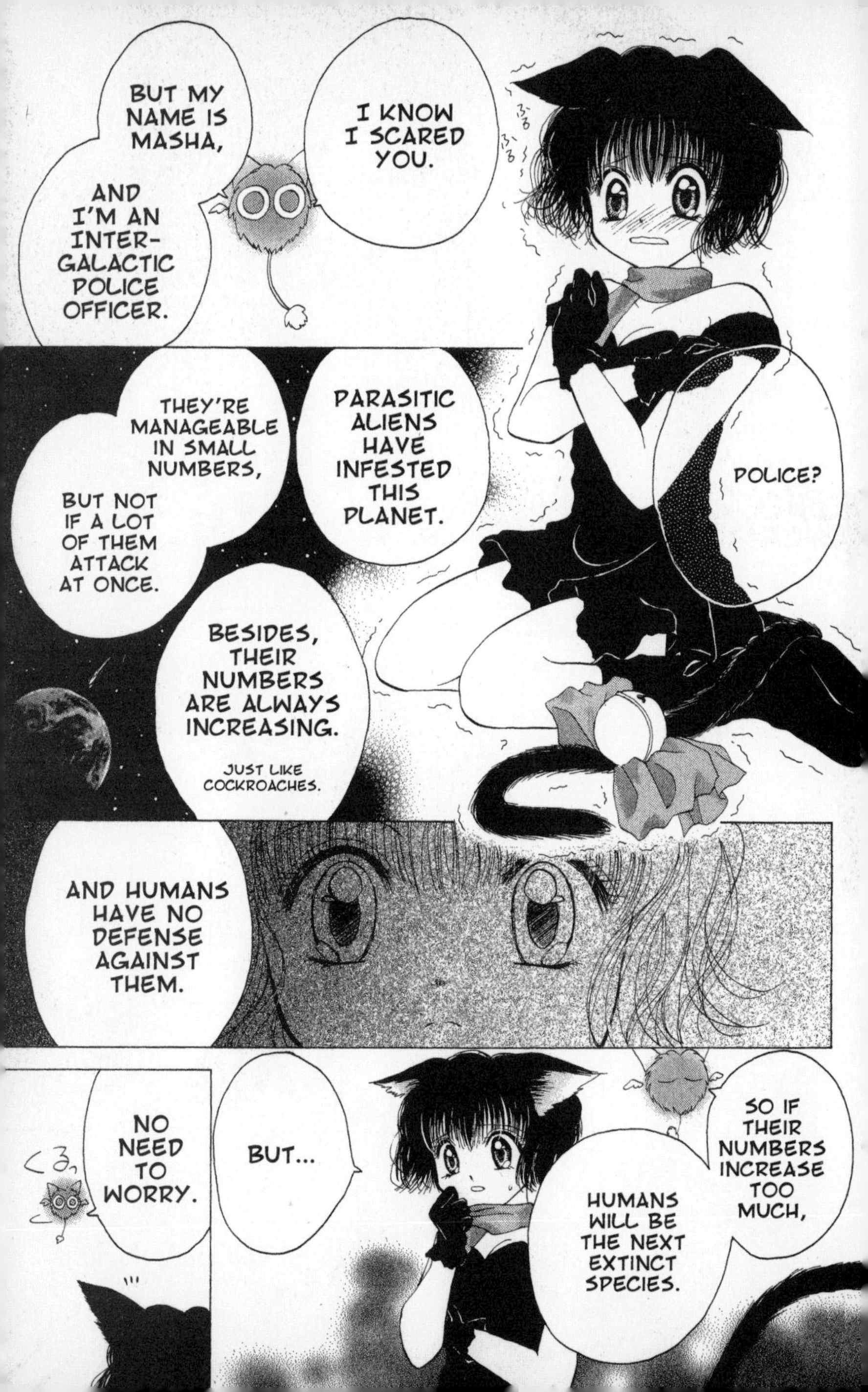
I KNOW I SCARED YOU.
BUT MY NAME IS MASHA,
AND I'M AN INTER-GALACTIC POLICE OFFICER.
POLICE?
PARASITIC ALIENS HAVE INFESTED THIS PLANET.
THEY'RE MANAGEABLE IN SMALL NUMBERS,
BUT NOT IF A LOT OF THEM ATTACK AT ONCE.
BESIDES, THEIR NUMBERS ARE ALWAYS INCREASING.
JUST LIKE COCKROACHES.
AND HUMANS HAVE NO DEFENSE AGAINST THEM.
SO IF THEIR NUMBERS INCREASE TOO MUCH,
HUMANS WILL BE THE NEXT EXTINCT SPECIES.
BUT...
NO NEED TO WORRY.
くる

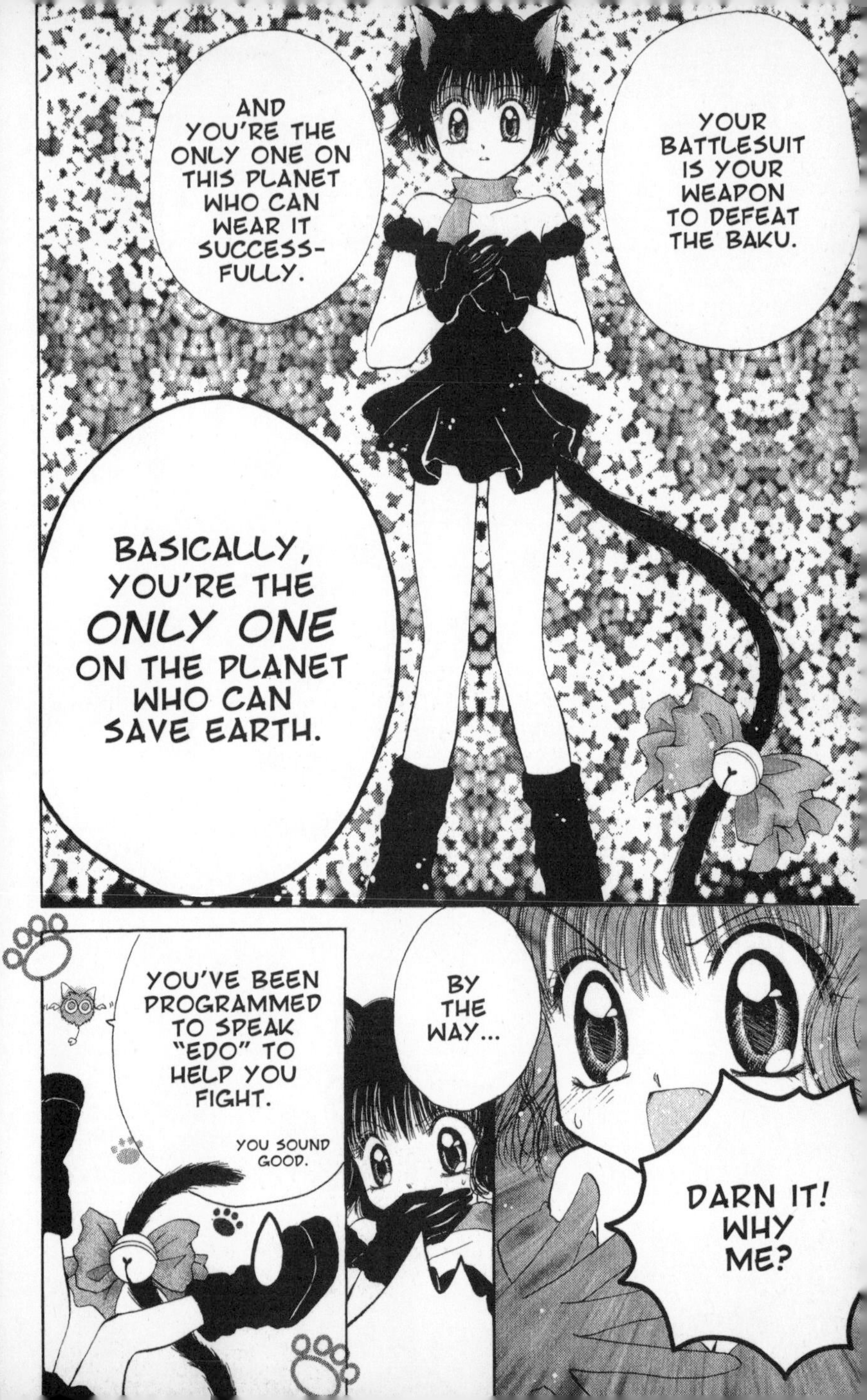
YOUR BATTLESUIT IS YOUR WEAPON TO DEFEAT THE BAKU.
AND YOU'RE THE ONLY ONE ON THIS PLANET WHO CAN WEAR IT SUCCESS-FULLY.
BASICALLY, YOU'RE THE ONLY ONE ON THE PLANET WHO CAN SAVE EARTH.
DARN IT! WHY ME?
BY THE WAY...
YOU'VE BEEN PROGRAMMED TO SPEAK "EDO" TO HELP YOU FIGHT.
YOU SOUND GOOD.

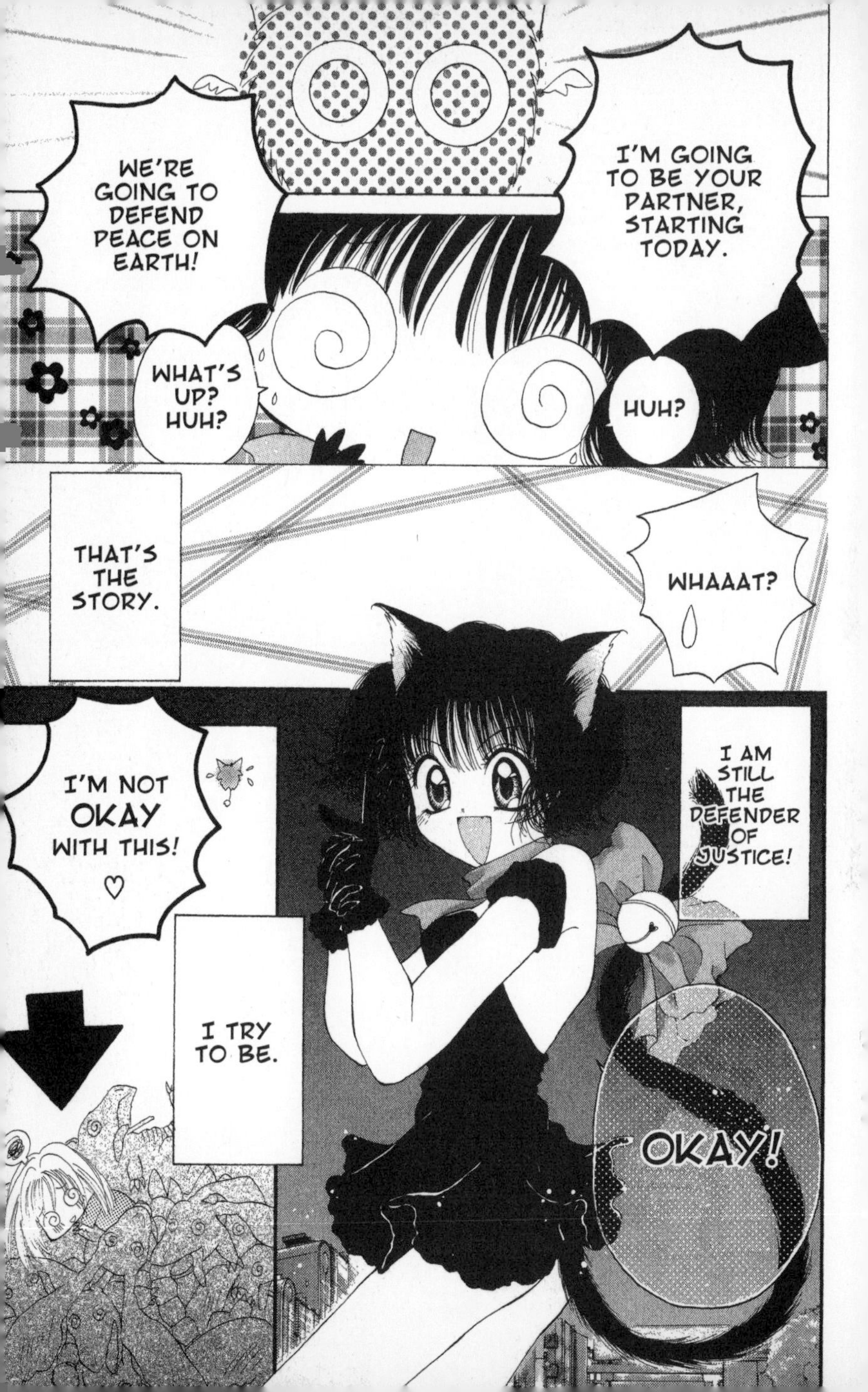
I'M GOING TO BE YOUR PARTNER, STARTING TODAY.
WE'RE GOING TO DEFEND PEACE ON EARTH!
HUH?
WHAT'S UP? HUH?
WHAAAT?
THAT'S THE STORY.
I AM STILL THE DEFENDER OF JUSTICE!
OKAY!
I TRY TO BE.
I'M NOT OKAY WITH THIS! ♡

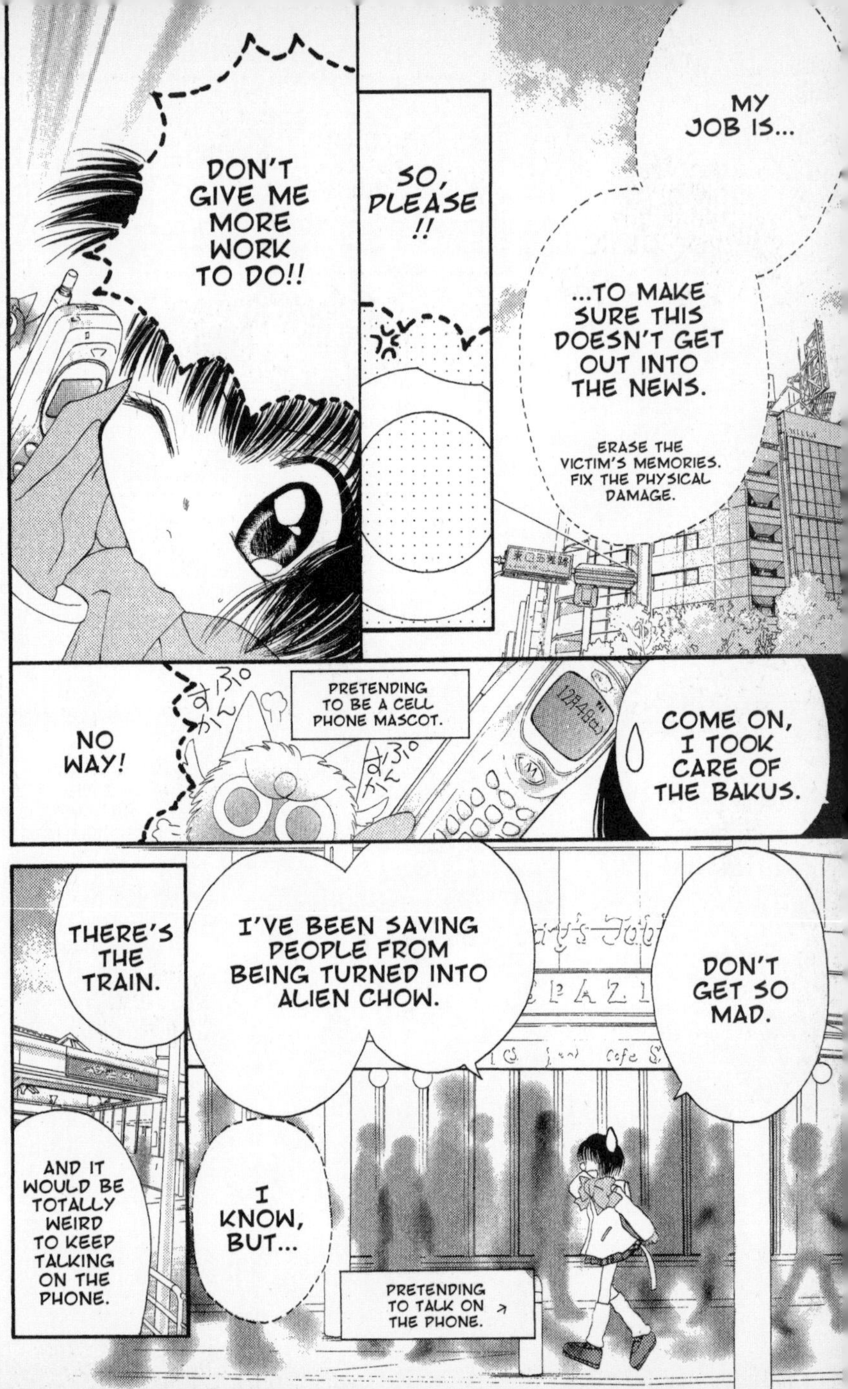
MY JOB IS...
...TO MAKE SURE THIS DOESN'T GET OUT INTO THE NEWS.
ERASE THE VICTIM'S MEMORIES. FIX THE PHYSICAL DAMAGE.
SO, PLEASE !!
DON'T GIVE ME MORE WORK TO DO!!
COME ON, I TOOK CARE OF THE BAKUS.
PRETENDING TO BE A CELL PHONE MASCOT.
NO WAY!
DON'T GET SO MAD.
I'VE BEEN SAVING PEOPLE FROM BEING TURNED INTO ALIEN CHOW.
THERE'S THE TRAIN.
PRETENDING TO TALK ON THE PHONE.
I KNOW, BUT...
AND IT WOULD BE TOTALLY WEIRD TO KEEP TALKING ON THE PHONE.

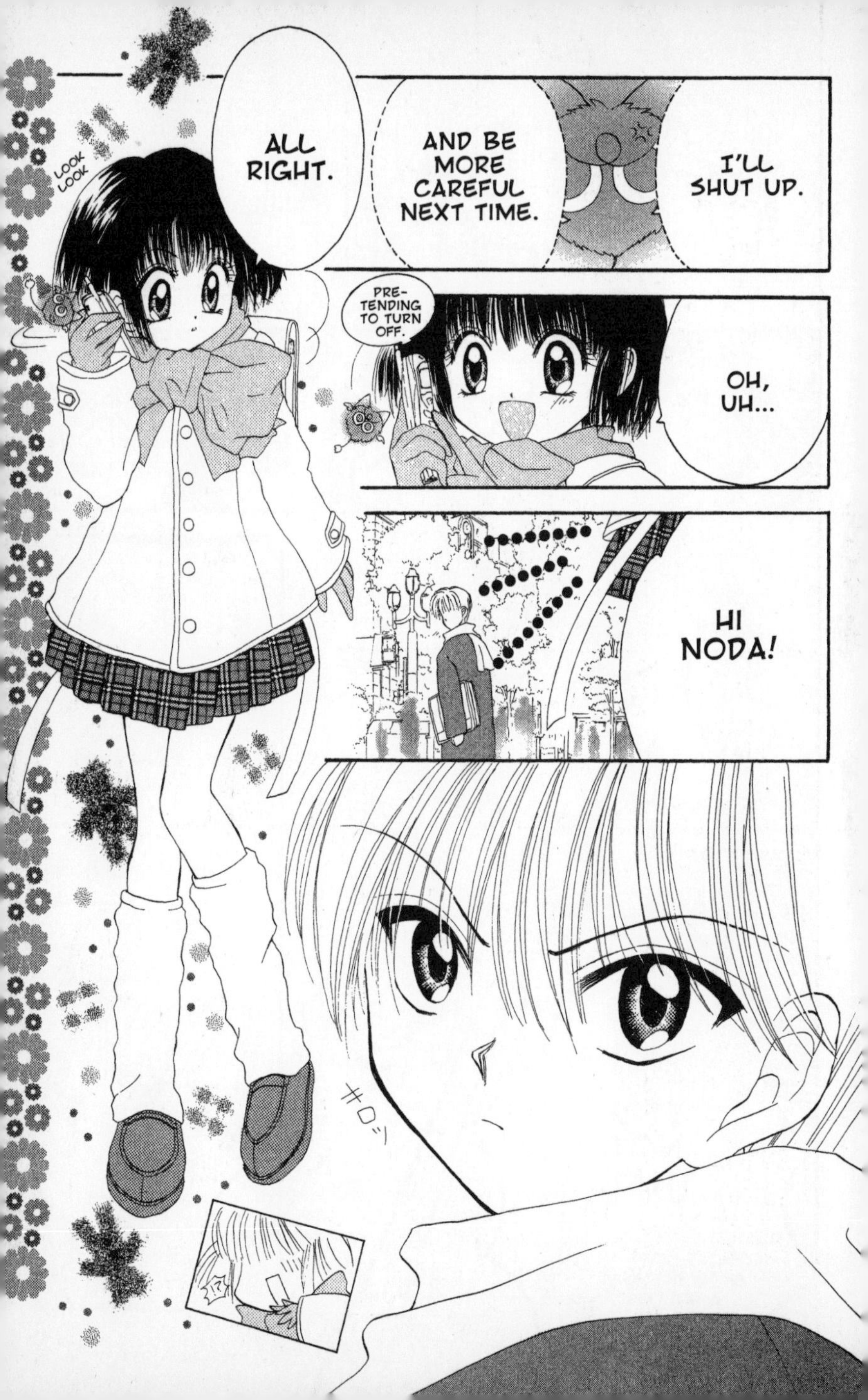
I'LL SHUT UP.
AND BE MORE CAREFUL NEXT TIME.
ALL RIGHT.
LOOK LOOK
OH, UH...
PRE-TENDING TO TURN OFF.
HI NODA!
キロッ
!?

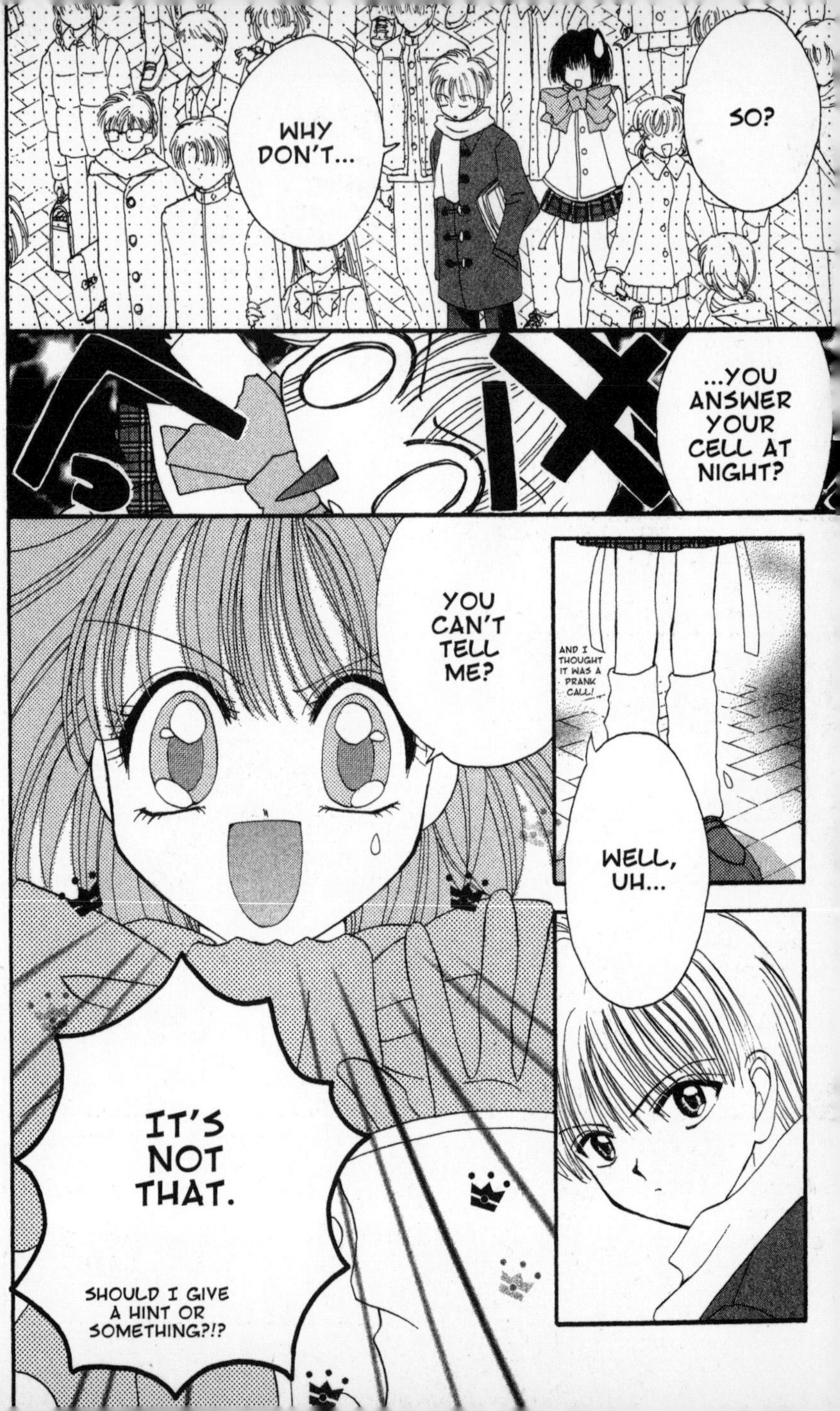
SO?
WHY DON'T...
...YOU ANSWER YOUR CELL AT NIGHT?
AND I THOUGHT IT WAS A PRANK CALL!
WELL, UH...
YOU CAN'T TELL ME?
IT'S NOT THAT.
SHOULD I GIVE A HINT OR SOMETHING?!?

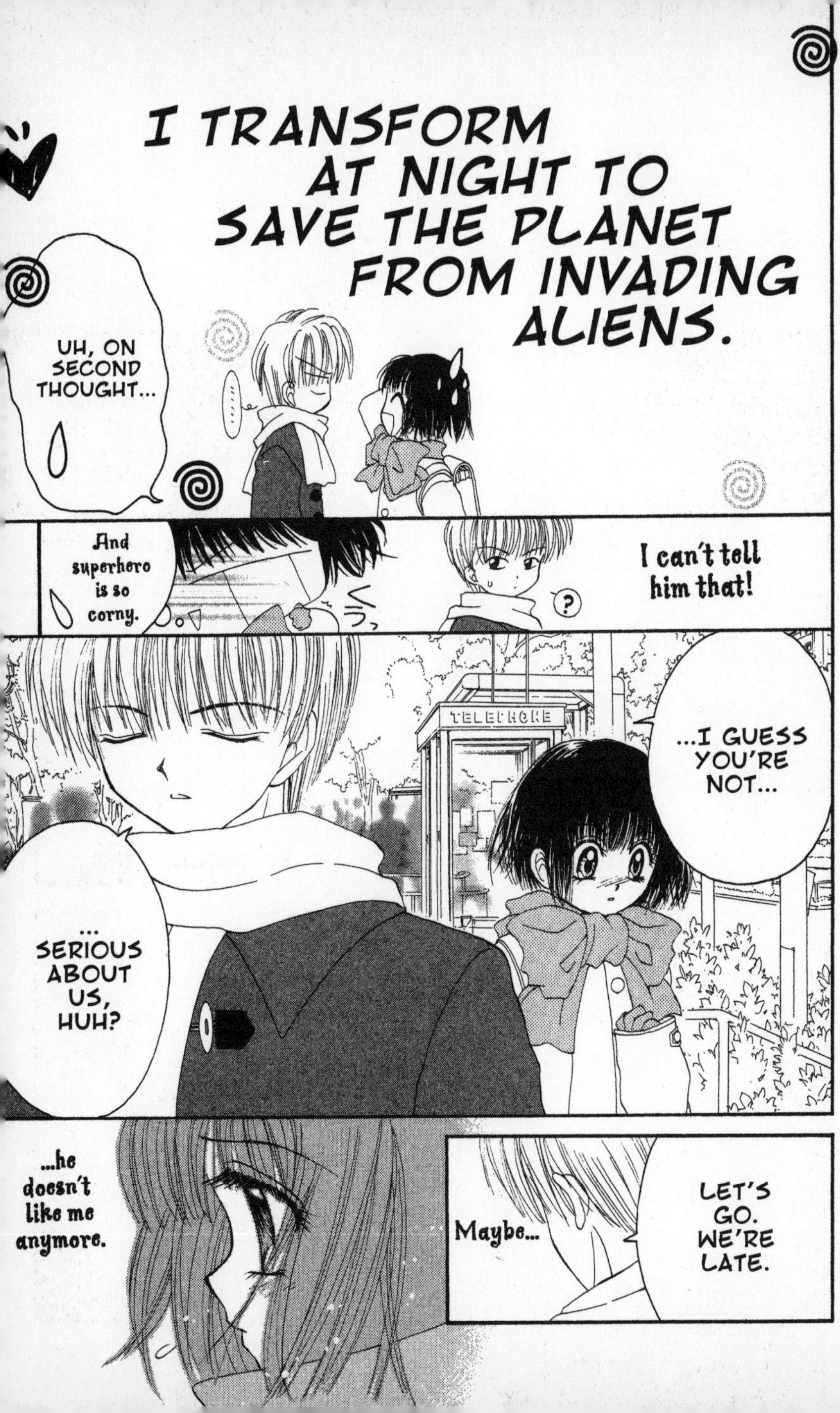
I TRANSFORM AT NIGHT TO SAVE THE PLANET FROM INVADING ALIENS.
UH, ON SECOND THOUGHT...
I can't tell him that!
And superhero is so corny.
TELEPHONE
...I GUESS YOU'RE NOT...
...SERIOUS ABOUT US, HUH?
LET'S GO. WE'RE LATE.
Maybe...
...he doesn't like me anymore.

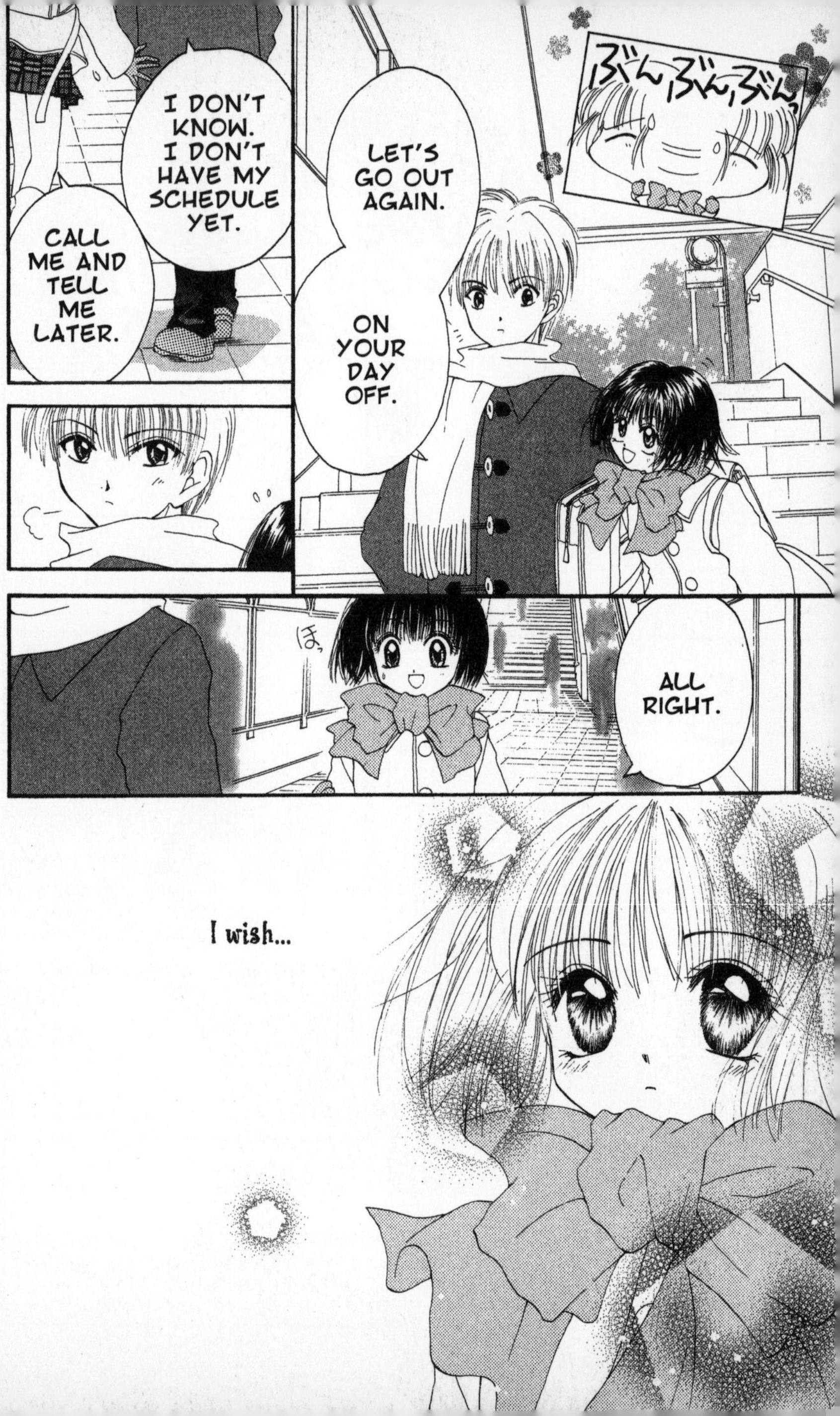
ぶんぶんぶん
LET'S GO OUT AGAIN.
ON YOUR DAY OFF.
I DON'T KNOW. I DON'T HAVE MY SCHEDULE YET.
CALL ME AND TELL ME LATER.
ALL RIGHT.
ほっ
I wish...

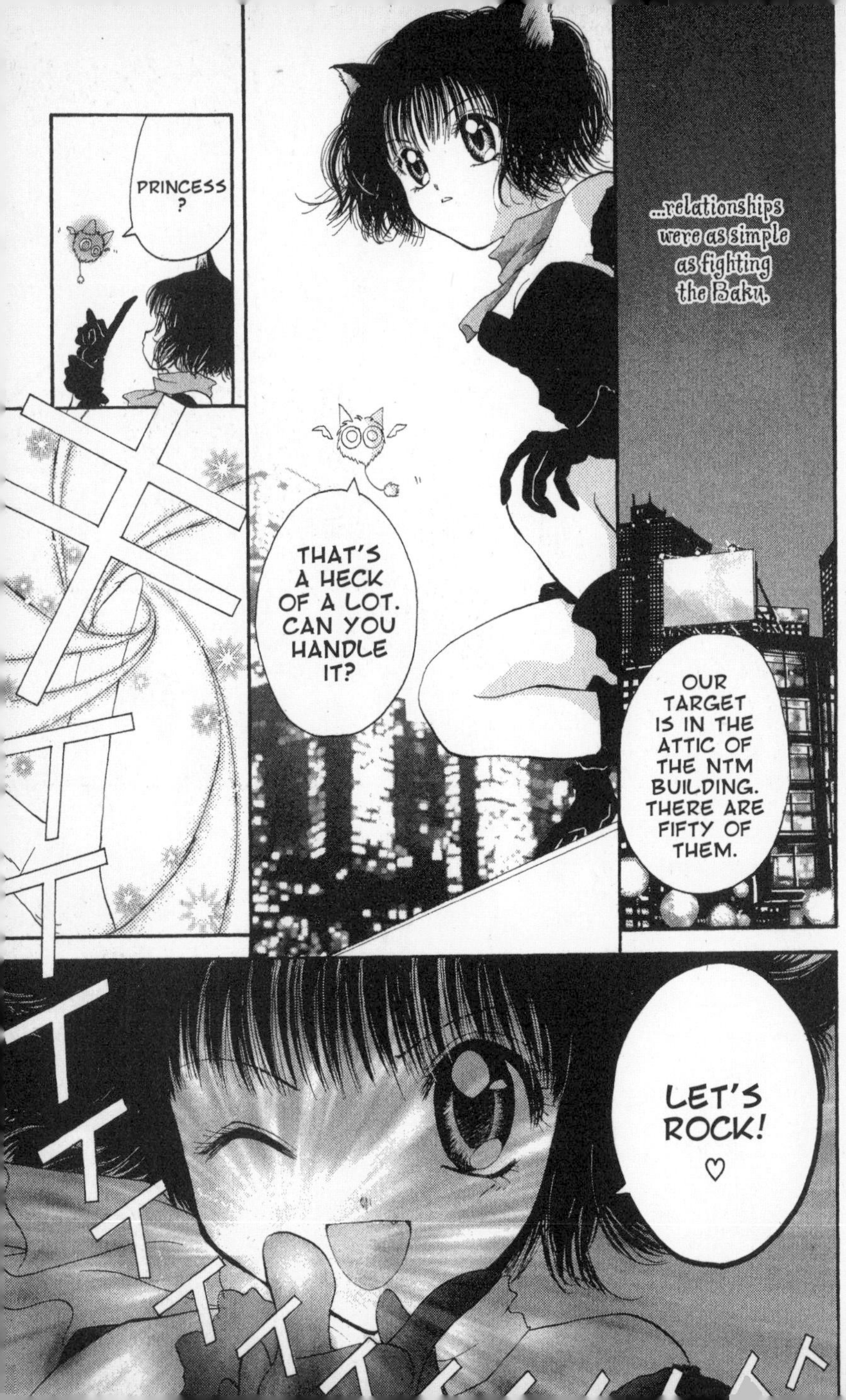
...relationships were as simple as fighting the Baku.
OUR TARGET IS IN THE ATTIC OF THE NTM BUILDING. THERE ARE FIFTY OF THEM.
THAT'S A HECK OF A LOT. CAN YOU HANDLE IT?
PRINCESS ?
LET'S ROCK! ♡

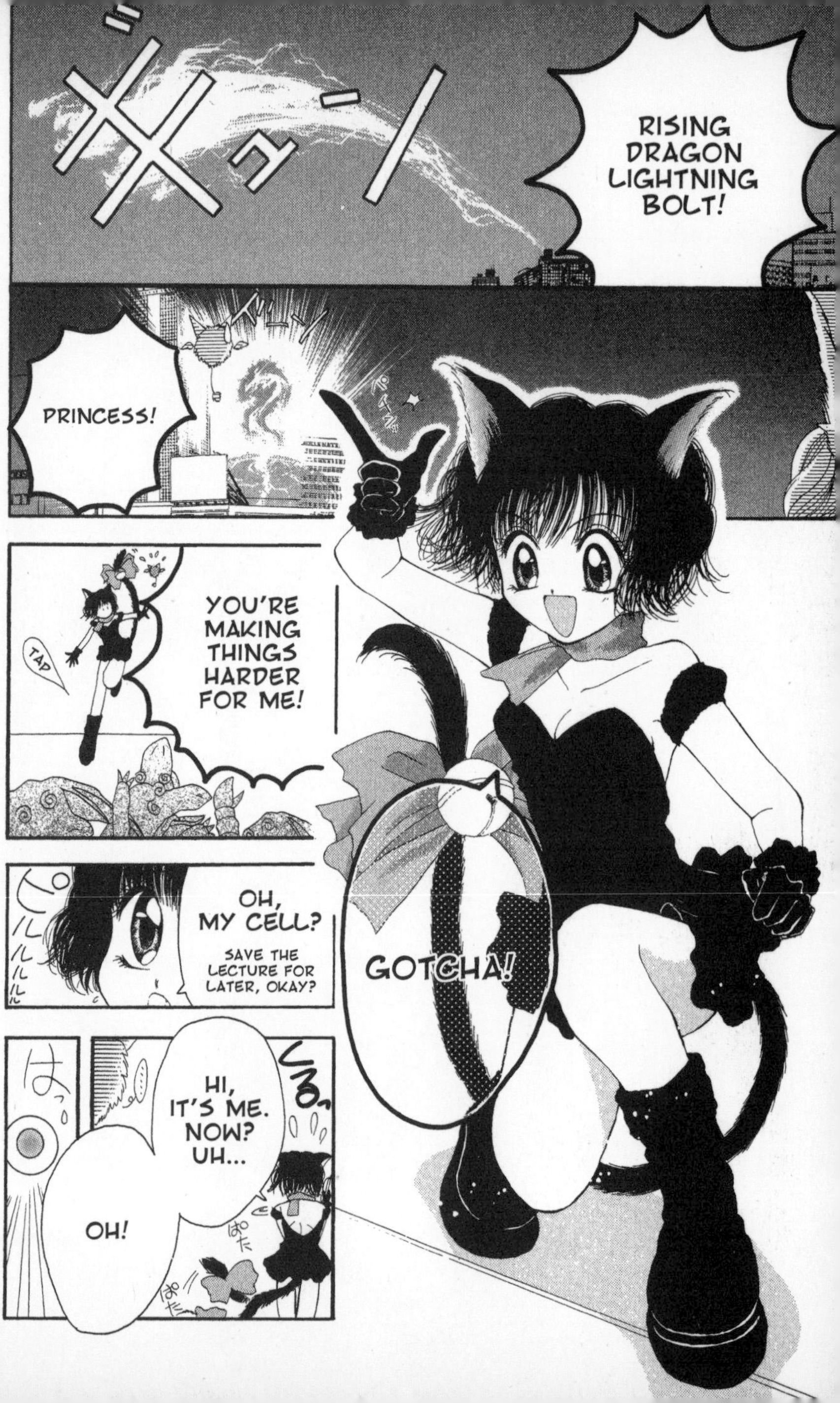
RISING DRAGON LIGHTNING BOLT!
PRINCESS!
GOTCHA!
YOU'RE MAKING THINGS HARDER FOR ME!
TAP
OH, MY CELL?
SAVE THE LECTURE FOR LATER, OKAY?
HI, IT'S ME. NOW? UH...
OH!

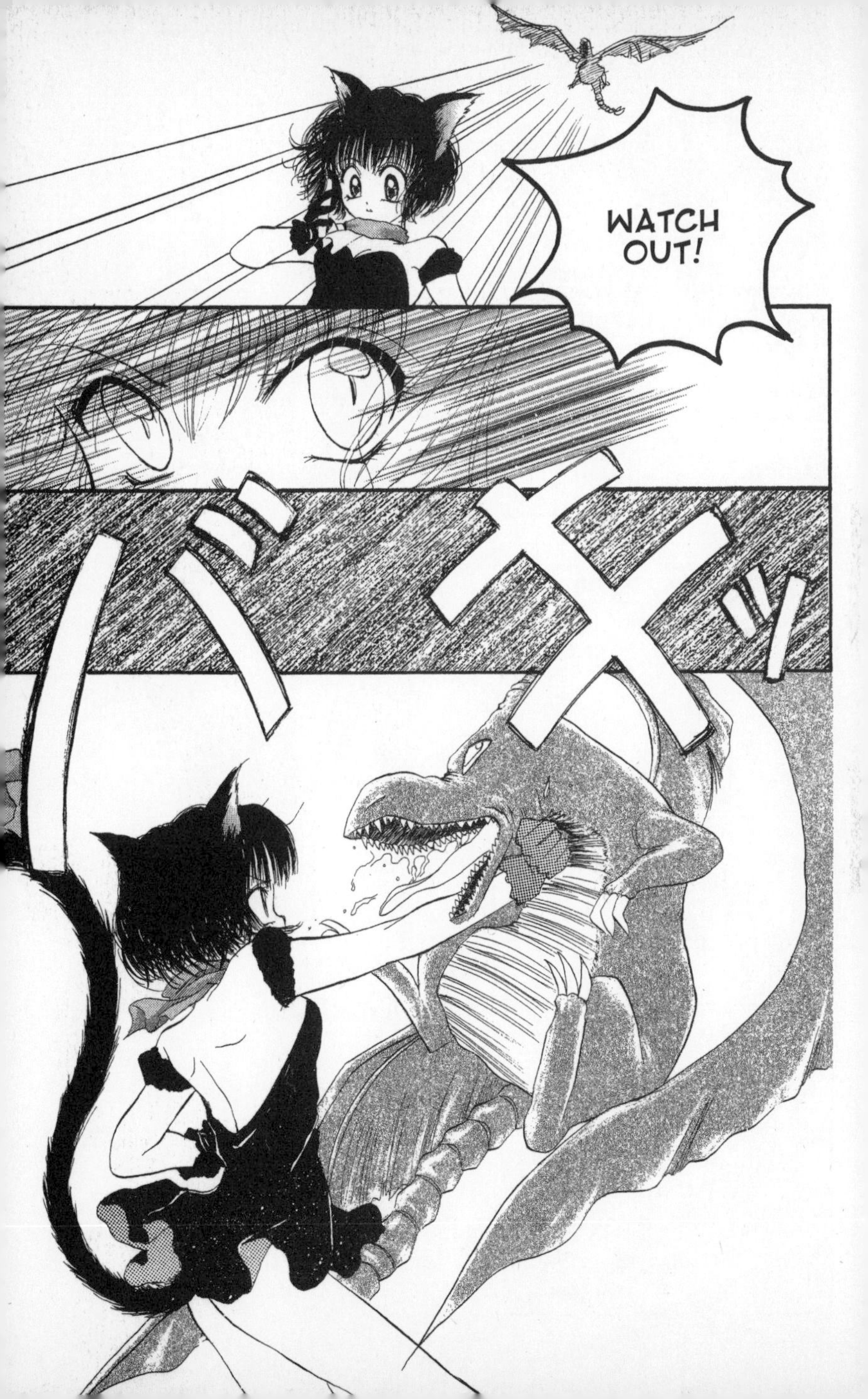
WATCH OUT!

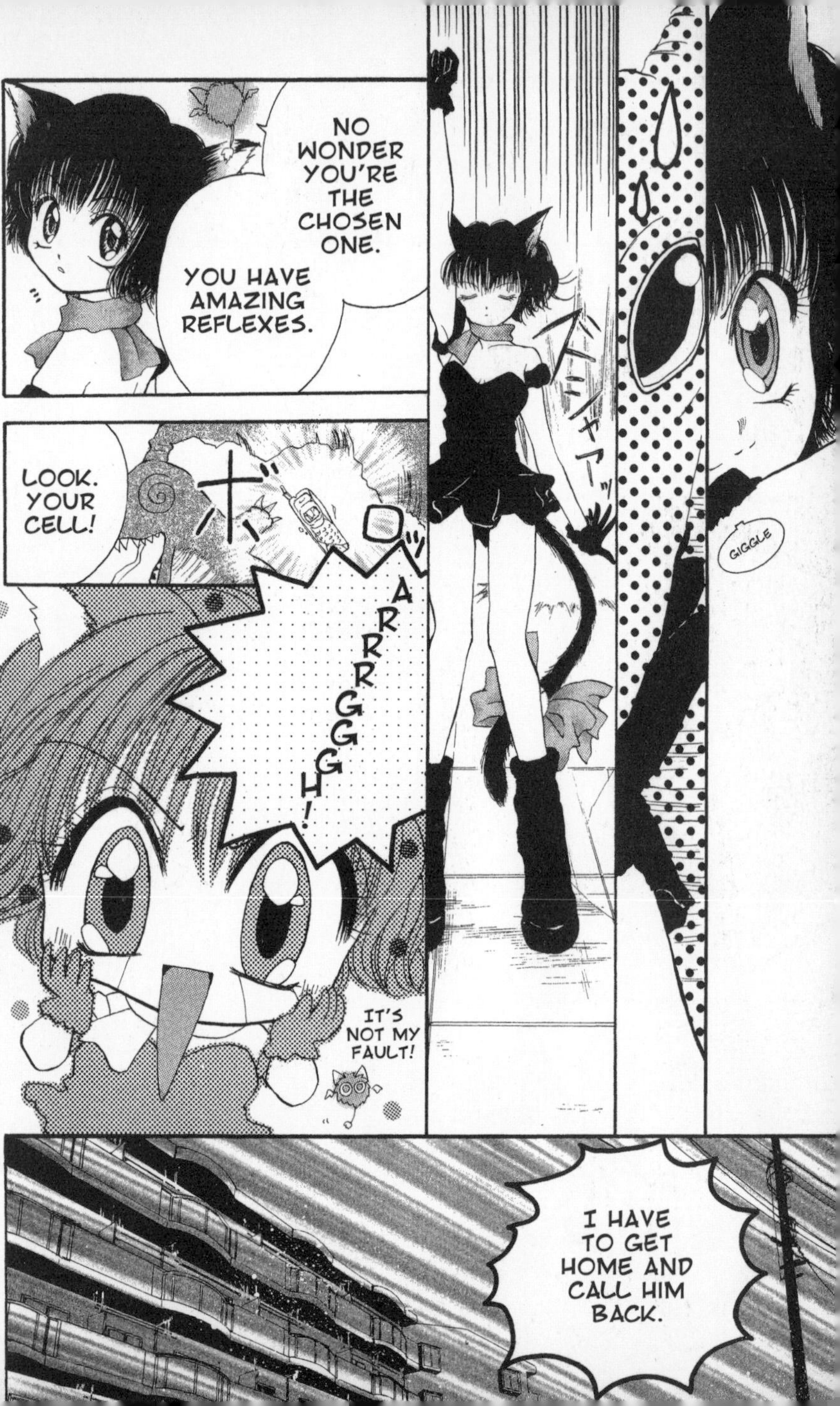
GIGGLE
NO WONDER YOU'RE THE CHOSEN ONE.
YOU HAVE AMAZING REFLEXES.
LOOK. YOUR CELL!
ARRRRGGGGH!
IT'S NOT MY FAULT!
I HAVE TO GET HOME AND CALL HIM BACK.

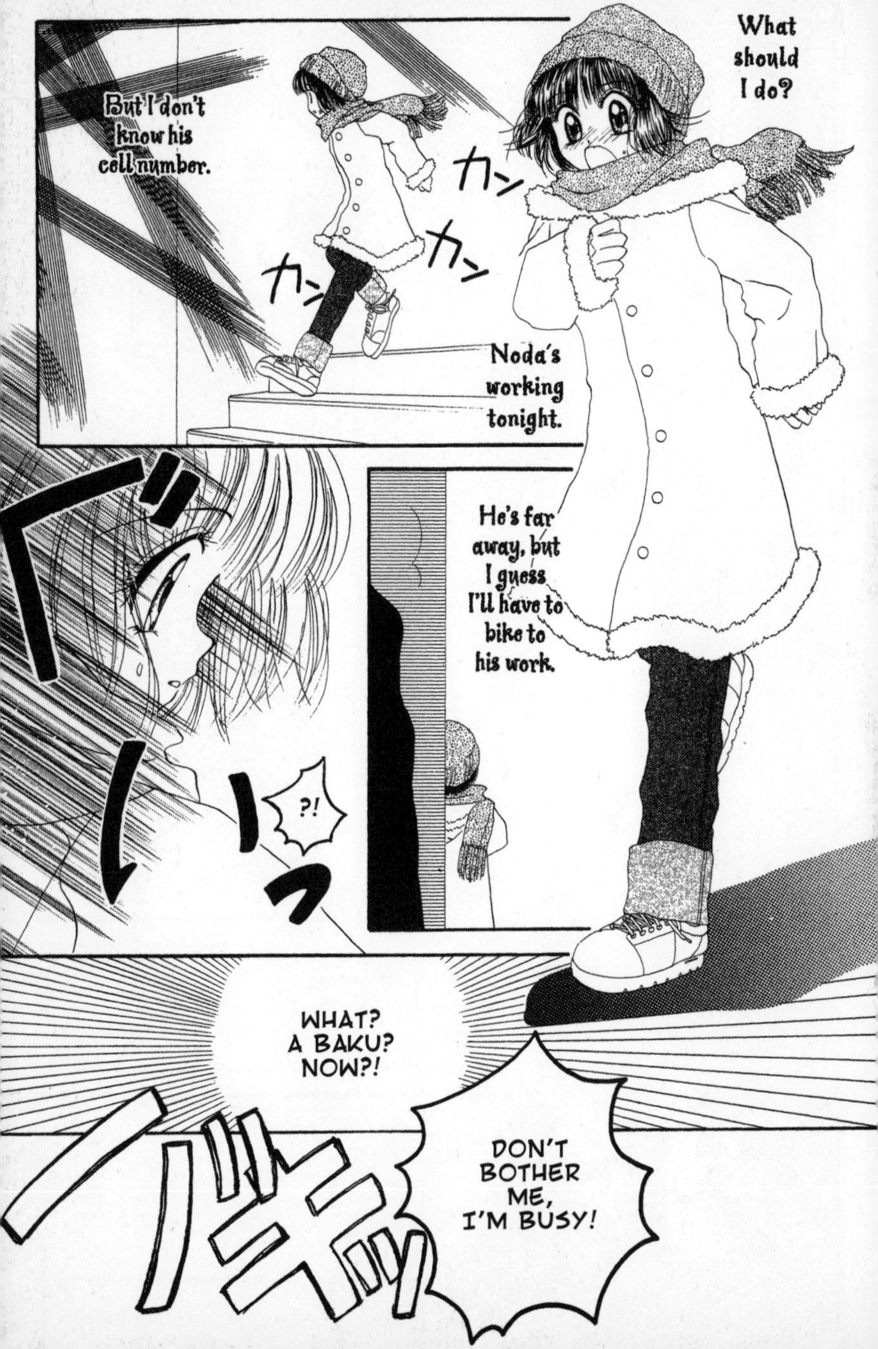
What should I do?
Noda's working tonight.
But I don't know his cell number.
カン
カン
カン
He's far away, but I guess I'll have to bike to his work.
?!
WHAT? A BAKU? NOW?!
DON'T BOTHER ME, I'M BUSY!

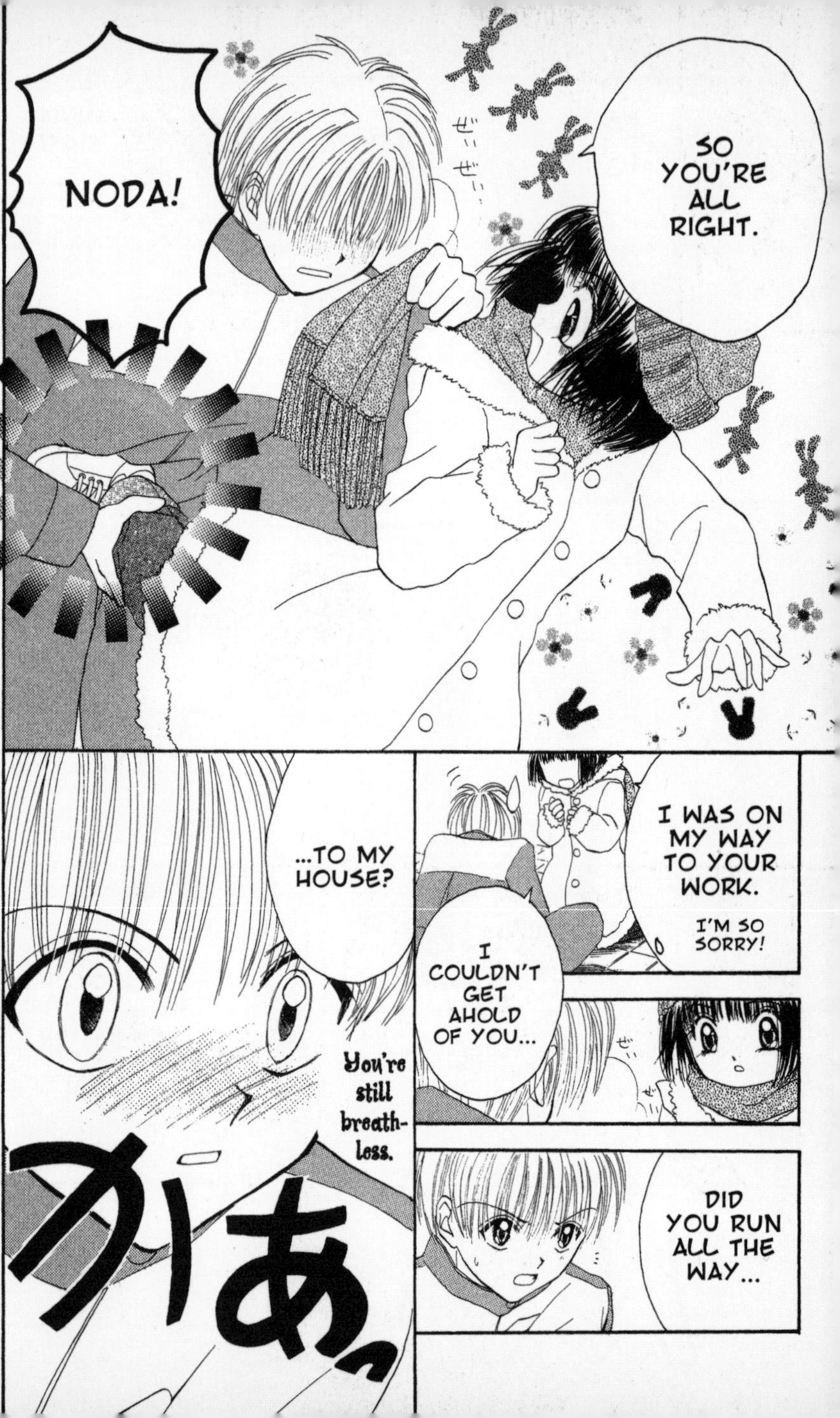
SO YOU'RE ALL RIGHT.
ぜいぜい
NODA!
I WAS ON MY WAY TO YOUR WORK.
I'M SO SORRY!
I COULDN'T GET AHOLD OF YOU...
DID YOU RUN ALL THE WAY...
...TO MY HOUSE?
You're still breath-less.
かぁ

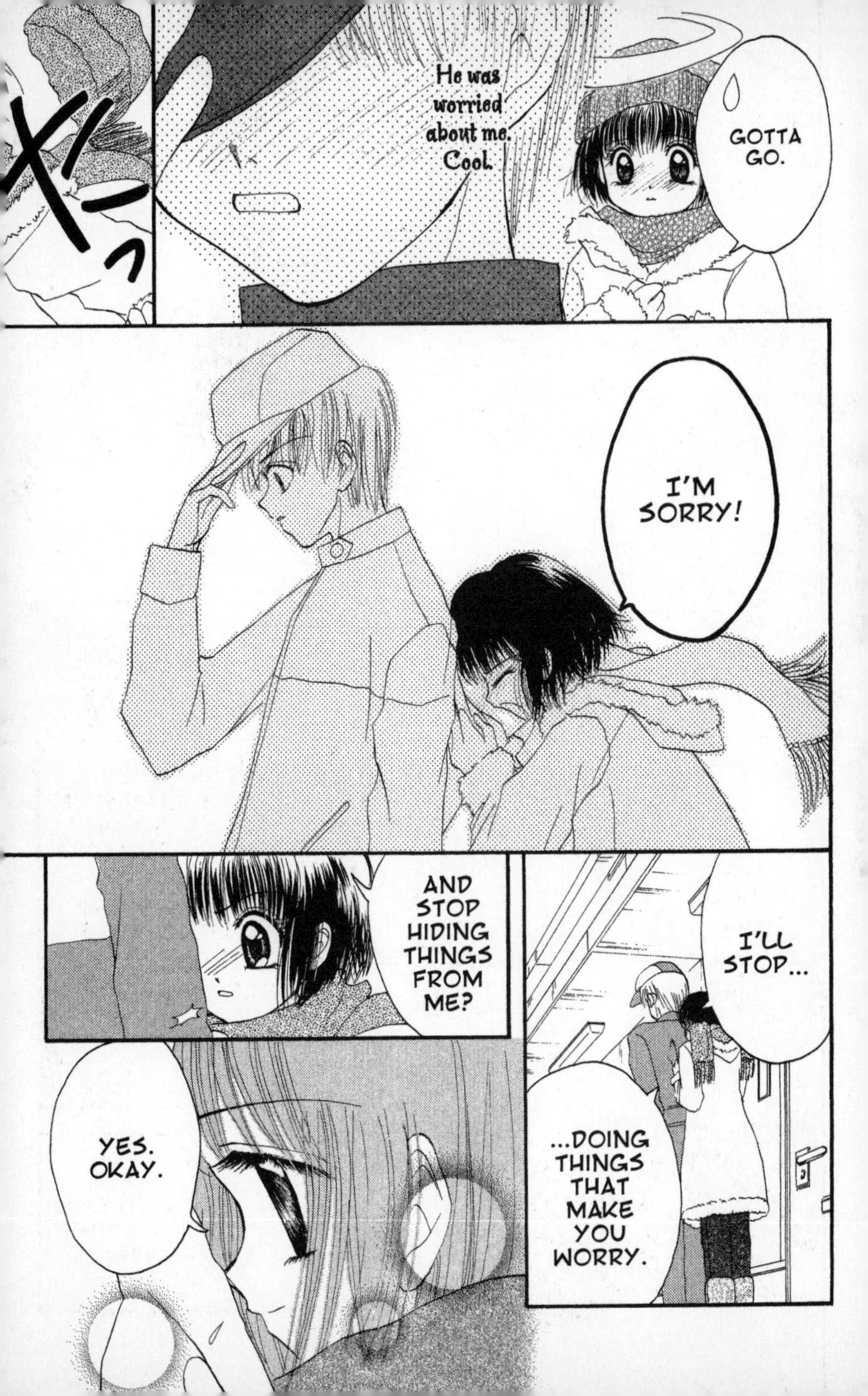
GOTTA GO.
He was worried about me. Cool.
I'M SORRY!
I'LL STOP...
...DOING THINGS THAT MAKE YOU WORRY.
AND STOP HIDING THINGS FROM ME?
YES. OKAY.

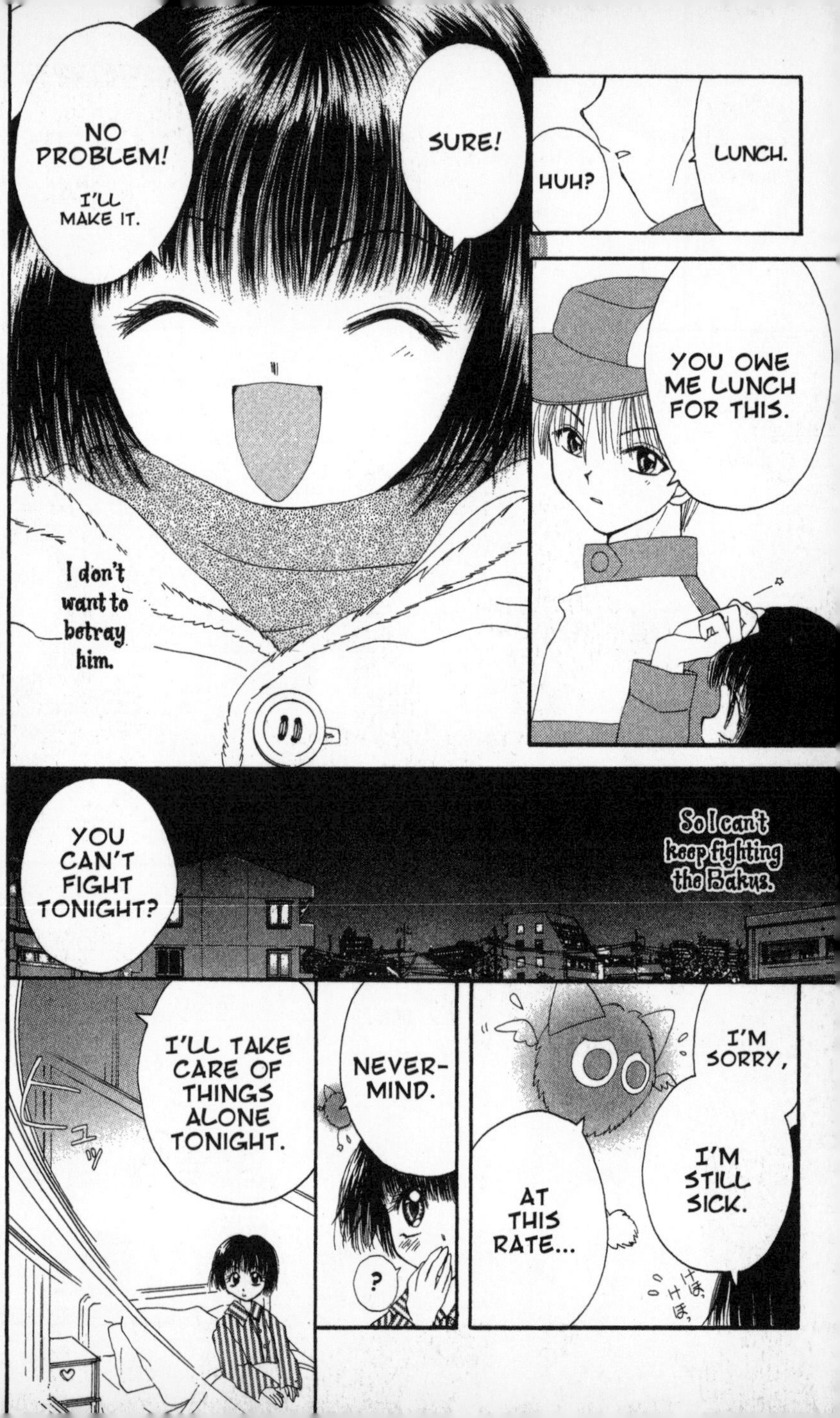
LUNCH.
HUH?
YOU OWE ME LUNCH FOR THIS.
SURE!
NO PROBLEM!
I'LL MAKE IT.
I don't want to betray him.
So I can't keep fighting the Bakus.
YOU CAN'T FIGHT TONIGHT?
I'M SORRY,
I'M STILL SICK.
けほ, けほ,
AT THIS RATE...
NEVER-MIND.
?
I'LL TAKE CARE OF THINGS ALONE TONIGHT.

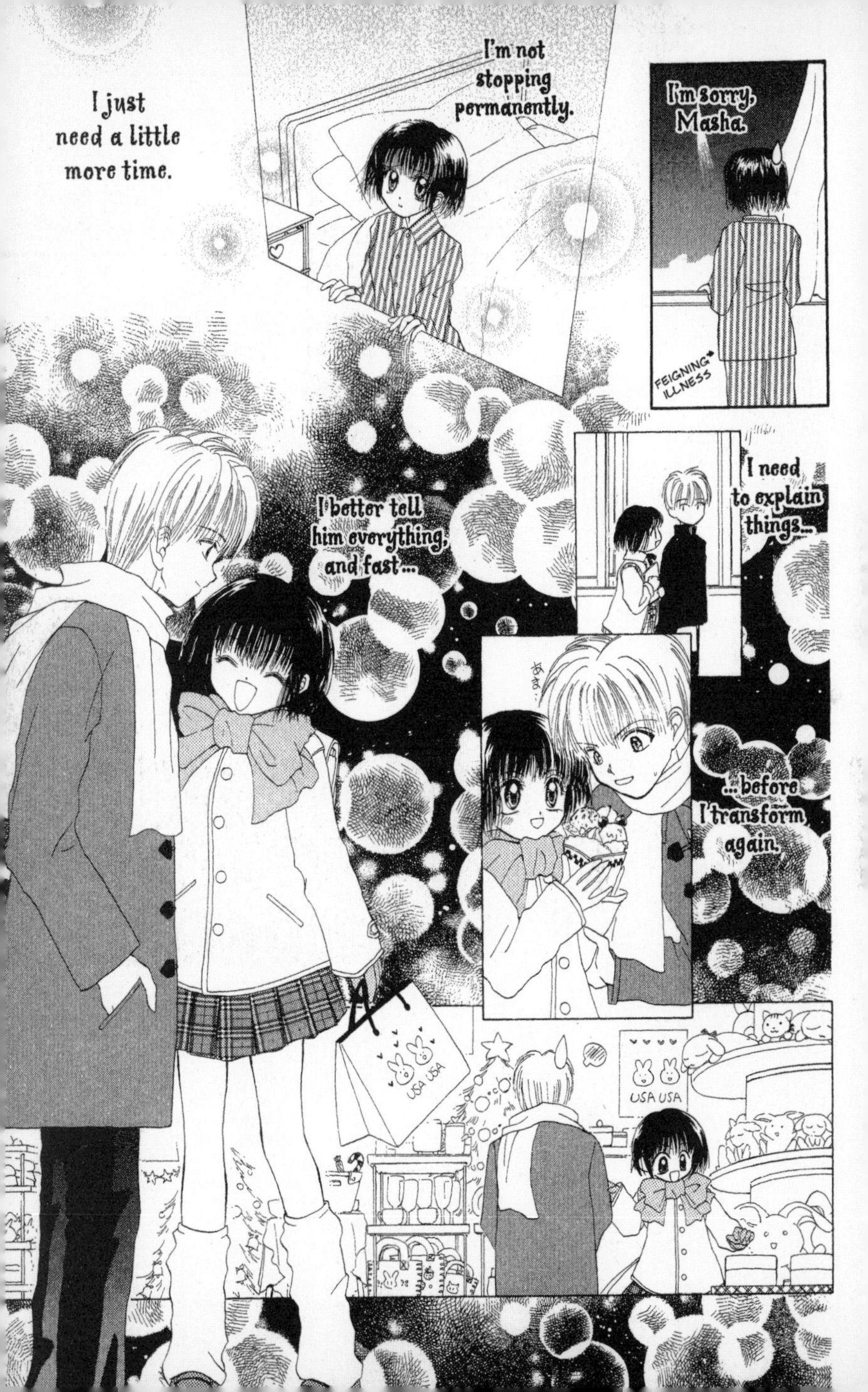
I'm sorry, Masha.
FEIGNING ILLNESS
I'm not stopping permanently.
I just need a little more time.
I need to explain things...
...before I transform again.
I better tell him everything, and fast...
USA USA
USA USA

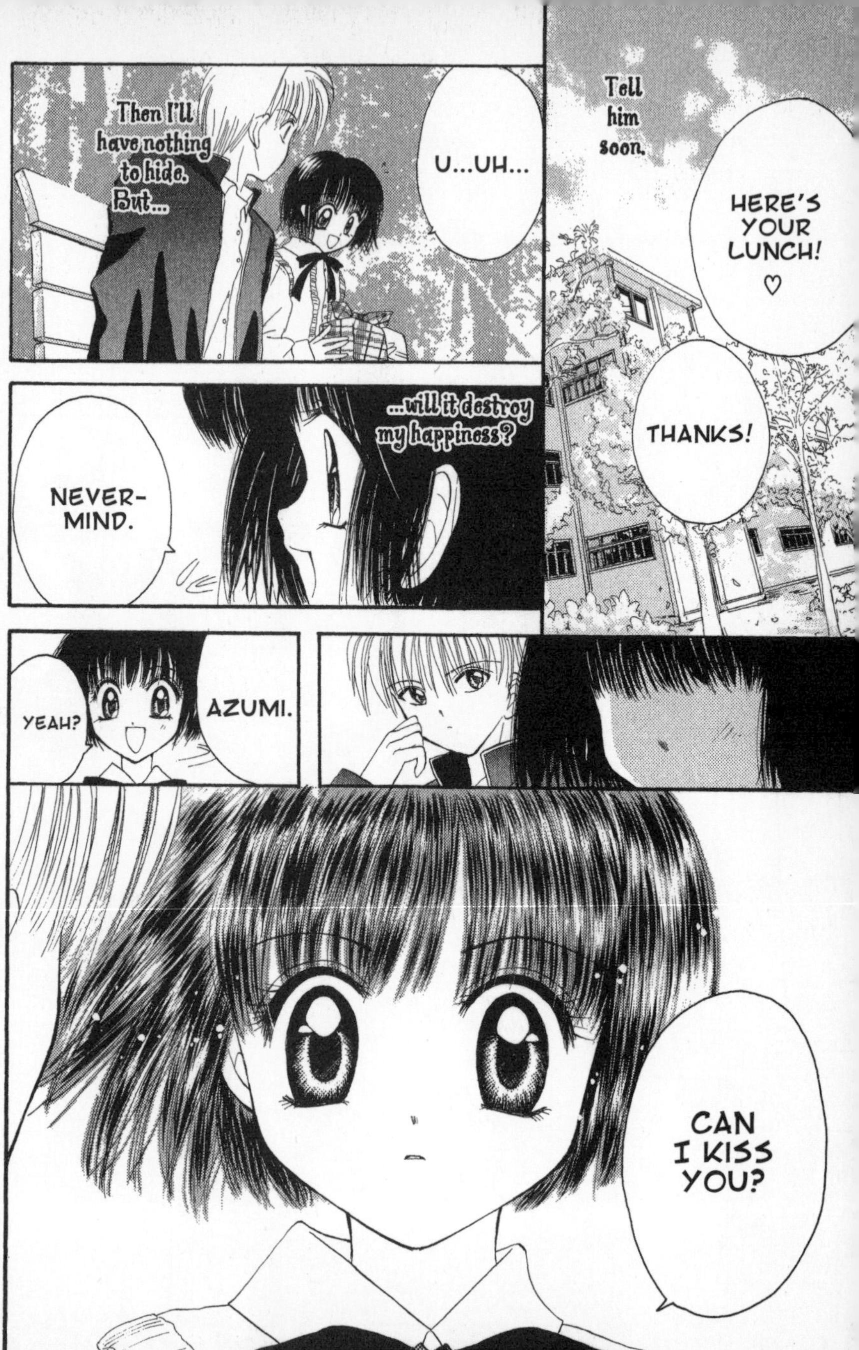
Tell him soon.
HERE'S YOUR LUNCH! ♡
THANKS!
U...UH...
Then I'll have nothing to hide. But...
...will it destroy my happiness?
NEVER-MIND.
AZUMI.
YEAH?
CAN I KISS YOU?

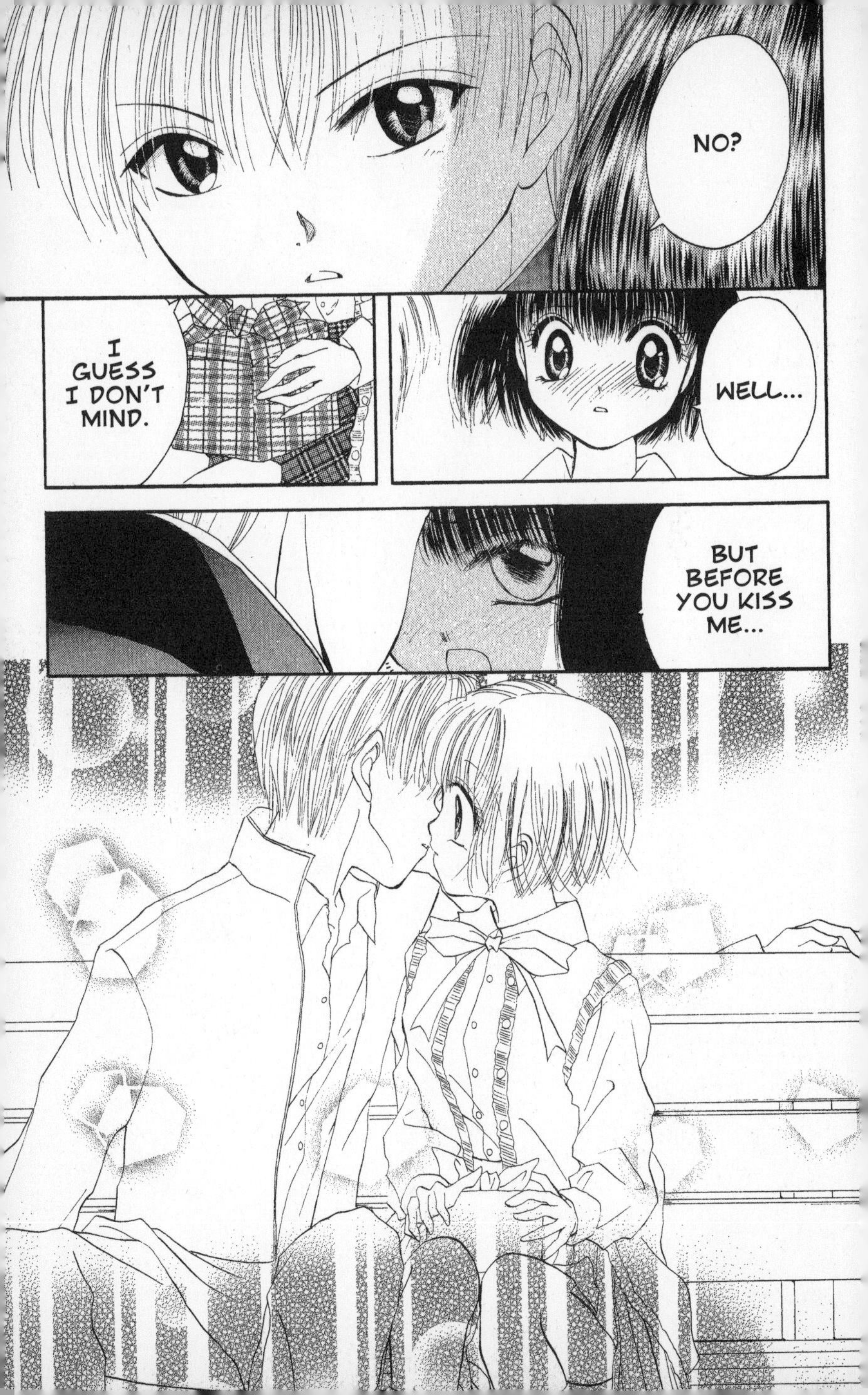
NO?
WELL...
I GUESS I DON'T MIND.
BUT BEFORE YOU KISS ME...

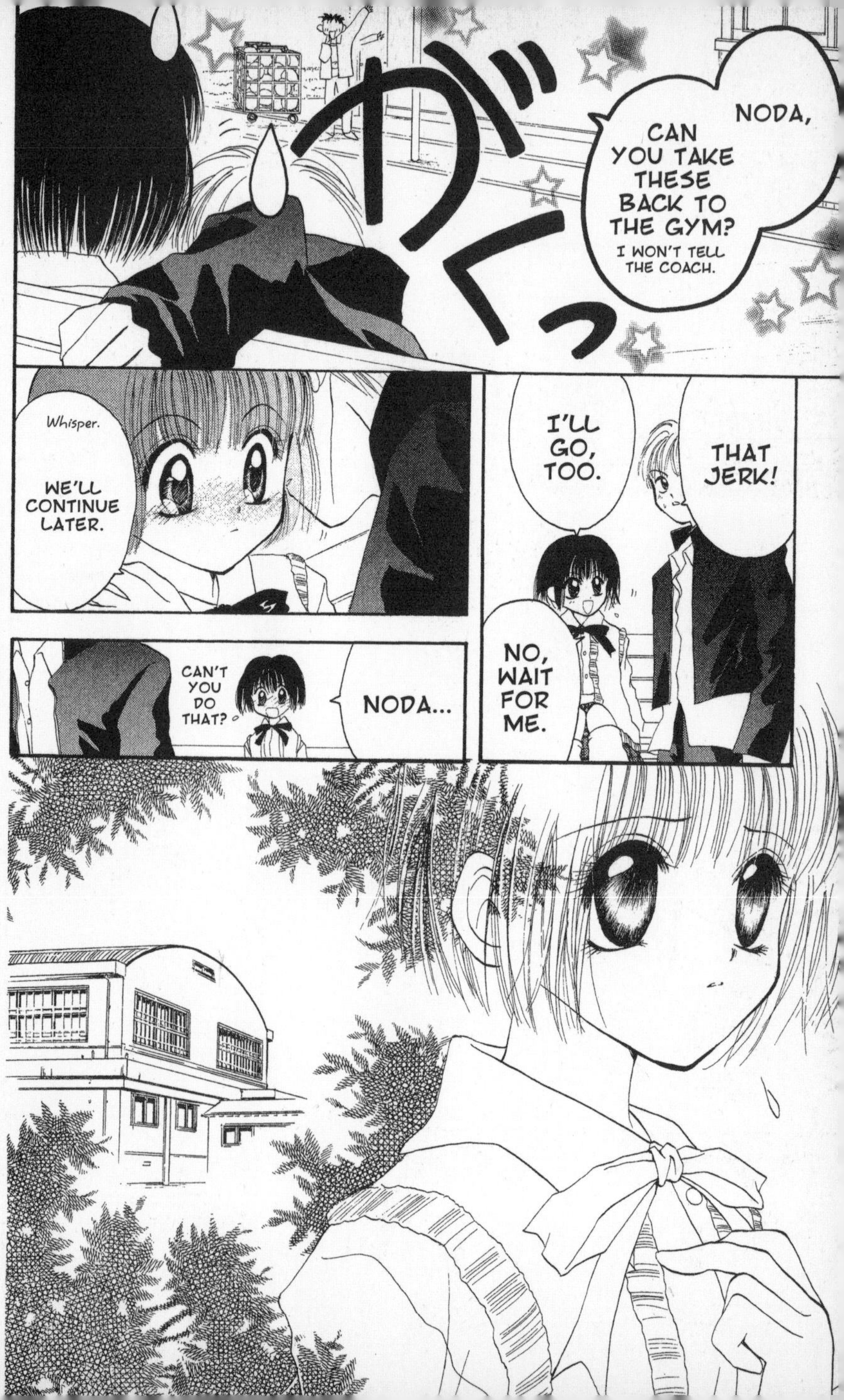
NODA, CAN YOU TAKE THESE BACK TO THE GYM?
I WON'T TELL THE COACH.
THAT JERK!
I'LL GO, TOO.
NO, WAIT FOR ME.
Whisper.
WE'LL CONTINUE LATER.
NODA...
CAN'T YOU DO THAT?

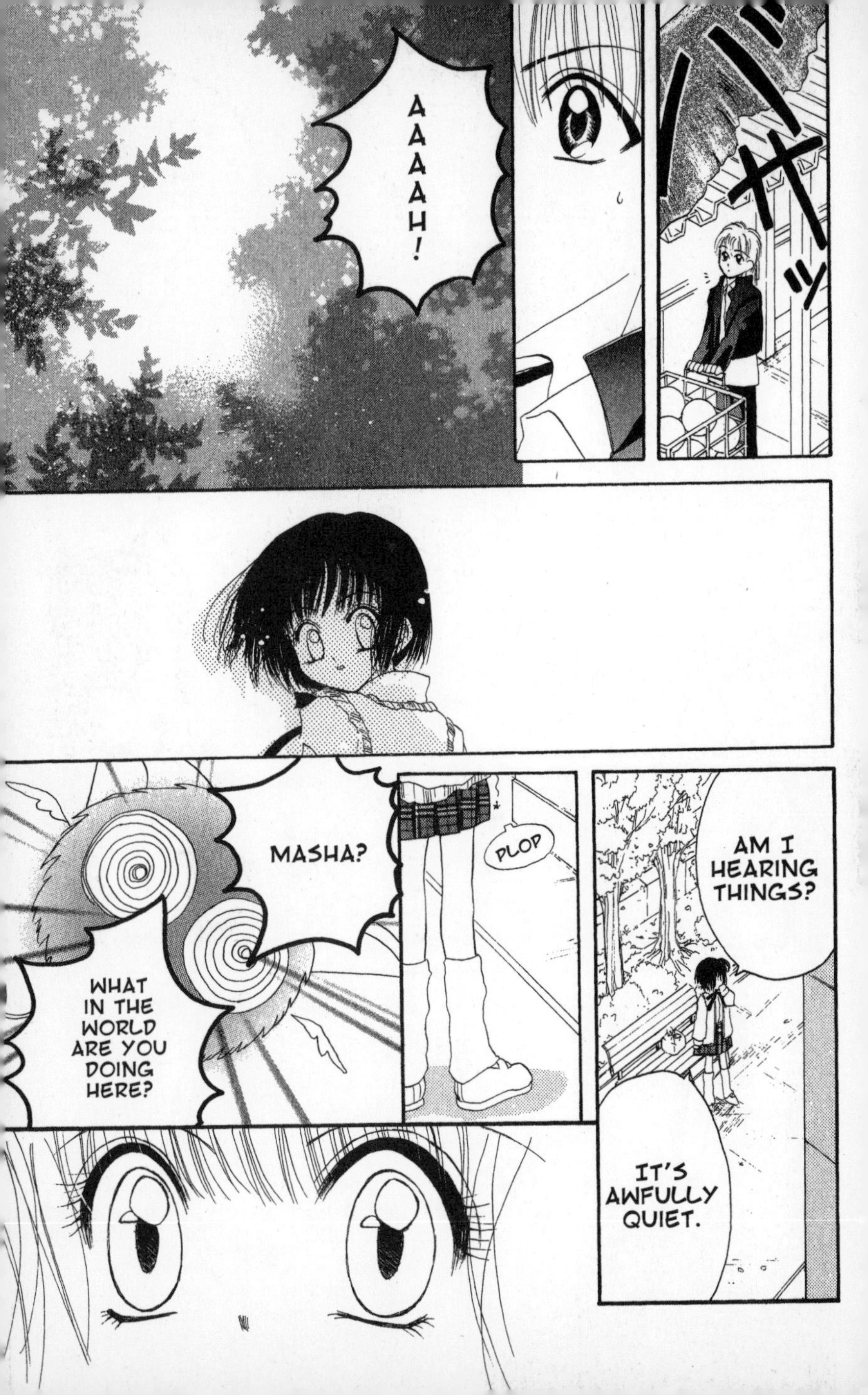

バサッ
AAAAAH!
AM I HEARING THINGS?
IT'S AWFULLY QUIET.
PLOP
MASHA?
WHAT IN THE WORLD ARE YOU DOING HERE?

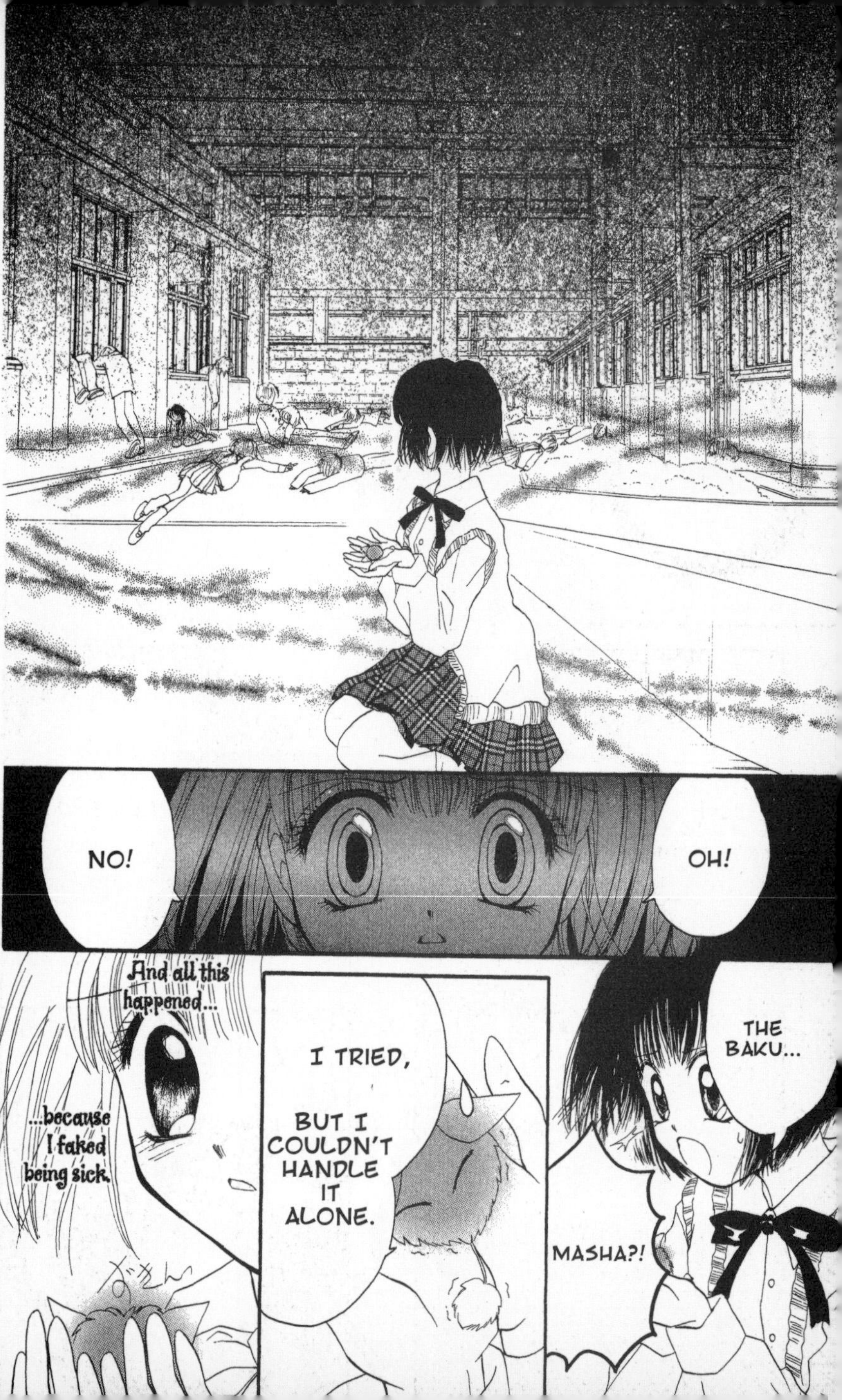
OH!
NO!
THE BAKU...
MASHA?!
I TRIED,
BUT I COULDN'T HANDLE IT ALONE.
And all this happened...
...because I faked being sick.

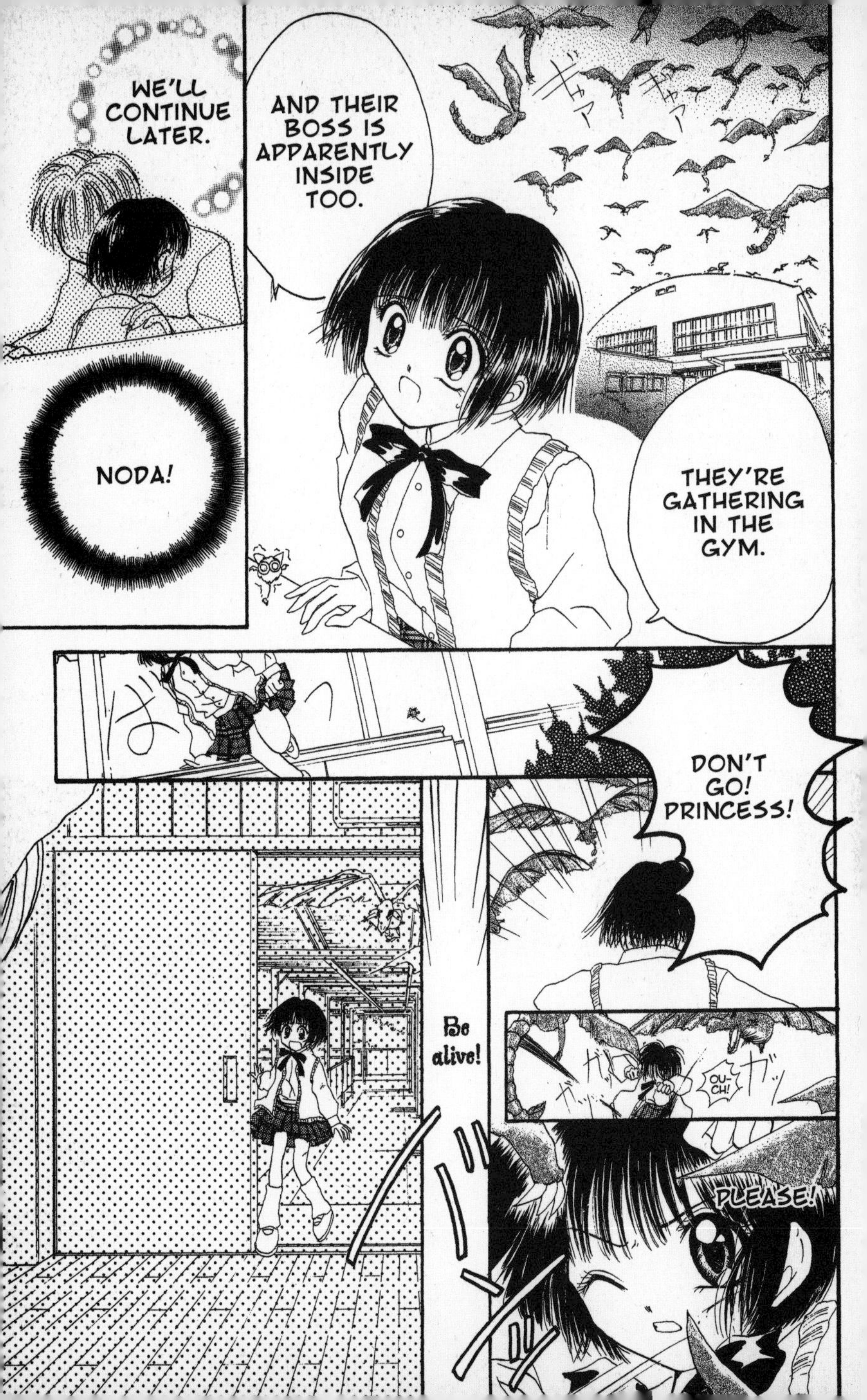
THEY'RE GATHERING IN THE GYM.
AND THEIR BOSS IS APPARENTLY INSIDE TOO.
WE'LL CONTINUE LATER.
NODA!
DON'T GO! PRINCESS!
OU-CH!
PLEASE!
Be alive!

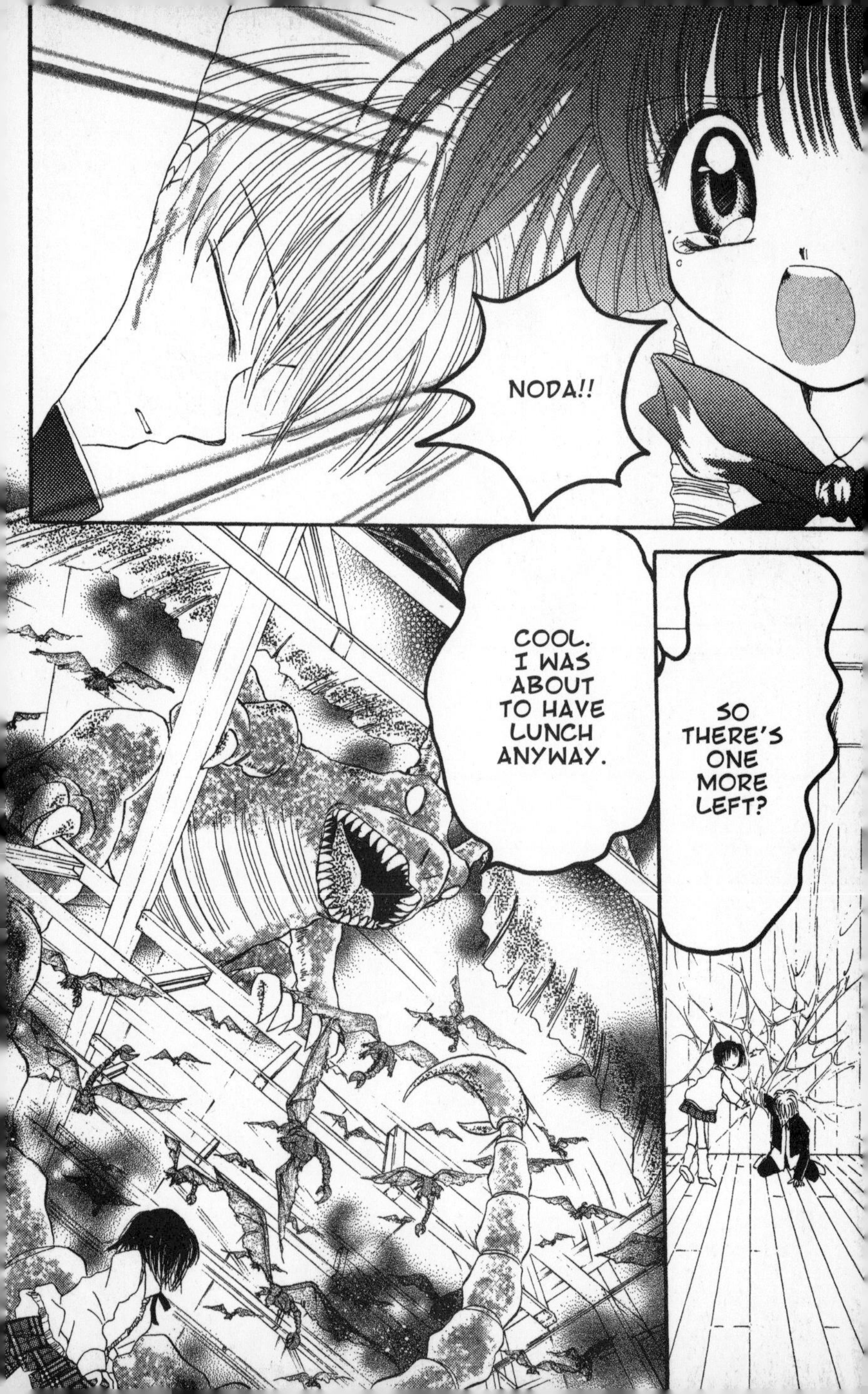
NODA!!
SO THERE'S ONE MORE LEFT?
COOL. I WAS ABOUT TO HAVE LUNCH ANYWAY.

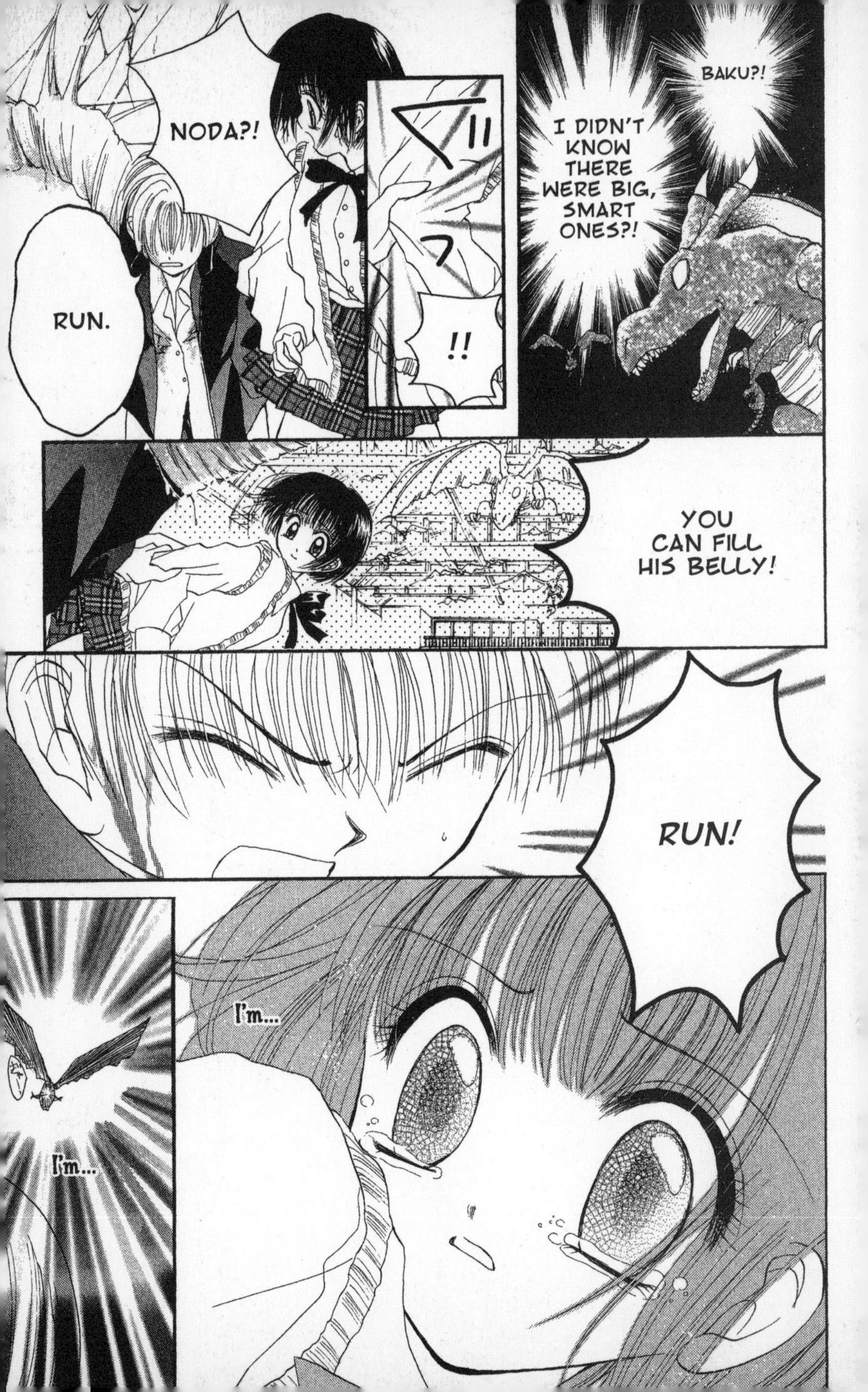
BAKU?!
I DIDN'T KNOW THERE WERE BIG, SMART ONES?!
!!
NODA?!
RUN.
YOU CAN FILL HIS BELLY!
RUN!
I'm...
I'm...

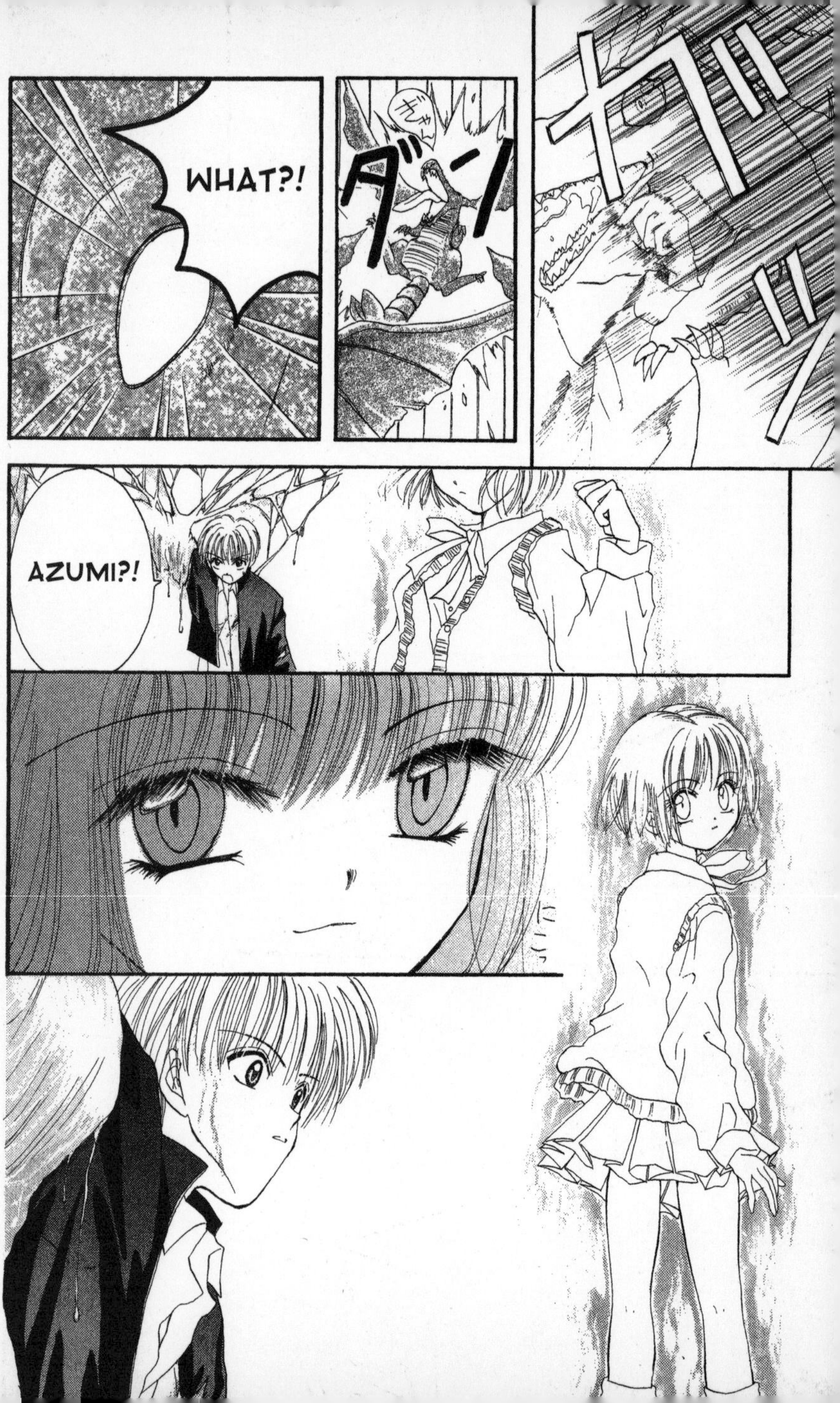
ダーン
WHAT?!
AZUMI?!

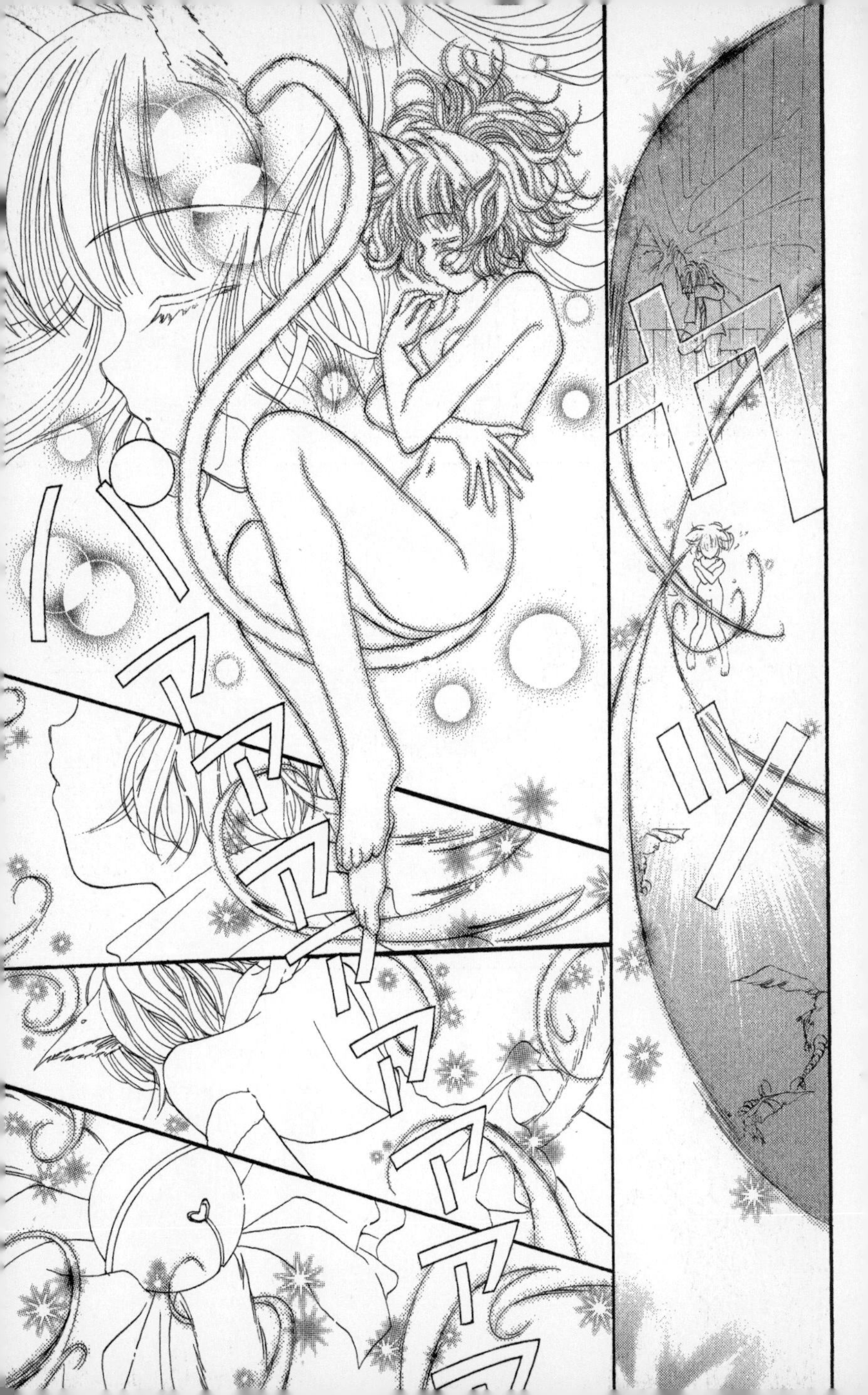

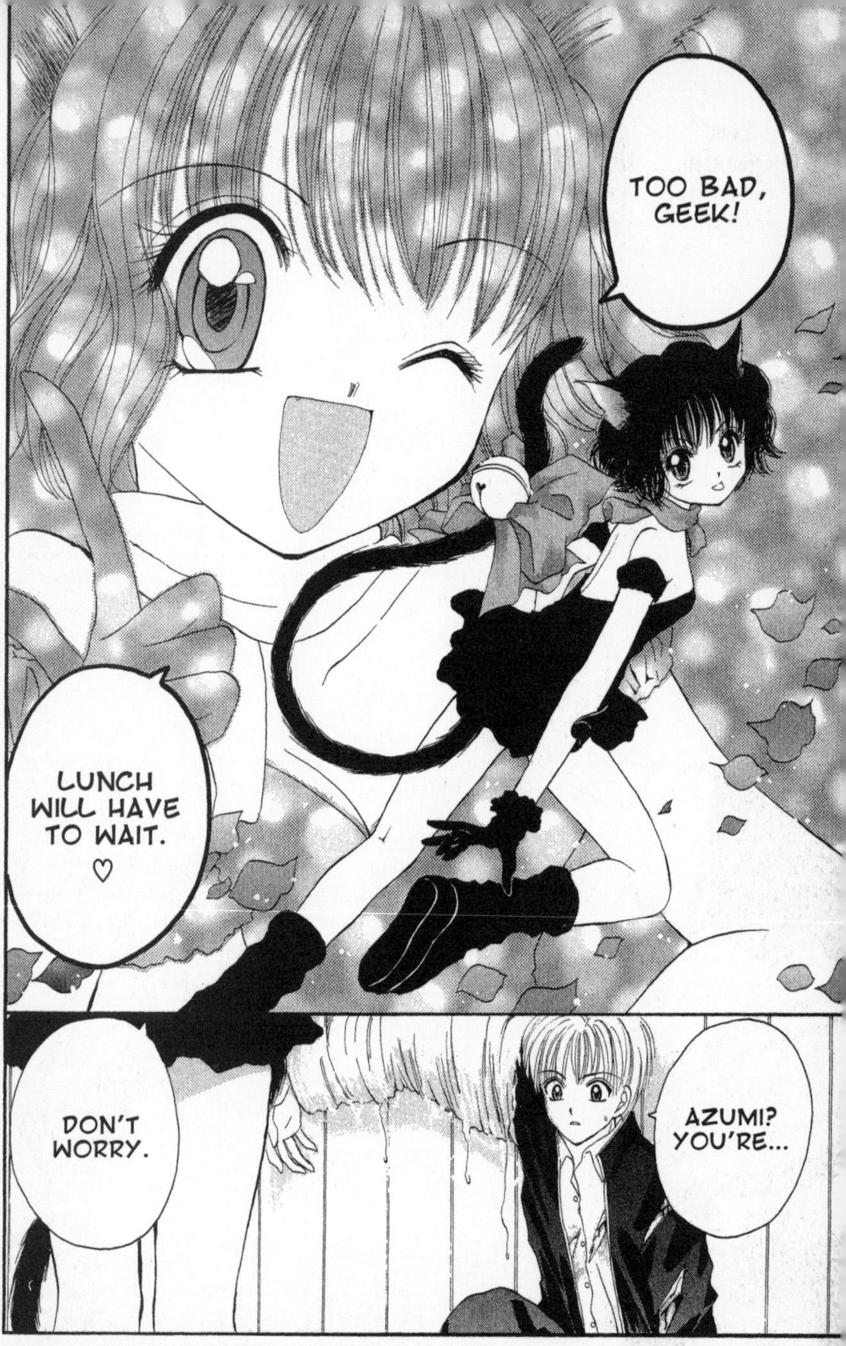
TOO BAD, GEEK!
LUNCH WILL HAVE TO WAIT. ♡
AZUMI? YOU'RE...
DON'T WORRY.

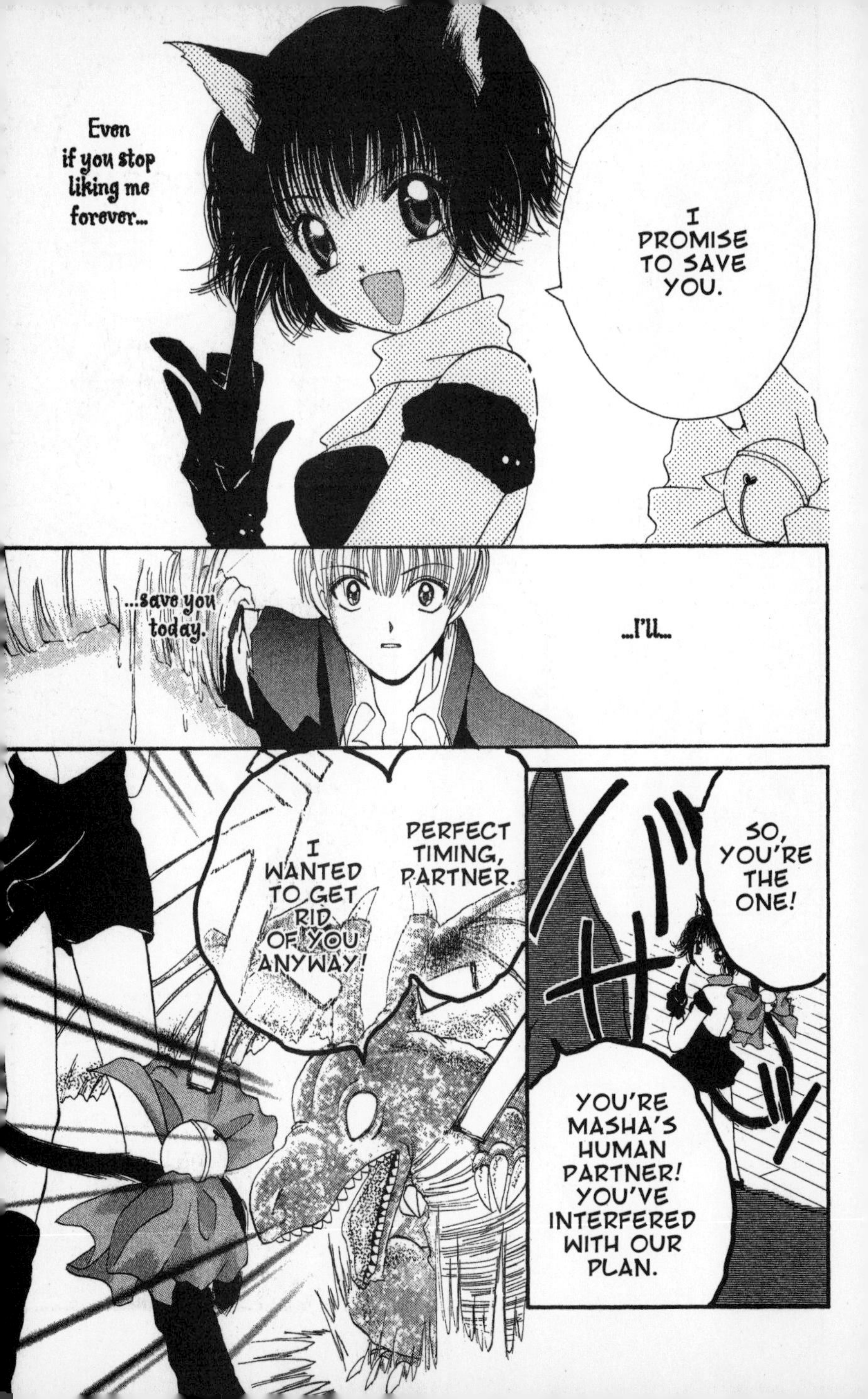
I PROMISE TO SAVE YOU.
Even if you stop liking me forever...
...I'll...
...save you today.
SO, YOU'RE THE ONE!
YOU'RE MASHA'S HUMAN PARTNER! YOU'VE INTERFERED WITH OUR PLAN.
PERFECT TIMING, PARTNER.
I WANTED TO GET RID OF YOU ANYWAY!

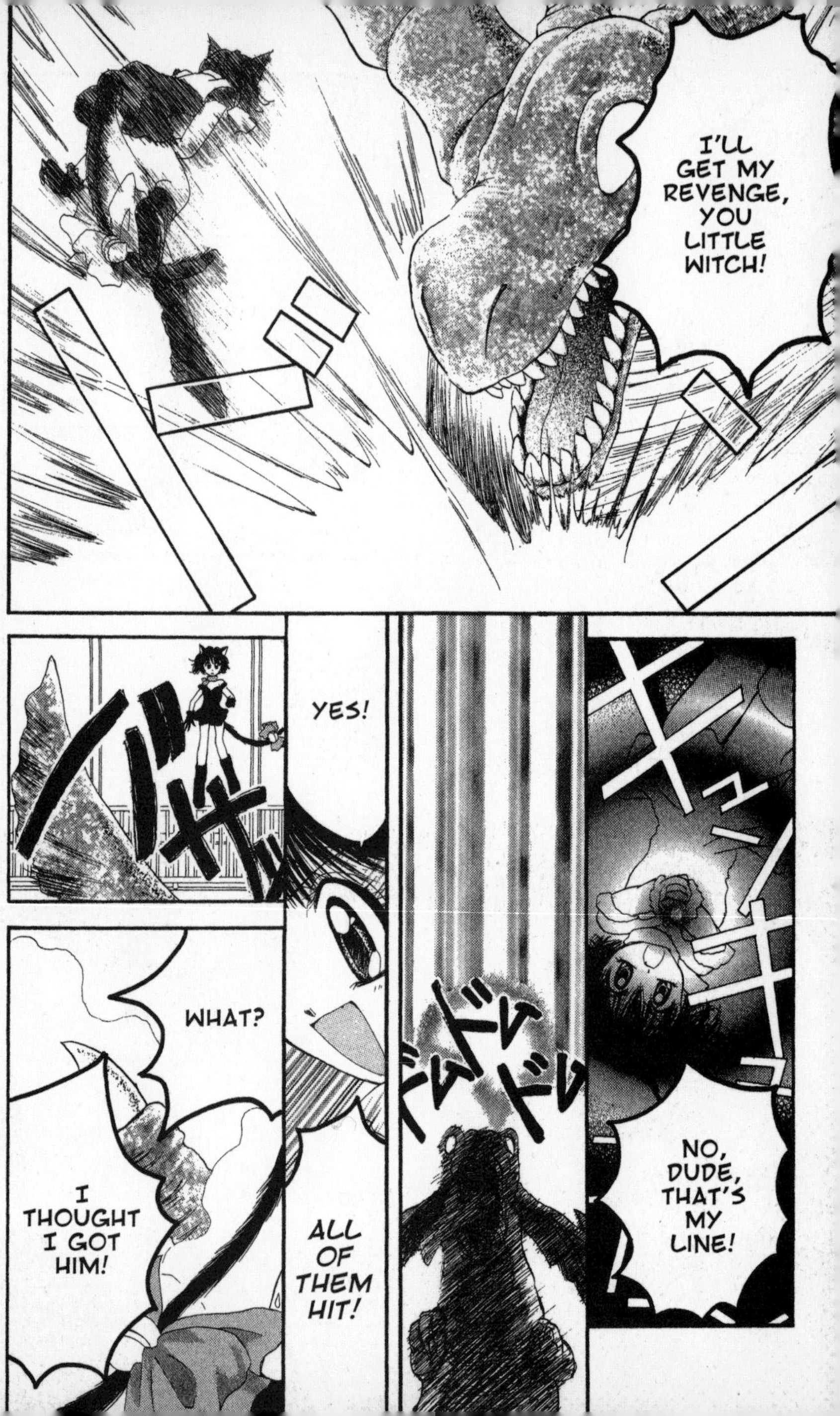
I'LL GET MY REVENGE, YOU LITTLE WITCH!
NO, DUDE, THAT'S MY LINE!
YES!
ALL OF THEM HIT!
WHAT?
I THOUGHT I GOT HIM!

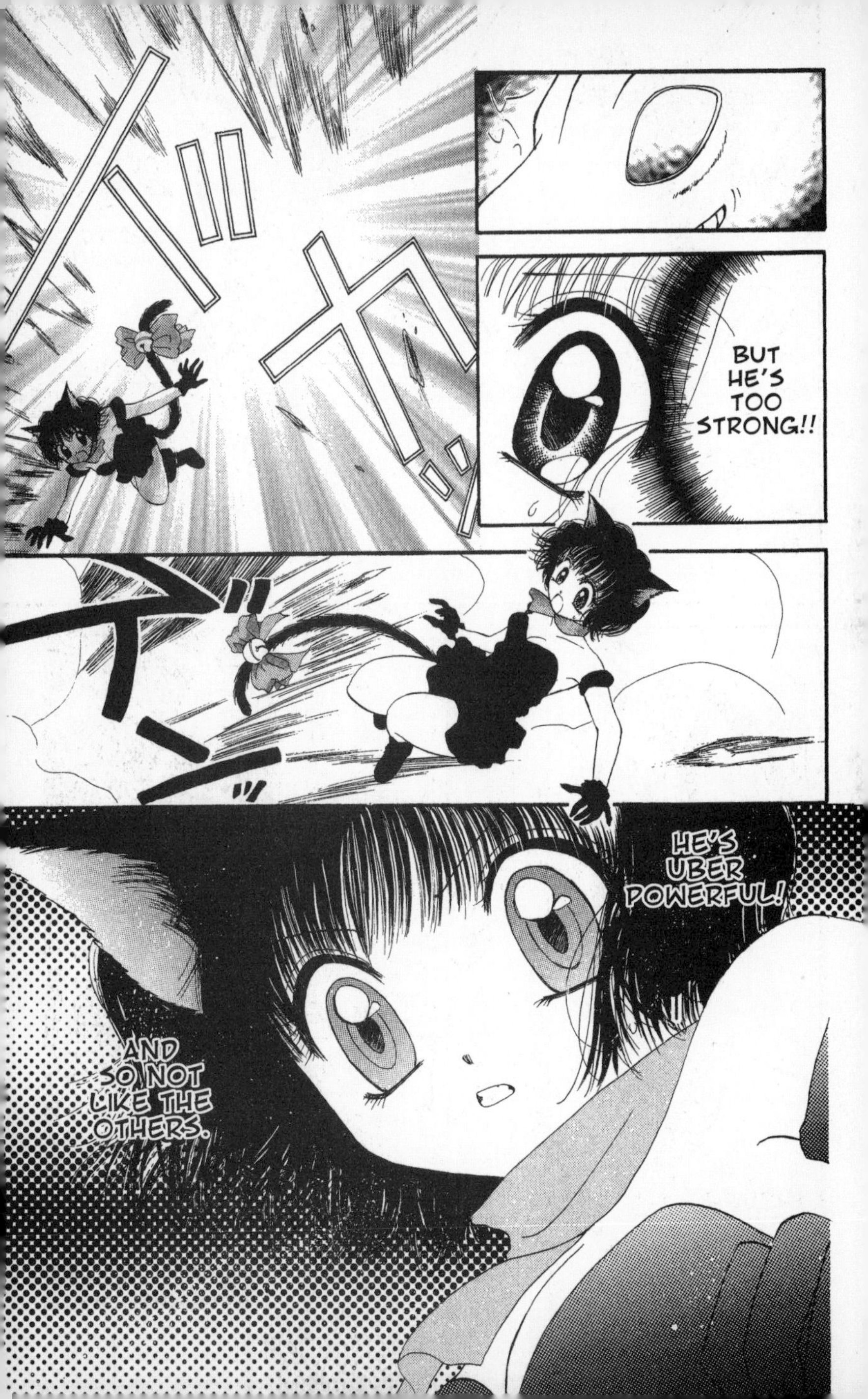
BUT HE'S TOO STRONG!!
HE'S UBER POWERFUL!
AND SO NOT LIKE THE OTHERS.

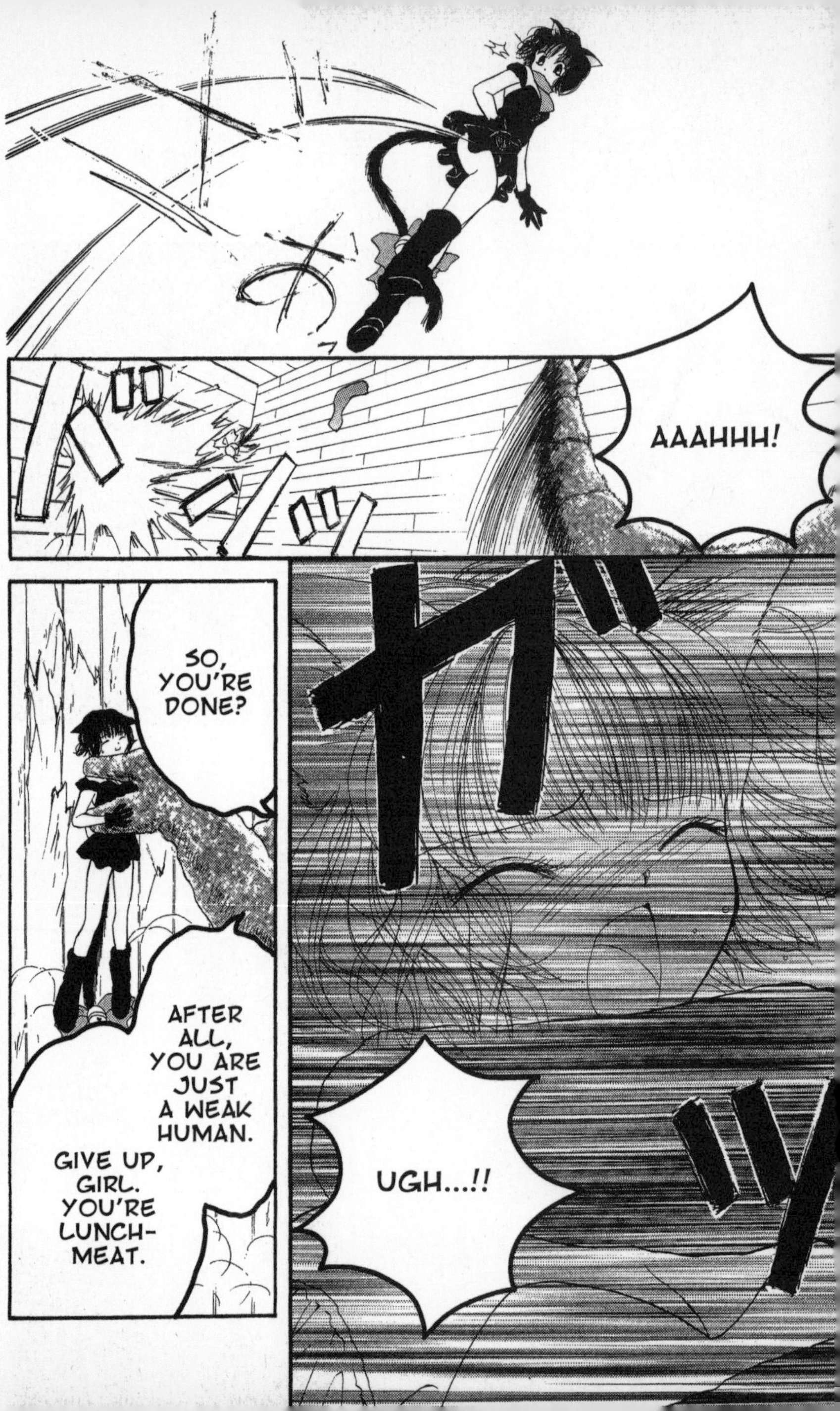
AAAHHH!
UGH...!!
SO, YOU'RE DONE?
AFTER ALL, YOU ARE JUST A WEAK HUMAN.
GIVE UP, GIRL. YOU'RE LUNCH-MEAT.

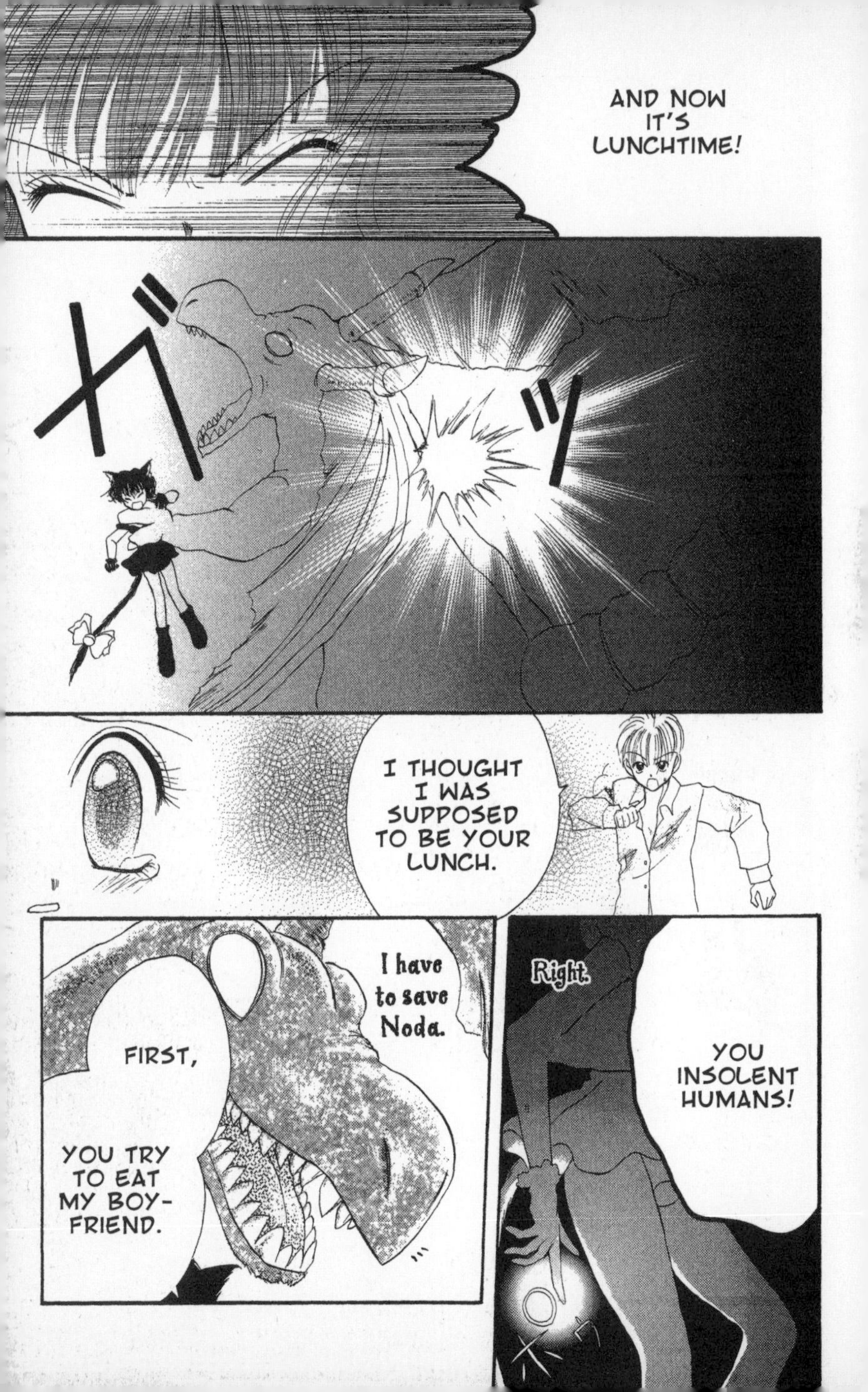
AND NOW IT'S LUNCHTIME!
ガッ
I THOUGHT I WAS SUPPOSED TO BE YOUR LUNCH.
YOU INSOLENT HUMANS!
Right.
I have to save Noda.
FIRST,
YOU TRY TO EAT MY BOY-FRIEND.

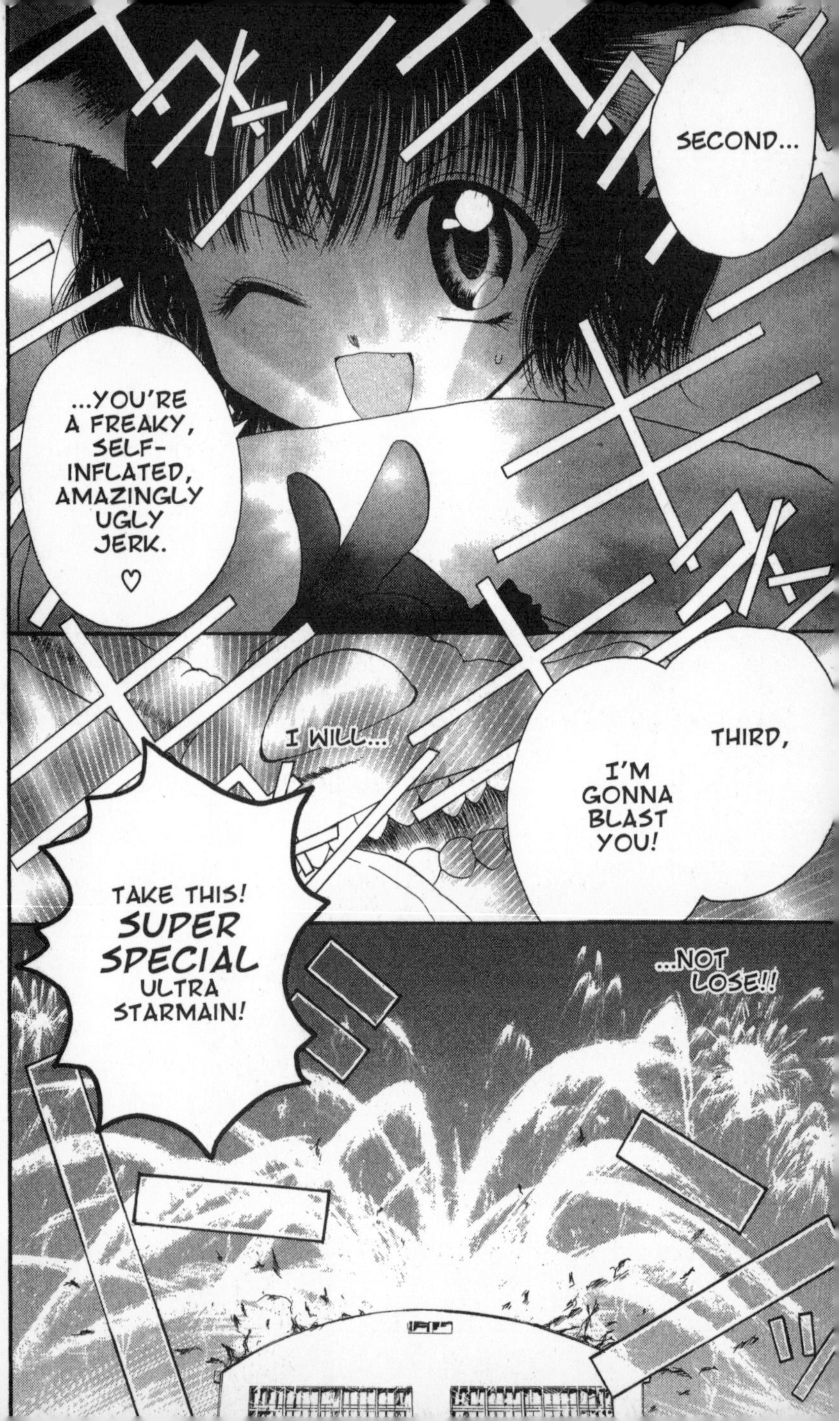
SECOND...
...YOU'RE A FREAKY, SELF-INFLATED, AMAZINGLY UGLY JERK. ♡
THIRD, I'M GONNA BLAST YOU!
I WILL...
TAKE THIS! SUPER SPECIAL ULTRA STARMAIN!
...NOT LOSE!!

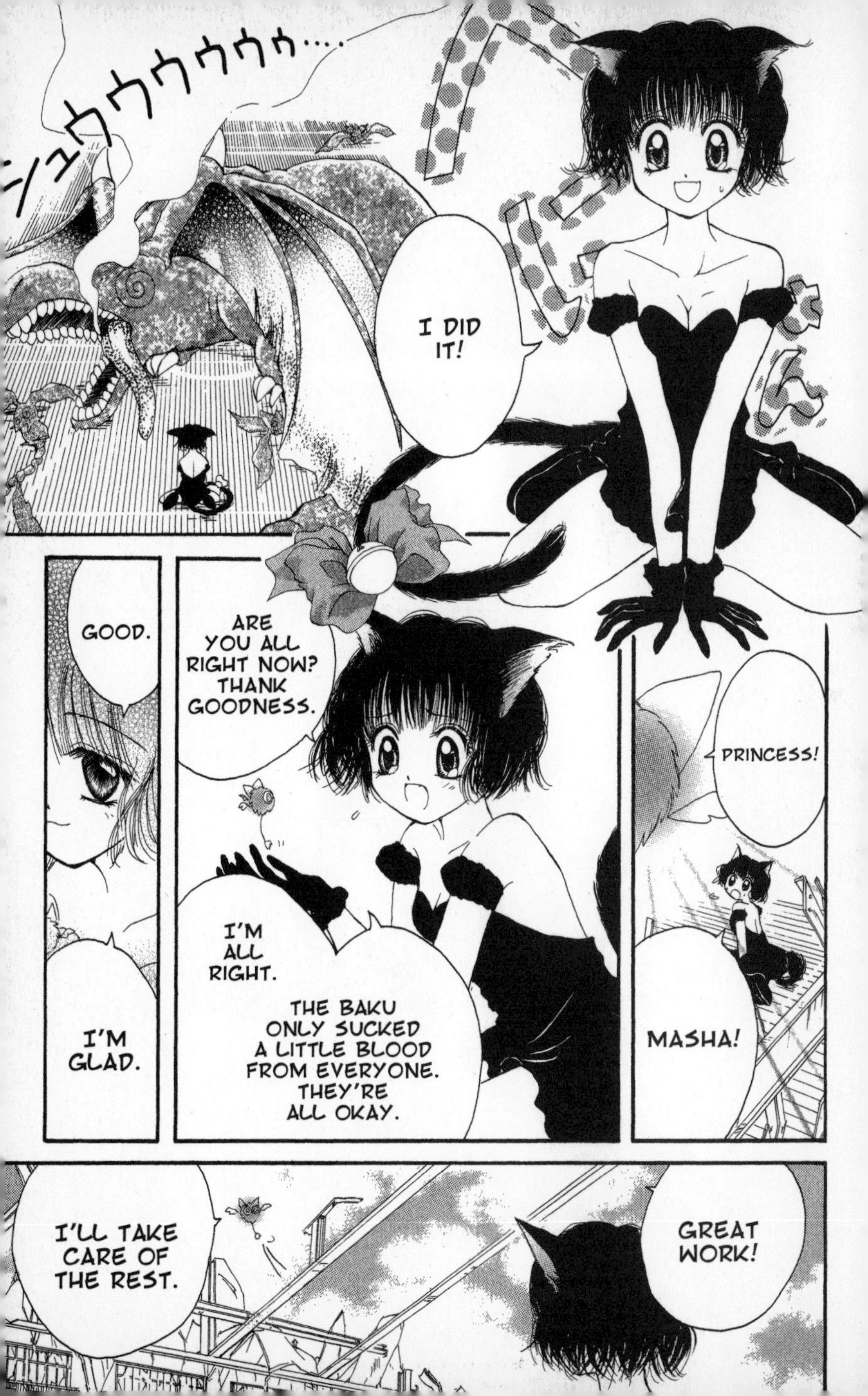
シュウウウウゥ….
I DID IT!
PRINCESS!
MASHA!
ARE YOU ALL RIGHT NOW? THANK GOODNESS.
I'M ALL RIGHT.
THE BAKU ONLY SUCKED A LITTLE BLOOD FROM EVERYONE. THEY'RE ALL OKAY.
GOOD.
I'M GLAD.
GREAT WORK!
I'LL TAKE CARE OF THE REST.

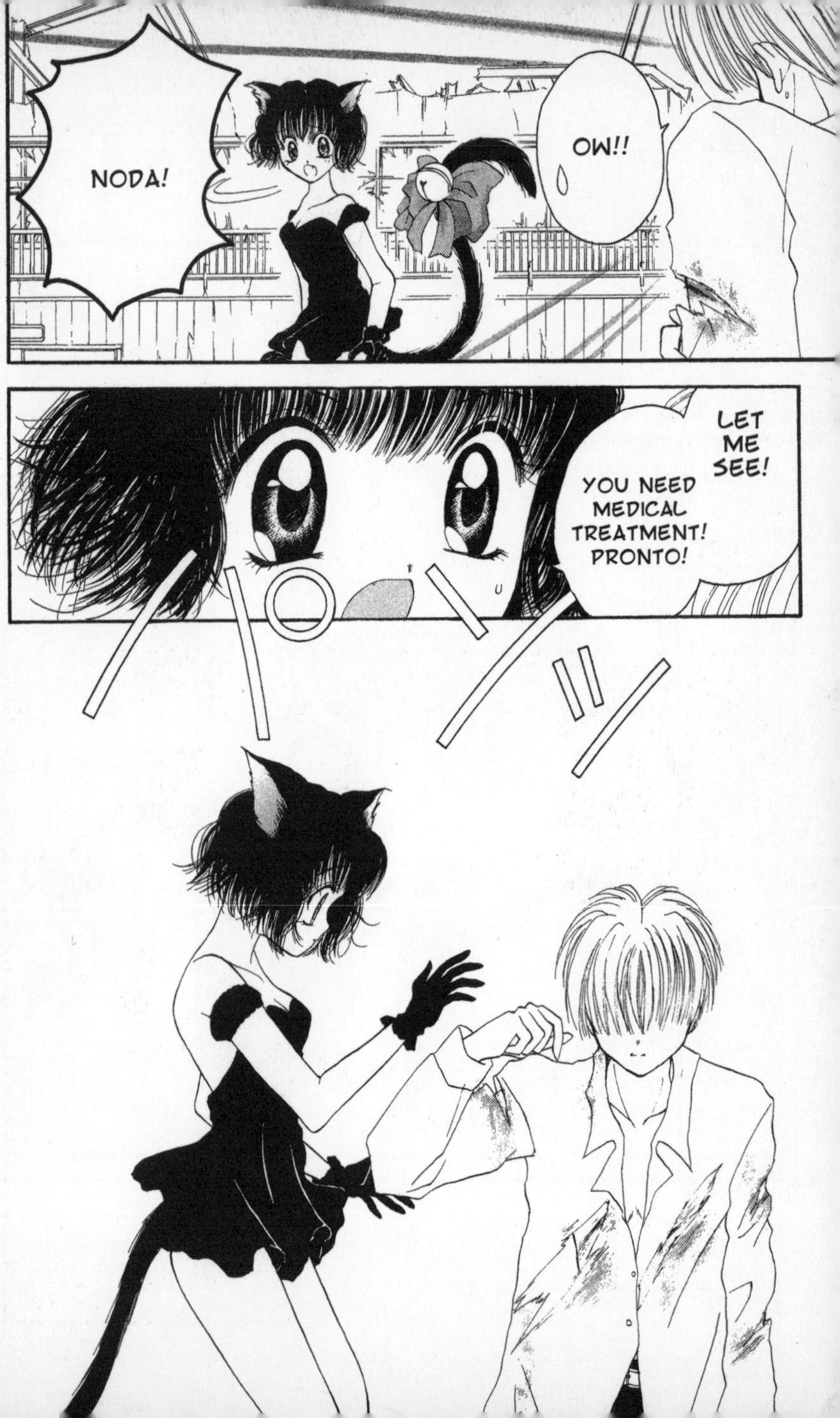
OW!!
NODA!
LET ME SEE!
YOU NEED MEDICAL TREATMENT! PRONTO!

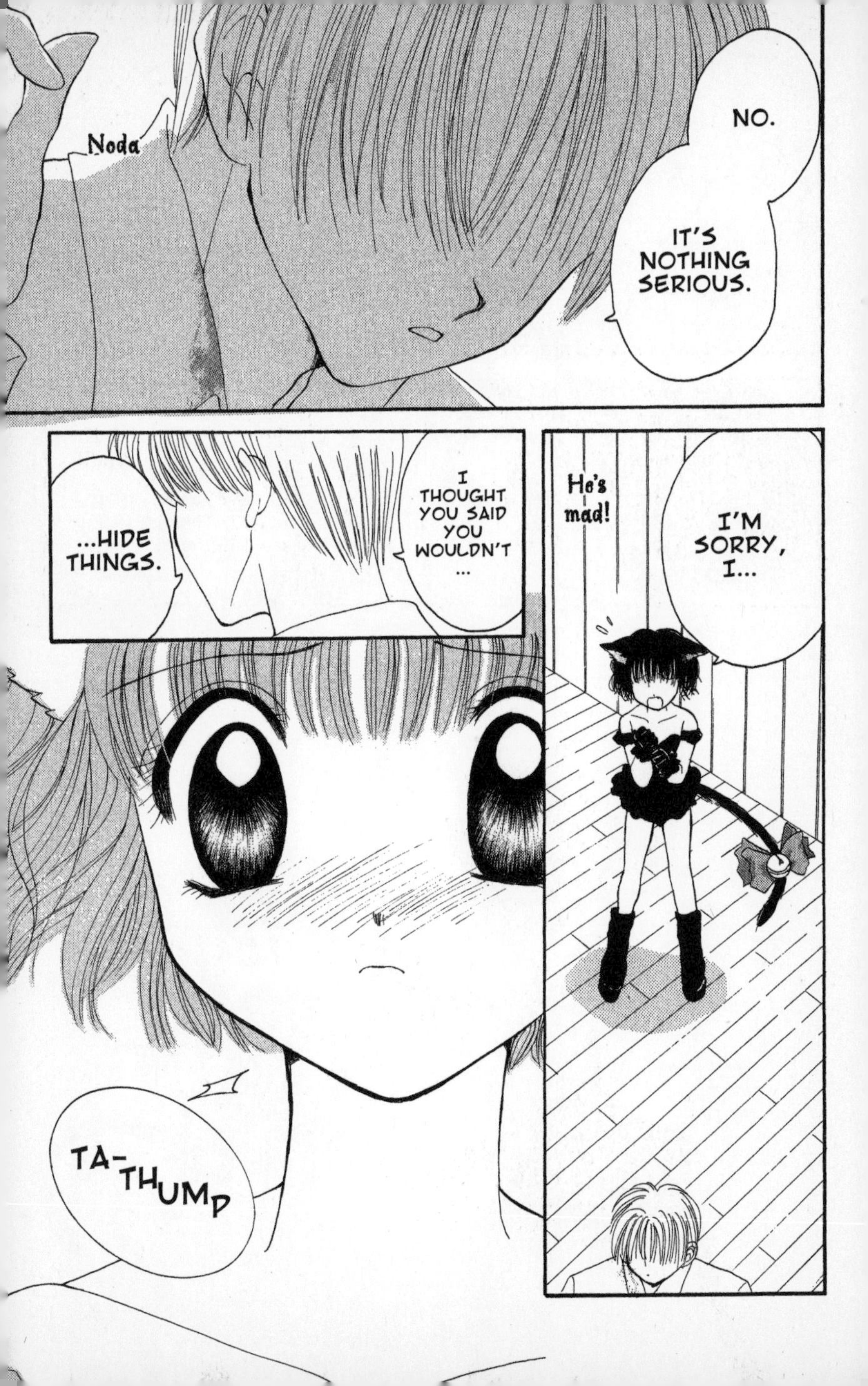

NO.
IT'S NOTHING SERIOUS.
Noda
I'M SORRY, I...
He's mad!
I THOUGHT YOU SAID YOU WOULDN'T ...
...HIDE THINGS.
TA-THUMP

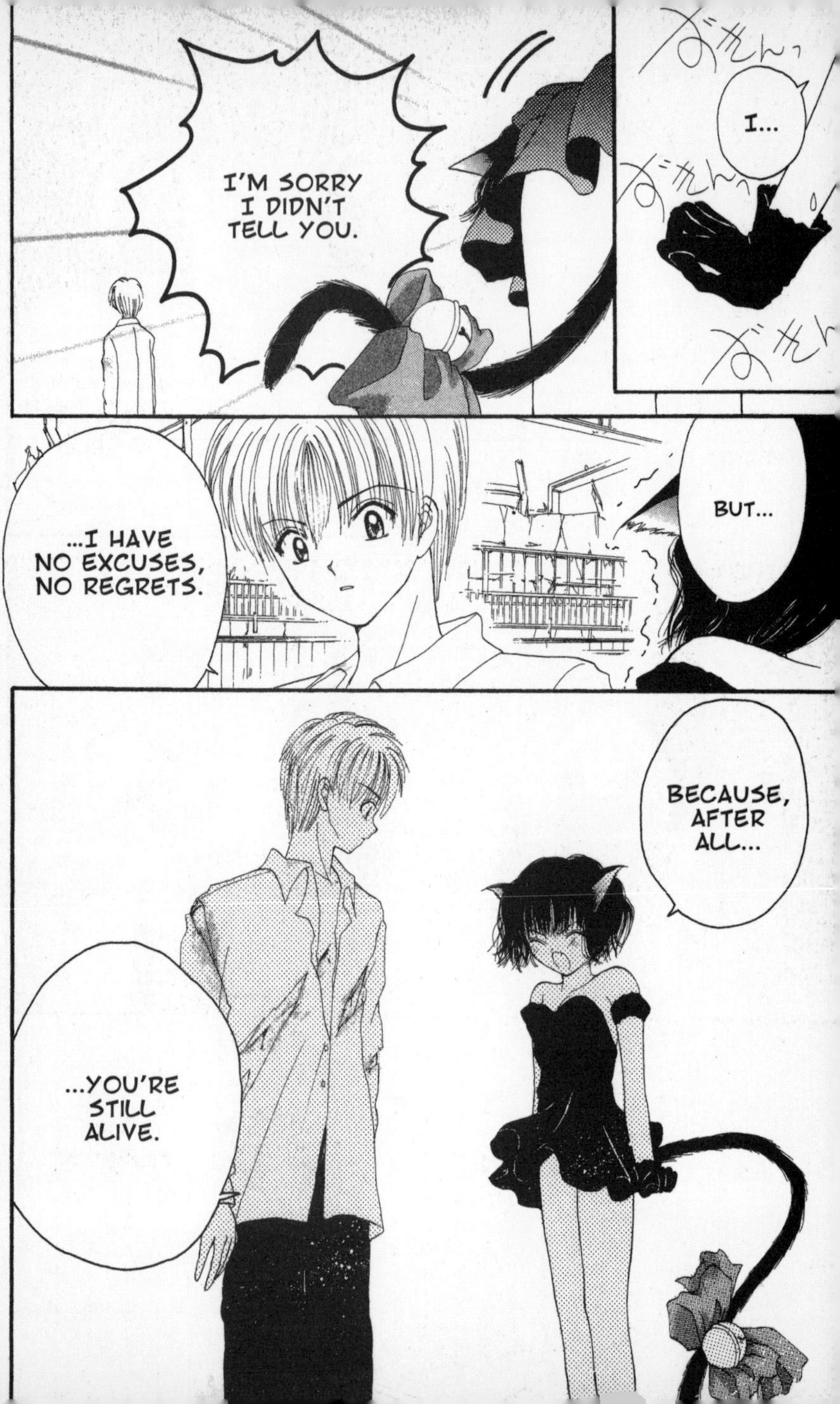
I...
I'M SORRY I DIDN'T TELL YOU.
BUT...
...I HAVE NO EXCUSES, NO REGRETS.
BECAUSE, AFTER ALL...
...YOU'RE STILL ALIVE.

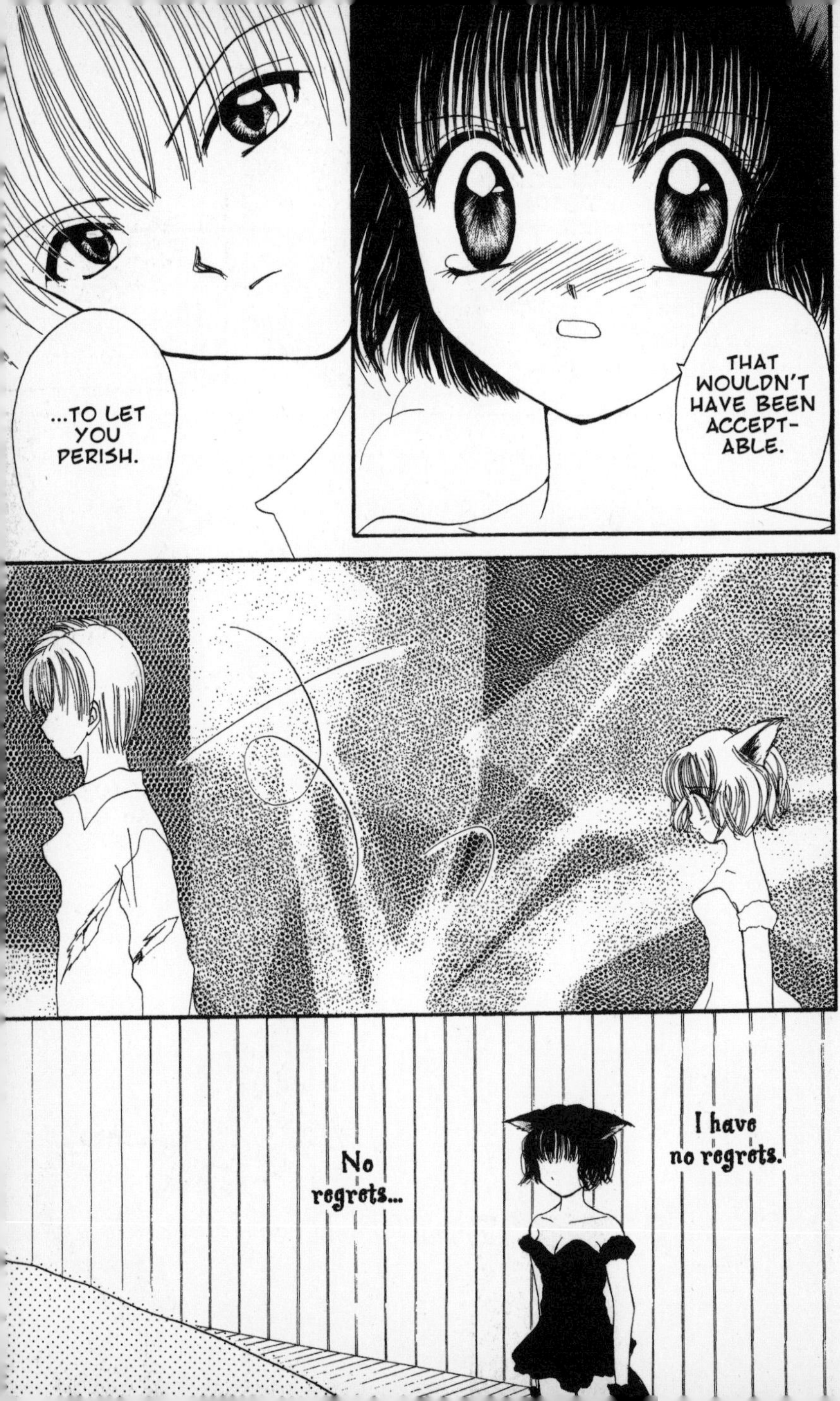
THAT WOULDN'T HAVE BEEN ACCEPT-ABLE.
...TO LET YOU PERISH.
I have no regrets.
No regrets...

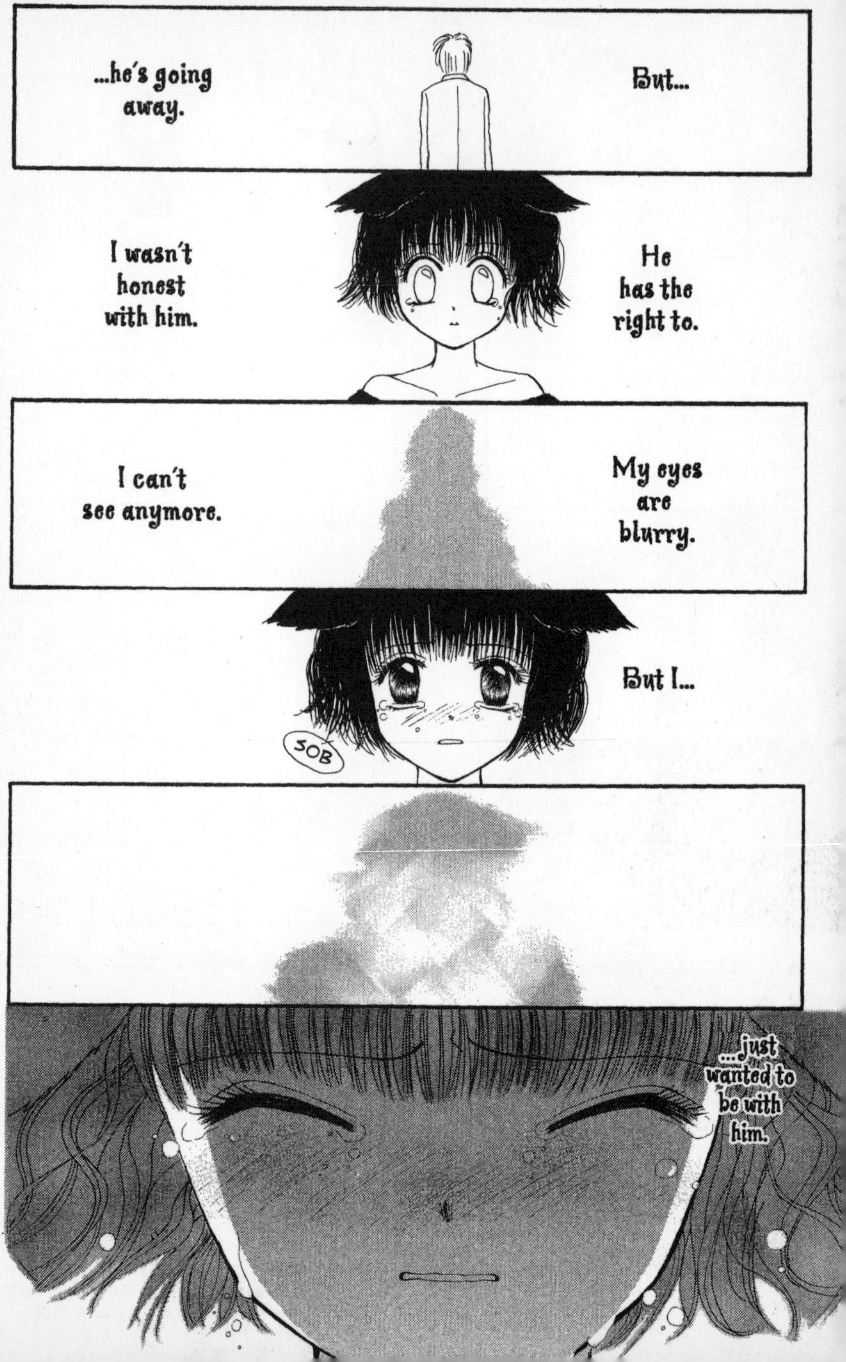
But...
...he's going away.
He has the right to.
I wasn't honest with him.
My eyes are blurry.
I can't see anymore.
But I...
SOB
...just wanted to be with him.

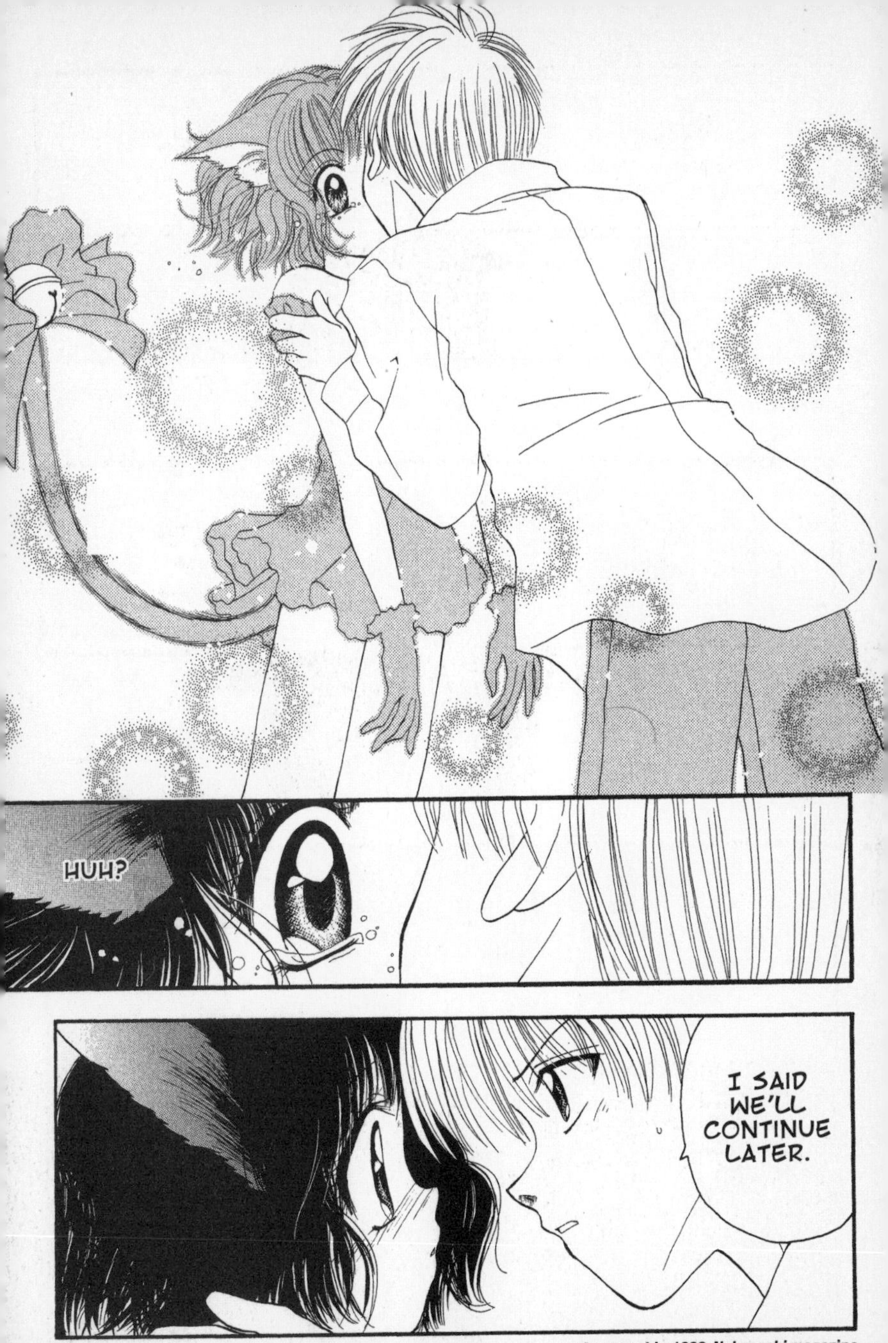
HUH?
I SAID WE'LL CONTINUE LATER.

Appeared in 1999 *Nakayoshi* magazine special Winter Break Land issue

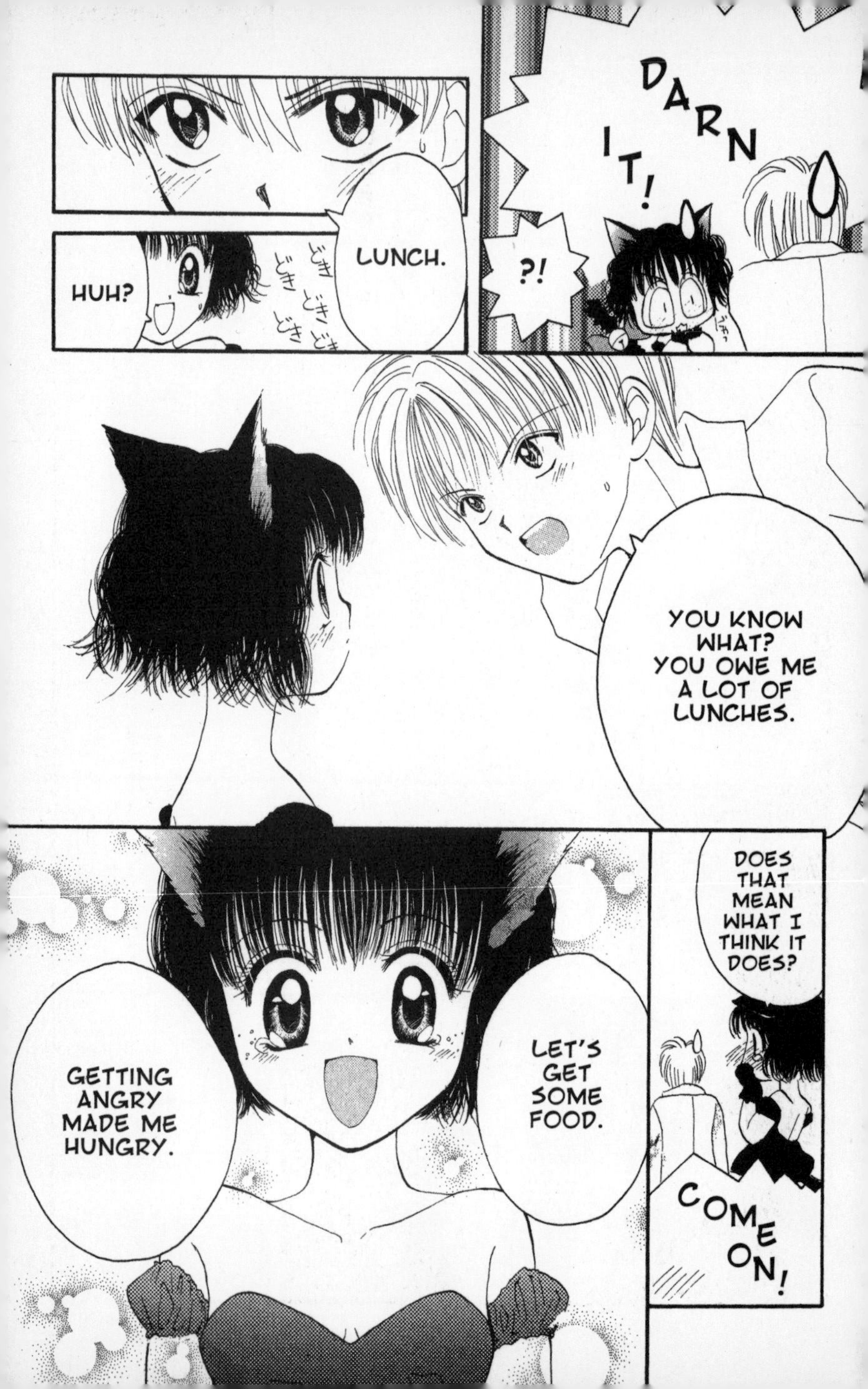
DARN IT!
?!
LUNCH.
どきどきどき
HUH?
YOU KNOW WHAT? YOU OWE ME A LOT OF LUNCHES.
DOES THAT MEAN WHAT I THINK IT DOES?
COME ON!
LET'S GET SOME FOOD.
GETTING ANGRY MADE ME HUNGRY.

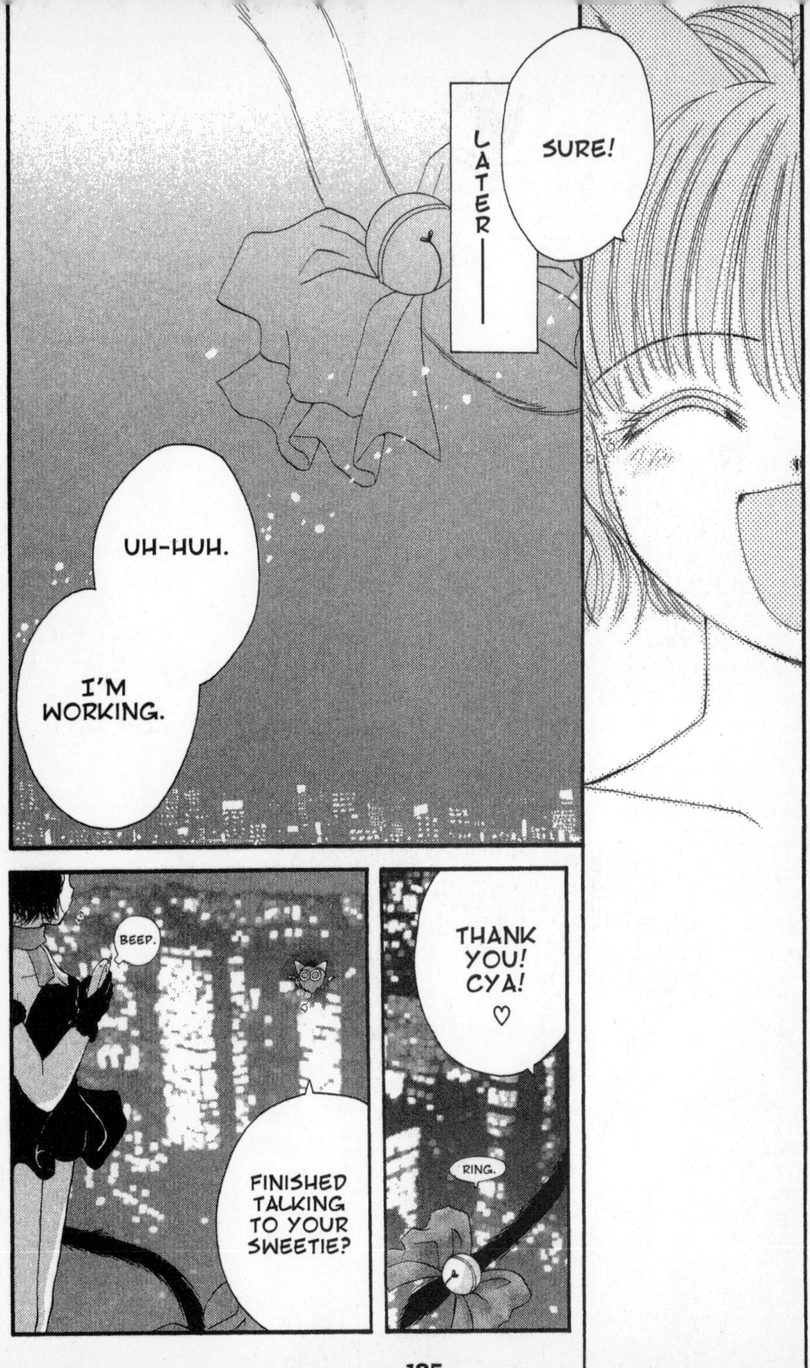
SURE!
LATER——
UH-HUH.
I'M WORKING.
THANK YOU! CYA! ♡
RING.
BEEP.
FINISHED TALKING TO YOUR SWEETIE?

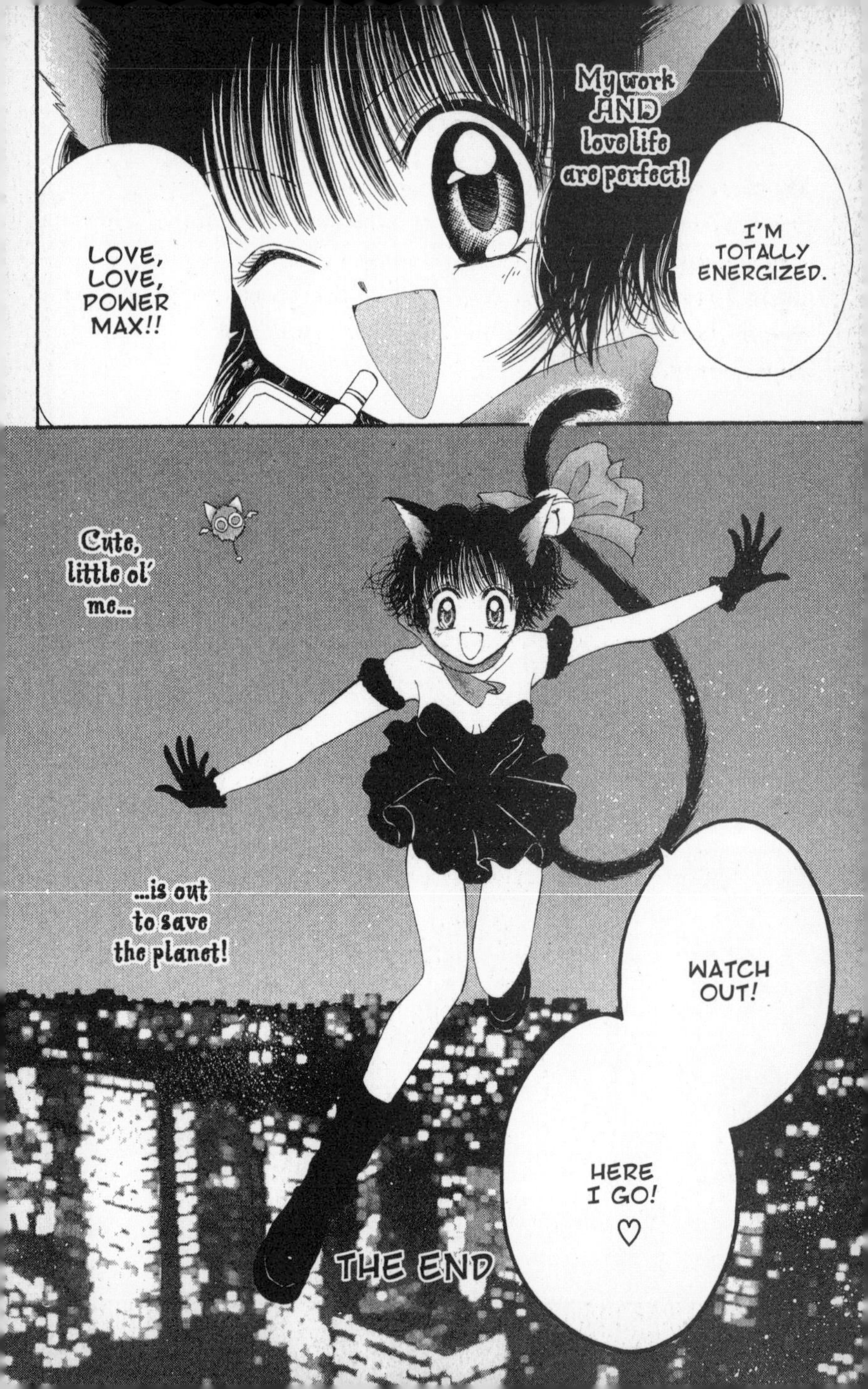
My work AND love life are perfect!
I'M TOTALLY ENERGIZED.
LOVE, LOVE, POWER MAX!!
Cute, little ol' me...
...is out to save the planet!
WATCH OUT!
HERE I GO! ♡
THE END

Afterward

The other day, I went by a store I haven't shopped in for a while. An older dude started the shop after being laid off by his company. When the store first opened, he was always frowning and mega-cranky. But this time, he gave me a shy, hesitant smile! That made me feel really good, since I'm sure he's going through a lot right now. That made me realize I have to smile, too! No matter what happens!

Finally...
To everyone who has read this series...
To everyone involved with this project...
To everyone who will help me in the future...
Thank you for your support!

02-21-2001
Mia Ikumi

COMING SOON...

VOLUME FIVE

Finally, Masaya and Ichigo are a genuine couple...and life is wonderful. But things don't stay too smooth for long. Suddenly, a Blue Knight appears and threatens to cause trouble for everyone. Will Ichigo be able to save the day in time?! Find out the fate of the Mew Mews in the next book, Volume Five!

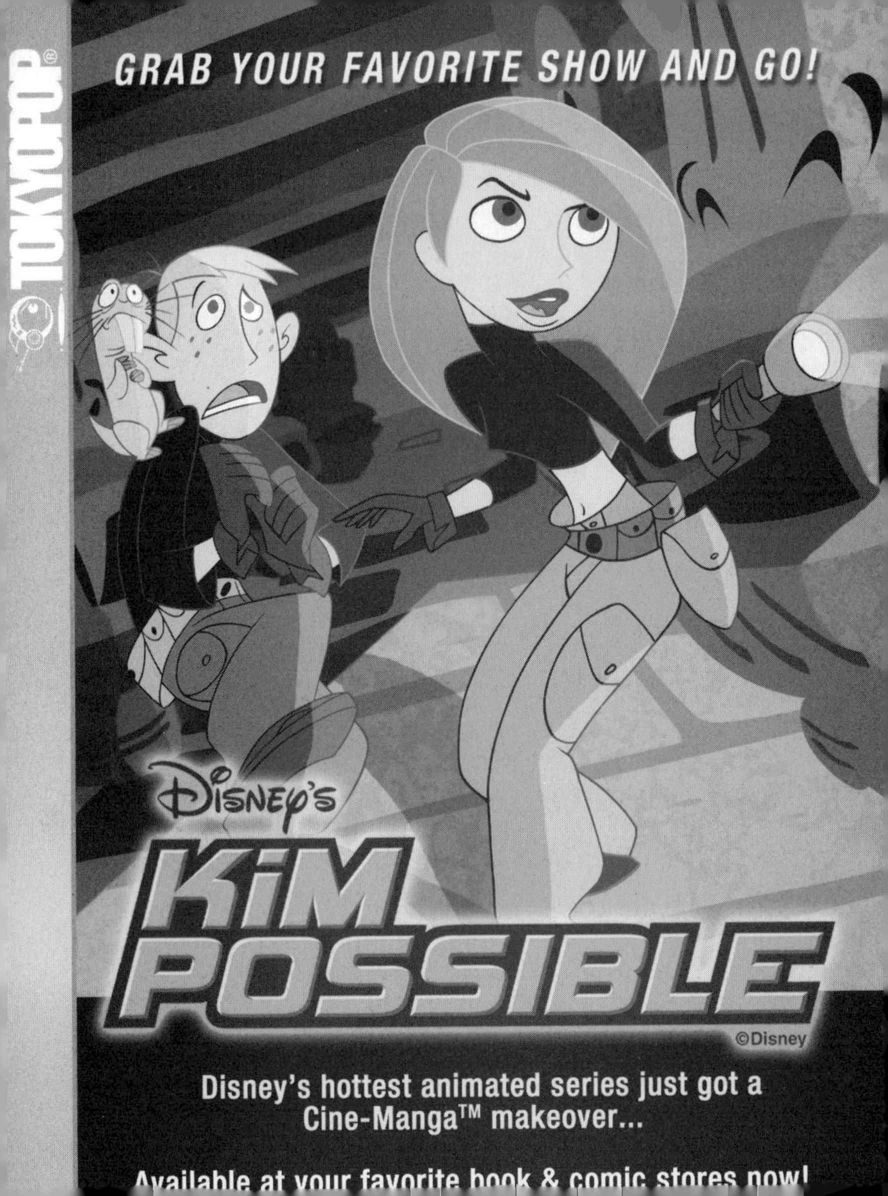
TOKYOPOP
GRAB YOUR FAVORITE SHOW AND GO!
Disney's
KIM POSSIBLE
©Disney
Disney's hottest animated series just got a Cine-Manga™ makeover...
Available at your favorite book & comic stores now!

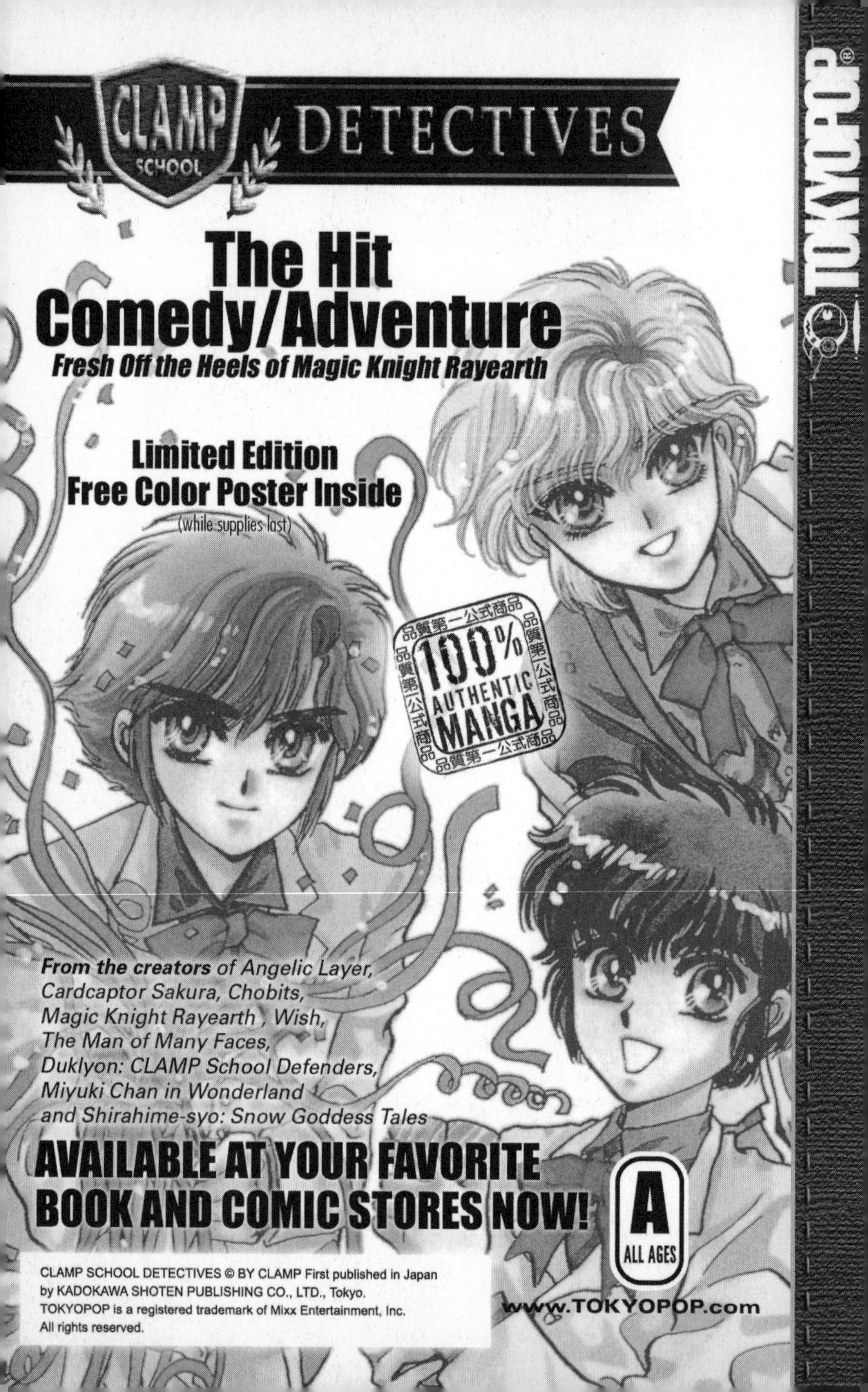
CLAMP SCHOOL
DETECTIVES
The Hit Comedy/Adventure
Fresh Off the Heels of Magic Knight Rayearth
Limited Edition
Free Color Poster Inside
(while supplies last)
品質第一公式商品
100% AUTHENTIC MANGA
From the creators of Angelic Layer, Cardcaptor Sakura, Chobits, Magic Knight Rayearth , Wish, The Man of Many Faces, Duklyon: CLAMP School Defenders, Miyuki Chan in Wonderland and Shirahime-syo: Snow Goddess Tales
AVAILABLE AT YOUR FAVORITE BOOK AND COMIC STORES NOW!
A
ALL AGES
CLAMP SCHOOL DETECTIVES © BY CLAMP First published in Japan by KADOKAWA SHOTEN PUBLISHING CO., LTD., Tokyo.
TOKYOPOP is a registered trademark of Mixx Entertainment, Inc.
All rights reserved.
www.TOKYOPOP.com
TOKYOPOP®

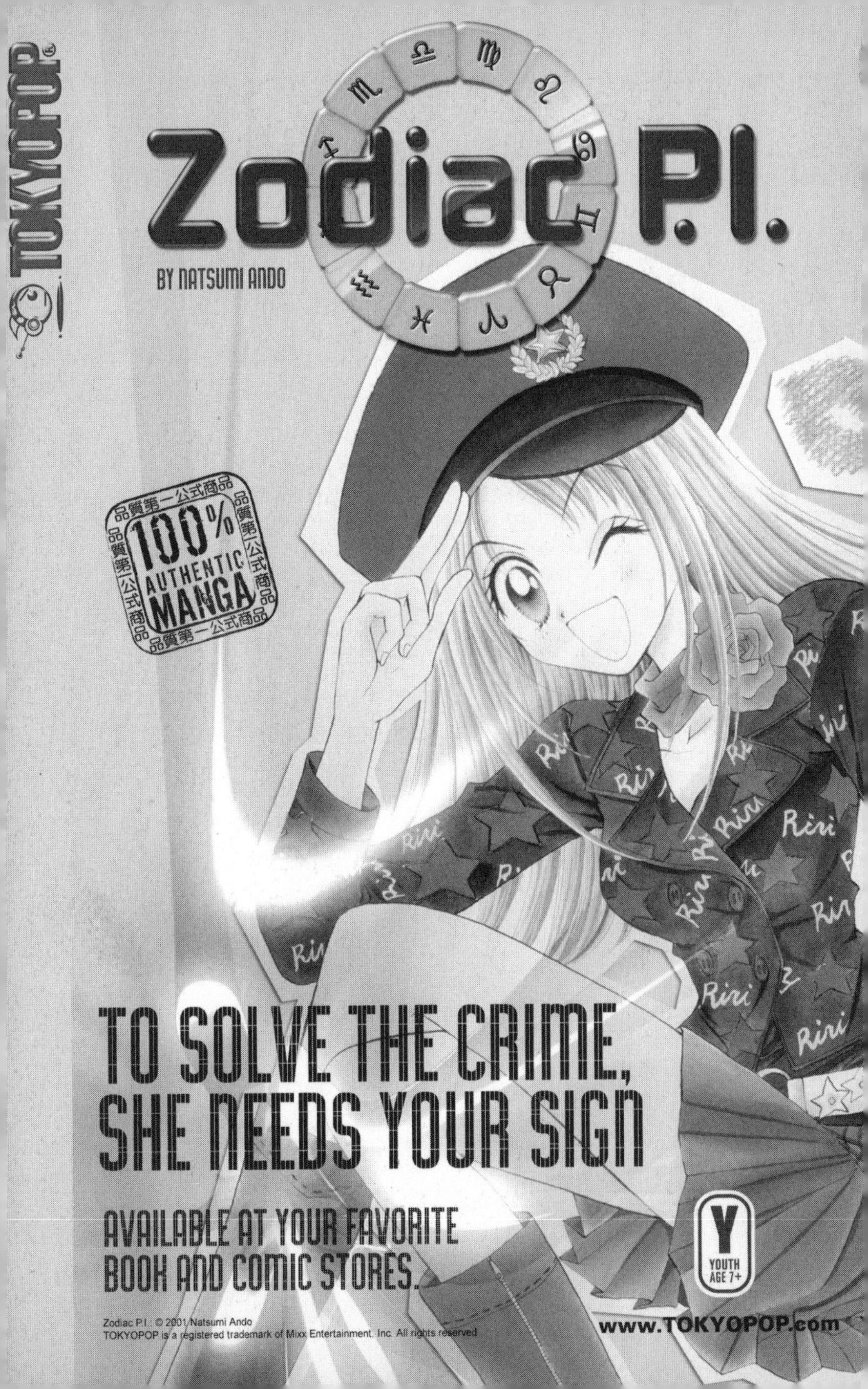
TOKYOPOP®
Zodiac P.I.
BY NATSUMI ANDO
品質第一公式商品
100% AUTHENTIC MANGA
TO SOLVE THE CRIME, SHE NEEDS YOUR SIGN
AVAILABLE AT YOUR FAVORITE BOOK AND COMIC STORES.
Y YOUTH AGE 7+
Zodiac P.I.: © 2001 Natsumi Ando
TOKYOPOP is a registered trademark of Mixx Entertainment, Inc. All rights reserved
www.TOKYOPOP.com

STOP!

This is the back of the book.
You wouldn't want to spoil a great ending!

This book is printed "manga-style," in the authentic Japanese right-to-left format. Since none of the artwork has been flipped or altered, readers get to experience the story just as the creator intended. You've been asking for it, so TOKYOPOP® delivered: authentic, hot-off-the-press, and far more fun!

DIRECTIONS

If this is your first time reading manga-style, here's a quick guide to help you understand how it works.

It's easy... just start in the top right panel and follow the numbers. Have fun, and look for more 100% authentic manga from TOKYOPOP®!